Stefano Della Torre · Sara Cattaneo ·
Camilla Lenzi · Alessandra Zanelli
Editors

Regeneration of the Built Environment from a Circular Economy Perspective

Editors
Stefano Della Torre
Architecture, Built Environment
and Construction Engineering—ABC
Department
Politecnico di Milano
Milan, Italy

Sara Cattaneo
Architecture, Built Environment
and Construction Engineering—ABC
Department
Politecnico di Milano
Milan, Italy

Camilla Lenzi
Architecture, Built Environment
and Construction Engineering—ABC
Department
Politecnico di Milano
Milan, Italy

Alessandra Zanelli
Architecture, Built Environment
and Construction Engineering—ABC
Department
Politecnico di Milano
Milan, Italy

https://doi.org/10.1007/978-3-030-33256-3

Preface

The chapters included in this book give a kaleidoscopic selection of conceptual, empirical, methodological, technical, case studies and research projects, which implement the concepts of circular economy to the regeneration of the built environment. This means enhancing the understanding of sustainability to a broader paradigm, developing a number of practices concerning energy, raw materials, waste, health and society. In particular, a set of theoretical and methodological contributions introduce the theme of the socio-economic development of territories, while the three following sections deal with the challenge of closing the loops of the construction sector—on the one hand, focusing at the larger scale of urban regeneration and, on the other hand, deepening new ways of activating sustainable and resilient paths at the level of the building materials' production, and eventually foreseeing novel policies, tools and organizational models of the building performances' improvement through the reusing, recycling, up-cycling and remanufacturing strategies, applied to the built environment.

This book belongs to a series, which aims at emphasising the impact of the multidisciplinary approach practised by ABC Department (Architecture, Built Environment and Construction Engineering) scientists to face timely challenges in the industry of the built environment. This book presents a structured vision of the many possible approaches—within the field of architecture and civil engineering—to the development of researches dealing with the processes of planning, design, construction, management and transformation of the built environment. Each book contains a selection of essays reporting researches and projects, developed during the last six years within the ABC Department of Politecnico di Milano, concerning a cutting-edge field in the international scenario of the construction sector. Following the concept that innovation happens as different researches stimulate each other, skills and integrate disciplines are brought together within the department, generating a diversity of theoretical and applied studies.

The papers have been selected on the basis of their capability to describe the outputs and the potentialities of carried out researches, giving at the same time a report on the reality and on the perspectives for the future. The cooperation of ABC Department scientists with different institutional and governmental bodies (e.g.

UNESCO, UIA, EACEA, EC-JRC, ESPON, DG REGIO) as well as their participation to sectoral boards and committees (e.g. ISO, CEN, UNI, Network Android-Disaster Resilient, IEA, Stati Generali della Green Economy, Green Public Procurement, Associazione Rete Italiana LCA, Lombardy Energy Cleantech Cluster) and their dialogues with institutions (e.g. national ministries, regional government, local administrations) led and motivated the selection of the essays.

Stefano Della Torre
Head of the Department Architecture
Built Environment and Construction Engineering
Politecnico di Milano
Milan, Italy
e-mail: stefano.dellatorre@polimi.it

Introduction

The regeneration of the built environment represents a prominent research field for all scholars and professionals interested in the creation, evolution and transformation of the urban environment and the relationships between urban, peri-urban and rural spaces. In spite of its well-established and long tradition, this field of enquiry has not yet become depleted but rather is receiving renewed attention and has become compelling in the scientific community for the co-occurrence of multiple trends and phenomena. First, recent times are characterised by an impressive rate of urbanisation, and projections forecast increased urbanisation for the future, especially in less developed and developing countries. Second, the increasing constraints on the widespread availability of economic, social and environmental resources push towards the ideation, prototyping and application of new solutions as to accommodate this quest for urbanisation. Third, the need to continue to take care of, adapt and maintain the heritage of historic cities, especially in advanced countries, and in the light of these constraints, require the experimentation of new approaches to the requalification and renewal, both material and functional, as well as new methodologies of intervention, more error-friendly and based on the reversibility of the current actions, in order to guarantee future generations the possibility of revising the approaches in view of more advanced tools and procedures.

This volume then aims to take on this challenge and proposes a reflection on the strategic importance and advantages of adopting multidisciplinary and multi-scalar approaches of enquiry and intervention on the built environment which are based on the principles of sustainability and on circular economy strategies. In fact, the regeneration of the built environment can represent an important cornerstone in the transition from a linear to a circular economy model through multiple actions that can take place at different scales, i.e. the recycling and reuse of building artefacts, products and components, the improvement of the quality and functionality of existing buildings, the valorisation of cultural heritage, the re-infrastructure and implementation of sustainable transport systems and the efficient use of local economic resources.

In order to address the abovementioned overarching research challenge, this volume identifies specific challenges according to a macro-to-micro unit of analysis ranging from the city itself as an aggregated unit of analysis, to the district/building, from sustainable innovative products and processes to be developed and deployed in the construction sector to multi-scalar strategies to improve building performances.

Starting from the most aggregated level of analysis, the first specific challenge addressed in this volume refers to the possible strategies to relaunch socio-economic development in urban environments through regenerative processes. The key concern, then, is how the regeneration of the built environment can promote not only economic growth processes but also the efficient use of local economic, social and environmental resources, from a circular economy perspective and consistently with sustainability principles.

The second specific challenge relates to the regeneration of urban spaces from a resilient and circular perspective. The key concern in this case is how regeneration of the built environment can be achieved through the reuse and requalification of existing buildings by developing efficient, structurally adequate, resilient, adaptive, flexible and convertible building systems; through the requalification of abandoned and peri-urban areas by planning construction and demolition, by managing and/or reusing building waste, by promoting sustainable buildings, by limiting land use, by activating virtuous and innovative circular processes between primary and secondary materials; and through the requalification of the urban fabric in minor centres by promoting the history and identity of rural villages and peri-urban areas as to favour their conservation and resilience with respect to risk factors such as earthquakes.

The third specific challenge is associated with the development and the deployment of innovative products and processes in the construction sector in the effort to move towards sustainable and circular principles. The key concern then refers to the ideation of new components, products, systems and processes starting from the reuse of existing products and materials that can lead to changes in the construction sector filière as well as to the use of innovative materials aimed at promoting the development of structural requalification technologies and techniques based on the use of materials that have been recycled or can be easily recyclable/convertible, according to a circular economy perspective.

The fourth and last specific challenge is linked to the development of multi-scalar (i.e. from the building to the city) approaches for enhancing the performances of the existing building stock, as well as of the new buildings. This concerns multi-scalar strategies as to mitigate climate change effects by limiting local metabolism, by improving energy efficiency practice, by integrating locally available resources, by diffusing smart buildings, systems and grids as well as by implementing actions to improve the existing buildings and public spaces with the aim of reducing risk factors for individual and collective health, of promoting built environment quality from both a social and environmental perspective along all phases from the project, to construction, from use to maintenance and dismantling.

Addressing these complex fields of research requires the availability and the integration of multiple disciplines that span from engineering to architecture and regional and urban economics and studies. Such multidisciplinary, in fact, enables to disentangle and to unpack the multidimensional nature of all processes impacting on built environment regeneration. The ABC Department of Politecnico di Milano, with its multidisciplinary faculty composition, is well-equipped to address all these research subjects and has launched over time a series of national and international research projects that explore and analyse in depth how these challenges can be addressed. Additionally, the international openness of the studies conducted at ABC enables a comparison with the most advanced research—basic, applied, technological and project-based—conducted abroad.

In particular, this volume offers a rich and kaleidoscopic selection of the most prominent conceptual, empirical, methodological, technical, case study and project-based researches conducted by the members of ABC and that are the outcome of national and international research projects carried in collaboration with other universities and research centres, also on behalf of institutional and governmental bodies (e.g. UNESCO, UIA, EACEA, EC-JRC, ESPON, DG REGIO); of participation to sectoral boards and committees (e.g. ISO, CEN, UNI, Network Android-Disaster Resilient, IEA, Stati Generali della Green Economy, Green Public Procurement, Associazione Rete Italiana LCA, Lombardy Energy Cleantech Cluster); of dialogues with institutions (e.g. national ministries, regional government, local administrations).

The design of this volume follows the challenge logic sketched above. Accordingly, the volume is organised in four main sections, each addressing one of the four specific challenges listed above and opening with an introduction written by the volume editors. Given the multidisciplinary nature of this volume, the allocation of each contribution in a specific section is not watertight but, in our view, the proposed structure of the volume serves as a useful structure of central themes in the research field on the regeneration of the built environment from a circular economy perspective.

Sara Cattaneo
Camilla Lenzi
Alessandra Zanelli

Contents

Reuse and Regeneration of Urban Spaces From a Resilient Perspective

About the Editors

Stefano Della Torre who graduated in Civil Engineering and in Architecture, is a Full Professor of Restoration at the Politecnico di Milano in Milan, Italy, and Director of the ABC Department (Architecture, Built Environment and Construction Engineering). He is the author of more than 360 publications. He served as an advisor to the CARIPLO Foundation (Cultural Districts), the Italian Government and Lombardy Region (policies on planned conservation of historical-architectural heritage). He has been President of BuildingSMART Italia – the national chapter of BuildingSMART International (2011-2017).

Sara Cattaneo has been Associate Professor of Structural Engineering at Politecnico di Milano since 2011, where she received both her MS and PhD in Structural Engineering. Since 2017 she has also been an Associate at the Construction Technologies Institute, Italian National Research Council (ITC-CNR). Examples of her wide-ranging research interests include fracture and damage of quasi-brittle materials, constitutive behavior, and the structural response of high-performance and self-consolidating concrete. She has been involved in a number of research projects at the national and European levels. Since 1999 she has spent periods at the Department of Civil Engineering of the University of Minnesota (Minneapolis, USA), where she has been a Visiting Professor. She is the author of more than 100 papers in international journals and international conference proceedings and serves as a reviewer for several international journals.

Camilla Lenzi has been an Associate Professor of Regional and Urban Economics at Politecnico di Milano since 2015. She holds a PhD in Economics from the University of Pavia and a Master of Science in Industry and Innovation Analysis from SPRU – University of Sussex, UK. From 2005 to 2008, she was a postdoctoral fellow in the Department of Economics of Bocconi University and CESPRI (now I-CRIOS). Her main research interests are in the fields of regional and innovation studies, urban economics, highly skilled worker mobility, and entrepreneurship. She has participated in several EU-funded projects and has published in various international refereed journals, such as the Journal of Urban Economics, the Journal of Regional Science, Urban Studies, Regional Studies, Papers in Regional Science, and Small Business Economics.

Alessandra Zanelli is an architect and Full Professor in the Department of Architecture, Built Environment, and Engineering Construction at Politecnico di Milano, where she teaches for both the School of Architecture, Urbanism, and Construction Engineering and the School of Design. She holds a PhD in the Technology of Architecture and the Environment. Since 2015 she has been coordinator of the Interdepartmental Research Laboratory of Textiles and Polymer Materials. She is also the Regional Representative and an Associate Partner of TensiNet, the thematic network for upgrading the built environment in Europe through tensile structures. She has been involved in many research projects co-financed by national and international bodies, focusing on the sustainable innovation of ultra-lightweight and flexible materials in both architecture and interior design. She is the author of more than 180 publications and holds four international patents.

Socio-Economic Development and Regeneration of Territories

Sara Cattaneo, Camilla Lenzi and Alessandra Zanelli

Introduction

This section of the volume focuses on the first challenge identified in the Introduction, in particular, on the possibility to relaunch the socio-economic regeneration and development of territories as to achieve sustainability and circularity goals (and not simply competitiveness ones). From this perspective, then, the regeneration of the built environment requires the capacity to gauge economic growth processes and the efficient (and circular) use of scarce local resources, where scarce resources include not simply economic ones, but also environmental ones.

Accordingly, the analysis of territorial regeneration requires a multidisciplinary perspective and the integration of different scientific competences including competences in spatial economic analysis, urban studies, evaluation studies, sustainable technological project design and development.

This section of the volume, thus, proposes a selection of contributions that covers all these different disciplinary fields. The contributions collected in this section are organized according to the perspective adopted, namely a comparative analysis at the aggregated urban scale across cities vs an in-depth analysis of single cities and areas within cities.

The first group of papers sets the analysis at the aggregated urban scale by adopting a comparative perspective on European cities. In particular, Camagni et al. provide a historical outlook on the evolution of economic thought concerning the development of cities and their performance with particular reference to the European context. Next, Capello et al. investigate the role of culture, cultural heritage and creativity as territorial assets and their impact on the socio-economic development of cities. Lenzi and Perucca complement these perspectives by examining the impact of urbanization, city size and city development on residents' well-being in European cities and for different types of cities. Lastly, Fratesi and Perucca propose an analysis of the role of different territorial endowments, i.e. territorial capital, for the resilience of European territories to the economic crisis and the effectiveness of local development policies in different contexts characterized by different territorial capital endowments.

The second group of papers sets as well the analysis at the urban scale while focusing on single areas/neighbourhoods within cities. Within this group, two subgroups can be identified depending on the specific dimension emphasized in the analysis. The former focuses on the analysis of territorial transformation in specific areas of a city while the latter concentrates on the technological project dimension of such transformations.

In the first subgroup, Merlini offers a conceptual reflection on the relationship between territorial regeneration and demolition. She proposes a new interpretation of this link that departs from the view of demolition as reparation or precondition for a valourization project. Instead, she proposes a view on demolition as a project tool for the reconfiguration and transformation of the built environment. Sdino et al. propose an overview of the state of the art of evaluation methods for the economic assessment of urban transformations complemented by the analysis of a peri-urban transformation in Italy.

In the second subgroup, Mussinelli et al. discuss public spaces valourization, urban landscape requalification, adaptive regeneration of degraded areas and advance a new approach to project development with the aim of targeting sustainability and resilience to climate change. Next, Mussinelli et al. reflect on the relevance of integrated and multidisciplinary approaches for peri-urban landscape project development, for architectural heritage valourization and for agriculture socio-economic value in the management of places. Lastly, Pavesi et al. propose a case study analysis on the possible drivers and strategies to improve real estate management, resources and processes and their valourization according to a social and circular economy perspective.

A Research Programme on Urban Dynamics

Roberto Camagni, Roberta Capello and Andrea Caragliu

Abstract Over the last three decades, the research group on regional and urban economics at the Politecnico di Milano has carried out studies on theoretical and empirical issues concerning the structure, competitiveness and growth of cities. A broad critical synthesis of this line of research is presented in Camagni et al. (Urban Empire, Edward Elgar, Cheltenham, 2019). In what follows, we focus on two crucial issues that the group has tackled, i.e. optimal city size theory and the empirics of central place theory. Although other issues, like self-organization dynamic models and the concept of city networks, have been elaborated by the group, they are not discussed in this paper.

Keywords Optimal city size · Urban hierarchy · Central place theory

1 Introduction

Over the last three decades, the research group on regional and urban economics at the Politecnico di Milano has carried out studies on theoretical and empirical issues concerning the structure, competitiveness and growth of cities. A broad critical synthesis of this line of research is presented in Camagni et al. (2019). In what follows, we focus on two crucial issues that the group has tackled, i.e. optimal city size theory and the empirics of central place theory. Although other issues, like self-organization dynamic models and the concept of city networks, have been elaborated by the group, they are not discussed in this paper.

The logical *fil rouge* connecting different contributions—sometimes explicit, sometimes only implicit and even hidden—became evident by developing this paper, which also allowed us to verify the logical consistency of the overall research programme progressed by the groups on these issues.

R. Camagni (✉) · R. Capello · A. Caragliu
Architecture, Built Environment and Construction Engineering—ABC Department, Politecnico di Milano, Milan, Italy
e-mail: roberto.camagni@polimi.it

S. Della Torre et al. (eds.), *Regeneration of the Built Environment from a Circular Economy Perspective*, Research for Development,
https://doi.org/10.1007/978-3-030-33256-3_1

The main inspiration for most of the work of our research group originates from a paper presented in 1984 at the Second World Congress of the RSAI (Camagni et al. 1986). This period was characterized by booming scientific creativity with ground-breaking works in fields such as the economics of urban size (Alonso 1971), city systems and urban hierarchy (Beckmann 1958), spatial interaction models (Wilson 1970) and the associated dynamic versions (Harris and Wilson 1978), complex systems, mathematical ecology and self-organization modelling (Prigogine and Stengers 1984; Allen and Sanglier 1981). Camagni et al. (1986) is a theoretical and methodological work, although it has also been supported by empirical verification through a computer simulation. In this work, all these traditionally separated research fields were somewhat merged. Also, the paper added a crucial dimension, i.e. Schumpeterian innovation declined in spatial terms. The result was an eclectic, supply-side self-organization model simulating the dynamics of an urban system (SOUDY).

The logical structure of the model paved the way for a few theoretical hypotheses which, on the one hand, improved existing models and theories on urban structure and growth, and, on the other hand, suggested new directions for further theoretical advances and empirical validations. In what follows, we will deal with two major fields of analysis in detail, using the SOUDY model as a guiding light.

2 On Optimal City Size

In the early 1970s, urban economics frequently dealt with the identification of an optimal city size, whereby the distance between benefits and costs is maximized. In particular, urban size optimality may be defined in terms of (i) minimum city size (corresponding to the size at which average benefits begin to outvalue costs); (ii) cost minimization (where, with benefits remaining constant, costs are minimized); (iii) per capita optimal city size (i.e. city size associated to the maximum vertical distance between average benefits and costs, usually interpreted as the optimal size for dwellers); (iv) benefits maximization; (v) socially desirable optimal city size, corresponding to the golden rule where marginal costs equal marginal benefits. This condition is usually interpreted as the view of the rational national planner; and (vi) maximum city size, corresponding to the largest city size whereby average costs equal average benefits (Alonso 1971).

Yet, since the late 1970s research on optimal city size received relatively little attention. Richardson first criticized the optimal city size theory, arguing that since cities do not perform the same functions, they differ in terms of both costs and benefits. This difference logically makes it impossible for cities to share the same optimal size. Later on, Henderson (1985) questioned the validity of the optimal city size theory, claiming that each city is characterized by a specific production function. In fact, the same critique was also discussed by Alonso (1971), acknowledging that an optimal size should be sought for each city. The logical consequence would be a unique optimal city size for each individual city.

Later research overcame some of the limitations mentioned above by focusing on the fifth class of city size optimality, where marginal location costs equal marginal location benefits. Within a system in spatial balance, a rational planner looks at urban optimal sizes through marginal conditions (Camagni et al. 2013). The model discussed in this last paper delivers a continuum of equilibrium city sizes, due to rational consumers deciding their locations on the basis of a classical "$MC = MB$"[1] optimal condition. This framework also allows for a comparison on a cross-section of cities solving the logical impossibility stemming from the Henderson critique. The model is also supported by an empirical assessment of the factors at the core of benefits and costs, determining equilibrium city size *irrespective of their dimensions*. These determinants encompass the quality of functions hosted but also other economic, social and environmental factors. The model strikes a balance between the dichotomy of "one vs. infinite optimal sizes": "*cities are supposed to share the same cost and production functions with heterogeneous, substitutable factors*" (economic functions and other context conditions). Also, "*each of them maintains its specificity and, consequently, its 'equilibrium' size, but comparability and possibility of running cross-sectional analyses is saved, and also possibility of devising policy strategies for urban growth and containment*" (Camagni et al., p. 313).

However, the remnants of these empirical estimates remain unexplained, or, to put it more accurately, amenable to alternative explanations. Along with true *i.i.d.* disturbances, residuals also capture potentially omitted variables such as good or bad governance, which may potentially sustain population levels above or below structural equilibrium ones.

3 On Urban Hierarchy and Central Place Theory

Central place theory (henceforth, CPT) explains the existence of urban systems as the result of the tension underlying centripetal and centrifugal forces, which create regular structures whereby cities of different ranks coexist and, in the Lösch version, can focus on performing different economic activities.

This theory introduced several fundamental advances in our understanding of urban systems. One such improvement lies in the role played by functions (in Christallerian contributions, specific per rank) in explaining the spatial distribution of cities across a system. The rank of a city explains its function, and therefore its size, leaving within an urban system space for cities of varying sizes. Paradoxically, this result was indirectly neglected for several years by the modern spatial equilibrium approach à la Von Thünen-Alonso-Fujita (Camagni 1992). Theoretical neoclassical models of stylized cities typically work on the assumption of location choice indifference, which posits that lower accessibility to the centre is compensated by lower rents and higher environmental quality. Extending the same approach to city systems equilibria, indifference in location choices is satisfied only when cities provide the

[1] MC: Marginal Costs; MB: Marginal Benefits.

same advantages and disadvantages to firms and dwellers. This condition remains valid only when cities share the same size (Camagni 1992, Sect. 6.6).

However, CPT is not free from shortcomings. One such limitation is related to their inherently static approach: proof being that in these models relative city rankings remain stable over time. While this result is acceptable over the short/medium run, it clearly cannot explain long-run urban growth processes. While some have tried to overcome this limitation at least in terms of comparative statics (Parr 1981), there is still a chance to explain the diverging development patterns of cities over the long run.

In this sense, following the newly developed self-organization approach to the dynamics of complex systems (Prigogine and Stengers 1984) and in particular its application to the evolution of urban systems (Allen and Sanglier 1981; Dendrinos and Mullally 1981; Bertuglia et al. 1987), the SOUDY model (Camagni et al. 1986) introduced a dynamic and evolutionary approach, in theoretical, mathematical and simulation terms. The dynamics of each city in the model, interacting within urban systems, happens through two distinct processes:

(i) a process of *constrained dynamics*, causing demographic growth (within efficient size intervals) towards an attractor (net urban benefits) and linked to the hierarchical level of each function;
(ii) a process of *structural dynamics*, engendered by an innovation leap achieved by each city. This happens through the acquisition of new functions, relating to a higher hierarchical level, allowing higher profits, balancing the superior costs of larger dimensions. In the SOUDY model, the probability of transition depends on an endogenous dynamic instability condition, where each city overcomes the size threshold for the appearance of the superior function. This can potentially lead to the acquisition of the new function (or to the loss of previous functions) and consequently to relevant bifurcations in the development path.

Following up to the conceptual novelties of the SOUDY model, the development path of cities determined by normal, multiplier-type dynamics and by *structural dynamics* led by internal innovation was empirically investigated identifying three hierarchical ranks (*small*, *medium* and *large* cities) in the European urban system (Camagni et al. 2015a, b). Interpreting urban growth as net returns to urban scale, the assumption of an inverted U-shaped relationship between city size and agglomeration economies inside each rank was found to be statistically significantly verified, along with the evidence of the possibility, for dynamic cities, to escape decreasing returns through innovation.

Moreover, Camagni et al. (2015a, b) find that:

(i) the intensity of the following factors determines increasing returns *irrespective of city size*: the quality of the activities hosted, the quality of production factors, the density of external linkages and cooperation networks, the quality of urban infrastructure—internal and external mobility, education, public services;
(ii) large, as well as medium and small cities, may experience a halt in their growth path, even a decline, when they grow without a simultaneous increase in the

endowment of these factors. This is what has been termed long-term *structural dynamics* (Camagni et al. 2015a).

This implies that some large cities escape agglomeration diseconomies, despite their large dimensions; by the same token, some small ones may face diseconomies if unable to implement innovative strategies and functional upgrading or to broaden their networks with other cities across short but also long distances through cooperative agreements relating to infrastructure, top public services or R&D facilities.

Within CPT, there is still considerable room for further advances. Particularly, there seems to be a general lack of consensus regarding the very definition of urban ranks. What do "large" and "medium" mean when defining urban ranks? While, from a general equilibrium perspective, city sizes are distributed along a continuum of functions and roles, structural breaks still seem to characterize urban systems, thus strengthening the case for the existence of different production functions, and different stocks of production factors for cities of different ranks. Ideally, theoretical models should follow suit and accommodate rank thresholds.

An important step forward in this sense is the critique of a number of theoretical shortcuts in neoclassical urban economics (Camagni et al. 2016) which assume that agglomeration economies (i.e. city size) automatically lead to urban growth (Krugman 1991; Glaeser et al. 2001; Glaeser 2011). Henderson (2010) argues that the "*association between urbanization and development (…) is an equilibrium not causal relation*" (p. 518) and that "*urbanization* per se *does not cause development*" (p. 515). The point made by the authors is that "*along an average productivity curve rising with urban size, reading the size-derivative as a time-derivative will be mistaken and, beyond that, implies a circular reasoning: 'if a city grows demographically it will grow economically*'" (Camagni et al. 2016, p. 134). A second critique also posed by the authors suggests the use of net rather than gross measures of urban efficiency when measuring agglomeration economies. This implies reaching beyond per capita GDP, productivity and wages in order to also include urban costs (as argued in Richardson 1978). Thirdly, in their empirical estimates (based on European metro areas), Camagni et al. (2016) find that:

(i) In static terms, net overall urban benefits (urban land rent) display a U-shaped relationship with urban size, suggesting the presence of net increasing returns to urban scale;
(ii) On the other hand, from a dynamic perspective, this relationship fails when it comes to interpreting urban growth. In fact, urban dynamics as measured by net benefit growth rates show no relation to initial urban size or density. Instead, results suggest that growth is positively associated with the upgrading of urban functions, the development of the nearby urban system and, once again, the capability of establishing long-distance cooperative agreements with other cities. These results call for a dynamic approach to explaining agglomeration economies (Camagni et al. 2016).

Despite consistent efforts, urban economics still has a long way to go. As frequently advocated (see e.g. Duranton and Puga 2004), the relative strength of agglomerative forces is still not fully understood. More specifically, there seems to be room to seek for more broadly defined dependent variables in agglomeration economy regressions (this is the case of the recent wave of studies on urban wellbeing and quality of life; see Lenzi and Perucca 2016, for a recent review) and independent variables (i.e. how to measure sources of urban efficiency).

4 Conclusions

The main goal of the present work is to present a selection of highlights from the scientific study of urban economics as carried out by the research group in regional science active at the Politecnico di Milano over the last thirty years, with a particular focus on optimal city size theory and on the empirics of central place theory. The specificity of this long-term research programme lies in taking the challenge launched by Alan Wilson in the early 1980s, i.e. the need to develop a unitary approach to urban economics, bringing together theoretical areas which were developed in total isolation. These have been labelled the five *principles* of urban economics (agglomeration, accessibility, interaction, hierarchy and development; Camagni 1992, Introduction).

The starting point of this journey was the construction of a theoretical and simulation model of urban system dynamics, driven by the capability to innovate in the functions hosted by each city (SOUDY model; Camagni et al. 1986). Schumpeterian innovation, generated both by private entrepreneurship and public leadership, and the consequent *structural dynamics*, were suggested as the main driving forces of urban growth. Subsequently, other issues were explicitly inserted into the picture: agglomeration economies, urban and environmental quality, city networks and high-level urban functions.

Attention was also paid to pinpointing the logical shortcuts of an automatic relationship between agglomeration economies and growth. Again, structural change is identified as the factor allowing faster growth of urban benefits to overcome the increase of urban costs, rather than sheer size. Remarkable empirical results have been achieved to prove these assumptions.

References

Allen, P. M., & Sanglier, M. (1981). Urban evolution, self-organization and decision-making. *Environment and Planning A, 13,* 167–183.

Alonso, W. (1971). The economics of urban size. *Papers and Proceedings of the Regional Science Association, 26,* 67–83.

Beckmann, M. J. (1958). City hierarchies and the distribution of city size. *Economic Development and Cultural Change, 3,* 243–248.

Bertuglia, S., Leonardi, G., Ocelli, S., Rabino, G., Tadei, R., & Wilson, A. (Eds.). (1987). *Urban Systems: Contemporary approaches to modelling*. London (UK): Croom Helm.

Camagni, R. (1992). *Economia Urbana: principi e modelli teorici*. Firenze: La Nuova Italia. French translation (1996): Principes et modèles de l'économie urbaine, Paris: Economica.

Camagni, R., Capello, R., & Caragliu, A. (2013). One or infinite optimal city sizes? In search for an equilibrium size for cities. *Annals of Regional Science, 51*(2), 309–341.

Camagni, R., Capello, R., & Caragliu, A. (2015a). The rise of second-rank cities: What role for agglomeration economies? *European Planning Studies, 23*(6), 1069–1089.

Camagni, R., Capello, R., & Caragliu, A. (2015b). Agglomeration Economies in large vs. small cities: Similar laws, high specificities. In K. Kourtit, P. Nijkamp, & R. Stough (Eds.), *The rise of the city* (pp. 85–116). Cheltenham: Edward Elgar.

Camagni, R., Capello, R., & Caragliu, A. (2016). Static vs. dynamic agglomeration economies: Spatial context and structural evolution behind urban growth. *Papers in Regional Science, 94*(1), 133–159.

Camagni, R., Capello, R., & Caragliu, A. (2019). A scientific program on urban performance and dynamics. In E. Glaeser, K. Kourtit, & P. Nijkamp (Eds.), *Urban empire*. Cheltenham: Edward Elgar.

Camagni, R., Diappi, L., & Leonardi, G. (1986). Urban growth and decline in a hierarchical system: A supply-oriented dynamic approach. *Regional Science and Urban Economics, 16*(1), 145–160.

Dendrinos, D., & Mullally, H. (1981). Evolutionary patterns of urban populations. *Geographical Analysis, 4,* 328–344.

Duranton, G., & Puga, D. (2004). Micro-foundations of urban agglomeration economies. In V. Henderson & J. F. Thisse (Eds), *Handbook of regional and urban economics* (Vol. 4, pp. 2063–2117).

Glaeser, E. L. (2011). *Triumph of the city: How our greatest invention makes us richer, smarter, greener, healthier, and happier*. New York: Penguin Books.

Glaeser, E. L., Kolko, J., & Saiz, A. (2001). Consumer city. *Journal of Economic Geography, 1*(1), 27–50.

Harris, B., & Wilson, A. (1978). Equilibrium values and dynamics of attractiveness terms in production-constrained spatial interaction models. *Environment and Planning A, 10,* 371–388.

Henderson, J. V. (1985). *Economic theory and the cities* (2nd ed.). Orlando (FL): Academic Press.

Henderson, J. V. (2010). Cities and development. *Journal of Regional Science, 50*(1), 515–540.

Krugman, P. (1991). Increasing returns and economic geography. *Journal of Political Economy, 99*(3), 483–499.

Lenzi, C., & Perucca, G. (2016). Are urbanized areas source of life satisfaction? Evidence from EU regions. *Papers in Regional Science, online first.*. https://doi.org/10.1111/pirs.12232.

Parr, J. B. (1981). Temporal change in a central-place system. *Environment and Planning A, 13*(1), 97–118.

Prigogine, I., & Stengers, I. (1984). *Order out of chaos*. New York (NY): Bantam Books.

Richardson, H. W. (1978). *Regional and urban economics*. London (UK): Penguin.

Wilson, A. G. (1970). *Entropy in urban and regional modelling*. London: Pion.

Cultural Heritage, Creativity, and Local Development: A Scientific Research Program

Roberta Capello, Silvia Cerisola and Giovanni Perucca

Abstract The present chapter reviews the recent studies of the ABC department surrounding the role of cultural heritage and creativity on local economic development. The research line covers the interpretation of culture as a territorial asset, its multifaceted dimensions, and impact on local development. An innovative definition of cultural capital was provided, jointly with empirical evidence on the relationship between cultural heritage and intangible cultural elements. The most interesting finding shows that culture, embedded within cultural heritage, plays a role in promoting prosperity only when tangible heritage is matched with intangible cultural assets. Among such intangible assets, creativity is particularly analyzed in terms of its link with the cultural heritage of places and their economic development. The assumption, both conceptually and empirically investigated, is that culture promotes creativity through emotional, esthetic, and inspirational mechanisms, driving individuals' ability to doubt, innovate, and think critically. In other words, creativity is an important mediator of the relationship between culture and socioeconomic development. Empirical evidence from Italian regions strongly supports this hypothesis. Future research directions are presented in the concluding section.

Keywords Cultural heritage · Creativity · Local development

1 Introduction

The economic role of culture nowadays is well recognized. From this perspective, culture does not just hold an esthetic and recreational value, as was the general opinion for a long time, but also an economic value, which makes culture a territorial asset of places.

R. Capello (✉) · S. Cerisola · G. Perucca
Architecture, Built Environment and Construction Engineering—ABC Department, Politecnico di Milano, Milan, Italy
e-mail: roberta.capello@polimi.it

S. Della Torre et al. (eds.), *Regeneration of the Built Environment from a Circular Economy Perspective*, Research for Development,
https://doi.org/10.1007/978-3-030-33256-3_2

From the seminal work of Throsby (1999), a long stream of research analyzed the mechanisms through which culture may influence economic development. These studies define culture in very distinct ways. The majority of them focused on tangible cultural heritage and the effect of these resources on the attractiveness of tourism flows (Fainstein et al. 2003). Other works, however, defined culture in different ways, concerning, for instance, the so-called cultural industry, the growth of which has outperformed, over the last decades, the more traditional sectors of the economy. Finally, other authors (Guiso et al. 2006) defined culture as the values shared in a community, such as religion, finding a positive effect on the reinforcement of trust and cooperation.

The research group in regional and urban economics developed a research program on the role of cultural heritage on economic development mainly due to two motivations, both concerning the nature of culture as an economic asset.

The first one, as suggested by the studies mentioned above, is that culture is a multidimensional asset. In other words, very different elements coexist under the label of "culture." Heritage represents a tangible form of culture, while other aspects are intangible, such as the values shared within a community. Moreover, other tangible forms of culture, like cultural industry, are conceptually different from cultural heritage, being private resources rather than public ones. It is therefore necessary, in order to fully understand the potential economic impact of cultural heritage, to develop a comprehensive and exhaustive definition of culture, embracing all its possible elements. The recognition and systematization of these multidimensional elements of culture will allow for the study of the joint effects through which cultural heritage generates economic prosperity. While several works, including the key CHCfE report (2015), recognize that cultural heritage affects economic development through various channels, it does not consider the role of intangible elements stemming from culture, like creativity, identity, sense of belonging in cultural heritage and its effects on the local area. We developed the impression that this position was underestimating the role of cultural heritage on local development, convinced that cultural heritage is able to generate a positive effect on local socioeconomic conditions in the presence of other cultural characteristics, like the shared values of the community.

The second reason of interest for this topic refers to the high differentiation of culture across space. The nonreplicability of cultural heritage, for instance, makes it unique and exclusive resources of each place. Therefore, the analysis of culture and economic development needs to adopt a regional perspective, able to compare territories characterized by different combinations of cultural elements of different varieties. Due to the difficulty in measuring culture and its different dimensions, such an approach is relatively rare in the literature, which is mostly focused on case studies analyzing single regions or cities.

Stemming from these considerations, the research program of the research group concentrated on:

1. *a definition and measurement of culture and the role of cultural heritage on local development*. The scope of this part is to provide a conceptually grounded definition of culture and its multidimensional elements, jointly with an empirical

measurement of these resources on a small territorial scale. The role of cultural heritage on local development was also measured;

2. *creativity as a mediator of the economic impact of cultural heritage.* A further element which is assumed to foster the economic role of culture is created. While creativity itself is not an element of culture, the two concepts are strictly related, being culture an expression of human creativity. Similarly to culture, creativity is also a rather vague concept, treated in the literature in several different ways, often without a conceptual framework on which a research hypothesis can be founded. The goals of this part of the project are therefore to conceptualize creativity and its connection with cultural heritage and to empirically test a set of assumptions on the mechanisms through which creativity can reinforce the effect of cultural heritage on local development.

The following sections review the two steps of the research program, pointing out the results achieved.

2 Culture as a Multidimensional Territorial Asset: Definition and Empirical Evidence

The recognition of a multidimensional nature of culture calls for a conceptual systematization of the different cultural elements. Inspiration came from the work by Camagni (2008), who systematized the elements constituting the territorial capital of places along two dimensions: materiality and rivalry. This approach is well suited for culture. The latter, in fact, is made up of both tangible and intangible components. At the same time, a number of cultural elements are close to public goods and therefore present a low level of rivalry, while others are comparable to private goods, as is the case of the cultural industry.

Taken together, these elements define the cultural capital of places. Figure 1 shows the taxonomy developed in Capello and Perucca (2017).

Cultural heritage is represented in boxes *a* and *b*. On both cases, the level of materiality is high, because monuments, galleries but also landscapes and aggregate tangible heritage have a material nature. On the other hand, these two elements differ in terms of rivalry. While aggregate tangible heritage (as for instance, the historical center of a city) is a public good, single goods (a monument, a museum) can be subject to congestion effects and are, therefore, characterized by an intermediate level of rivalry.

Empirically, the measurement of the elements of the taxonomy for Italian NUTS3 regions allowed for the identification of the different typologies of intangible cultural environments. In a nutshell, the variation across regions of the intangible elements of cultural capital was analyzed, with the aim of identifying groups of regions that were similar in their characteristics. Three were identified: areas endowed with intangible cultural elements embedded within individual behavior, areas endowed with intangible cultural elements embedded within institutional behavior and areas which

Rivalry ↑		Tangible goods (hard)	Mixed goods (hard + soft)	Intangible goods (soft)
(High)	Private goods	*c* Private Cultural Capital: stock of capital invested in the cultural industry	*i* Private Mecenatism: Arts patronage, foundations and agencies supporting cultural activities	*f* Cultural capital embedded in human beings: Human capital, individual cultural attitudes
	Club goods, impure public goods	*b* Tangible Cultural Assets: monuments, museums, galleries	*h* Cultural Cooperation Networks: Public/private partnerships in the provision of cultural goods and services	*e* Cultural capital embedded in social relations: cultural networks
(Low)	Public goods	*a* Public, Aggregate, Tangible Culture: landscapes, aggregate tangible heritage	*g* Urbanization Economies: Types of agglomeration	*d* Cultural values embedded in the society: Inherited cultural values shared within the community such as religion, folklore
		(High)	Materiality →	(Low)

Source: Capello and Perucca, 2017.

Fig. 1 A taxonomy of cultural capital elements

are poor in intangible cultural assets, i.e., with low values of intangible elements. While the first two groups characterize northern Italy, the latter is peculiar of southern regions (Capello and Perucca 2017).

Having categorized the alternative intangible cultural settings characterizing Italian provinces, the research question addressed concerned the way in which these settings mediate the impact of cultural heritage on economic growth. Economic growth is empirically defined by real GDP growth between 2004 and 2008 in Italian provinces.

The results of the estimates of an econometric economic growth model point out that the pure endowment of cultural heritage has no significant effect on regional economic growth. In other words, regions with a higher density of cultural heritage did not perform better than the others. However, the effects differ in different areas. In particular, areas that are poor in intangible cultural assets are not able to generate an economic return from their endowment of cultural heritage. The opposite applies to the areas endowed with intangible cultural elements embedded within institutional behavior; here, the impact of cultural heritage on economic growth is positive. Finally, in areas endowed with intangible cultural elements embedded within individual behavior, the effect of cultural heritage on economic growth is not statistically significant.

This result once again highlights the importance of a good, wise, and efficient governance of public monuments and cultural goods in general for their efficient exploitation. Without appropriate local conditions, investing in cultural heritage does not necessarily generate an economic return; in order to achieve such a goal, investments must be coupled with policies enhancing and preserving the sociocultural environment in which cultural heritage and industries are located.

3 Creativity as a Mediator of the Economic Impact of Cultural Heritage

Particular attention has been devoted by the research group to a specific intangible element through which the role that could be played in socioeconomic development by cultural heritage could take place: creativity. In recent literature, the linkage between the impacts of socioeconomic development by cultural heritage on the one hand and by creativity on the other has been widely recognized at both academic and institutional levels.[1]

The spatial dimension, specifically, has gained great relevance within these topics, through the emphasis on the importance of history and cultural heritage in shaping local systems and in affecting their economic outcomes.[2] Moreover, history, culture, physical setting, and overall operating conditions also shape the creative capacity of a place (Csikszentmihalyi 1988).

Two parallel theoretical traditions have developed, one regarding the link between cultural heritage and economic performance and the other focusing on creativity and economic performance. Up to now, however, they have remained mainly separate and overall inconclusive.

As for the relationship between creativity and regional development, the mixed empirical evidence is due to the objective difficulties in defining and measuring creativity. As for cultural heritage and regional development, on the other hand, the link is often just assumed. When a transmission channel is considered, this is often exclusively cultural tourism, according to a linear and mechanical "tourism → demand → income multiplier effect → production → development" model.

Drawing on such limitations within the existing literature, this part of the research program suggests that an effort should be made to link the two streams. The added value of the research group work lies specifically in bringing the two theoretical traditions together, highlighting for the first time that cultural heritage and creativity do in fact interact on a territorial level and can concur to push economic development, mutually reinforcing their interpretative potential.

Cultural heritage could indeed inspire local creativity, which could—in turn—have a positive impact on economic development through the generation of new and original ideas (Cerisola 2019a, b).

In this sense, the main research question that this part of the research program attempts to answer is whether creativity mediates the effect of cultural heritage on economic development.

[1]E.g. European Council ESDP (1999), Florida (2002) UNCTAD (2010).

[2]E.g. Pratt (2008), JPI (2014).

In order to address the issue, the general thought process starts by taking into account the (potential) direct relationship between cultural heritage and economic development, which is usually assumed in the existing literature. The idea is that the mere presence of cultural heritage is unlikely to be effective, but that there could be some more indirect channels through which cultural heritage could affect local development. Following this line of thought, the relationship between cultural heritage and creativity is subsequently explored, according to the idea that cultural heritage—through its *inspirational role*—can contribute to the shaping of the peculiar creativity of a local area. Finally, the—expectedly positive—relationship between creativity and economic development is investigated.

The overall reasoning is thus based on the potential *mediating* role of creativity between cultural heritage and economic development: cultural heritage could affect regional development through its *inspirational role* in shaping local creativity and, by this mechanism, influence economic performance.

This perspective is empirically tested using employment growth as the main dependent variable and Italian provinces as the units of analysis. Italy is in fact a country with a rich endowment of cultural capital, the exploitation of which strongly differs from one area to another. Thus, it is an interesting case study where this innovative framework can be applied.

To address, both conceptually and empirically, the research question presented above—*does creativity mediate the effect of cultural heritage on economic development?*—this part of the research program develops:

i. an investigation of the potential direct link between cultural heritage and economic development;
ii. an analysis of the effect of cultural heritage on (different types of) local creativity;
iii. an exploration of the role of creativity in regional development; and
iv. an overall comprehensive model meant to shed light on the cultural heritage → creativity → development nexus.

According to this logical framework, the work starts by analyzing the potential direct effect of cultural heritage on economic development. Drawing on Camagni (2008) and Capello and Perucca (2017), cultural heritage is considered a tangible and common element. In particular, its tangibility can be interpreted in terms of physical representation of the history of a given place and people, since immovable units of heritage also carry intangible meanings (Carta 1999). Moreover, cultural heritage is considered a public good, thus characterized by nonexcludability and by a low level of rivalry. In this sense, the variable representing cultural heritage refers to the presence of immovable tangible cultural heritage in the area, thus to the degree of residents' exposure to tangible cultural heritage.

Since this first step of the analysis shows that there is no generalized direct impact of cultural heritage per se on economic development, the work moves on with the line of reasoning, exploring some more sophisticated channels through which cultural heritage could indirectly affect regional performance. It could play, for instance, an inspirational role on local creativity.

To investigate this idea, the work provides a conceptual framework that allows for the identification and measurement of different types of creative talents (artistic, scientific, and economic) and all their possible interactions, according to the belief that it is the "mental cross-fertilization" (Andersson et al. 1993; Camagni 2011) between different creative talents that generate innovative and ground-breaking ideas and—through this mechanism—drives economic development. Creativity is thus defined as *ideation based on talents of different types, i.e., stemming from different domains* (Cerisola 2018a).

In an attempt to restrain the limitations of the different existing approaches (e.g., UK-DCMS 2001; WIPO 2003; Santagata 2009; UNCTAD 2010; Florida 2002), a new measurement of different types of creativity is proposed and the potential inspirational role played by cultural heritage on the different creative talents is econometrically explored, along with other possible determinants of different types of creativity (Cerisola 2018b). The initial expectations and previous results are confirmed in the empirical (econometric) studies: cultural heritage does not seem to play any generalized direct role on economic development, but it has an indirect effect on regional performance through its significant inspirational impact on artistic and scientific creative talents.

4 Conclusions: Future Research Directions

The research program does not stop at this level. Two additional new research streams are put forward and will provide interesting results over the upcoming years. The first one is to investigate in greater depth the idea of intangible elements mediating the link between cultural heritage and local development, by focusing on another very important element, i.e., sense of belonging in local communities (Perucca 2019). The results of this additional intangible element may give more robustness to the results obtained with creativity and to the general idea that intangible cultural elements are indeed important mediators of cultural heritage and local development. The results are crucial for the launching of successful cultural policies on a local level. The second stream of research relates to cultural and creative industries (CCIs), with respect to their location behavior and their support to local productivity. Despite the vast literature on the issue, a large effort in an operational definition of CCIs is required. Implications for the right strategies relating to such industries exist and call for effective and well-thought-out conceptual and empirical analyses.

References

Andersson, Å. E., Batten, D. F., Kobayashi, K., & Yoshikawa, K. (1993). Logistical dynamics, creativity and infrastructure. In Å. E. Andersson, D. F. Batten, K. Kobayashi, & K. Yoshikawa

(Eds.), *The cosmo-creative society: Logistical networks in a dynamic economy*. Berlin: Springer-Verlag.

Camagni, R. (2008). Regional competitiveness: Towards a concept of territorial capital. In R. Capello, R. Camagni, B. Chizzolini, & U. Fratesi (Eds.), *Modelling regional scenarios for the enlarged Europe: European competitiveness and global strategies* (pp. 33–48). Berlin: Springer Verlag.

Camagni, R. (2011). Creativity, culture and urban milieux. In L. Fusco Girard, T. Baycan, & P. Nijkamp (Eds.), *Sustainable city and creativity*. Farnham: Ashgate.

Capello, R., & Perucca, G. (2017). Cultural capital and local development Nexus: Does the local environment matter? In *Socioeconomic environmental policies and evaluations in regional science* (pp. 103–124). Singapore: Springer.

Carta, M. (1999). *L'armatura culturale del territorio. Il patrimonio culturale come matrice di identità e strumento di sviluppo.* Milano: Franco Angeli.

Cerisola, S. (2018a). Creativity and local economic development: the role of synergy among different talents. *Papers in Regional Science, 97*(2), 199–216.

Cerisola, S. (2018b). Multiple creative talents and their determinants at the local level. *Journal of Cultural Economics, 42*(2), 243–269.

Cerisola, S. (2019a). A new perspective on the cultural heritage—development nexus: the role of creativity. *Journal of Cultural Economics, 43*(1), 21–56. https://doi.org/10.1007/s10824-018-9328-2.

Cerisola, S. (2019b). *Cultural heritage, creativity and economic development*. London: Edward Elgar.

CHCfE Cultural Heritage Counts for Europe. (2015). Accessed 2 May 2019 at http://blogs.encatc.org/culturalheritagecountsforeurope//wp-content/uploads/2015/06/CHCfE_FULL-REPORT_v2.pdf.

Csikszentmihalyi, M. (1988). Society, culture, and person: a systems view of creativity. In J. Sternberg (Ed.), *Sternberg, in R.* The nature of creativity: Cambridge University Press.

European Council of Ministers, European Spatial Development Perspective (ESDP) (1999). Towards balanced and sustainable development of the territory of the european union. Accessed 22 Oct 2019 at http://ec.europa.eu/regional_policy/sources/docoffic/official/reports/pdf/sum_en.pdf

Fainstein, S. S., Hoffman L. M., & Judd D. R. (2003). Making theoretical sense of tourism, In S. S. Fainstein, L. M. Hoffman, amp; D. R. Judd (Eds.), *Cities and Visitors: Regulating People, Markets and City Space* (pp. 239–253). Oxford: Blackwell.

Florida, R. (2002). *The rise of the creative class: And how it's transforming work, leisure, community and everyday life*. New York: Basic Books.

Guiso, L., Sapienza, P., & Zingales, L. (2006). Does culture affect economic outcomes? *Journal of Economic perspectives, 20*(2), 23–48.

JPI Cultural Heritage and Global Change. (2014). Strategic Research Agenda (http://www.jpi-culturalheritage.eu/wp-content/uploads/SRA-2014-06.pdf).

Pratt, A. C. (2008). Creative cities: The cultural industries and the creative class. *Geografiska Annnaler: Series B, Human Geography, 90*(2), 107–117.

Perucca, G. (2019). Residents' satisfaction with cultural city life: Evidence from EU Cities. Applied Research in Quality of Life, 1–18. https://doi.org/10.1007/s11482-018-9623-2.

Santagata, W. (2009), *Libro bianco sulla creativita. Per un modello italiano di sviluppo*. White paper on creativity. For an Italian development model, Universita Bocconi Edizioni.

Throsby, D. (1999). Cultural capital. *Journal of Cultural Economics, 23*(1), 3–12.

UK-DCMS. (2001). Creative industries mapping document. https://www.gov.uk/government/publications/creative-industries-mapping-documents-2001.

UNCTAD. (2010). Creative economy report. http://unctad.org/en/Docs/ditctab20103_en.pdf.

WIPO. (2003). Guide on surveying the economic contribution of the copyright-based industries, World Intellectual Property Organization.

Urbanization and Subjective Well-Being

Camilla Lenzi and Giovanni Perucca

Abstract This chapter proposes a review of the most recent works developed by the authors on the association between urbanization and subjective well-being. While most previous studies point out a strong dichotomy between urban and rural areas, the latter being characterized by higher levels of well-being than the former, the research program presented here aims at overcoming this perspective. Specifically, it focuses on three elements that are assumed to influence the role of urbanization on subjective well-being: the nature of externalities generated by cities of different kinds, the spatial accessibility to these externalities and the temporal dimension. Empirical results show that all these factors are important determinants of individuals' well-being, whose association with urbanization is more complex than generally assumed.

Keywords Subjective well-being · Urbanization · European regions

1 Introduction

The investigation of the determinants of human well-being has always been one of the main scopes of economic theory. The definition of well-being itself, however, evolved over time. Purely economic measures, mostly represented by income growth, have been progressively integrated by other indicators of quality of life which, taken together, contribute to the individual's self-perception and overall well-being (Stiglitz et al. 2009). While political interest in this issue is relatively recent (Veneri 2019), it is rooted in a scientific debate dating back at least to the seminal work of Easterlin (1973).

Easterlin's contribution was particularly influential because, for the first time, it pointed out a tension between objective (economic) and subjective well-being (SWB), where the latter is typically measured by survey studies asking respondents about their satisfaction with life. This result, labelled as the Easterlin paradox, was in

C. Lenzi · G. Perucca (✉)
Architecture, Built Environment and Construction Engineering—ABC Department, Politecnico di Milano, Milan, Italy
e-mail: giovanni.perucca@polimi.it

S. Della Torre et al. (eds.), *Regeneration of the Built Environment from a Circular Economy Perspective*, Research for Development,
https://doi.org/10.1007/978-3-030-33256-3_3

strong contradiction with the mainstream assumption about a positive and straightforward association between income growth and well-being (Ferrara et al. 2019). More recently, this paradox has been transposed and reshaped into a spatial setting (Graham 2012) through the metaphor of the 'happy peasant and the miserable millionaire'. A long stream of research demonstrated that, at least in developed countries, subjective well-being tends to be higher in less dense settings than in crowed environments, in spite of worse job opportunities and income conditions (Sørensen 2014).

While the empirical evidence of the urban/rural divide in subjective well-being is rather robust and exhaustive, less is known about its determinants. Why are large cities sources of dissatisfaction? The research program developed by the authors in recent years aims at answering this question, by addressing three issues left partially underexplored by the literature:

- *the effect of differently ranked urban functions on SWB*: cities of different size host different activities, providing different goods and services to the resident. Previous studies analysed the relationship between size (usually measured in terms of population density or categories) and SWB without a clear reference to the positioning of cities along the urban hierarchy (Christaller 1933) and, as a consequence, to the set of advantages they provide to the resident population.
- *the indirect effect of urbanization on SWB*: the dichotomy between urban and rural settings hides a deeper level of complexity, because it does not account for their spatial distribution and interconnections. For instance, rural areas may be more or less close to larger cities, and the effect of this relative distance on the well-being of the resident population has been almost entirely ignored in the literature.
- *the evolution of the association between urbanization and SWB over time*: the empirical analysis of the negative link between urbanization and SWB extensively covered the years from 2000 on, but without taking a temporal perspective, i.e. focusing on the change of this association over time. However, the social and economic structure of cities is constantly evolving, and it is therefore interesting to understand whether, in the long term, SWB also varied accordingly.

The next sections of the present chapter review the results of the studies focused on these three issues. Conclusions follow in the last section.

2 The Effect of Differently Ranked Urban Functions on SWB

While previous studies provided broad and robust evidence of an urban/rural divide in SWB, less is known about the determinants of this imbalance. The rich literature on agglomeration economies, on the other hand, has identified the many benefits deriving from urbanization in terms of productivity and wages, learning and knowledge exchanges, innovation and creativity, as well as public services and amenities that may influence life satisfaction positively. All these benefits are partially balanced by negative externalities, such as land rent and cost of living, pollution and congestion, unregulated urban expansion. The effects of urbanization are significantly different for different kinds of cities, according to the place in the urban hierarchy they occupy (Christaller 1933). For instance, the set of externalities generated on the resident population by metropolitan areas is entirely different from those available in medium-size cities.

An innovative approach to the analysis of the association between urbanization and SWB should therefore conceptualize the measurement of city size, with a clear reference to the rank of cities and, as a consequence, with a clear interpretation in terms of agglomeration economies/diseconomies generated by each kind of urban environment.

As mentioned in the introduction, the common approach to the topic makes use of survey data where a sample of respondents is asked to define his/her level of overall life satisfaction, choosing among different options.[1] This empirical measurement of SWB is expected to be a function of some individual characteristics (such as age, gender, education, income) and regional features (per capita GDP, demographic structure, etc.), among which the most interesting variable is represented by the degree of urbanization of the respondent's region of residence:

$$\mathrm{SWB}_i = f\left(\text{individual characteristics}_i, \text{regional characteristics}_r, \text{urbanization}_r\right) \tag{1}$$

where i stands for the individual and r for his/her region of residence. While the measurement of urbanization is often represented by population density, in our approach it consists of a categorical variable capturing the positioning of each area along the urban hierarchy. This approach allows us to interpret the results not only in terms of city size but also with a reference to the set of urbanization economies and diseconomies that each group of cities is assumed to generate.

The first study applying this perspective is an analysis of SWB and urbanization in Romania (Lenzi and Perucca 2016a). Romania is a particularly interesting case study because its development path from 2000 onwards was dominated by the role of its capital (Bucharest) in fostering national economic growth. Moreover, the urban structure in Romania is highly differentiated, with several rural and urban areas other than the capital region.

Romanian NUTS2 regions were classified according to the size of their biggest city. Results show that, separating out the effect of the capital city from that of the other large cities, (i.e. cities with more than 200,000 inhabitants), people living in these areas are happier than those residing in less-populated regions, suggesting the existence of an urban–rural divide in life satisfaction favouring relatively larger cities. Nevertheless, living in the capital city is detrimental to life satisfaction. With the exception of Bucharest, therefore, Romanian people living in larger cities

[1]The most common sources of data on SWB are, for European countries, Eurobarometer (http://ec.europa.eu/commfrontoffice/publicopinion/index.cfm) and the European Values Survey studies (https://europeanvaluesstudy.eu/).

seem happier than others. Compared with the findings from previous studies, this evidence suggests that urbanization per se is not a source of dissatisfaction. Rather, agglomeration benefits seem to prevail over agglomeration costs, but only up to a certain threshold, when increased population size generates more disadvantages than advantages, as in the case of Bucharest.

In order to test the generality of these results, a similar approach was applied to a sample including all European countries (Lenzi and Perucca 2018, 2019a). As before, in each region, the number of people living in larger urban zones (LUZ) allowed us to define a ranking of areas, from the most (more than 1.5 mln people living in a LUZ) to the least (less than 300 k people living in a LUZ) urbanized.

Results show that, taking the least urbanized regions as reference, SWB is lower in the most urbanized ones (first rank) and the higher ones in second rank regions, i.e. those with a degree of urbanization immediately below the maximum. This finding, consistent with the one uncovered in Romania, suggests the perceived effect of the disadvantages arising in metropolitan areas, such as congestion, pollution and greater costs of living to prevail with respect to the perception of its advantages. On the other hand, the opposite mechanism remains in regions characterized by an intermediate urbanization level (i.e. second rank).

Taken together, the findings from the previous studies pointed out a positive effect of urbanization on SWB, at least until a certain threshold of agglomeration are reached. In order to fully understand the mechanisms associating urbanization and SWB, it is fundamentally important to analyse the characteristics of cities (i.e. advantages and disadvantages) and their effect on individuals' well-being.

Among these factors, a prominent role is played by innovation. Economic literature, whatever the level of analysis adopted (from individuals to firms, from cities to regions, from countries to continents), and the time span considered, pointed out that innovation is the key to competitiveness. The innovation process, however, is strictly related to urbanization. Cities play a primary role in the development of new ideas and the introduction of innovations into the market. Moreover, highly innovative places tend to attract creative and more educated individuals. Despite these premises, very little is known about the relationship between innovation, urbanization and SWB.

In our research, we explored this nexus and empirical findings indicate that different types of innovation play different roles in differently urbanized contexts: more technology-intensive innovations (i.e. patents) impact on SWB only in highly urbanized areas, whereas less technology-intensive innovations (i.e. trademarks) are associated with greater SWB in all settings. The interpretation of these results is linked to the different natures of the two types of innovation. In order to make technology-intensive innovation have an impact on SWB, a more sophisticated demand and, possibly, a certain scale to conduct research activities efficiently are needed. These conditions are typical for the most urbanized areas. On the other hand, less technology-intensive innovations, closer to the commercialization stage, are, on average, more easily appreciated by market demand, less radical and often do not require a substantial scale for their creation.

These results add to our previous findings (Lenzi and Perucca 2016a, 2018) and suggest that the opposite impact on SWB of innovation in settings of different ranks does not depend solely on the *quantitative* net balance between the advantages and disadvantages of urbanization. Rather, these externalities are also *qualitatively* different in cities of different kinds, and this is a further channel through which they contribute to individuals' SWB.

3 The Indirect Effect of Urbanization on SWB

The association of low levels of urbanization with higher SWB was often interpreted in the literature as the demonstration that living in rural settings is always beneficial for individuals' well-being.

This assumption, however, does not consider the relative location of rural settings compared with more urbanized areas. Urbanization effects, in fact, are not constrained within the boundaries of the city producing them. Rather, they spread to the neighbouring environment, with an intensity and nature that is highly differentiated based on the rank of the city, as theoretically suggested by central place theory (Christaller 1933). Rural communities embedded in urbanized regions, for instance, are expected to benefit from the positive externalities, without suffering the disadvantages that are typical of urban settings.

The investigation of this hypothesis represented the second research line undertaken by the authors. A first study (Lenzi and Perucca 2016a) focused on the analysis of SWB in different kinds of rural communities and classified according to the urbanization level of the NUTS2 region they were pertaining to.

Results showed that people living in rural communities embedded in both first and second rank regions (i.e. highly urbanized) are, on average, more satisfied than those living in the urban settings of the same regions. On the other hand, living in a rural setting within third-rank regions, (i.e. those characterized by the lowest level of urbanization) is associated with lower SWB than the residents in the urban settings of the same regions. In short, rural inhabitants tend to be more satisfied than others, consistently with the literature, but only if they live in highly urbanized regions (i.e. first rank and second rank).

A more complex and detailed approach to this research question was applied in Lenzi and Perucca (2020). This study assumed that SWB depends not only on the urbanization level of the community of residence, among other things, but also on the distance, in terms of travel time, to the closest city of a higher rank. Empirical findings also pointed out, besides the *direct* effect of urbanization on the SWB of the resident population, an *indirect* effect which cities generate on the SWB of individuals living in other regions and in urban settings of a lower rank. While the direct effect, as largely demonstrated by previous studies and by the authors themselves, is generally negative for the largest cities, the indirect effect of urbanization on SWB is positive. This implies that keeping other things constant, the shorter the distance to a city of higher rank compared with that of one's place of residence, the higher one's own level of SWB will be.

The interpretation of this result is that living outside highly urbanized areas is beneficial to SWB only if the individuals have access to the services and goods provided by large cities. Rurality per se, on the contrary, does not necessarily lead to higher levels of well-being.

4 The Evolution of the Association Between Urbanization and SWB Over Time

A last issue rarely addressed by the literature on urbanization and SWB concerns its evolution over time. Most studies adopted a short-term perspective, using empirical evidence from 2000 onwards. However, the social and economic characteristics of cities deeply vary over time, and major changes occurred in the last thirty years in developed countries, corresponding to processes of industrial reconversion from manufacturing to service sectors. Therefore, the last question addressed in our research agenda refers to the role of time within the association between urbanization and SWB. The analysis of this issue focused on two quantitative case studies, both relative to countries that experienced deep institutional and economic changes.

The first case study is represented by Romanian regions between 1996 and 2010 (Lenzi and Perucca 2016b). In this period, following the fall of the Iron curtain and the collapse of the Soviet Union, the country experienced a process of institutional, social and economic reconversion from a planned economy to one which was market-based, culminating with access into the European Union (EU) in 2007. This process was matched by an increase in the polarization of income in favour of urban areas and, in particular, the capital city.

The empirical analysis shows that the economic transition period (1996–2004) was marked by a neutral role of urbanization on SWB, with the exception of Bucharest. While living in the capital city was already associated with lower SWB, no significant difference was found for residents in rural settings and medium-rank cities. On the road to EU accession (2004–2010), however, significant differences emerged, and individuals in medium-rank cities appeared to be more satisfied than those living in rural settings, while living in the capital was still associated with lower SWB. This period is marked by the increase in disparities in economic growth, favouring urban areas above others. Hence, the interpretation of our results is related to the fact that the benefits of urbanization (i.e. jobs, average income, etc.) increased, leading to higher SWB compared to rural areas. This happened only in medium-size cities, where these benefits were not counterbalanced by negative externalities (cost of living, crime, etc.) which are what occurred in the capital.

The second case study involves Italian regions between 1980 and 2010 (Lenzi and Perucca 2019b). In the thirty years considered in the analysis, Italy undertook a process of economic reconversion from manufacturing to service sectors. The outcome of this process was highly differentiated across regions and, in particular, between North and South. In the former case, this was more successful than in the latter, resulting in a widening of the differences, in terms of average income and occupation, between the two macro-areas. The research hypothesis tested is whether the association between urbanization and SWB was constant over the time span considered and in the two parts of the countries.

Results showed that the urban/rural divide in SWB is not constant, which suggests once more that urbanization is not a source of dissatisfaction per se; rather, the combination of positive and negative externalities and their impact on perceived well-being do indeed vary over time. Moreover, our findings showed that the negative association of urbanization and SWB concerns only large cities in southern Italy from 1990 onwards, i.e. when their gap in economic growth compared to northern regions started to widen. This suggests, consistently with the implications about Romania discussed above, that the urban/rural divide arises when the most urbanized settings are less effective in providing the expected positive externalities (mainly job opportunities) to the resident population.

5 Conclusions

The research program on urbanization and SWB led to some relevant and innovative conclusions along the three research lines discussed in the previous section.

Summing up, the main finding from these studies is that urbanization is not, per se, a source of dissatisfaction, just as much as living in a rural area cannot be said to be beneficial for individuals' well-being. This conclusion is extremely relevant in a literature often marked by a simplistic, if not ideological, dichotomy between the city and the countryside.

A much higher degree of complexity characterizes the mechanisms associating with one's own place of residence and SWB. The research program identified three elements of complexity: the kind of externalities generated by cities, the spatial accessibility to these externalities and the temporal dimension.

References

Christaller, W. (1933). Die zentralen Orte in Süddeutschland: eine ökonomisch-geographische Untersuchung über die Gesetzmässigkeit der Verbreitung und Entwicklung der Siedlungen mit städtischen Funktionen. University Microfilms.

Easterlin, R. A. (1973). Does money buy happiness? *The public interest, 30,* 3.

Ferrara. A. R., Nisticò, R., & Lombardo, R. (2019). Subjective and objective well-being: Bridging the gap. *Scienze Regionali – Italian Journal of Regional Science, 18*(3s): 35–70.

Graham, C. (2012). *Happiness around the world: The paradox of happy peasants and miserable millionaires.* Oxford University Press.

Lenzi, C., & Perucca, G. (2016a). Life satisfaction across cities: Evidence from Romania. *The Journal of Development Studies, 52*(7), 1062–1077.

Lenzi, C., & Perucca, G. (2016b). Life satisfaction in Romanian cities on the road from post-communism transition to EU accession. *Region: The Journal of ERSA, 3*(2), 1–22.

Lenzi, C., & Perucca, G. (2018). Are urbanized areas source of life satisfaction? Evidence from EU regions. *Papers in Regional Science, 97,* S105–S122.
Lenzi, C., & Perucca, G. (2019a). The nexus between innovation and wellbeing across the EU space: What role for urbanisation? *Urban Studies*. https://doi.org/10.1177/0042098018818947.
Lenzi, C., & Perucca, G. (2019b). Subjective wellbeing over time and across space—Thirty years of evidence from Italian regions. *Scienze Regionali—Italian Journal of Regional Science*, 18(3).
Lenzi, C., & Perucca, G. (2020). Not too close, not too far: Urbanization and subjective well-being along the urban hierarchy. Mimeo.
Sørensen, J. F. (2014). Rural–Urban differences in life satisfaction: Evidence from the European Union. *Regional Studies, 48*(9), 1451–1466.
Stiglitz, J. E., Sen, A., & Fitoussi, J. P. (2009). Report by the commission on the measurement of economic performance and social progress Commission on the Measurement of Economic Performance and Social Progress.
Veneri, P. (2019). The OECD framework and database to measure regional well-being. *Scienze Regionali – Italian Journal of Regional Science, 18*(3s), 117–125.

EU Regional Policy Effectiveness and the Role of Territorial Capital

Ugo Fratesi and Giovanni Perucca

Abstract The present chapter reviews the recent studies of the group of regional and urban economics on the impact of the European Union regional policy on regional development. In particular, the focus of the research program is on the identification of the mechanisms through which the local territorial characteristics mediate the effect of public investments. Results show a strong relationship between the territorial capital of regions and the effectiveness of the EU regional policy. This evidence conveys relevant implications for policy makers. In particular, it suggests that regions should invest in those assets that are complementary to the ones which they already have, in order to build a balanced economic system.

Keywords EU regional policy · Territorial capital · Economic resilience

1 Introduction

The European Union (EU) allocates every year about one-third of its budget to regional policies, i.e., to actions aimed at promoting the development of places in various fields, from transport infrastructure to ICT, from firms' competitiveness to social inclusion. The allocation of funds across regions, however, is not distributed equally. About 51% of the budget is allocated to less developed regions, i.e., those with a level of per capita gross domestic product (GDP) lower than 75% of the EU average. Remaining funds are invested in transition regions (per capita GDP between 75 and 90% of the EU average) and more developed regions (per capita GDP above 90% of the EU average).

This asymmetric allocation of funding mirrors the redistributive principle of the benefits from economic integration which, since its establishment, guides EU

U. Fratesi · G. Perucca (✉)
Architecture, Built Environment and Construction Engineering—ABC Department, Politecnico di Milano, Milan, Italy
e-mail: giovanni.perucca@polimi.it

S. Della Torre et al. (eds.), *Regeneration of the Built Environment from a Circular Economy Perspective*, Research for Development,
https://doi.org/10.1007/978-3-030-33256-3_4

regional policy. In the words of Jacques Delors, "all regions of the Community ought to be able to share progressively in these benefits. (…) It is for this reason that the 'transparency' of the large market should be facilitated by supporting the efforts of regions with ill-adapted structures and those in the throes of painful restructuring. Community policies can be of assistance to these regions, which in no way absolves them from assuming their own responsibilities and from making their own effort" (Delors 1987, p. 7).

Therefore, the ultimate goal of regional policy is, through the promotion of socioeconomic development in regions less favored by European integration, to reinforce territorial cohesion within the EU. For this reason, the EU regional policy is often labeled as Cohesion Policy.

The assessment of Cohesion Policy is fundamental to understand whether this target has been achieved. A long stream of research has focused on this issue, with the aim of measuring the net impact of EU regional policy on the development of regions, mainly interpreted in terms of GDP and employment growth. Empirical evidence of a positive association between CP funding and economic prosperity, however, appeared to be inconsistent across studies (Dall'Erba and Le Gallo 2008; Becker et al. 2012), especially because there are empirical and conceptual issues which cannot yet be reconciled (Fratesi 2016): Whether Cohesion Policy had a positive effect on regional development or not, is still an open question in the literature.

The group of regional and urban economics formulated a hypothesis for explaining the divergence of empirical results from previous studies. According to this hypothesis, the way in which Communitarian policies are implemented and their effectiveness, can change substantially due to certain specific territorial assets characterizing EU regions. In other words, the territory and, more specifically, the *territorial capital* of regions, is not neutral in the mechanism through which policy implementation generates development. Instead, specific characteristics of regions mediate the impact of Cohesion Policy, and it is therefore necessary to keep them in mind in the policy assessment.

Stemming from this assumption, the aim of the research program of the group of regional and urban economics was to understand and measure the differentiated effects of EU regional policy across different territories. More precisely, the association between the territory and Cohesion Policy addressed three main issues:

- *territorial capital and the allocation of Cohesion Policy funds*: As stated above, Cohesion Policy focuses on a variety of policy targets. It is therefore important to study the relationship between regional characteristics and the allocation of funding across different policy needs because it allows us to understand and improve the allocation mechanisms.
- *territorial capital and the effectiveness of Cohesion Policy*: The effect of EU regional policy on regional development is assumed to be differentiated, according to the regional endowment of territorial capital.
- *territorial capital and the development of regions*: Apart from the direct association between territorial capital and Cohesion Policy, it is relevant to fully understand

the role of the territory on the development of regions, i.e., on the overall contexts in which policies are implemented.

The next section will discuss the conceptual and methodological approach adopted, with a clear explanation of what is meant by "territorial capital" and how it could be related to Cohesion Policy. The other sections will summarize the results of the study of the three issues defined above.

2 Territorial Capital and EU Regional Policy

The identification of the sources of endogenous local development is one of the main issues of regional economics. Human capital, physical infrastructures and social capital are all examples of single territorial assets having been proved to positively affect prosperity. A comprehensive and general approach to this topic, however, requires a coherent and exhaustive classification of all potential endogenous sources of development.

In this perspective, OECD (2001) firstly introduced the concept of territorial capital, defined as the system of territorial assets having economic, cultural, social and environmental nature. In order to succeed, regions and territories have to exploit the potential of this complex set of locally based factors. Camagni (2008) provided a taxonomy for these elements, based on the dimensions of materiality and rivalry. Instead of providing just a list of local assets, this approach explicitly defines their properties, allowing to identify potential interactions and policy implication.

The taxonomy is reported in Fig. 1, showing how territorial capital includes very different assets, from physical infrastructures (box a) to human capital (box f) to social capital (box d).

This classification of regional assets was chosen to study the relationship between regional characteristics and the implementation of Cohesion Policy. The idea that the local context of implementation mediates the effects of EU regional policy is not new in literature. In fact, some studies tested, for example, whether policy effectiveness is higher in more developed regions (Cappelen et al. 2003) or in areas with high-quality institutions (Rodríguez-Pose and Garcilazo 2015). The innovative aspect of the approach of the research group, however, relies on its ability to consider, at the same time, the whole set of territorial characteristics, and therefore their joint effect on the outcome of Cohesion Policy.

Rivalry		Tangible goods (hard)	Mixed goods (hard + soft)	Intangible goods (soft)
(high)	*Private goods*	*c* Private fixed capital stock Pecuniary externalities Toll goods	*i* Relational private services operating on: - external linkages of firms - transfer of R&D results	*f* Human capital and pecuniary externalities
↑	*Club goods*	*b* Proprietary networks and collective goods: - landscape - cultural heritage	*h* Cooperation networks Governance on land and cultural resources	*e* Relational capital
(low)	*Public goods*	*a* Resources: - natural - cultural Social overhead capital: infrastructure	*g* Agglomeration and district economies Agencies for R&D transcoding Receptivity enhancing tools Connectivity	*d* Social capital: - institutions - behaviors - trust - reputation
	Materiality	**(high)**	**→**	**(low)**

Fig. 1 Territorial capital: a taxonomy. *Source* Camagni (2008)

3 Territorial Capital and the Allocation of Cohesion Policy Funds

A further element of complexity in the identification of an empirical association between territorial capital and the effectiveness of Cohesion Policy relies on the fact that regions may differ not just in terms of their territorial characteristics but, also, in the mix of policies they decide to implement (Rodríguez-Pose and Fratesi 2004). Regions are likely to adopt different growth strategies, investing the Cohesion Policy funds received in those territorial assets which they hope will maximize the local growth potential.

In order to shed light on this issue, this first step of the analysis (Fratesi and Perucca 2016) collected, at a fine territorial scale (NUTS3),[1] statistical data on territorial capital endowment (Perucca 2013). This data covered the categories of assets

[1]The NUTS (nomenclature of territorial units for statistics) classification is the official classification adopted in the EU for the administrative sub-national regions.

is reported in Fig. 1. Matching this data with evidence on the Cohesion Policy expenditure on 19 axes[2] over the Programming Period 2000–2006,[3] the goal of the analysis was (i) to classify EU regions according to their territorial capital and (ii) associate this endowment with the allocation of funds across different axes of expenditure.

Empirical results (Fratesi and Perucca 2016) highlight that regions with different endowments of territorial capital allocate their funds in a different way. Core metropolitan areas, characterized by the highest levels of territorial capital, allocate, on average, 26.9% of their funds to the support of Small and Medium Enterprises (SMEs) and the craft sector, i.e., to investments aimed at increasing the competitiveness of their firms. At the same time, these regions are those allocating more resources in actions on human capital, from the labor market to social inclusion. On the other hand, regions characterized by the lowest endowments of territorial capital are also those devoting more resources to investments in basic infrastructure such as transport, energy and environmental infrastructure.

Summing up, less developed regions tend to invest relatively more in basic infrastructural assets, i.e., in those resources that are still lacking in the region. Richer areas, already endowed with infrastructures, tend to pay more attention to social and economic issues. Even if different typologies of regions tend to allocate their funds differently across axes of expenditure, it is not possible to say whether this choice is the most efficient. In other words, we do not know whether the allocation strategy is associated with a higher impact on investments. This issue is the focus of the second step of the analysis, discussed in the following sections.

4 Territorial Capital and the Effectiveness of Cohesion Policy Funds

The assumption on the association between territorial capital and Cohesion Policy is that specific territorial characteristics foster the effectiveness of the EU regional policy. The empirical verification of this assumption requires, in the first place, the definition of what is meant by the term *effectiveness*. In our approach, the outcome of Cohesion Policy is defined in terms of increased GDP growth: the higher the statistical impact on economic growth in the years after the policy implementation, the higher the effects of Cohesion Policy.[4] This choice is based on the fact that EU

[2]An axis of expenditure is the thematic field in which the policy intervenes. Tourism, ICT, transport, energy and environment, female labor participation are all examples of aces of expenditure. See Fratesi and Perucca (2016) for the full list.

[3]The Multiannual Financial Frameworks set the annual budgets for seven-year periods. A Programming Period is, as a consequence, a seven-year period characterized by a given budget and rules for Cohesion Policy.

[4]This relationship has to be controlled for all the other factors, apart from Cohesion Policy investments, that may affect GDP growth. See Fratesi and Perucca (2014) for a detailed description of the methods and of how this issue was addressed in the empirical analysis.

regional policy is aimed, in the first place, at reducing economic disparities within the EU, by increasing income in lagging-behind regions.

The methodological approach was similar to the one described in Sect. 2. Territorial capital for all EU NUTS3 regions was measured, jointly with data on Cohesion Policy funding across different axes of expenditure. Then, an empirical model was estimated, where GDP growth in the years after the end of the Programming Period 2000–2006 is assumed to be a function, among other characteristics, of the territorial capital of regions, the funds they received and the interactions between the two elements. This analysis allowed us to check whether Cohesion Policy investments had an impact on regional economic growth and if this impact was differentiated for regions with different endowments of territorial capital. Given the structural differences between eastern and western EU countries, the analysis was carried out separately for the two groups of nations.

In eastern EU countries (Fratesi and Perucca 2014), policy investments in immaterial assets (boxes d, e and f in Fig. 1) are characterized by increasing returns, i.e., they tend to be more effective where regions are more endowed. For instance, labor market policies are only effective when in the region there is a presence of high-value functions. Similarly, policies on workforce flexibility, entrepreneurship, innovation and ICT are only effective when the regions are endowed with human capital.

On the other hand, the effect of investments in tangible assets (boxes a, b and c in Fig. 1) is mediated mainly by regions' level of urbanization and agglomeration economies. In this case, decreasing returns emerge, since intermediate urban areas (and neither metropolitan nor rural areas) gain from those where Cohesion Policy is most effective. In general, the fact that Cohesion Policy is more effective in correspondence to higher endowments of territorial capital, implies that investing policy funds in regions that already more developed can pay more than investing them in weaker regions. This suggests the existence of a potential trade-off between the effectiveness of policies and the achievement of territorial cohesion.

Evidence from western EU countries (Fratesi and Perucca 2019), where data depth allows a more systemic analysis, suggests different and more complex mechanisms compared with those presented above. First of all, the idea that policies tend to have larger effects where territorial capital assets are present remains because many policies have higher impacts in regions which are rich in territorial capital, while some decreasing returns also exist in areas such as R&D and telecommunication infrastructure.

Even more interesting is the observation that policies which invest in assets which are complementary to those already present in regions. For example, areas characterized by high levels of collective goods, human capital and behavior exhibit lower returns than other clusters in fields making intense use of assets of this kind. Finally, areas which are very poorly endowed with territorial capital tend to have lower returns in all assets but those, such as SMEs, directly related to the private firm establishment, most likely because firms in areas lacking territorial capital are more in need of assistance than firms elsewhere.

The way in which support to firms interacts with territorial capital has been further investigated in Bachtrögler et al. (2019), thanks to collaboration with the Vienna

University of Economics and Business and the WIFO. In this case, the analysis was developed thanks to a database of firms put together by our partner for many European countries for the Programming Period 2007–13.

An EU-wide analysis based on propensity score matching shows that the impact of Cohesion Policy support to firms is highly impactful on the firms' size (in terms of GVA and employment), yet, while the impact on productivity is still significant, it turns out to be much smaller. Going down to the individual countries, the analysis shows important differences, in terms of magnitude and significance of the effects.

Finally, the analysis goes down to the regional NUTS2 level, showing that the impacts of firm support are differentiated within countries as well and in different ways in the different countries. It seems that, for some countries, the impact of firm support depends on needs, i.e., is higher where regions lack complementary assets.

5 Territorial Capital and Regional Development

The framework of territorial capital can also be fruitfully applied to the explanation of growth tout court. Following ten years of crisis with sluggish recovery, the research group addressed the issue of resilience, which is an engineering concept which has now been widely adopted in economics to show the capability of economies to react to crises.

Different measures of resilience exist on a regional level, and these were analyzed by Fratesi and Perucca (2018) in view of dependence on the territorial capital endowment of regions.

The analysis shows, first, that regions with different endowments of territorial capital are differently resilient in quantitative terms because those with more territorial capital are also more resilient and, second, that the typologies of territorial capital are relevant, because depending on the presence of one or the other, they are also resilient in different ways (e.g., in terms of resistance or recovery). In particular, different territorial capital assets have different effects, and those more closely linked to resilience measures are those that have an intermediate level of materiality and/or rivalry (see Fig. 1). The second result is the confirmation of the expectation that less mobile factors of both a private and public nature are more linked to resilience, being difficult to transfer from one region to the other.

The paper hence concludes that the structure of regions is an important determinant of how they can afford periods of distress.

6 Conclusions and Future Research Directions

The research program on territorial capital and regional policies has already offered many hints which will be helpful to policy makers, for example, the fact that regions should invest in those assets that are complementary to the ones which they already have, in order to build a balanced economic system.

At the same time, the research already accomplished paves the way for further research, along with a number of directions.

The first direction is the systematic study of the determinants of regional policy effectiveness under different conditions, in order to provide policy makers with a matrix of which policy interventions are helpful in each situation.

The second direction is the microeconomic study of the micro-territorial determinants of regional policy effectiveness. The presence of other firms nearby, with complementary or synergic possibilities, and the presence of territorial assets are expected to play a role which takes place on a scale which is smaller than the regional one. Although the theory is aware of the fact that regions are far from homogenous internally, they are often treated as such in the econometric analyses, where each of them is a single observation.

Finally, the research program has demonstrated the fruitfulness of the territorial capital concept, which was developed within the research group, for the analysis of regional growth and regional policy. Our conceptual understanding of the link between local territorial assets, policies and other assets in neighboring regions can still be deepened with the study of the actual mechanisms by which the effects take place.

References

Bachtrögler, J., Fratesi, U., & Perucca, G. (2019). The influence of the local context on the implementation and impact of EU Cohesion Policy. *Regional Studies, forthcoming and on-line*. https://doi.org/10.1080/00343404.2018.1551615.

Becker, S. O., Egger, P. H., & Von Ehrlich, M. (2012). Too much of a good thing? On the growth effects of the EU's regional policy. *European Economic Review, 56*(4), 648–668.

Camagni, R. (2008). Regional Competitiveness: Towards a Concept of territorial capital. In R. Capello, R. Camagni, B. Chizzolini, & U. Fratesi (Eds.), *Modelling regional scenarios for the enlarged Europe: European competitiveness and global strategies,* (pp. 33–48). Berlin: Springer Verlag.

Cappelen, A., Castellacci, F., Fagerberg, J., & Verspagen, B. (2003). The impact of EU regional support on growth and convergence in the European Union. *JCMS: Journal of Common Market Studies, 41*(4), 621–644.

Dall'Erba, S., & Le Gallo, J. (2008). Regional convergence and the impact of European structural funds 1989-1999: A spatial econometric analysis. *Papers in Regional Science, 87*(2), 219–244.

Delors, J. (1987). The Single Act: A New Frontier for Europe. Communication from the Commission to the Council. COM (87) 100 final, 15 February 1987. Bulletin of the European Communities, Supplement 1/87.

Fratesi, U. (2016). Impact assessment of European cohesion policy: Theoretical and empirical issues. In S. Piattoni & L. Polverari (Eds.), *Handbook on cohesion policy in the EU* (pp. 443–460). Chelthenham: Edward Elgar. ISBN 978-1-78471-566-3.
Fratesi, U., & Perucca, G. (2014). Territorial capital and the effectiveness of cohesion policies: An assessment for CEE regions. *Investigaciones Regionales, 29,* 165–191.
Fratesi, U., & Perucca, G. (2016). Territorial capital and EU Cohesion Policy. EU Cohesion Policy. In: J. Bachtler, P. Berkowitz, S. Hardy, & T. Muravska, (Eds.), *EU cohesion policy (open access): Reassessing performance and direction.* Taylor & Francis.
Fratesi, U., & Perucca, G. (2018). Territorial capital and the resilience of European regions. *The Annals of Regional Science, 60*(2), 241–264.
Fratesi, U., & Perucca, G. (2019). EU regional development policy and territorial capital: A systemic approach. *Papers in Regional Science, 98*(1), 265–281.
OECD (2001): OECD Territorial Outlook, Paris.
Perucca, G. (2013). A redefinition of Italian macro-areas: The role of territorial capital. *Rivista di Economia e Statistica del Territorio, 2,* 37–65.
Rodríguez-Pose, A., & Fratesi, U. (2004). Between development and social policies: the impact of European Structural Funds in Objective 1 regions. *Regional Studies, 38*(1), 97–113.
Rodríguez-Pose, A., & Garcilazo, E. (2015). Quality of government and the returns of investment: Examining the impact of cohesion expenditure in European regions. *Regional Studies, 49*(8), 1274–1290.

Demolition as a Territorial Reform Project

Chiara Merlini

Abstract The widespread conditions of obsolescence and risk emerging in many parts of our country pose new questions to the territorial project and entail a review of its operational tools. In this sense, even demolition can acquire a new meaning, soliciting a technical and cultural reflection that has repercussions on future of the contemporary territory.

Keywords Decline · Demolition · Urban planning · Volumetric transfer · Urbanity

1 Introduction: Decline and Risk

The following notes will argue that the territorial project can usefully reconsider demolition as its operational tool and that, more generally, the notion itself of demolition must be reconceptualised. The assumption is that the current conditions of our country push us to consider in new ways potential removal actions of built heritage, giving them a broad spectrum of meanings and recovering the complexity of a term too often used in reductive ways (Terranova 1997; Criconia 1998; Nigrelli 2005; Merlini 2008, 2019).

Two main aspects can be called upon as a reference background, in relation also to a substantial convergence of representations provided by the latest urban and territorial studies (Calafati 2014; Munarin and Velo 2016; Fabian and Munarin 2017; De Rossi 2018).

First of all, the issue of decline, which is today, linked in a new way to surplus built space. In some parts of the country, housing stock is in excess compared to the people's request, with the resultant occurrence of underutilization and abandonment phenomena. In particular, a new phenomenology arises in which the peculiar entanglement between economic crisis and demographic contraction broadens the

C. Merlini (✉)
Architecture, Built Environment and Construction Engineering—ABC Department, Politecnico di Milano, Milan, Italy
e-mail: chiara.merlini@polimi.it

S. Della Torre et al. (eds.), *Regeneration of the Built Environment from a Circular Economy Perspective*, Research for Development,
https://doi.org/10.1007/978-3-030-33256-3_5

set of impoverishing objects. To the traditional emptying of large urban 47 equipment and to the 20th-century production dismantling, territorial situations are added characterized by the obsolescence of smaller and dispersed buildings (Lanzani 2015).

What we are thus called upon to face is therefore not only a quantitatively significant phenomenon, linked to the growing disproportion between the space availability and concretely actionable demand, which is of course connected to the drastic reduction in public and private resources. It is precisely the specific nature of the artefacts affected by underutilisation and/or abandonment that must be highlighted. More and more we are dealing with ordinary and anonymous buildings, essentially devoid both of value, and of those elements of suggestion that had sometimes the big factories protagonists of the first phases of urban dismantling.

There are several examples: the condominium incorporated in many urban centres after World War II; the prefabricated industrial building on the edge of production areas or along roads that no longer ensure adequate levels of services and appropriate accessibility; the family home in città diffusa settlement in which the system of expectations and preferences has drastically changed with the generational change; the second home in tourist areas made less attractive by climate change or by congestion; the shopping centre along market streets that are no longer sufficiently dynamic, and so on. Buildings that in the phase of the country's intense growth that is now behind us have incorporated significant economic and symbolic investments and now suffering from the crisis. These are artefacts that are poor in terms of architectural and construction quality, poorly placed on the territory, without recognizable surroundings or a proximity space; in effect the result of urban policies that is not very context-conscious and of construction processes often conducted in economics. Aged prematurely, they often witness a drastic reduction in the property value, that makes their fate very uncertain.

Secondly, it is now evident that large portions of our country disclose increasingly dramatic risk conditions (Fabian and Munarin 2017). It is a territorial fragility expressed in a variety of ways: hydrogeological instability, deficient maintenance and static uncertainty of buildings and infrastructures, seismic risk, construction sites never completed, and air and soil pollution. Recent reports on the state of the territory measure some of the effects of the long cycle of urbanisation, investigating the relationships with the broader dynamics of climate and demographic change. What emerges, beyond the obvious territorial differences, is an increasingly more fragile country where the very elements that over the long-term have built it main structure, such as hydrographical and infrastructural networks, fall into a crisis.

Faced with these issues—abandoned building stock and risk—the question is whether generalized actions of securing the country and urban regeneration are really viable, or whether there we should not rather consider that this may not always be possible. There are plentiful reasons: the growing uncertainty of real estate transactions based on replacement building, the difficult management of reuse and recycling processes, often unsustainable in terms of economic investments, seemingly shape up a rather uncertain situation (Micelli 2014).

The complexity of the current conditions pushes us, in other words, to advance different working hypotheses, which consciously take note of territorial situations that are not always recoverable, which must therefore eventually be removed or accompanied in a process of decline. Not everything can be saved, reused, enhanced from a recycling perspective (Corbellini and Marini 2016). And this of course raises considerable problems in a cultural context marked by the centrality of memory and by the symmetrical distrust about future (Andriani 2010; Bauman 2017). There is an entire research field that should probably be reformulated, and in which, even demolition can regain an important planning role. And this of course involves technical questions as questions pertaining to the value assigned to the inherited assets and to the possible redefinition of contemporary settlements.

2 Demolition, Between Failure and Promise

A demolition is a violent act: destruction is its constitutive and unavoidable part, and so its ambition to be a conclusive action. But it is also an act of repair, a kind of compensation and/or promise. In the recent history of urban transformation, at least in our country, demolition has acquired, somewhat simplistically, a dual meaning. On the one hand, it was considered an event, an anomaly reserved for a few exceptional cases loaded with symbolic meaning; on the other, it was the slightly hidden face of a more ordinary transformation process that has perhaps overestimated the qualitative effects of building replacement interventions.

The first case includes those demolitions that take up a compensatory value, either because they have the effect of correcting for the violation of a rule and damage suffered, as occurs with the removal of illegal buildings in a valuable landscape (Curci et al. 2017), or because they put an end to a recognized failure, as in the case of some buildings that represent the problematic legacy of modernity. In the second case, there are the demolitions describable as a precondition of a real estate development process. The tabula rasa is considered here an opportunity, as can be read in the debate on industrial dismantling (Russo 1998; Dansero et al. 2001), but also in ordinary demolition action often guided by an economistic logic or from the safeguarding constraints. To make a tabula rasa to rebuild was, in other words, a non-problematized process, both in relation to what was removed, and in relation to the new building production, often architecturally modest, not very ecologically virtuous and incapable of defining articulated and complex urban relationships.

Two ways of considering demolition often made even more ambiguous by a further simplification, which reduced the urban quality to the removal of the "ugly" with the conviction that it was a necessary step in a process of modernization. Deviation from the norm, removal of an aesthetic damage, recovery of a public asset, promise of an urban development responding to new housing needs and capable of supporting the construction industry: these were the main terms of a discourse on demolition that oscillated between overexposure and indifference. Hence, the need for conceptual and operational repositioning (Merlini 2019).

3 Reorganization. Remove on One Side, Remit It on the Other

Facing a demolition's representation of this kind, the current territorial conditions introduce inevitable elements of complexity and force us to reformulate the terms. For the urban project, two perspectives emerge in particular.

On the one side, a partial and selective demolition, like what has been done in recent public housing redevelopment projects, in which the residual value assigned to the building and the recycling of the materials removed is accompanied by the redefinition of urban relations (Infussi and Orsenigo 2008; Laboratorio città pubblica 2009; Di Palma 2011; Lepratto 2017). On the other side, an idea of demolition where the building's value is dematerialised and transferred elsewhere, becoming the tool for a broader territorial reorganisation design.

This second aspect deserves to be more investigated by referring, for example, to the role that demolition could play in the redevelopment of those parts of the città diffusa that are facing a greater crisis today. The generally modest quality of these territories, the loss of attractiveness, the social composition with increasing amounts of elderly population, the high levels of pollution, and soil waterproofing, poses new challenges to urban planning.

In particular, underutilisation phenomena emerge, often linked to a general redefinition of relations between living spaces and workplaces. This is attested, for example, by the changing of the family house, which has had a big impact on the urbanisation processes between the 1960s and 1990s, both in the single-house format and in hybridisations with working spaces. A space that is no longer able to intercept the preferences and investments of the new generations, who sometimes see that inheritance more as a burden than as an advantage (Merlini and Zanfi 2014). Or it is attested—to give another example—by the production building in which add up the obsolescence, the inefficient accessibility, the dearth of support services for the company, the criticality of a landscape impact.

These buildings do not always show advanced degradation conditions, but nevertheless it is difficult to imagine them in a redevelopment perspective what restores them to a new life cycle (Zanfi and Curci 2018). In such situations, a responsible judgment is forced to be selective and also consider the possibility of demolition, because of a number of factors that consider the scarcity of available economic resources, while also promoting a territorial vision aimed at restoring security and urbanity conditions. For the urban design, a reflection therefore opens up that primarily seeks to recognize those situations in which it is possible to recover and transfer value, through mechanisms of subtraction and addition of volumes. It is essentially a case of promoting a reorganisation process based on identifying source areas and areas of fall in volumes, made operational through volumetric transfer mechanisms, while also evaluating the factors that ensure economic feasibility (Lanzani et al. 2014).

Demolition is in this case the tool of a territorial reorganisation that recognizes a divergence of values. On the one hand, buildings that decline and that might have a future only through the value generated by their volumetric rights; on the other, more dynamic situations where new volumes could be an opportunity for urban consolidation. The task of urban planning would naturally be to identify and adjust areas of departure and relapse of the volumes, responding not only to the need to restrict the soil consumption bat, more generally, to issues relating to safety and urbanity of settlements.

This territorial reorganization should have a dual requirement. First, it is a matter of removing buildings that are in decline, abandoned or located in improper places, which cause problems of insecurity, or involving unsustainable maintenance and management costs. Demolition would be based on a very relevant technical topic—what produces risk must be demolished—which reconfigures its terms. At the same time, it would generate volumes to consolidate parts of the existing city, especially where the settlements are less defined and where they could benefit from the introduction of new volumes. In essence, a demolition and a densification that, through specific intervention rules, can contribute to the necessary reflection on the urbanity forms of contemporary territories.

But it's not just about this. A further element emerges in this territorial reorganization project. When a building in decline or an impermeable soil is removed, a naturalization and remediation action (granted in fact by the presence, elsewhere, of an improvement) should be combined (Girot 2005). The terms of the problem are: more security, more urbanity, but also more nature.

The development of a procedural mechanism allowing volumetric transfers should, in this sense, be part of a wider territorial vision, which could partially redefine our very idea of nature. Some partial demolition could in fact collaborate in defining a new landscape in the città diffusa contexts. A re-naturalization that takes its distances from a restoration idea (unthinkable in a landscape that has drastically changed the original agricultural use and hybridized its expressive codes), and can also be activated through actions that, like the demolitions might be partial.

The removal of the most critical elements from an environmental viewpoint, accompanied by low-cost interventions (for example, simple carry-over of land and sowing), could trigger a reconfiguration process with significant landscape effects and, at the same time, might change our imaginary. Partial removals, even small and episodic, could give shape to parts of non-domesticated nature, offered to visual perception but subtracted from use (Clément 2005).

4 Conclusions

What is synthetically exposed is a change of perspective that has unavoidable technical and cultural complexities opening up reflections in multiple directions. For example, it becomes necessary to review the regulatory framework traceable to the waste cycle (Rigamonti 1996), redefine the organization of the dismantling and demolition sites that could be temporarily shape up as storage depots, and more generally rethink the concept of risk.

This takes us back to a more general theme, which cannot of course be developed here. The phenomena mentioned at the beginning urge a reflection on the possible presence, in next future, of buildings destined to decline because no transformation will be activated on them, and no economic resources will be available, not even for their demolition. For them, perhaps only a scenario of permanent abandonment opens up. This will have to be managed knowing that the possibility that they can turn into ruin with a certain symbolic and testimonial value is limited, and that, more likely, we will be forced to coexist with waste and rubble (Augé 2004; Broggini 2009; Lanzani and Curci 2018).

References

Andriani, C. (Ed.). (2010). *Il patrimonio e l'abitare*. Roma: Donzelli.

Augé, M. (2004). *Rovine e macerie. Il senso del tempo*, (2003). Torino: Bollati Boringhieri.

Bauman, Z. (2017). *Retrotopia*. Roma-Bari: Laterza.

Broggini, O. (2009). *Le rovine del Novecento. Rifiuti, rottami, ruderi e altre eredità*. Reggio Emilia: Diabasis.

Calafati, A. (Ed. 2014), *Città tra sviluppo e declino: un'agenda urbana per l'Italia*. Roma: Donzelli.

Clément, G. (2005). *Manifesto del terzo paesaggio, (2004)*. Macerata: Quodlibet.

Corbellini, G., & Marini, S. (Eds.). (2016). *Recycled theory*. Quodlibet, Macerata: Dizionario illustrato.

Criconia, A. (Ed.). (1998). *Figure della demolizione. Il carattere instabile della città contemporanea*. Genova Milano: Costa & Nolan.

Curci, F., Formato, E., & Zanfi, F. (Eds.). (2017). *Territori dell'abusivismo. Un progetto per uscire dall'Italia dei condoni*. Roma: Donzelli.

Curci, F., Zanfi, F. (2018). "Il costruito, tra abbandoni e riusi". In A. De Rossi (Ed.), *Riabitare l'Italia. Le aree interne tra abbandoni e riconquiste* (pp. 207–231). Roma: Donzelli.

Dansero, E., Giaimo, C., Spaziante, A. (Eds.). (2001). *Se i vuoti si riempiono. Aree industriali dismesse: temi e ricerche*. Firenze: Alinea.

De Rossi, A. (Ed.). (2018). *Riabitare l'Italia*. Donzelli, Roma: Le aree interne tra abbandoni e riconquiste.

Di Palma, V. (2011). *Demolizione e ricostruzione nei programmi di riqualificazione urbana*. Roma: Aracne.

Fabian, L., & Munarin, S. (Eds.). (2017). *Re-Cycle Italy*. Lettera Ventidue, Siracusa: Atlante.

Girot, C. (2005). "Vers une nouvelle nature". In Aa. Vv, *Landscape Architecture in Mutation. Essay on Urban Landscape* (pp. 19–33). Zurich: Eth.

Infussi, F. & Orsenigo, G. (Eds.). (2008). "Progetto di demolizione. Viaggio ai confini del moderno". In *Territorio*, n. 45, pp. 9–62.

Laboratorio Città Pubblica (2009). *Città pubbliche. Linee guida per la riqualificazione urbana*, Bruno Mondadori, Milano.

Lanzani, A. (2015). *Città territorio urbanistica tra crisi e contrazione*. Milano: Angeli.

Lanzani, A., Merlini, C. & Zanfi, F. (2014). "Quando 'un nuovo ciclo di vita' non si dà. Fenomenologia dello spazio abbandonato e prospettive per il progetto urbanistico oltre il paradigma del riuso". In *Archivio di Studi Urbani e Regionali*, n. 109, 28–47.

Lanzani, A., Curci, F. (2018). "Le Italie in contrazione, tra crisi e opportunità". In A. De Rossi (Eds.), *Riabitare l'Italia. Le aree interne tra abbandoni e riconquiste* (pp. 79–107). Roma: Donzelli.

Lepratto, F. (2017). *Bricolage urbano. Il progetto contemporaneo per trasformare la residenza collettiva del secondo dopoguerra: obiettivi, metodi, strumenti*. Dottorato di ricerca in Architettura, Urbanistica e Conservazione dei luoghi dell'abitare e del paesaggio, Politecnico di Milano.

Merlini, C. (2008). "La demolizione tra retoriche e tecniche del progetto urbano", in *Territorio*, n. 45, pp. 49–55.
Merlini, C. (2019). "L'eventualità della demolizione. Forme, situazioni e linguaggi". *Archivio di Studi Urbani e Regionali*, n. 124, pp. 26–48.
Merlini, C., & Zanfi F. (2014). "The family houses and its territories in contemporary Italy: present conditions and future perspectives". In *Journal of Urbanism, 9*, pp. 221–244.
Micelli, E. (2014). "L'eccezione e la regola. Le forme della riqualificazione della città esistente tra demolizione e ricostruzione e interventi di riuso". In *Valori e Valutazioni*, n. 12, pp. 11–20.
Munarin, S., & Velo, L. (Eds.). (2016). *Italia 1945–2045. Urbanistica prima e dopo. Radici, condizioni, prospettive*. Roma: Donzelli.
Nigrelli, F. C. (Ed.). (2005). *Il senso del vuoto*. Manifestolibri, Roma: Demolizioni nella città contemporanea.
Rigamonti, E. (1996). *Il riciclo dei materiali in edilizia*. Sant'Arcangelo di RomagnaL: Maggioli.
Russo, M. (1998). *Aree dismesse. Forma e risorsa della "città esistente*". Napoli: Edizioni Scientifiche Italiane.
Terranova, A. (Ed.). (1997). *Il progetto della sottrazione*. Roma: Croma Quaderni n. 3.

The Evaluation of Urban Regeneration Processes

Leopoldo Sdino, Paolo Rosasco and Gianpiero Lombardini

Abstract The conditions why processes of urban regeneration can be developed in modern-day cities have changed enormously over the last decade. Unlike the recent past, where the reuse for urban uses of former industrial areas was only based on maximising the amount of space, after the housing bubble begun in 2008, the profit margins for operators were reduced, and today, they faced to a sharp contraction in demand and a surplus of supply. Consequently, the framework within which we carry out the investment decisions is increasingly complex and is characterised by the opposition of a potential conflict between two forces. On the one hand, the public administration which seeks to take full advantage of the urban transformation processes to improve the quality of live for citizens; on the other, the private entity that has the aim of maximising the profits obtainable from the intervention and to the minimise business risk. Therefore, to ensure the overall feasibility of an intervention, urban viability must correspond to an economic and financial sustainability. The paper analyses the role of the economic evaluation in urban regeneration interventions through the analysis of a case study in the city of Genoa.

Keywords Urban regeneration · Economic and financial feasibility · Cost-Revenue analysis

1 Introduction

The conditions why processes of urban regeneration can be initiated in modern-day cities have changed radically over the last two decades, especially after the 2007–2010 crisis (Nespolo 2012; Cutini and Rusci 2016). While until the end of the last century the economic growth dynamics, although progressively weaker and unstable,

L. Sdino (✉)
Architecture, Built Environment and Construction Engineering—ABC Department, Politecnico di Milano, Milan, Italy
e-mail: leopoldo.sdino@polimi.it

P. Rosasco · G. Lombardini
Department of Architectural and Design—DAD, University of Genoa, Genoa, Italy

S. Della Torre et al. (eds.), *Regeneration of the Built Environment from a Circular Economy Perspective*, Research for Development,
https://doi.org/10.1007/978-3-030-33256-3_6

allowed interventions on the existing urban area that could be based on significant increases in real estate value, the economic conditions after the early 2000s changed, reducing the economic profit for private investors. This was caused by the crisis in the real estate markets, mainly caused by excess of supply (De Gaspari 2013), repeated crises, economic stagnation and the state's fiscal crisis which has led to a drastic reduction in public and private investment.

So if initially, the urban transformation projects could be self-sustaining financially through the implementation of the changes of intended uses and the exploitation of agglomeration economies determined by the "positional income", with the passing of time and the change of economic conditions, these possibilities gradually are failed.

In this context, only big cities included in the large circuits of the flow economies and high finance are really attractive to financial capitals (Sassen 2001, 2018; Dicken 2003). In addition, the reduction in public investment makes local contexts increasingly dependent on private and international capital.

The location preferences for these "seeking value" capitals are extremely selective, as well as time-varying. The medium-sized cities have been pushed to the edges of the major processes and urban renewal projects. The strategies adopted by them are based on becoming as attractive as possible on the international markets of urban transformation (Ombuen 2018).

The transformation and urban redevelopment projects move within a framework characterised by actors who have, at least potentially, objectives and requirements that are opposed to one another:

- Public Administration, pursuing the maximum competitive advantage from the new regional planning and the improvement of environmental quality and the lives of citizens (Palermo and Ponzini 2012);
- Private Investors, which through real estate investing seek the maximisation of profits (Brenner and Theodore 2002).

The mission of the governance of urban transformation in this context therefore resides in the development of strategies to bring together other resources, more and more often by private investors, from which is possible obtain economics resources for creating infrastructure and services for the community.

2 From the "Blueprint" Project to "Levante Waterfront" in Genoa

The "Levante Waterfront" project is one of the most significant operations that lie ahead for the city of Genoa. It was conceived in the early twenty-first century to restore the sea area overlooking the city along the coastal stretch from Porto Antico (designed by Renzo Piano for the 1992 Expo) to the Corso Italia promenade.

Currently, the whole area is taken up by different functions (exhibition, production and port) and is in fact separated from the rest of the city.

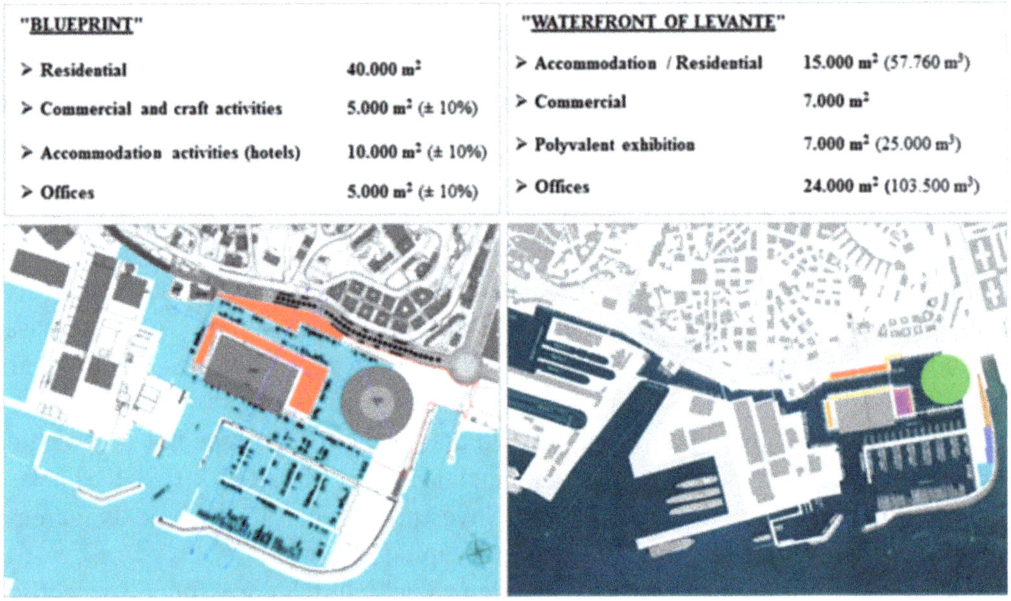

Fig. 1 Areas affected by the redevelopment project and square metres

The redevelopment projects began with the acquisition of areas and buildings of the exhibition site by the Municipality of Genoa in 2000 (for a value of 18.6 million euros). After a long period of pilot projects (among which the most important is the "Affresco" project developed in 2014 by Renzo Piano that redesigns the entire Genoese coastal strip), the urban transformation operation entered into an operational phase in 2014. In that year, Renzo Piano developed a first master plan for the coastal strip to the east of the city called the "Blueprint".

The transformation, conceived in this first phase, involved the construction of a new waterway (navigable channel) near the ancient city walls obtained by excavating existing pier sections and demolishing some disused buildings such as the ex-Nira building as well as some of the exhibition centre's obsolete.

The pedestrian walkway was placed along this dock, which should have been the missing link between Porto Antico and the Corso Italia promenade (in the eastern part of the exhibition area).

The total surface area for the new intended uses is equal to 48, 300 sqm.

With regards to the general design, the scope appearing to be the most complex among those identified was the one in the (ex) exhibition area: in accordance with the provisions of the urban plan of Genoa, the volumes of the demolished buildings use can be reconstructed in this area.

In 2016, the Municipality of Genoa established that the implementation of the "BluePrint" project (Fig. 1—left) should take place by means of a design competition developed in the areas owned by the municipality and SPIM.[1] (the company

[1] Society for the Promotion of Heritage Property in the City of Genoa.

designated as a guidance subject for the transformation). In July 2016, a competition notice was then issued which saw the participation of over 70 national and international groups of design.

The work of the appointed Selection Committee led to the conclusion of the procedure with no winner. Following the outcome of this competition and from the evolving urban dynamics of the city, a new project proposal has therefore been reached, the result of a reworking of the assembly design again by Renzo Piano, now called the "Levante Waterfront".

The changes to the "Blueprint" have maintained the idea of bringing the water near to the city but decreasing the building dimensions (Fig. 1—right).

The Municipality of Genoa has decided to proceed with the assessment by selling the entire compendium by evaluating the proposal in two different stages: in a first stage, the best compliance with the design idea of the "Levante Waterfront"; in a second phase, the technical and economic proposal (the latter regarding the tender for purchasing the areas).[2]

Within the pre-qualification questionnaire, it is confirmed that the Private Investor will take charge of the demolition of the former trade fair pavilions and the construction of the waterway[3] (excluding the first part—at the west—which will be built by the municipality after the demolition of the ex-Nira[4] building).

Between August and September 2018, the commission assessed the six proposals received, regarding only one as being eligible for the second phase (the most specifically designed and financial), the one from the Company EM2C from Lyon (France).

The French company, based on the economic elaborate checks, then notified about withdrawing the proposal in February 2019, considering the canal's construction cost as not being financially viable, which was required by the Municipality of Genoa.[5]

3 The Economic Sustainability of the "Levante Waterfront"

The feasibility of the project on the former Genoa exhibition area is therefore based not only on the urban and architectural plan but also on economical and financial

[2]Evaluated according to the most economically advantageous offer with the best value for money. As indicated in the tender documents, the price will fluctuate between 20 and 25 million euros (approximate values and not binding).

[3]The notice establishes a channel width of 40 m and a depth of 3.5 m.

[4]The public funds used are from the "Pact for Genoa", signed in November 2016 between the national government and the Municipality of Genoa, which provides for a budget of 110 million euros for direct investment to be made in the city of Genoa. Specifically, for the Waterfront project, 13.5 million euros have been allocated in addition to the 15 million euros that were previously allocated.

[5]From the newspaper "Il Secolo XIX" (6 and 8 March 2019), the cost estimated by EM2C is about 70 million euros.

Table 1 Intervention costs and contact persons

Municipality of Genoa	Private investor
Demolition of the former Nira building	Acquisition areas
Waterway construction	Waterway completion
Elevated stretch substitution (500 m)	Reuse of the S Pavilion (sports hall)
	Creation of new buildings, facilities and docks for mooring boats (53,000 sqm of SA)
	Public pedestrian footpaths and areas
	Parking for residents, businesses, moorings
	Urbanisation works (public car parks, etc.)
Total cost: 50 million euros	

sustainability; it must ensure the Private Investor who will develop the intervention an adequate profit margin for the capital invested.

In order to verify what the economic and financial viability conditions of the "Levante Waterfront" project are, a Cost-Revenue Analysis model (CRA) is developed, assuming the quantities of intended uses indicated by the Municipality of Genoa for various intended uses (residential, tertiary, etc.) (Fig. 1—right).

According to the instructions given in the tender documents and in the attached documents, costs were attributed to the two main parties according to Table 1.

According to the CRA, the evaluation of economic and financial sustainability is developed on the basis of two indicators (Prizzon 1995; Sdino et al. 2016):

- Net Present Value (NPV), which is the difference between revenues and discounted costs compared to the time of the assessment and estimated within the intervention/investment time period (55 years);
- Internal Rate of Return (IRR), which is the average percentage of the investment profitability referring to the time base assumed for the analysis of costs and revenues (one year, two months, etc.).

4 The Evaluation of Costs and Revenues

To estimate the construction costs for the buildings with different intended uses, a synthetic methodology[6] is adopted while for the connecting channel with the Expo area of Genoa, a summarised bill of quantities is developed. Apart from the design

[6]The costs have been estimated on the basis of unit values taken from the price list for building typologies of the DEI for similar types and interventions.

Table 2 Estimated construction costs

Intended use	Cost	
	Min.	Max.
Purchase areas (€)	25,000,000	30,000,000
Residential (€/sqm)	1100	1800
Commercial (€/sqm)	900	1700
Offices (€/sqm)	1025	1500
Hospitality (€/room)	70,000	85,000
Outdoor areas (€/sqm)	70	140
Underground car parks (€/car park)	15,000	18,000
Waterway (€)		67,500,000
Jetty dock (€)		10,000,000
Planning fees (€)		20,000,000

costs[7] and marketing costs,[8] the general overheads of the Private Investor[9] as well as the unexpected expenses[10] are considered.

The assumed unitary costs are shown in Table 2.

Regard to the cost of the areas—which is the subject of the economic offer to be presented in the second phase—is considered equal to the average value among those indicated by the Municipality of Genoa.[11]

In the economic evaluation of a real estate development project, the forecast of the constructed real estate market values is one of the most critical factors that influence the value of sustainability indicators (Calabrò and Della Spina 2014; Napoli 2015; Rebaudengo and Prizzon 2017).

For the estimation of unit market values for the residential properties, an analysis of some property realities was developed which have some similarities to the one in question in terms of their urban planning and housing characteristics; in particular are analysed the unitary residential values of buildings located in the Ligurian and Tuscan coasts, served by major public transport services and located in the immediate vicinity of port facilities for recreational medium-large boating (with more than 50 moorings).

The survey conducted shows that the values range from a minimum of 3980 €/sqm to a maximum of 5850 €/sqm.

[7]Estimated at 7% of the construction cost.

[8]Estimated at 2% of the real estate value.

[9]Estimated at 3% of the construction cost.

[10]Estimated at 10% of the construction cost.

[11]As indicated in the tender documents, the price will fluctuate between 25 and 30 million euros (values are not binding for the municipality); the value taken in the CRA amounted to € 27.5 million euros.

Table 3 Unit values estimated for sale and leasing

Intended use	Unitary value	
	Min.	Max.
Sale		
Residential (€/sqm)	3900	5800
Commercial (€/sqm)	2000	4500
Car park (€/car park)	45,000	70,000
Offices (€/sqm)	2000	3000
Moorings (€/mooring)	35,000	100,000
Lease		
Commercial (€/sqm/month)	204	290
Hospitality (€/room/day)	140	220
Managerial (€/sqm/year)	120	150
Moorings (€/space/year)	4500	18,000

In the CRA, it was assumed that the values of residential properties range from a minimum of 3900 €/sqm and a maximum of 5800 €/sqm.[12] With regard to other intended uses (commercial, offices, hospitality and moorings), the sales and rental values assumed were gathered by observers in the housing market or from the offers listed on major real estate deals sites[13] for the Foce area[14] or by the companies that manage facilities for recreational boating in the Ligurian area.

Table 3 shows the unit values assumed in the CRA model.

It is expected that the sale of the property will take place within the six years after the closure of the building site.

The evaluation of the economic sustainability of the project is developed in relation to a "sale and management" real estate scenario that considers five years for the construction of buildings (residences, offices, shops and hotel) and subsequent six years for sale; the Sports Hall (Pavilion S) and part of parking located in Piazzale Kennedy are considered in management concession—to the Private Investor by the Municipality of Genoa—for fifty years. At the end of the concession (the 56th year), they will go back to being fully owned by the Municipality of Genoa.

5 Results

The analysis of the indicator values (NPV and IRR) obtained by the CRA models highlights limit conditions of economic and financial sustainability (Table 4). For

[12]The variability takes into account the different locations of the properties inside the buildings (floor level, view, brightness, etc.).

[13]Casa.it; Immobiliare.it.

[14]Genoa District where the intervention is located.

Table 4 Scenarios and financial sustainability indicators (NPV and IRR)

Scenario	Waterway cost	Planning fees	Quantity (sqm)	NPV (million €)	IRR (%)
Sale and management	100% PI	YES (20 million €)	Residential: 15,000 Tertiary: 24,000 Commercial: 7000 Expo 7000	21.2	3.8
Alternative scenarios					
1	50% M 50% PI	NO	Residential: 15,000 Tertiary: 24,000 Commercial: 7000 Expo 7000	62.5	6.3
2	50% M 50% PI	NO	Residential: 29,000 Tertiary: 10,000 Commercial: 7000 Expo 7000	88.5	7.5
3	50% M 50% PI	NO	Residential: 35,000 Tertiary: 10,000 Commercial: 7000 Expo 7000	101.7	8.2
4	50% M 50% PI	NO	Residential: 40,000 Tertiary: 10,000 Commercial: 7000 Expo 7000	111.0	8.6
5	100% M	YES (20 million €)	Residential: 40,000 Tertiary: 10,000 Commercial: 7000 Expo 7000	125.1	10.0
M = Municipality of Genoa					
PI = Private investor					

the "sale and management" scenario, the NPV is positive (although low) while the IRR is below the minimum acceptable limits for this type of real estate investments (12.5%).[15] The cost of the waterway (67.5 million euros) has the greatest negative impact on the sustainability indicators; the expected revenue relating to selling and renting moorings[16] is unable to sustain the high cost. Five alternative scenarios are therefore established and configured according to a different combination of some variables such as: the planning fees to be paid to the municipality[17]; the allocation of the construction costs of the waterway; the amount of the areas for the intended uses (Table 4).

The economic sustainability indicators's values show that only the scenario 5 can be considered sustainable: the NPV value is equal to 125.1 million euros while the IRR is equal to 10.0%, close to the minimum acceptability threshold.

This scenario was configured considering that the waterway will be constructed entirely by the municipality (and leased for 50 years), that Private Investor will pay the planning fees (estimated at € 20 million) and that the distribution of the areas will be aligned with the one indicated in the previous "Blueprint" competition notice (Fig. 1—left) with 40,000 sqm of residential area.[18]

6 Conclusions

The economic and financial evaluation of the "Levante Waterfront" in Genoa point out that the configured scenario based on the indication of the tender documents is not economically sustainable for a private investor; the construction cost of the waterway connecting with the Porto Antico area is the work that has the most negative impact on the economic feasibility of the intervention.

The only scenario that is feasible, despite having an IRR value slightly below the minimum threshold, is the one that provides for the construction of the entire waterway by the Municipality of Genoa and the subsequent concession of the moorings for 50 years to the Private Investor (scenario 5); the scenario also provides for an increase in the residential area (from 15,000 to 40,000 sqm) and a decrease of the tertiary area (from 24,000 to 10,000 sqm).

---

[15]The value is determined by the sum of three components (Prizzon 1995): the profitability of an alternative low-risk investment (1.5%—thirty-year Italian treasury bonds); inflation contingency (1%); investment property inherent risk (10%).

[16]It is considered that 50% of the moorings are sold in the first six years and the remaining 50% are rented for 50 years, after which they will be sold. In the alternative 1–4 scenarios, the number of leased and sold moorings is reduced by 50% because half of the waterway is considered public property; in scenario 5, they are considered in concession for 50 years.

[17]Quantified by mutual agreement between the Municipality of Genoa and the Private Investor at the time of preparation of the Operative Urban Plan (PUO).

[18]In relation to the characteristics of the real estate market of Genoa, the residential use is the one that guarantees a higher profit margin.

The results obtained, however, must be carefully evaluated in relation to some uncertainty factors which could further affect the feasibility of the intervention, including:

- the costs of disposing of the materials from the demolition, where the presence of pollutant substances may be identified (asbestos, etc.);
- the potential demand for buildings that will be constructed and their corresponding sales timing, in relation to a Genoese real estate market that has been characterised by lower prices and a lack of vibrancy in trading activity for over a decade in relation to the entire existing housing stock;
- the permitting timelines and any requirements that might affect the economic feasibility conditions.

Also, if the feasibility conditions can be guaranteed by a massive use of public resources, it is permissible to ask what the overall social benefits obtained from an operation conceived in this way are and whether they are justified compared to a "fair" allocation of public economic resources.

In other words, in another vision of sustainability understood as being fair to work, an intervention should first be true (economically feasible), good (socially correct) and beautiful (environmentally acceptable) (Sdino et al. 2018).

References

Brenner, N., & Theodore, N. (Eds.). (2002). *Spaces of neoliberalism: urban restructuring in North America and Western Europe*. Malden: Blackwell.

Calabrò, F., & Della Spina, L. D. (2014). "The public-private partnerships in buildings regeneration: A model appraisal of the benefits and for land value capture" in *Advanced Materials Research. Trans Tech Publications Ltd., 931–932,* 555–559.

Cutini, V., & Rusci, S. (2016). Ai tempi della crisi, il mercato immobiliare e le influenze sulla pianificazione. *Archive of Urban and Regional Studies*, (116), 91–114.

De Gaspari, M. (2013). *Bolle di mattone. La crisi italiana a partire dalla città. Come il mattone può distruggere un'economia*. Milan: Mimesis.

Dicken, P. (2003). *Global shift: reshaping the global and economic map in the 21st century*. New York: Guilford Press.

Napoli, G. (2015). "Financial sustainability and morphogenesis of urban transformation project". In *Lecture Notes in Computer Science (including subseries Lecture Notes in Artificial Intelligence and Lecture Notes in Bioinformatics)* (Vol. *9157*, pp. 178–193). Springer.

Nespolo, L. (2012). *Rigenerazione urbana e recupero del plusvalore fondiario. Le esperienze di Barcellona e Monaco di Baviera*. Florence: IRPET.

Ombuen, S. (2018). "Rendite e finanziarizzazione nelle economie urbane". In: *Urban@it National Centre of Studies for urban policy—Fourth Report on the cities. Il governo debole delle economie urbane*. Bologna: Il Mulino.

Palermo, P., & Ponzini, D. (2012). At the crossroads between urban planning and urban design: Critical lessons from three Italian case studies. *Planning Theory & Practice, 13*(3), 445–460.

Prizzon, F. (1995). *La valutazione degli investimenti immobiliari*. Turin: Celid.

Rebaudengo, M., & Prizzon, F. (2017). "Assessing the investments sustainability after the new code on public contracts". In *Lecture Notes in Computer Science (including subseries Lecture Notes in Artificial Intelligence and Lecture Notes in Bioinformatics)* (Vol. *10409*, pp. 473–484). LNCS.

Sassen, S. (2001). *The global city*. New York: London, Tokio, Princeton University Press, Princeton.
Sassen, S. (2018). *Cities in a world economy*. New York: Sage.
Sdino, L., Rosasco, P., & Magoni, S. (2016). "The financial feasibility of a real estate project: the case of the Ex Tessitoria Schiatti". In F. Calabrò, L. D. Della Spina (Eds.), *Procedia Social and Behavioral Sciences* (Vol. *223*, pp. 217–224).
Sdino, L., Rosasco, P., & Magoni, S. (2018). *True, fair and beautiful: Evaluative paradigms between the encyclical letter laudato Sì and Keynes* (pp. 87–98). Green Energy and Technology: Springer.

New Paradigms for the Urban Regeneration Project Between Green Economy and Resilience

Elena Mussinelli, Andrea Tartaglia, Daniele Fanzini, Raffaella Riva, Davide Cerati and Giovanni Castaldo

Abstract Starting from a PRIN 2015 study, the paper addresses the themes of adding value to public spaces, quality to the urban landscape, redeveloping degraded areas and proposing a sustainable and resilient design approach to cope with the effects of climate change. Specifically, this study focuses on the key role public space can play in urban resilience processes, with the aim of not only providing results in qualitative terms, but also measuring the feedback in environmental and economic terms.

Keywords Nature-based solution · Green infrastructure · Public space · Environmental design

1 Climate Change and Urban Crises

The intense urbanisation processes that have characterised the development of human settlements in recent decades have played a decisive role in the modification of the mankind–environment relationship: cities are in fact one of the most significant sources of impact, with relevant effects in the consumption of natural resources, in polluting emissions and in the overall alteration of natural and climatic balances. It is therefore necessary to start from the cities, from their management and operating models in order to define policies, strategies and concrete action that can guarantee more sustainable forms of development, including from a social and economic point of view. As clearly stressed in a recent publication by the European Political Strategy Centre (2018), the climate change issue, which was perceived as a long-term danger, is instead already showing its impact all over the world, in Europe as well (European Commission 2006). In most of the European Countries, the increase in temperature from the last century is almost of one degree, with a trend that, as a minimum, will soon double the limit of the Paris Agreement signed in 2016. Climate-related catastrophes—such as floods, storms and droughts—have become more and

E. Mussinelli (✉) · A. Tartaglia · D. Fanzini · R. Riva · D. Cerati · G. Castaldo
Architecture, Built Environment and Construction Engineering—ABC Department, Politecnico di Milano, Milan, Italy
e-mail: elena.mussinelli@polimi.it

S. Della Torre et al. (eds.), *Regeneration of the Built Environment from a Circular Economy Perspective*, Research for Development,
https://doi.org/10.1007/978-3-030-33256-3_7

more recurrent in our territories, with negative impacts also on urban environments and health. Flooding and urban heat islands sum their negativities to other issues, such as air, soil and water pollution, land-use change and soil sealing increasing the criticalities of life in urban areas.

The progressive awareness of these increasingly evident criticalities pushed the European Union to develop new policies and actions, initially aimed at urban sustainability,[1] later at urban resilience[2] and now stressing the role of urban robustness.[3] Within the broad panel of policies and instruments that can now be used to combat the deterioration of urban environmental quality and climate change, in recent years, the so-called nature-based solutions (NBS) have emerged. NBS are a set of technical solutions based on natural resources (vegetation, water, soil, etc.) to regenerate buildings and urban spaces in a resilient key, even with the formation of real "ecological corridors" (green and blue infrastructures GBI) able to reconstitute, through suitable reconnections, the continuity of environmental systems. NBS and GBI are in fact configured as multifunctional tools, capable of generating environmental and economic benefits, of delivering ecosystem services and, at the same time, of contributing to the formation of more functional, comfortable and healthy built spaces.

2 The Role of Public Spaces: Environment and Life Quality

Hence, the interest of this research in exploring the applicative potential of these solutions in relation to a specific dimension of the city, that of public spaces, which—for various reasons and for several years now—is experiencing a process of significant delay (Mussinelli 2018).

---

[1] *"According to the European Commission (2006), urban sustainability is defined as the challenge to 'solve both the problems experienced within cities and the problems caused by cities', recognizing that cities themselves provide many potential solutions"* moreover *"sustainable urbanization is a dynamic process that combines environmental, social, economic and political-institutional sustainability. It brings together urban and rural areas, encompassing the full range of human settlements from village to town to city to metropolis, with links on national and global level"* (Shen et al. 2011: 18).

[2] *"Urban resilience is the capacity of urban systems, communities, individuals, organisations and businesses to recover, maintain their function and thrive in the aftermath of a shock or a stress, regardless of its impact, frequency or magnitude"* (Urban Resilience. A concept for co-creating cities of the future URBACT Resilient Europe).

[3] *"Robust systems include well-conceived, constructed and managed physical assets, so that they can withstand the impacts of hazardous events without significant damage or loss of function. Robust design anticipates potential failures in systems, making provision to ensure failure is predictable, safe, and not disproportionate to the cause. Over-reliance on a single asset, cascading failure and design thresholds that might lead to catastrophic collapse if exceeded are actively avoided"* (The Rockefeller Foundation and Arup 2014:5).

The research unit of the ABC Department has been involved in the PRIN 2015 study entitled "Adaptive design and technological innovations for the resilient regeneration of urban districts under climate change"[4] which intended to investigate, also through experimental demonstrating projects, the applicability of strategic guidelines and technological and environmental design solutions able to obtain positive repercussions from the reduction in exposure to climate risks and from the socio-economic sustainability of cities. Specifically, the local unit of the Politecnico di Milano focused on the topic of identifying tools and defining and implementing actions for revamping and redeveloping the public space. In fact, the environmental quality and usability of public spaces are still a too much underrated aspect of the urban project, which tends to focus mainly on the morphological configuration of the settlements and the functional and energy performances of the buildings with poor outcomes with regard to the open space structure. These spaces—squares, roads, urban gardens, etc.,—often become a "result", frequently achieved in significantly dilated timeframes compared with the construction of buildings, to be functionalised ex-post, through furnishings and object layouts that support its use.

Public spaces—if approached through a multidisciplinary lens that considers its formal, environmental and user values—pave the road towards a way in which to cope positively with climate change issues and the needs of social cohesion. Within this mindset, this study has systematically integrated multidisciplinary inputs and structures relating to methods and tools for the design and implementation of NBS in the ecological requalification of public spaces, with criteria and indicators for monitoring and evaluating their multifunctionality and environmental effectiveness; models and tools to manage and enhance public spaces as a common cultural heritage, endowed with identity values, supporting full and conscious accessibility in physical (multisensorial) and cultural terms; strategies, planning criteria, name and technical solutions for the promotion of liveability and psycho-physical well-being and for the containment of risk and the management of public space safety (UN Habitat 2004).

The area of cross-fertilisation amongst the various disciplinary contributions derives from the use of research action and co-design methodologies that combine analysis/programming strategies and spontaneous forms of bottom-up participation (SWOT analysis, strategic planning and good demonstrative practices and projects) and from the common goal of achieving the development of integrated tools for the qualitative-quantitative evaluation of the expected benefits and the effectiveness of the proposed solutions, measurable by their cultural, social and economic value.

[4]PRIN 2015 principal investigator: M. Losasso, Università degli Studi di Napoli "Federico II". Local unit Politecnico di Milano, ABC Department: E. Mussinelli (coordinator), R. Bolici, G. Castaldo, D. Cerati, D. Fanzini, M. Gambaro, M. Mocchi, R. Riva, A. Tartaglia.

3 Solutions and Indicators

Nowadays, all European policies are characterised by targets (as in those focused on climate and energy) and by impact assessment tools and methods used to estimate the possible economic, social and environmental impacts of decisions and laws. This approach works quite well on the macro-scale and can lead and control the effects of policies on a territorial and urban scale, but it is not suitable to support the decisional process related to local and specific single interventions.

At any rate, on this same scale, "the role of analytical-assessment processes is central for verifying the achievement of goals aimed at ecological improvement and greater resilience through nature-based solutions" (Mussinelli et al. 2018:120). This is essential in the transformation of urban settlements and public spaces in which contemporary needs found in the NBS and GBI are one of the most requested and applied solutions. Even if NBS are not the only tool and cannot alone solve climate change-related issues,[5] because of their multifunctionality they have a strategic role in European policies. In fact, in 2013, the EU adopted the Communication on GI[6] and, amongst the eight actions listed in the strategy on adaptation to climate change, stressed the importance of a "full mobilisation of ecosystem-based approaches to adaptation". Moreover, the report entitled Towards an EU Research and Innovation policy agenda for Nature-Based Solutions and Re-Naturing Cities published by the European Commission specifies that "enhancing sustainable urbanisation through nature-based solutions can stimulate economic growth as well as improving the environment, making cities more attractive, and enhancing human well-being" (Directorate General for Research and Innovation 2015:4). In particular, NBS and GBI are considered cost-effective alternatives to traditional grey infrastructure, capable of producing direct and indirect economic and financial advantages and, in the meantime, bringing about environmental benefits, well-being for people and an improvement in social cohesion. The use of these solutions in public space has the potential to activate or reactivate a wide panel of ecosystem services that represent a major element of cities' resilience.

The analysis of almost 50 case studies around the world stresses that in the majority of cases, decisions have been taken with a poor level of quantitative assessment or even with no attention at all given to the environmental impacts deriving from design alternatives, often focusing only on a single specific benefit related to the use

---

[5]The European Commission stresses that *"forests and agricultural lands currently cover more than three-quarters of the EU's territory and naturally hold large stocks of carbon, preventing its escape into the atmosphere. EU forests, for example, absorb the equivalent of nearly 10% of total EU greenhouse gas emissions each year. Land use and forestry – which include our use of soils, trees, plants, biomass and timber – can thus contribute to a robust climate policy"* (https://ec.europa.eu/clima/policies/forests_en). However, considering this value, it is also evident that a widespread action of forestation and urban forestation will never be enough to compensate the European emission of CO_2 related to human activities and to invert the trends in climate change.

[6]Communication from the Commission to the European Parliament, the Council, the European Economic and Social committee and the Committee of the Regions "Green Infrastructure (GI)—Enhancing Europe's Natural Capital"—COM/2013/0249 final.

of NBS and often not applying any monitoring of ex-post results of the interventions. In particular, the case studies analysed by the study (38% in Europe, 12% in Asia and 50% in North America) stress that: in 40% of the cases, the interventions were carried out for socio-cultural purposes (regenerating the landscape and providing new green spaces); in 38%, to create a particular regulatory ecosystem service (specifically for the management of water and the prevention of floods). Moreover, only 50% of the interventions were supported by quantitative data about possible obtainable environmental benefits (they were mostly North American cases; only in three European projects, there was a quantitative anticipation of the researched benefits).

This scenario contradicts the fact that "the long-time sustainability of decisions can be pursued only by following performance-based approaches capable of integrating environmental, economic, productive and socio-cultural components" (Tartaglia 2019). For this reason, the research activities were carried out first by identifying and, when necessary, developing performance indicators, able to both support the decisional process during the project activity for public spaces on a local scale and monitor and assess the benefits obtained.

4 Environmental Design and Measurement of the Impact of Alternatives

The understanding and anticipation of the potential results, their scalability and the ex-post assessment relating to local and punctual interventions are essential to build a link that connects European policies, national and regional programming, urban planning, local action and single projects. The environmental design, based on a systemic approach to problems and solutions, finds in the quantitative measurement of the impacts which is a necessary tool for its theoretical armoury. It is not only a problem of state indicators as the attention must be focused on performance indicators to have a complete operative design tool, easily applicable and not limited to highly specialised researchers. In particular, the research has focused on a core set of environmental indicators able to synthesise the effects of the decisions in terms of direct and indirect environmental benefits, also in indirect economic outcomes (avoided costs). In fact, as already anticipated, the ecological reconstruction of an urban environment is an economic opportunity both to reduce the costs of adaptation and management and to stimulate the birth and the development of companies in the field of green economy. From this perspective, there are interesting North American cases in which the increase of NBS in urban settlements and the application of GI instead of grey solutions have been estimated from an economic standpoint as well.[7]

[7] Particularly interesting are the experiences of the city of Philadelphia described in the report "Triple Bottom Line Assessment of Traditional and Green Infrastructure Options for Controlling CSO Events in Philadelphia's Watersheds" by Stratus Consulting (2009).

The green reconstruction of urban environments instead of the existing brownfields, open and public spaces, mobility infrastructures and in general grey infrastructure is finalised to a better use of soil, to a multifunctional usability of public resources and to increase the robustness of urban environments.

5 Experimental Case Study: South Milan

In this scenario, the south-east sector of the metropolitan area of Milan has been identified as an applicative case for design experimentation and the testing of the evaluation model proposed and defined by the study. This choice is related to many factors: indeed, this urban sector has undergone important transformation processes, is well equipped with infrastructure for local and supra-local mobility (Mussinelli and Castaldo 2015) and is also directly connected to the rural fringes and the Agricultural South Milano Park (Schiaffonati 2019; Tartaglia and Cerati 2018). Moreover, in this sector, in coherence with the strategic view of the Municipality (VVAA 2017) regarding urban resilience, many experimental projects and activities have been funded and activated.[8] In the meantime, it shows the main environmental criticalities that characterise the city territory and the Po valley, such as air pollution, the sewage system during acute meteorological phenomena, periods of drought and an increase in temperatures during the summer period, with urban canyons as well.

The whole sector has been analysed to identify areas of criticality where regeneration interventions can be proposed through the use of NBS (Fig. 1).

Specifically, the activity carried out concerned the morphological/typological and functional aspects (building heights, green areas and trees presence, public and private assets, presence of urban canyons, relationships between green areas, total surface area between permeable and impermeable surfaces, etc.), together with reliefs on the materials characterising the paving and vertical fronts of buildings and other structures above ground, as well as the solar exposure of open public spaces (streets and squares) during the summer period. All the analyses have been codified through the GIS tool, in such a way as to conform to the modelling tool of the urban microclimate (with ENVI MET software), according to stratigraphy and materials that characterise the open spaces and buildings (Mussinelli et al. 2018b).

[8]Among the different initiatives, the project "Sharing cities" for the experimentation of smart and integrated solutions in the area of Porta Romana; the competition "Reinventing Cities" (area of via Serio) for the realisation of an innovative building with regard to the reduction/zeroing of the carbon footprint in which the ABC Department was involved in a participating team as environmental experts (Andrea Campioli, Elena Mussinelli, Monica Lavagna, Andrea Tartaglia, Davide Cerati, Giovanni Castaldo, Anna Dalla Valle, Serena Giorgi and Tecla Caroli); the project "OpenAgri: New Skills for new Jobs in Peri-urban Agriculture" in the area of Porto di Mare-Parco della Vettabbia; the "100 Resilient Cities—Urban cooling" resilient workshop to explore resilient urban cooling solutions and technologies appropriate and coherent with communities' expectations with the participation of the ABC Department (Elena Mussinelli, Davide Cerati).

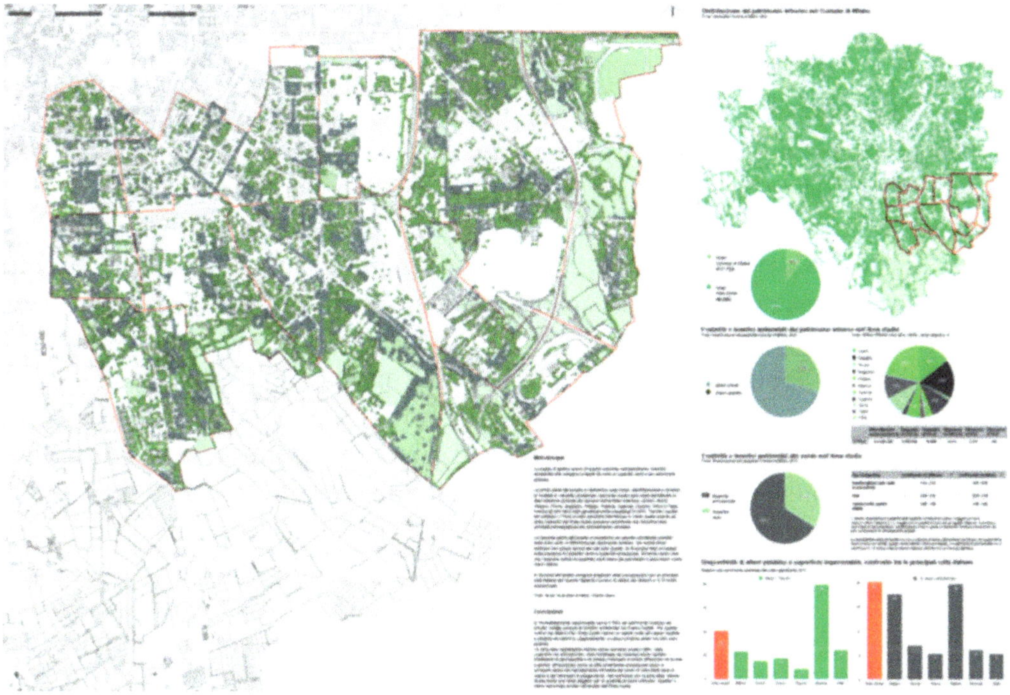

Fig. 1 Environmental values in the area of the applicative case

Elements such as the presence of green areas, accessibility, pollution, temperature and predicted mean vote (PMV) during the summer period have been used both to select the design case studies and to evaluate the possible results of the natural/natural and artificial alternatives for the construction of green infrastructures. The design proposals involved different kinds of public spaces to cover the alternative which can commonly be found in an urban settlement (avenues or lineal systems, squares or point systems, brownfields and infrastructure to be revamped). The parallel use of parametric evaluations and modelling tools has been used to assess the benefits related to air pollutants and greenhouse gases, direct and indirect absorption of CO_2, urban heat islands and rainwater management, arriving at an economic evaluation. Specifically, the quantification of indirect economic benefits, defined as lower costs for the implementation of other services that are essential for the functioning of the city, has in fact confirmed to the involved stakeholders (municipalities four and five of the city of Milan) that the savings obtained can be compared with the costs for the maintenance of new green infrastructures. In particular, the test areas have been the two linear systems of Corso Lodi and of Via Brenta; the punctual system of the San Luigi Square; the brownfield of Via Toffetti; the building and related open spaces of the project for the call "Reinventing cities" in Via Serio.

6 Conclusions

In a phase characterised by a narrowness of public resources and a limited capacity in managing the time–cost–quality ratio of public works, the project action should be strongly based on principles of necessity and rationality. In this scenario, the urban green project can find its proper integration within the overall regeneration actions, enhancing, where necessary, the use of trees, hedges, green walls and parterres and bio basins as multifunctional elements able to offer ecosystem services, to contribute to a comfortable use and to architecturally connote urban space. The design and management of these components must therefore be based on a principle of necessity, which means acting as a correct response to the demand for use, comfort and decor, ease of maintenance, high durability, reliability and safety, integration and environmental efficiency. The pursuit of these objectives cannot be achieved by involving actions that are reduced to the "tactical" dimension, but by activating processes of social and design re-appropriation that can really raise the level of knowledge, awareness and competence of citizenship, in order to produce structural and lasting results.

The study has allowed us to benefit from a more in-depth view of the ways in which to transform public spaces, to produce lasting socio-spatial effects and to contribute environmental improvement. In fact, the goal is to trigger virtuous processes of renewal of both contents and containers for the production of new culture and spatial regeneration. A central aspect of the intervention on public spaces concerns in fact the methods of triggering regeneration processes: further research developments are looking at new approaches that combine real estate investments and the creation of social value to move from typically compositional and "regulatory" design logics to logics of a promotional and "experimental" type, to create a trading zone within and to initiate demonstrations to accompany the processes. A new design paradigm for urban regeneration combines two levels: the long-term strategic vision and the short-medium term experimental vision.

References

Directorate General for Research and Innovation-European Commission. (2015). *Towards an EU Research and Innovation policy agenda for Nature-Based Solutions & Re-Naturing Cities*. Publications Office of the European Union.

European Commission. (2006). *Targeted summary of the European sustainable cities report for local authorities*. European Commission.

European Political Strategy Centre. (2018). 10 *trends reshaping climate and energy*. European Union.

Mussinelli, E. (2018). Il progetto ambientale dello spazio pubblico. *EcoWebTown*, *8*(II), 13–20.

Mussinelli, E., & Castaldo, G. (2015). Design and scale issues in the new metropolitan city: a study of the south-east Milan homogeneous zone. *Techne-Journal of Technology for Architecture and Environment, 10,* 153–160.

Mussinelli, E., Tartaglia, A., Bisogni, L., & Malcevschi, S. (2018a). The role of nature-based solutions in architectural and urban design. *Techne-Journal of Technology for Architecture and Environment, 15,* 116–123.

Mussinelli, E., Tartaglia, A., Cerati, D., & Castaldo, G. (2018b). Qualità e resilienza ambientale nelle proposte di intervento per il sud Milano: un'analisi quanti-qualitativa delle infrastrutture verdi. *Le Valutazioni Ambientali-Valutare la rigenerazione urbana, 2,* 79–98.

Schiaffonati, F. (2019). *Paesaggi milanesi*. Lupetti, Milano: Per una sociologia del paesaggio urbano.

Shen, L. Y., Ochoa, J. J., Shah, M. N., & Zhang, X. (2011). The application of urban sustainability indicators e a comparison between various practices. *Habitat International, 35,* 17–29.

Tartaglia, A. (2019). The valorisation of the resource system in rural and periurban areas. In D. Fanzini, A. Tartaglia, & R. Riva (Eds.), *Project challenges: sustainable development and urban resilience*. Santarcangelo di Romagna (in press): Maggioli.

Tartaglia, A., & Cerati, D. (Eds.). (2018). *Design and enhancement of the metropolitan rural territories*. Santarcangelo di Romagna: Maggioli.

The Rockefeller Foundation, Arup. (2014). *City Resilience Framework.*

UN Habitat. (2004). *Urban indicator guidelines*. UN Habitat.

VVAA. (2017). *Proposte e progetti per il Sud Milano. Il ruolo dei Municipi*. Municipio 4, Urban Curator TAT and Municipio 4. Cambiago: Notizie dal Comune sas.

The Technological Project for the Enhancement of Rural Heritage

Elena Mussinelli, Raffaella Riva, Roberto Bolici, Andrea Tartaglia, Davide Cerati and Giovanni Castaldo

Abstract Based on the results of three research experiences in rural contexts, this paper proposes an integrated and multidisciplinary approach to the themes of the peri-urban landscape project, the enhancement of architectural heritage and the economic and social value of agriculture in land management. Starting from the potential and criticalities identifiable in peri-urban and rural contexts and recognized by the scientific literature, the selected experiences define a theoretical and operational framework based on a technological project approach aimed at integrating the ecological-environmental, landscape-fruitive, economic-productive and socio-inclusive values with the objective of enhancing the rural heritage.

Keywords Rural heritage · Peri-urban territories · Landscape enhancement · Fruition · Environmental design

1 Potentialities and Criticalities of Peri-Urban and Rural Territories

In order to fully understand the meaning of sustainable development, it is necessary to frame the issue within a broader and more articulated context. Indeed, it is not sufficient to refer to the scale of green building, but we must widen our focus to the scale of the green city and moreover to that of the green economy, in line with the objectives of the 2030 UN Agenda for sustainable development, the *Strategia Nazionale per lo Sviluppo Sostenibile* and the proposals of the Sustainable Development Foundation and of the Green City Network.

The economic model of the green economy is based on the protection of natural capital, the improvement of the ecological quality of the urban systems, the increase of cultural capital, the enhancement of technological capital and the safeguard of social capital (work group policy of the architecture for the green economy in the

E. Mussinelli (✉) · R. Riva · R. Bolici · A. Tartaglia · D. Cerati · G. Castaldo
Architecture, Built Environment and Construction Engineering—ABC Department, Politecnico di Milano, Milan, Italy
e-mail: elena.mussinelli@polimi.it

S. Della Torre et al. (eds.), *Regeneration of the Built Environment from a Circular Economy Perspective*, Research for Development,
https://doi.org/10.1007/978-3-030-33256-3_8

cities 2017). A marked tendency towards an "ecological conversion" derives from this, where a key role is assumed by the management of non-urban anthropized landscapes, mainly consisting of rural and peri-urban territories, which constitute the natural capital to insert an effective green infrastructure of the territory, while at the same time offering the cities a mix of ecosystem and social-cultural services.

Since these transition areas between anthropized and natural spaces are currently under strong transformative pressure, in the metropolitan sprawl, the characteristics of the urban and of the rural have basically merged, making up a diffused and polycentric landscape which led to the formulation of the concepts of "urban-rural agricultural eco-system" (Council for Agricultural Science and Technology 2002) and "urban bioregion" (Magnaghi and Fanfani 2010). These areas are a strategic resource for the regeneration of the built environment, due to the fact they can play a primary role for the creation of regional and super-local ecological networks. However, a number of specific critical issues remain to which the project must respond: in these territories, relevant effects of ecological and environmental degradation are particularly relevant, due to soil consumption from urban expansion as well as the construction of new infrastructures, while also deriving from a crisis in the agriculture sector, characterized by small-sized companies not being able to face the general reduction in EU subsidies and the competition of the global market. Thus, the peri-urban rural areas are fragile contexts, where the value of agricultural productivity is always less than the income derivable from urbanization. The real risk is that of further erosion processes, with a drastic reduction in environmental, ecological and productive values, in addition to the degradation of the landscape and of cultural heritage and to the consequent crumbling of the social structures typical of rural communities.

European policies have recognized the structural role of these contexts, promoting a development of a "suburban agriculture" characterized by multi-sectorial design and by the integration of economic-productive values, environmental and landscape peculiarities and social-cultural identities (Mussinelli and Cerati 2017).

These issues traditionally belong to the culture of environmental design, and they characterize the activities of the research group "Governance, design and enhancement of the built environment" of the ABC Department-*Politecnico di Milano*, previously coordinated by Fabrizio Schiaffonati and today by Elena Mussinelli. Relevant and remarkable experimentations regarded, for instance, the integrated planning of the *Parco Naturale della Valle del Ticino piemontese*, with actions for the management of its environmental and landscape resources and for the territorial development of the pre-park areas, as well as experiences of territorial marketing plans in the Mantua Moraine area in the Oltrepò area, from which also derived initiatives for the establishment of cultural districts and for the promotion of territories through ecomuseums.[1] More recently the research group carried out a more in-depth study of the issue of enhancing rural heritage, specifically in the contexts of the Oglio Po area, of the peri-urban area of Mantua and of the metropolitan area of Milan.

[1] For further information, see Schiaffonati et al. 2015.

2 The Project for the Landscape Fruition of the Oglio Po

Significant on a territorial scale is the experience developed with the LAG *Terre d'Acqua Oglio Po* within the framework of the inter-territorial and transnational cooperation project LANDsARE "Landscape Architectures in European Rural Areas: a new approach to local development design",[2] for the identification and promotion of innovative modalities for the fruition of rural heritage and for adding both economic value, as a lever of attractiveness for tourist flows, and social value, by reconnecting elements of the territory's identity.

The territory of Oglio Po is a context with a prevalent agricultural vocation, located between the provinces of Cremona and Mantua, characterized by the presence of noteworthy environmental, landscape and historical-cultural peculiarities, as well as by a diffused fabric consisting of rural buildings only partially still working and productive. The SWOT analysis conducted for the characterization of this context outlined, on the one hand, the excellence of the heritage and, on the other hand, the need to define a strategy of integrating the enhancement of this heritage, not adequately used and in some cases entirely neglected, as a basic condition for the economic development and for the tourism-focused promotion of the area.

The first phase of the project is focused on landscape heritage through the establishment of a database for the classification of historical and architectural heritage with its relationships with the system of environmental resources, a catalogue of the collected information, a selection of character-defining elements on which to develop emblematic actions of rural heritage enhancement, a survey of the conditions of degradation of the selected heritage and thus the identification of intervention priorities. The second phase, presenting an experimental nature, consisted in the organization of the design workshop "Land-LAB" and of the "Call for ideas for the restoration and enhancement of rural heritage of the LAG Oglio Po territory", aimed at collecting design proposals for the implementation of tourist fruition ideas for the area. Eventually, the third phase launched actions of dissemination and the presentation of the achieved results, through traditional channels (exhibition, catalogue, public presentation) as well as innovative solutions (digital devices and the cohesion platform).

[2]"Realization of a survey for the knowledge of the landscape heritage of the area of the Oglio Po and its conditions of degradation" (2013), LANDsARE Project–Measure 421 "Inter-territorial and transnational cooperation" of the PSR 2007–2013 of the Lombardy Region—FEASR. Project of transnational cooperation "LANDsARE", research contract between Territorial Pole of Mantua of the *Politecnico di Milano* and LAG *Terre d'Acqua Oglio Po*, scientific responsible R. Bolici, operative coordinators G. Leali and S. Mirandola, work group E. Mussinelli, F. Schiaffonati, A. Poltronieri, D. Fanzini, M. Gambaro, A. Tartaglia, R. Riva, G. Castaldo, C. Giordano, L. Mora, R. Scalari. The outcomes are published in: Bolici 2015; Mussinelli et al. 2015; Fanzini et al. 2019.

3 The Enhancement Project of the *Corti Bonoris* in Mantua

In the context of the UNESCO city of Mantua and with reference to the peri-urban scale, the project of rural heritage enhancement for the *Corti Bonoris* in the Mincio Natural Park is emblematic.[3] This is an agricultural area of 600 ha, located between Mantua and Porto Mantovano, owned by the *Fondazione Conte Gaetano Bonoris*, a non-profit institution operating in favour of minors suffering from disabilities. The area is of extraordinary environmental, landscape and production interest, between the Bosco Fontana State Natural Park and the northern shore of the Superior Lake of the city of Mantua, one of its kinds in terms of dimension, undivided property and strategic location. It includes ten rural courts dating back in some cases to the mid-eighteenth century, partly in a state of abandonment or underuse.

In this case, the project faced, on the one hand, the high level of protection due to the exceptional environmental and landscape heritage and, on the other hand, the need to enhance its rural heritage, both in terms of increasing rent, with technological adaptation interventions for the management of agricultural funds and livestock, and through opening up to tourism and the non-profit sector, within which the Foundation operates. An enhancement cannot be postponed, due to the consequent condition of abandonment and the loss of a huge cultural and landscape heritage, the maintenance costs of which become sustainable only if they are framed within a more comprehensive intervention of modernization, innovation and qualification of agricultural production, including new functions capable of producing income at the same time. The project involved the activation of a process of participation with the engagement of different public and private actors, stakeholders and institutions of the third sector—first of all the Foundation and its tenants, the *Parco del Mincio*, the *Sovrintendenza*, the *Caritas Ambrosiana*, the *Provincia di Mantova* and citizens—also through the organization of a series of design workshops. The outcome of this process has led to the definition of a general master plan, of guidelines for thematic sub-areas and to the development of pilot projects.

The investigation conducted through site surveys, analysis of plans and program documents, meeting with stakeholders and questionnaires, allowed researchers to identify the polarities of the territory, outlining the relationships between themselves, the criticalities, the potential, the constraints and the tendencies of the local system development. Starting from this fact-finding basis, the project aimed at strengthening the connections between the city, rural areas and protected areas, through the provision of a system of ecological corridors, a network of slow mobility paths, equipped areas as well as providing courts with new agricultural, social, tourist, educational

---

[3]"Studies for the rehabilitation and the use, environmental and landscape enhancement of the heritage of the *Fondazione Bonoris*, in territorial context of the Mincio Natural Park" (2012–14), research contract between Department of Built Environment Science and Technologies BEST *Politecnico di Milano* and the *Fondazione Conte Gaetano Bonoris*, scientific coordinator E. Mussinelli, coordinator R. Riva, work group C. Agosti, R. Bolici, D. Fanzini, A. Poltronieri, collaborators A. Bezzecchi, A. Chirico, C. Giordano, R. Scalari, advisors B. Agosti (*Parco del Mincio*), M. Castelli (*Provincia di Mantova*), A. G. Mazzeri (*Sovrintendenza*). The outcomes are published in: Mussinelli 2014a, b; Agosti and Riva 2014; Schiaffonati et al. 2015; Mussinelli et al. 2015.

and cultural functions. A mapping of the interventions of functional updating of the courts has been conducted, with the identification of disused buildings for the proposal of regeneration projects, realizable also in different steps in accordance with the financing opportunities and the interest of investors, fostering a true flexibility for these transformations. The synthetic framework of these interventions depicts the master plan of the project. The second step of analysis concerned the development of guidelines for landscape redevelopment, accessibility and usability, the diversification of the tourism offer and energy requalification. Finally, the third level has developed two pilot projects for the enhancement of the *Corte San Giovanni Bono*, now fallen into disuse, under the "Gate of Mantua" project, with the realization of an agri-camping and tourist accommodation services. Furthermore, the enhancement of the area made up of *Corte Canfurlone* and *Corte Ca' Bianca*, under the "Gate of the environmental system" project, with accommodation and restaurant activities integrated with collective services, such as an agri-nursery school, museum spaces and a centre for environmental education managed by *Bosco Fontana* and *Parco del Mincio*, as well as a bike-sharing station with a cycle workshop under the Roundabike association management.

For the *Fondazione Bonoris* and the *Parco del Mincio*, the project constitutes a replicable model of intervention in other rural contexts within the Park, thus proposing itself as a good project practice for the peri-urban landscape, triggering economic regeneration processes and promoting greater social cohesion.

4 The Project of Strategic Development of the Peri-urban Rural Heritage of the *Ospedale Maggiore* in Milan

The strategic plan FILARETEAM (For Innovation of Landscape and Agriculture: Renewable Energy, Territorial Economy and Amelioration Management) was developed in the Milan metropolitan peri-urban context, in collaboration with the *Fondazione IRCCS Ca' Granda* and the *Fondazione Sviluppo Ca' Granda*, respectively, as owner and as manager of the rural assets of the *Ospedale Maggiore* in Milan.[4] The overall rural heritage consists of about 200 agricultural farmsteads (8500 ha) concentrated for the 60% in the metropolitan area of Milan. As for the *Corti Bonoris*, in this case, we are also facing a vast rural heritage, of great historical and cultural importance and with undivided property. Cross-checking the internal policies of the *Fondazione Sviluppo Ca' Granda* and those of municipal and metropolitan programming, the strategic plan has identified four macro-areas of action, on which to conduct

[4]The strategic plan FILARETEAM is the first result of the "Framework agreement for the research and the education between *Politecnico di Milano* and *Fondazione Sviluppo Ca' Granda*" (2015–21), with the financing of one Scholarship for the 31st Doctoral "Environmental design and resilient approaches for the redevelopment of landscape heritage in metropolitan peri-urban and rural areas", supervisors E. Mussinelli, A. Tartaglia, Ph.D. student D. Cerati. The outcomes are published in: Malcevschi et al. 2017; Mussinelli and Cerati 2017; Tartaglia and Cerati 2018; Fanzini et al. 2019.

specific in-depth studies, pre-feasibility studies and actions aimed at acquiring financing. The macro-areas are: the creation of new agro-productive models; the activation of a food quality brand through sustainable processes involving short supply chains; the enhancement of heritage for tourism and cultural use; the experimentation of housing and social work models in the agricultural area.

The first phase of experimentation concerned the rural heritage of the Abbiatense area, south of the metropolitan area, which represents a strategic context, representative of the strong historical-cultural link with the city of Milan. The analysis of the territory, of the infrastructural connections, of the existing and planned productive and commercial activities, of the historical agricultural system and of the environmental aspects, has provided the knowledge base on which to structure a smart specialization strategy called "Agro-Active Landscape". The strategy identifies two lines of action and then declined into pilot projects. The first line of action, "Agriculture-woods-energy" (AWE), is aimed at implementing the arboreal heritage along the Bereguardo Canal and near the Ticino River, in order to produce environmental results both in terms of CO_2 capture to compensate for greenhouse gas emission from the urban heritage of the Foundation and in terms of absorption of nitrates present in the agricultural subsoil, in view of an eco-environmental balance between the city and the suburban rural area. The second line of action, "Channels-connections-production" (CCP), focuses on the redevelopment of the Bereguardo Canal, of the connected basins and of the hydraulic artefacts, with the aim of allowing its navigability in a productive, tourist-oriented key, also representing itself as a hydraulic mitigation intervention during extraordinary events. Both lines of action provide for an active involvement of farmers and stakeholders, called on to implement good practices for the production of quality goods and the provision of an ecosystem and multifunctional services for the territory.

5 A Methodology for the Enhancement of Rural Heritage

The experiences described show how an increase in multi-functionality and an enhancement of ecosystem services and the benefits of rural heritage represent possible levers for actions to regenerate a built environment, verified in their feasibility and sustainability even with respect to the increase in the resilience of urban areas and subways. *"The concept of multi-functionality, which is inherent to resilience, well interprets the need to improve a territory's environmental effectiveness, meanwhile increasing the level of awareness of the local social system. The putting into effect of resilience strategies is, in this sense, a particularly functional tool for the redevelopment of suburban rural territories in which the critical points grow in the environmental, cultural, social and economic aspects"* (Mussinelli and Cerati 2017:252).

The presented cases allow us to derive a replicable methodology that sees as the first fundamental step, the systemization, formalization and management of knowledge and information on the territorial context, aimed at highlighting critical issues and the potential of the considered areas. Starting from this formalization, it is therefore possible to activate cooperation and active participation processes involving local institutions, stakeholders, economic operators and local communities, to gather ideas, needs and willingness to participate in the implementation of the interventions. This type of process is not immediate, especially in contexts that express a lack of dialogue and the search for a balance between different interests, but it can find supports through the dissemination of best practices and the direct comparison with "virtuous" local systems (Riva 2017). Therefore, the results of the participation process can be translated into a strategic plan for the enhancement of the rural heritage that expresses an integrated and organic vision in the broad territorial context, structured through the sharing of lines of action and pilot projects, selected on the basis of the significance of the interventions, on their replicability and on the financing opportunities that can be activated. The more the projects will be able to balance and integrate the ecological-environmental, landscape-fruitive, economic-productive and socio-inclusive values, the higher will be the possibility of triggering long-lasting processes of enhancement of rural heritage, with positive effects for the urban environment as well.

References

Agosti, C., & Riva, R. (2014). Rehabilitation and enhancement among culture, nature and landscape. Master plan and guidelines for Bonoris Courts heritage in Mantua. In R. Amoêda, S. Lira & C. Pinheiro (Eds.), REHAB 2014. In *Proceedings of the international conference on Preservation, maintenance and rehabilitation of historical buildings and structures* (pp. 9–18). Barcelos: Green Line Institute for Sustainable Development.

Bolici, R. (Ed.). (2015). *Il progetto tecnologico per la valorizzazione del patrimonio rurale*. Maggioli, Santarcangelo di Romagna: Nuove prospettive per il paesaggio dell'Oglio Po.

Council for Agricultural Science and Technology. (2002). *Urban and agricultural communities: Opportunities for common ground*. Ames, Iowa: Task Force Report 138.

Fanzini, D., Tartaglia, A., & Riva, R. (2019). *Project challenges: sustainable development and urban resilience*. Maggioli: Santarcangelo di Romagna (in press).

Gruppo di lavoro "Policy dell'Architettura per la Green Economy nelle Città" (2017). *Verso l'attuazione del Manifesto della Green Economy per l'architettura e l'urbanistica. Obiettivi, ambiti di indirizzo, strategie prioritarie*. Consiglio Nazionale della Green Economy.

Magnaghi, A., & Fanfani, D. (2010). *Patto città campagna: un progetto di bioregione urbana per la Toscana centrale*. Firenze: Alinea.

Malcevschi, S., Mussinelli, E., Tartaglia, A., & Andreucci, B. (2017). Safeguard of the environment and the agricultural soil, enhancement of the water capital and green infrastructures. In E. Antonini & F. Tucci (Eds.), *Architecture, cities and territory towards a Green Economy*. Milano: Edizioni Ambiente.

Mussinelli, E., & Cerati, D. (2017). The potential of rural suburban systems for metropolitan resilience. Research and experimentation in Milan's context. In V. D'Ambrosio & M. F. Leone (Eds.), *Environmental Design for Climate Change adaptation* (pp. 250–263). Napoli: CLEAN.

Mussinelli, E. (2014a). Improvement of heritage and landscape in periurban and rural areas. In *Proceedings of the 1st international conference Preservation and improvement of historic town* (pp. 257–275). Beograd: Jp Službeni glasnik.

Mussinelli, E. (Ed.). (2014b). *La valorizzazione del patrimonio ambientale e paesaggistico*. Maggioli, Santarcangelo di Romagna: Progetto per le Corti Bonoris nel Parco del Mincio.

Mussinelli, E., Tartaglia, A., Riva, R., & Agosti, C. (2015). Design and strategies for rural heritage enhancement. In P. Iglesias & L. Manuel (Eds.), Reuso 2015. *III Congreso internacional sobre documentación, conservación y reutilización del patrimonio arquitectónico y paisajistico* (pp. 1812–1819). València: Editorial Universitat Politècnica de València.

Riva, R. (Ed.). (2017). *Ecomuseums and cultural landscapes*. Maggioli, Santarcangelo di Romagna: State of the art and future prospects.

Schiaffonati, F., Mussinelli, E., Majocchi, A., Tartaglia, A., Riva, R., & Gambaro, M. (2015). *Tecnologia Architettura Territorio*. Maggioli, Santarcangelo di Romagna: Studi ricerche progetti.

Tartaglia, A., & Cerati, D. (2018). *Design and enhancement of the metropolitan rural territories*. Maggioli, Santarcangelo di Romagna: Proposals for the South-Abbiatense.

Real Estate Assets for Social Impact: The Case of the Public Company for Social Services "ASP City of Bologna"

Angela S. Pavesi, Andrea Ciaramella, Marzia Morena and Genny Cia

Abstract In 2016, the Public Company for Social Services of the Municipality of Bologna "ASP City of Bologna" requires the ABC Department to analyze its huge real estate portfolio with the aim to identify efficiency strategies to free up resources to be reinvested in the offer of personal social services. Corporate governance sets up its strategy by coherently matching: the statutory values, the corporate mission and the growing need to respond to the needs expressed by the community in terms of providing personal services. The collaboration found strong foundations of understanding in the intention to pursue the mission of general social interest with environmental and economic sustainability, in a research path that made explicit the values of transparency and accountability of the Company. On the one hand, the research outlined the levers for making management, resources and processes more efficient, and on the other, strategies for enhancing assets in a social and circular economy perspective (see Bilancio Sociale ASP 2017).

Keywords Evaluation and enhancement of real estate assets · Management optimization of public company · Real estate infrastructure for personal services · Models for the management of real estate assets · Social economy and circular economy

[1]According to the ASP Statute, the Shareholders' Meeting monitors and controls the ASP's activity and performs various functions including: "*[...] defines the general guidelines of the ASP; approves the transformation of the assets from unavailable to available, as well as the disposals of available assets [...].*"

A. S. Pavesi (✉) · A. Ciaramella · M. Morena · G. Cia
Architecture, Built Environment and Construction Engineering—ABC Department, Politecnico di Milano, Milan, Italy
e-mail: angela.pavesi@polimi.it

S. Della Torre et al. (eds.), *Regeneration of the Built Environment from a Circular Economy Perspective*, Research for Development,
https://doi.org/10.1007/978-3-030-33256-3_9

1 Introduction

In October 2016, the Public Company for Social Services of the Municipality of Bologna—ASP Città di Bologna (hereinafter "ASP")—brings to the Shareholders Meeting[1] the proposal of a research path aimed to evaluate, analyze its own available assets and its management model in order to identify strategies/opportunities to make the assets profitability more efficient and to free up resources to increase the supply of services to citizens. The proposal of a research project with these aims immediately outlines the highly strategic view of ASP governance[2] that challenges its model to best adhere to its statutory mission. Subsequently, ASP identifies in ABC Department of Politecnico di Milano the qualified partner with which to start the path[3], and, right from the start, the collaboration finds very strong bases of understanding precisely in that proactive intentionality with which, not only governance, but all the manpower involved in the various functions, pursuing the aim of sustainable innovation, in a virtuous combination that distinguishes the Company for transparency and accountability.

Starting from these assumptions and in pursuing the research aims, the ABC Department started a path of support for the Company lasting over a year, adapting results to progressive requests, up to the elaboration of a final research report which clearly outlines:

- levers for improving the management model and optimizing the Company's[4] resources and processes;
- value of available real estate portfolios;
- enhancement strategies for strategic porfolio;
- strategies for management and energy efficiency;
- strategies for innovation of welfare models (services provided).

Furthermore, some experiments have been started on specific assets of the Company.

[2]Gianluca Borghi, formerly Sole Director and Elisabetta Scoccati, formerly General Manager of ASP.

[3]December 2016: entrusted to the ABC Department of the research project for the enhancement of the real estate assets of ASP Città di Bologna through the study of an adequate management model with respect to the aims of the Entity. "Scientific coordinator: professor A. S. Pavesi. Research group: professor A. Ciaramella and M. Morena and ingg. G. Cia and M. Gechelin."

[4]by Asset Management and Corporate Real Estate Companies benchmarks.

2 The ASP Città di Bologna Mission and Its Real Estate Portfolio as a Social Infrastructure for a Resilient City

ASP Città di Bologna is the Public Company for Social Services of Bologna set up by resolution of the Council of the Emilia-Romagna Region no. 2078 of 12/23/2013 following the merger of the Public Company of Poveri Vergognosi, the Public Company of Servizi alla Persona Giovanni XXIII, and the Public Company of IriDes.

ASP is a non-economic public entity governed by regional law, with legal status governed by public law, statutory, managerial, patrimonial, accounting and financial autonomy, within the framework of rules and principles established by regional law and regional indications. It is a non-profit organization. The ASP partners are the Municipality of Bologna (97%), the Metropolitan City of Bologna (2%), and Fondazione Carisbo (1%).

Art. 4 of the Statute shows the mission of the Company: "*ASP has as its purpose management and provision of social, social-health services to elderly, adult and minor persons who are in conditions of difficulty, hardship, disability or non self-sufficiency, according to the different needs defined by local programming*".

To pursue its statutory mission, ASP owns heterogeneous real estate portfolio, deriving from bequests and inheritances and is distinguished in available or unavailable assets depending on whether it is alienable or not. This subdivision comes from the, i.e., art. 5 paragraph 1 of the Regional Law 12/2013 and provides:

- buildings used to pursue statutory and welfare purposes, i.e. unavailable assets;
- assets which, in consideration of their valuable characteristics, or because they are susceptible to entrepreneurial use, are destined to income and to support the provision of services of social initiatives, i.e., assets available for income;
- buildings used for: housing needs, social activities, activities carried out by non-profit entities, i.e., assets available for housing needs;
- agricultural assets destined to favor youth entrepreneurship or made available to non-profit entities that perform social recovery and assistance purposes for weak subjects, i.e., social agricultural assets;
- and historical and artistic heritage.

The assets characteristics have been made explicit in a quantitative and qualitative desktop analysis carried out by the research group alongside ASP, which was subsequently optimized in properties evaluation phase.

From a quantitative point of view and according to the survey concluded in October 2017 (see Table 1), the ASP real estate portfolios consist of 1462[5] real estate units—located mainly in the city of Bologna, about 2000 ha of agricultural land and about 130 farm buildings—located in the province of Bologna.[6]

---

[5]Dynamic data.

[6]The research group developed a survey of the rural portfolio, identifying its main characteristics. These cards represent the first step in defining ad hoc valorization strategies. The theme of rural portfoliola des can be the subject of in-depth analysis of a phase 2 of the research that consists in the census and analysis of best practices in the field of valorization of rural buildings, in the

Table 1 Recognition of ASP real estate portfolio in October 2017 (*source* Research report)

Category	N. property January 2017	N. property October 2017
Houses	665	665
Offices	67	67
Care facility	**22**	**23**
Public offices	2	2
School and laboratories	**2**	**3**
Libraries, museums, and galleries	1	1
Shops	50	50
Stores	94	94
Laboratories	11	11
Sports facilities	2	2
Garages	**256**	**334**
Closed and opened roofs	4	4
Factory	14	14
Hotels	2	2
Theater, cinema	1	1
Agricultural buildings	136	132
Religious buildings	2	2
Other	55	55
Total	1386	1462

As mentioned, a part of the work carried out by the ABC Department consisted in rationalization of real estate database of ASP, by a desktop work on the spreadsheet that represented the IT management system used.

In the spreadsheet, each row corresponded a real estate unit identified through land register reference and in which were reported data of different nature: cadastral, administrative, economic, financial, and technical.

This work was a preliminary step to the subsequent phases of the project, highlighting areas of potential improvement, including:

- identify the most suitable management system to make data management more efficient, based on need to enhance real estate assets;

identification and analysis of the main tools and in the definition of the strategy more suitable for ASP.

- define Quality plans for database management (definition of data entry, updating processes, etc.);
- carry out technical and administrative due diligence for buildings not yet surveyed or for which a valorization strategy has been defined;
- establish plans and programs for building and plant maintenance (Maintenance and Energy Management);
- consolidate technical and operational skills, and managerial ones.

The active management of real estate assets is crucial if we manage to adequately monitor information and time. It is only through knowledge that it is possible to define lines of action, plan interventions, deliberate, and take decisions. The preliminary analysis of assets, aimed at understanding the characteristics of the properties, lays the foundations for strategic management phase (Ciaramella 2016).

3 Survey and Scenario: Clustering and Evaluation of Real Estate Assets

The choice of the most appropriate valorization strategies cannot be separated from the mission of Institution, the role that single asset plays in the core business and real estate value both as balance sheet value and market value. Asset management should focus on two levels of performance: the increase in revenues and the increase in profitability (Burns 2002), in which the quantification of both a reduction in expenses, but also, a more efficient use of resources available, in order to maximize business purposes. According to Huffman (2003), the management strategies of real estate derive from the set of corporate strategies.

Based on these statements and thanks to the highly strategic view of ASP governance, an assessment of the most probable market value of the Company's available assets was necessary.

The Client, with the support of the research group, made a selection of the assets available which did not play a key role in the provision of services and in pursuit of the corporate mission but could have an attractiveness toward the market and allow new resources to be introduced in order to improve the offer of services.

As better outlined in the social balance (2017), ASP conceives the management of assets "*according to criteria of efficiency, transparency and fairness, has the objective of enhancing the available assets, both real estate and agricultural, to generate resources to be allocated to citizen welfare. The action of optimization and effectiveness is expressed through recovery of arrears, maximization of profits also resulting from actions of organizational rationalization and transparency in the leasing process*". The asset management perspective is therefore not attributable to pure economic efficiency, but to sustain, through the profitability of the assets, the costs of the citizen welfare system.

Following the patrimony survey, the Client and the ABC group selected the real estate units by linking them to homogeneous clusters by use, location, and in-depth assessment levels, on the basis of which the public tender was drawn up and the technical specifications for the selection of the most suitable market subject to perform this activity.[7] Scenari Immobiliari[8] won the tender.

The complexity of real estate portfolio and information necessary to perform the evaluation activity required periodic meetings among the parties. The first phases of research—relating to the analysis of the real estate database—highlighted the difficulty in tracing and identifying the source of the data, its accuracy and its level of updating, therefore the correctness of the data stored in relation to the condition of the asset during this analysis phase.

An in-depth knowledge of real estate portfolio is essential for the correct attribution of market value.

4 Strategies for Optimizing Asset Profitability: From Administrative Management to a New Efficient Management Model

The problem faced in the management of real estate portfolios such as ASP is a problem of choice: every good manager must make decisions orienting them to managerial choices to maximize added value (Ciaramella 2016).

Considering the characteristics of real estate assets of ASP, the optimization of profitability derives from two main areas: administrative and operations management (Property and Facility management) and the management model adopted. The first one requires a system of diversified skills that condition the second one. The management of rents, monitoring and containment of costs are typically property manager's activities and requires technical-administrative and commercial skills. The planning of maintenance requires technical, project and facility management skills. The adopted management model is strongly influenced by the professionalism and skills in company workforce and is attributable in part to the so-called Social Management typical of social housing interventions (Pavesi et al. 2017).

In the case of ASP' portfolio, a part of management activities is oriented to safeguarding the profitability of the assets, another part, to managing the main maintenance activities in addition to managing and providing welfare services.

Administrative activity includes management of rents and costs, with the aim to maximize net operating income and to manage new rentals for vacant spaces, with the aim to reduce vacancy rate.

[7]The writing of call for tender was carried out by Contracts-Service Contracts, services and supplies under the advice of A. S. Pavesi. In this phase, the ABC group carried out the project management activity.

[8]Scenari Immobiliari | Independent Institute of Studies and Research. www.scenari-immobiliari.it.

During the analysis, the analysis of the gross yield,[9] of the potential yield[10] as well as the analysis of the vacancy rate was evident, representing the margins of improvement in the management of the assets.

The study of vacancy has made it possible to compare available data with the results of studies on the trend of rental market in the city and for different functional types, verifying the positioning of one's portfolio with respect to market benchmark.

This comparison made it possible to set a management strategy in line with the market needs and influencing the investment choices.

In fact, the management of operations is always attributable to the whole series of maintenance activities (ordinary and extraordinary maintenance), which has the aim to maintain or improve the conservation status of buildings and consequently to maintain over time the value of the assets.

With a view to optimizing the profitability of assets and resources used, it was appropriate to reflect on the ways in which administrative management and operations (property and facility management) were carried out by ASP. The objective was to identify which management model (internal, outsourcing or mixed) could be more suitable for the Company, both in relation to the state of the art and in a perspective view of efficiency.

The analysis showed that the management model adopted was attributable to the "internal management model." The internal staff of ASP was completely dedicated to asset management (regulatory compliance, cost and expense planning, management and supervision of external suppliers, management and coordination of services provided with internal staff) and, to a small extent, operational activities (technical maintenance).

With respect to this topic, the research group analyzed and evaluated alternative management models: outsourcing management model and hybrid management model with the outsourcing of operating activities only. The first model prefigures the outsourcing of all services to a single supplier (so-called Integrated Services). This model favors economies of scale and a reduction in costs, but in the same time, determines the loss of control over the process, on quality management in the provision of services, in particular of maintenance ones.

The second model provides for the outsourcing of operational services to different suppliers and the presence of an internal function in the Company dedicated to the management of contracts, with the task of coordinating, administering, and supervising the supplies. On the one hand, this model provides for an increase in organizational flexibility and a greater ability to control service costs, and on the other, it requires considerable coordination by the staff involved in the management.

The widespread orientation to outsourcing by different groups and organizations for the management of real estate assets is essentially connected to the possibility of transforming fixed costs (employees) into variable costs (external contracts). This choice, which in many ways can be shared in its general principles, cannot, however,

[9]Gross Yield is calculated as the ratio among current fee, sum of MV and capex.

[10]Potential Yield is the return that could be obtained if all the vacant spaces were leased to market rents.

disregard the vision of the owner or manager. Very often the choices of outsourcing brought unsatisfactory results; in several cases, it may be appropriate to aim at the enhancement of properties and, at the same time, of people involved in.

Based on features, real estate portfolio and ASP organization model, the "internal management model with outsourcing of operating activities" was evaluated as viable because it is capable to obtain the enhancement of the real estate assets, a better use of resources involved. The recommendation is, whatever the choice, the supervision of the information, and the governance and the control of activities were maintained by ASP.

5 Strategies for Optimizing the ASP Management Model from a Circular and Social Economy Perspective

The constant question that has always guided investigations and research work has been: "What does ASP need?" The collaboration between the research group and ASP has found strong bases of understanding in the intention to pursue the mission of general interest of the Company through criteria of environmental, social, and economic sustainability. The results of the research have, on the one hand, outlined the levers for making management, resources, and processes more efficient, and on the other hand, identified enhancement strategies for assets in a social and circular economy perspective, as expressed in the ASP Social Balance (2017).

The research results outline the following strategic levers for ASP:

- introduction of specialized figures in the field of Property and Asset Management and Real Estate Analyst (for business plans, feasibility studies, coordination of advisor figures, evaluation of new investments, etc.).
- Optimization of the Facility system through the investment in the field of information services for dynamic asset management, maintenance optimization, etc.
- Creation of an ASP brand through the implementation of a "smart" platform aimed at citizens, to give voice to ideas, needs, new trends and specialize services.
- Optimization of condominium management also through experimentation according to new models of urban welfare (Social management).
- Strategic management of assets through greater diversification with respect to emerging needs or new trends.

The question whether the contribution of assets to an impact finance fund could be the most effective solution to achieve these objectives has remained in the background.

The characteristics of ASP real estate portfolio allow, such as:

- the targeted alienation of some assets more suited to the market to free resources to be reinvested in the development of innovative services spread throughout the territory (social mix);

– the targeted alienation of some assets that are more suited to the market to free up resources to be reinvested in scheduled asset maintenance.

Under these conditions, it seemed more challenging to apply the best management model from virtuous SGRs to the existing corporate structure.

In fact, ASP acts as a benefit corporation because it creates a sort of public benefit in the community in which it operates and has a concrete positive impact on people and the environment (an area that is certainly to be improved); in ASP, "the shareholders" (and the citizens themselves) can also evaluate qualitative and quantitative performances, based on declared objectives.

ASP was found to have all the features to accept the challenge of creating a model of a Public Company of excellence, able to activate forms of private–public partnership according to a welfare scheme that makes the most of its assets as a tool to create positive impacts in the areas of corporate governance, human resources, communities and the environment, through the services offered to the city of Bologna. It represents the public subject that addresses its services to the weaker groups and at the same time is able to specialize them toward more profitable areas in a dynamic cycle, thanks to the variety and size of the real estate stock it administers in respect of the legacy of those who have been able to donate to their own city.

The demonstrated ability to administer ASP with seriousness, competence, and sense of responsibility of the people who work there, together with the vision of governance, represents the virtuous case of Public Company, a best practice and a scalable model in the more general society responsible for the provision of welfare services.

References

ASP Città di Bologna. (2017). Bilancio Sociale. Available on http://www.aspbologna.it/bilancio-sociale/asp-citta-di-bologna/bilancio-sociale/bilancio-sociale-2017.

Burns, C. M. (2002). Analysing the contribution of corporate real estate to the strategic competitive advantage of organisations, working papers. Available at: www.occupier.org/papers/working_paper10.pd.

Ciaramella, A. (2016). *Corporate Real Estate. Strategie, modelli e strumenti per la gestione attiva del patrimonio immobiliare aziendale*. Milano: FrancoAngeli.

Huffman, F. E. (2003). Corporate real estate risk management and assessment. *Journal of Corporate Real Estate, 5*(1), 31–41.

Pavesi, A. S., Ferri, G., Zaccaria, R., Gechelin, M. (2017). Abitare Collaborativo: percorsi di coesione sociale per un nuovo welfare di comunità. *TECHNE Journal of Technology for Architecture and Environment, 14* (Architettura e innovazione sociale. Firenze).

Reuse and Regeneration of Urban Spaces From a Resilient Perspective

Sara Cattaneo, Camilla Lenzi and Alessandra Zanelli

Introduction

Reuse and regeneration are two different approaches in terms of scale of intervention—the first at the punctual scale of the single building or urban block, and the second at the larger and more complex urban scale—but both aimed at raising the capacity for adaptation and resistance of contemporary cities. This ability to adapt even to dramatic changes that can occur over the years—also defined in terms of resilience—is nowadays one of the key factors of the urban development policies and essentially involves three challenges: resource saving, increasing of the special quality of both confined spaces and open-air zones and, not least, social inclusion.

The resilient perspective, with which this section interprets both reuse and regeneration interventions, takes into consideration the intensive and intentional processes, on the one hand, and the extensive and spontaneous ones, on the other hand.

This section intends to address the following topics in particular:

(a) the reuse and redevelopment of buildings with the objective of developing and defining efficient systems that are structurally adequate, resilient, adaptable and flexible over time, easily re-convertible;

(b) the redevelopment of disused areas and suburbs, planning construction and demolition works, managing the disposal and/or reuse of demolition waste, favouring building replacement, limiting land consumption and activating virtuous and innovative processes of circularity between raw and second materials;

(c) the redevelopment of urban fabrics in the historic districts of cities, of villages and traditional rural landscapes, of peri-urban contexts to enhance their history, memories and identities and to promote their conservation with respect to the main risk factors (e.g. earthquakes) in a resilient key.

Participated Strategies for Small Towns Regeneration. The Case of Oliena (Nu) Historic Centre

Laura Daglio, Giuseppe Boi and Roberto Podda

Abstract Dealing with the issue of depopulation and abandonment of villages and small towns in Italy and Europe is amongst the goals of the economic and social policies aimed at investigating and experimenting new strategies for the regeneration and reactivation of urban space. An extensive literature collects researches aimed at analysing the problem, exploring diverse management and design approaches, alternative measures to stop the phenomenon and innovative legislative incentives and economic tools. This paper has the aim of reporting an ongoing research experience concerning participated solutions aimed at developing new possible models for the regeneration of Oliena's historic centre, in Sardinia.

Keywords Participatory design · Depopulation · Historic villages · Regeneration strategies

1 Background

Forestalling population decline and the abandonment of small towns in Italy and in Europe is the goal of economic and social policies aimed at investigating strategies for the re-qualification and reactivation of urban space. An extensive literature endorses researches intended at exploring management, typological and technological approaches (Castagneto and Fiore 2013), new possible programs (Di Figlia 2016) and innovative legislative and economic tools (Flora and Crucianelli 2013; Maietti 2008).

L. Daglio (✉)
Architecture, Built Environment and Construction Engineering—ABC Department, Politecnico di Milano, Milan, Italy
e-mail: laura.daglio@polimi.it

G. Boi
Milan, Italy

R. Podda
Department of Architecture, Xi'an Jiaotong – Liverpool University, Suzohu, China

S. Della Torre et al. (eds.), *Regeneration of the Built Environment from a Circular Economy Perspective*, Research for Development,
https://doi.org/10.1007/978-3-030-33256-3_10

The recent exhibition at the 16 Venice Biennial Italian Pavilion, 'Arcipelago Italia', curated by Mario Cucinella showcased the issue of the territories which are '*spatially and temporally distant from the large urban areas*',[1] especially characterised by a lack of services and infrastructures. Inner areas, fragile territories, abandoned landscapes, shrinking cities (Oswalt et al. 2006) the diverse definitions present in the literature and in the media highlight the urgent problem of these areas, which possess an inestimable cultural heritage both tangible and intangible but no economic wealth. Albeit not a novel question, it has been harshened by the consequences of the economic crisis as well as the rapid ageing of the population, increasing the differences and the unbalances between regions of the same country.

A rich literature focuses on this topic presenting an evolution in the approaches and in the models of possible actions, which can be classified and recognised according to some selected criteria such as initiative and permanence. Bottom-up rather than top-down projects are featured, involving participatory design as a potential approach, and strategic or tactical solutions are experimented, including the time variable in the proposal and realisation of activities, events, new constructions and renovations. However, all these projects have to deal with the task of reinterpreting the built environment and of defining the appropriate solutions to intervene on the existing heritage. In fact, together with the problem of geographical isolation, these ancient settlements suffer not only from a physical decay due to the lack of maintenance and the abandonment, but also from a functional obsolescence. Conceived to host the activities of societies and rural or industrial economies, that do not exist anymore, the built environment requires an upgrading and renovation to respond to the changed demands of the potential new inhabitants. Thus, a dialogue with the authorities and the rules regulating the modes and approaches of renovation of historic heritage are required, also considering that the introduction of new regulations and constraints to limit and define these interventions often caused the freezing of the heritage, limiting the transformation and introducing complex and long-lasting procedures.

In spite of these common features, these areas are extremely different from the point of view of the geographic, economic, social, cultural and historical background. In addition, a considerable number were also abandoned due to the occurrence of natural disasters, now raising the issue of the opportunity for the renovation, in terms of resources to be employed.

The ongoing debate and recent case studies disclose the increasing application of participatory processes to develop measures for the redevelopment projects, whilst solutions involving the top-down creation of a new building or activity, also requiring a significant investment, are almost disappearing.

The lively emergence of participatory design initiatives is aimed at determining the new demand (Sennet 2012), developing new strategies with co-design activities to create and share new meanings and goals and frequently employ tactical urbanism methodologies (Lydon and Garcia 2011) to anticipate possible scenarios, to raise awareness and a sense of belonging in the inhabitants.

---

[1]Cf. the exhibition and project site at http://www.arcipelagoitalia.it/en/home (accessed May 5th 2019).

This paper has the aim of reporting a recent research experience concerning shared solutions aimed at enquiring new possible models for the reactivation of Oliena's historic centre, in Barbagia. The research, still ongoing, is patronised by the Municipality and the GAL Barbagia; these institutions endorsed the activities and offered economical and operative support, believing in the participatory methodology as a means to trigger change in mentality and built environment.

2 Problems and Potentials of the Oliena Region

The characters of the depopulation phenomenon in Oliena are slightly different from the recurring elements to determine the abandonment. In fact, the small town (approximately 7000 inhabitants) is in the centre of Sardinia, thus far from the developed touristic coastal areas, in the mountain zone of Supramonte, with a lack of infrastructures for transportation—as mainly all the Mediterranean Island towns—but adjacent to the province capital of Nuoro. The majority of the population is in fact employed in the public sector or in the administration, in agriculture and in the breeding industry, and they are not affected by major economic issues either by massive migration processes to the coast or to other national or international destinations.

However, the historic centre of Oliena is characterised by an ongoing abandonment. Since the seventies and the eighties, inhabitants moved towards the outer expansion areas, where they built low-density single-family housing settlements that better responded to contemporary lifestyles. Accordingly, the transformation of the town centre into a periphery is a consequence of the inadequacy of the historic urban fabric and of the roads and of the functional obsolescence of the existing buildings. In addition, the zoning ordinance transformed the town centre into a conservation area (Zone A), without producing specific guidelines for renovation, thus freezing the old town and hindering the potential for transformation. Currently, this large heritage, which extends for more than 27 ha, is undergoing a significant physical decline, revealed by the increasing number of condemned buildings and ruins (Fig. 1).

The historical documentary value of the ancient centre relies in the morphological, typological and technological characteristics of the urban fabric, since the presence of artistic landmarks and monuments is limited.

The ancient settlement, in between the Monte Corrasi and the fertile valley of the Cedrino River, is organised in closed courtyards belonging to a large family, where all the main past social and productive activities took place. The so-called *Cortes* represent the legacy of a rural society based on family clans, currently disappeared, intrinsically tied to their region (Fig. 2). This relationship of belonging and identity is still very strong in the present population, as the belief that the ancient centre cannot be adapted to contemporary requirements of use without major significant intervention of replacement and reconstruction and is therefore doomed to an inescapable abandonment.

For this reason, the research team realised that any proposal to trigger the physical transformation of the centre solution should tackle with the transformation of

Fig. 1 The number of condemned building is progressively increasing (*source* photo by the Authors)

its perception by the people who inhabit it, according to the European Landscape Convention (European Council 2000), and therefore with their involvement and participation.

This was the origin of the research activity, dealing with the definition of possible scenarios of intervention, emerging from the local identity and the social and cultural peculiarities of the place.

Accordingly, the research path encompasses, on the one hand, an analytical phase dedicated to understanding the place, its problems and potentials, as well as a review of the scientific literature on the topic of regeneration models and strategies on a national and international scale. The goal of these steps is to define possible strategies, approaches and solutions for the renovation of the historic centre.

On the other hand, participatory initiatives were developed as a tool for deepening the investigation of the landscape, understanding the demands, sharing the results of the design solutions explored and encouraging an increasing awareness of the value of the abandoned places and of a spontaneous re-appropriation of the space.

Fig. 2 Aerial view showing the urban fabric characterised by the building grouped around semipublic courtyards (*Cortes*) (*source* Sardegna Geoportale)

The analysis of the Oliena region revealed potentials and problems: potentials related to the lush and fertile agricultural territory characterised by the high quality of its food products, wine and oil in particular; to the beauty of the natural mountain landscape with its limestone karst highlands, excavated by the underground waters to create caves and sinkholes; to the rich ancient and diverse culture still present in the handicraft and witnessed by the many archaeological sites, *menhirs* and Palaeolithic villages. However, the investigation also highlighted that the main issues hindering the exploitation of these aspects to trigger economic development rely on the lack of networks and of systemic strategies to put together and connect the different small fragmented activities into a bigger collective operator with increased investment capacity in resources, infrastructures and marketing. Simultaneously, a similar networking of the existing touristic resources (natural, historical and experiential) could call visitors from the seaside areas or activate new all-year-round modes of holidaying in the region. In addition, the ownership of the historic centre buildings is extremely fragmented and therefore requires the development of any initiative to be shared and agreed with the many owners.

Once again the analysis highlighted the need to raise awareness in the population to generate a new perception of their homeland in order to start change as well as the requisite of finding solutions to gather consensus on a wide basis.

These initial results pointed to the elaboration and enhancement of the specific approaches for the possible design proposals and to the organisation of diverse participated events, each to stimulate a different reaction in the local population.

3 Development of the Methodological Approach

The research defined two different intertwined paths for the development of the activities to stimulate the involvement of the local population: on the one hand, the exploration of the capacity of the existing urban texture to accommodate different new facilities emerging from the features of the social, economic and geographic context. This testing was applied on some typical selected plots of the historic centres with different locations and slightly different morphologies. Following the analytical phase, new possible functions were identified in relation to the potentials relying in the beauty of the landscape (tourism and sport facilities), in the excellence of the wine and food products (exhibitions and food processing), in the handicraft (exhibitions and enterprises) and in the proximity to the 'blue zone'[2] (homes for the elderly and health). The design entailed not only the urban and architectural renovation of the existing buildings but also the design of the process, the definition of the different possible stages of the transformation and reactivation, the involved stakeholders in each phase and the possible funding to assess the concrete feasibility of the proposal. Moreover, all the projects portray a multiscalar, multidimensional feature investigating the proposal as part of a larger network of diverse activities and places spread on the local territory as well as linked to wider structures through ICT technologies, in order to promote synergies and to create systems as unavoidable approach for the reactivation of the area. Finally, also the issue of defining the appropriate approach towards the refurbishment and renovation of the historic heritage was examined, experimenting architectural solutions that, whilst ensuring the recognition of the existing heritage, revisited and tested its adaptability to the changing needs of the contemporary living through a 'grafting' practice.

On the other hand, public events were organised with the twofold aim of presenting the results of the design exploration through exhibitions and of discussing the potentials, methods, feasibility and opportunity within workshops and seminars open to the citizens. The different initiatives were organised over the years to deepen the involvement and the exploration in conjunction with the annual '*Cortes Apertas*' fair in September, which for over 20 years has summoned a large public of visitors from all Sardinia and national and international tourists. Hence, the fair displaying the local products was an opportunity also to present the results of the research and to host the debate and raise the awareness in the inhabitants towards the models and the scenarios for the re-appropriation of the historic centre. Three workshops were organised and conceived with an increasing engagement of the citizens.

The first was intended as a round table[3] involving scholars from around Italy to discuss the issue of the regeneration of historic centres. Internationally renowned

---

[2]Barbagia and Ogliastra regions in Sardinia are included in the so-called Blue Zones: regions of the world where people live much longer than average because of the social geographical food and lifestyle features.

[3]The seminar was held in Oliena on 10 September 2016 and was attended by A. Sanna, C. Atzeni (University of Cagliari), E. D'Alfonso, L. Daglio, P. Mei, R. Podda (Politecnico di Milano), S. Garattini (M. Negri Institute), G. Onni, P. Pittaluga and F. Spanedda (Università di Sassari).

Fig. 3 The 2018 edition of the participatory workshop took place in one of the ancient courtyards (*source* photo by the Authors)

scholars and experts from different fields and disciplines were invited in the week-long workshops[4] organised in the two following consecutive years to present their work and projects with the aim of collecting case studies and experiences on similar contexts and to deepen the knowledge of the characters and potentials of the region.

During the last workshop,[5] a site-specific installation inside one of the ancient *Cortes* (courtyards) (Fig. 3) was designed and constructed as one of the fair's installations to highlight the physical and cultural heritage of the village (Fig. 4). Simultaneously, local producers and farmers and local associations related to sports (speleology, climbing and cycling), culture (tourist guide associations and local experts) and leisure were consulted during the workshops in order to understand their needs, criticalities and potentials. In particular, visits and activities were organised together with these stakeholders in order to share their experiences and directly comprehend their everyday life. Such immersive practices by the researchers team having a different culture and background also allowed for a different interpretation of the context, the emergence of a different perspective to see and analyse the local culture and landscape and to disclose original potentials.

[4]The 2017 edition was open to the Master Degree students in Architecture at Politecnico di Milano and Architecture and Building Engineering and Architecture and Ph.D. students of the University of Cagliari, Sassari, seat of Alghero, the Politecnico di Milano, the University of Alcalá de Henares, the University of Lisbon and the Tianjin University.

[5]In the last workshop, the School of Design and the School of Architecture Urban Planning Construction Engineering of Politecnico di Milano, together with the Tianjin University, were involved.

Fig. 4 The visits to the site-specific installation in 2018 (*source* photo by the Authors)

4 Conclusion

The success of the yearly workshops in terms of public participation to the meetings and to the initiatives testifies the achievement of the goal of raising awareness in the inhabitants. Ordinary people followed and participated in the seminars, attended to the lectures and discussed with the young teams of researchers that involved (master course, just graduated and Ph.D. students) the proposals and their specific needs, expectations and the geographical and economic constraints of the region.

The Municipality, and the counsellors albeit changed after the elections, promote and patronise the events organised by the research team, also participating in the debates during the workshops and seizing the opportunity to start a direct dialogue with the citizens.

Moreover, after the first two workshops, the owners of the historic centre's buildings did realise the potentials of networking and of starting bottom-up actions and gathered in a new association called Oliena Centro, with the aim of strengthening their initiatives and sharing problems and opportunities. This has also created the basis for a crowdfunding to start concrete actions.

Finally, the workshops became also a meeting place for the participants to trigger a dialogue amongst the too often separated operators, to know each other better and to foster new synergies and collaborations and to start working together for the common good.

The lessons learned from the case study of Oliena are important in terms of methodology enhancement. In particular, the participatory tools were differently declined to include: discussions/debates with the citizens aimed at analysing their demands and expectations as well as their perception of their home land and culture; the creation of a two-way dialogue and direct exchange between Municipality and citizens; disruptive cognitive reactions generated on the one hand by the supply of external expertise to the inhabitants and on the other hand by the provision of know-how and intangible heritage experiences to the research team. The latter appeared as the main trigger towards innovation and change, raising awareness and the commitment to the village centre regeneration in the locals and suggesting original paths to define possible feasible strategies.

References

Castagneto, F., & Fiore, V. (Eds.). (2013). *Recupero, valorizzazione, manutenzione nei centri storici: un tavolo di confronto interdisciplinare*. Siracusa: Lettera Ventidue.

Consiglio d'Europa. (2000). Convenzione Europea del Paesaggio. [Online] Available at: http://www.convenzioneeuropeapaesaggio.beniculturali.it/uploads/2010_10_12_11_22_02.pdf. Accessed May 10, 2019.

Di Figlia, L. (2016). Turnaround: Abandoned villages, from discarded elements of modern Italian society to possible resources. *International Planning Studies, 21*(3), 278–297.

Flora, N., & Crucianelli, E. (Eds.). (2013). *I borghi dell'uomo: strategie e progetti di ri-attivazione*. Siracusa: Lettera ventidue.

Lydon, M., & Garcia, A. (2011). *Tactical urbanism: Short-term action for long-term change*. Washington DC: Island Press.

Maietti, F. (Ed.). (2008). *Centri storici minori: progetti di recupero e restauro del tessuto urbano*. Maggioli: Santarcangelo di Romagna.

Oswalt, P., Beyer, E., Hagemann, A., & Rieniets, T. (2006). *Atlas of shrinking cities*. Ostfildern: Hatje Cantz Pub.

Sennet, R. (2012). *Together. The rituals, pleasures and politics of cooperation*. Yale: Yale University Press.

Living and Learning: A New Identity for Student Housing in City Suburbs

Oscar E. Bellini, Matteo Gambaro and Martino Mocchi

Abstract The role of student housing in academic formative paths is rapidly changing and increasing in importance. According to international trends, university residencies are shifting their function from mere dormitories for students to more open structures for urban territories and the local population and are starting to be considered as important opportunities for enhancing and revitalizing the peripheral and problematic contexts in which they often are located. The case of the Politecnico di Milano is emblematic, due to the large investments the university injected into this sector over recent years, leading to the opening of three new residencies in the suburbs of Milan. This chapter reports on the activities developed by the authors over the last few years, aiming at fostering a more direct relationship among academic knowledge, educational strategies, and urban contexts. This comes via the experimentation of new forms of didactic and research, which attach great importance for university residencies for their possibility to share services, facilities, knowledge among students and the local population. The research focuses on the consequences of this change not only in sociological terms, but also in architectural ones, considering the new implications for the morpho-techno-typological design of structures. The results aim at going beyond the rigid constraints of the current regulation, developing a more open approach to design, which could be a starting point for the advisable revision of the law 338/2000, which is now 20 years old.

Keywords Student housing · Urban regeneration · Social capital · Human capital · Multicultural processes

---

O. E. Bellini (✉) · M. Gambaro
Architecture, Built Environment and Construction Engineering—ABC Department, Politecnico di Milano, Milan, Italy
e-mail: oscar.bellini@polimi.it

M. Mocchi
Milan, Italy

S. Della Torre et al. (eds.), *Regeneration of the Built Environment from a Circular Economy Perspective*, Research for Development,
https://doi.org/10.1007/978-3-030-33256-3_11

1 New Perspectives for Student Housing[1]

The role of student housing in academic formative paths is rapidly changing and increasing in importance, with a view of the broadening of learning and educational processes, triggering new forms of socialization, developing sharing habits, fostering emancipation from families (Micheli 2008; Rosina et al. 2007; Agnoli 2010) increasing the sense of responsibility, promoting exchange and dialogue among students coming from different cultures and traditions, also from the standpoint of their involvement in public life (Livi Bacci 2008; Abidin et al. 2011; Costa 2014; Naji et al. 2014; Eikemo and Judith Thomsen 2018).

In encouraging a new way of living, based on the acceptance of rules, timetables and deadlines, student housing contributes to developing the moral and civic quality of individuals, enhancing their social disposition and fostering an idea of "education as life" (Simmel 1995) in which interpersonal relationships and relational context become key elements to increase the individual's faculties and skills in an economic, cultural, and social perspective. Not surprisingly, the ability to meet the student housing demand is affirming itself as an increasingly relevant factor in the definition of international rankings and in the evaluation of the quality of universities (Downing et al. 2017).

This raises the question of the effectiveness of the policies implemented in our country over the last decades, aiming at increasing the overall number of students' matriculations, without specific reflections on structures and strategies to raise a higher level of social and collective education. This situation needs to find a solution quickly, fostering new consideration for student housing, both from a morpho-techno-typological perspective (Bellini 2015, 2019a, b; Newman 2016) and from a social one. The new users of residencies, their crescent variety in terms of age, nationality, academic role, education raise the necessity to adapt the functional and organizational offer of these structures to the new social and cultural scenario (McBride 2017) (Fig. 1).

Far from being considered as mere structures dedicated to temporary accommodation for foreign students, student housing should be regarded as a public service: a fundamental element to support academic, didactic, and research activities as well as to provide facilities and services for the collective cultural and recreational growth of population, generating new human and social capital (Ciaramella and Del Gatto 2012; Laudisa 2013; Bellini et al. 2015; Bosio et al. 2018; Eversley 2019).

[1]The present paper illustrates activities and studies made possible by the collaboration between the ABC Department and the ATE—Area Tecnico Edilizia—of the Politecnico di Milano.

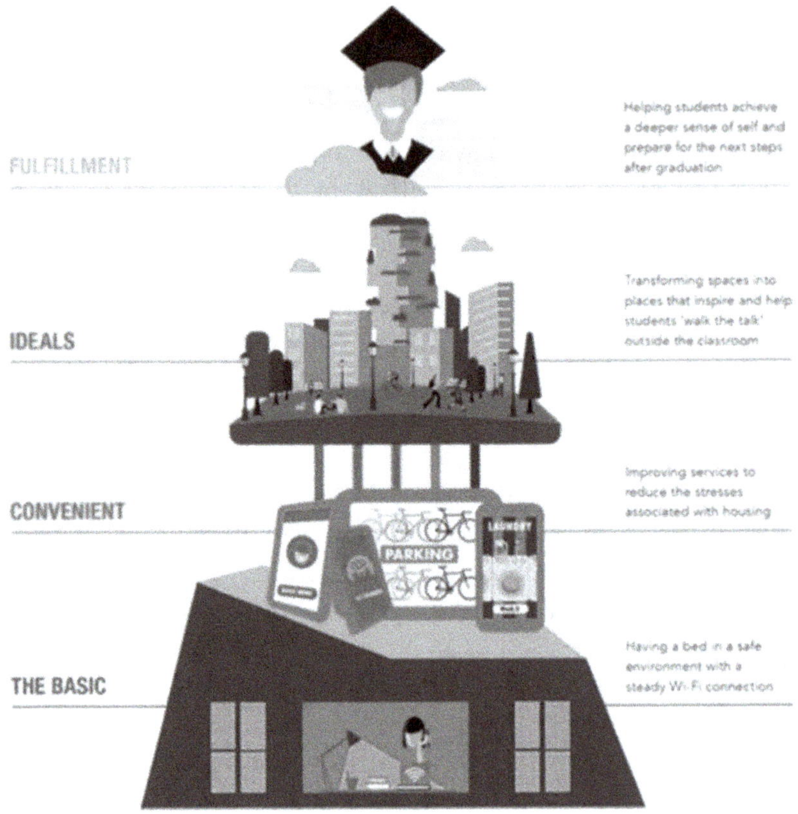

Fig. 1 Maslow pyramid of student accommodation

2 The Case of the Politecnico di Milano

This reflection frames the strategic investment of the Politecnico di Milano, which over the last decades doubled the sleeping accommodation for its students, by activating to date seven new student residencies in Milano, Lecco, and Como.[2] The result has been achieved both through the renovation of existing structures and the realization of new ones that enhance the outstanding supply (Fig. 2).[3] This situation

[2]The success of the initiative is a result of the significant financing located by MIUR—Ministry of Education through the law 338/2000 for the development of student housing in Italy. As it clearly appeared in the text of the law, the Ministry aimed at favoring an integration between student residencies and urban contexts, requiring a continuum in the social and services fabric of the city (Del Nord 2014). Despite these intentions, the rigidity in the following implementation procedures and the definition of unavoidable spatial and functional requirements made a real experimentation difficult, both in the design of new spaces adequate for a new type of users and in the development of new educational paths (Bellini and Mocchi 2016).

[3]With funding from the law 338/2000, the Politecnico di Milano could increase its student housing offer by 1515 sleeping units, among which 1150 in Milan. The residencies involved are Galileo Galilei (406 beds, Corridoni Street, Milan), Adolf Loos (200 beds, Ghislanzoni Street, Lecco), La Presentazione (165 beds, via Zezio, Como), Leonardo da Vinci (333 beds, Romagna Avenue, Milan), Isaac Newton (258 beds, Mario Borsa Street, Milan) Vilfredo Pareto (232 beds, Maggianico Street, Milan), and Albert Einstein (214 beds, Einstein Street, Milan). All these interventions provide a

Fig. 2 Student residence "Isaac Newton" of the Politecnico di Milano, in the Gallaratese District

is destined to grow as a consequence of the fourth implementation procedure of the law 338/2000, which will allow the Politecnico di Milano to realize three new interventions, adding 834 new sleeping accommodations to its offer.[4] The importance and the size of this venture, as well as the urban placement of the new buildings, make the case particularly meaningful to understand the new management praxis and the operational procedures involved in the phenomenon (Bellini et al. 2016).

The first interesting point is the tendency to locate new student housing facilities in peripheral areas of the city as well, characterized by the lack of common services and difficulties in social integration and cultural dialogue among citizens. This is also produced by the situation of the historical center, denoted by strict building heritage protection, determining a general growth of the price of real estate and limited flexibility in its reconversion.

In this scenario, the authors initiated a study to focus on the proactive role of student housing in urban regeneration processes, both at a physical level—in relation to the common spaces and facilities that they provide to districts—and at a social one—considering the importance of students in understanding the multicultural problems of citizens who live in suburbs. After a general analysis, the more suited residence for starting the experimentation turned out to be the Newton one, in the Gallaratese District (Fig. 2). Due to its urban, social, and historical context, as

significant contribution in the requalification of their urban contexts, often in the suburbs of the city, characterized by environmental and social problems.

[4]Law 338/2000 on student housing, IV implementation procedure (D.M. n. 937/2016), ranking of accepted projects for financing approved by the Commission on July 5, 2018 (report n. 11/2018 all. n. 4), published in the Official Gazette of Italian Republic on March 29, 2019, Serie generale n. 75.

well as its morpho-techno-typological traits, the residence represents the best qualities for a field trial. The choice is determined by the heavy social and territorial problems of Gallaratese,[5] confirmed by its inclusion among the five areas of the competition "Bando alle periferie" fostered by the Municipality of Milano in 2017.

In this scenario, Newton residence introduces 258 students from 20 different nationalities, becoming an integral part of the urban fabric—on average, students live in the district for more than one year. The students represent a micro-community, in some respects bound together by the same problems of the local community—difficulties of integration and cultural comprehension, linguistic barriers, distance from home—in others characterized by original traits—high cultural profile, belonging to a young and homogeneous age range. If not properly considered and treated, this resource risks becoming a negative factor for the population and the urban environment, fostering undesirable processes such as "studentification".[6]

In order to avoid this situation, the research group focuses on the definition of an innovative multidisciplinary and multi-scale strategy, able to foster a reciprocity among academic knowledge, technical apparatus and local fragilities, fostering a shared environmental and social atmosphere as the condition for promoting a sense of belonging for individuals to their urban context and local community. According to international studies and experimentations (Ferrante 2012; Hassan et al. 2012; Khajehzadeh and Brenda 2016; Kader 2017), this approach could produce significant consequences for urban territories, also in view of the participation and sensibilization of local people on urgent topics such as social integration, environmental sustainability, food education, waste reduction, sustainable mobility (Fig. 3).[7]

[5]"Gallaratese San Leonardo" District (corresponding to NIL—Local Identity Unit 65) has a population of 31,481 units (source: Municipality of Milano, Piano Servizi, rev. 2016) and characterized by the presence of elderly residents (35.3% against the average of 23.7% in the whole city) with a significant percentage of over-85-year-olds. The impact of foreigner citizens is relatively low (8.8% against 18.8%), even if it increases among underaged people (22%). In particular, the urban area close to the residence, including ALER housing in Bolla Street, is characterized by strong degradation, with social conflicts, illegal occupation of apartments, lack of health facilities, sport and educational services, and infrastructures (Piano dei Servizi of PGT of Milano).

[6]According to the literature on gentrification (Borlini and Memo 2008; Semi 2015), "studentification" represents a recent phenomenon, characterized by speculative trends in local rental markets, changes in the commercial activities and services in favor of students' needs, processes of marginalization of old citizens.

[7]As demonstrated by a number of examples: Stanford University (Sustainable Stanford), Harvard (Water Taste Test, Food Better, Mount Trashmore), Ball State (Energy Action Team, Dinner Dark, America Recycles Day Party), Yale (Sustainable Yale), Lausanne University (VolteFace, Troc-o-Pole, Carrot City), University of York (Fairtrade), University of Melbourne (Bokashi Bucket). All these actions started from the idea of "sustainable campus" (https://www.international-sustainable-campus-network.org/), using student housing facilities to foster a dialogue between university and local urban environments (Radder and Han 2009).

Fig. 3 Public space facilities in Newton student residence

3 Ongoing Projects

The ongoing projects are the result of a study conducted by the authors over recent years, which has already produced publications on the topic (Bellini 2015), participation in seminars and conferences (Bellini and Mocchi 2016; Bellini 2019b; Mocchi 2019), field classes and activities.[8] The results so far achieved confirm a dynamic situation, made up of cooperative students and a local network of stakeholders, associations, and players already active in the area.[9]

[8]The "Building Technology Studio" 2018/19 (prof. Gambaro, Aceti) concentrates on the design of the open spaces of the Newton student residence, aiming at defining public areas and services dedicated to both students and local people. During the course, specific on-field activities were organized as well as seminars involving experts and operators of student housing (Adolfo Baratta, Fabrizio Schiaffonati, Francesco Vitola, Oscar Eugenio Bellini, Maria Teresa Gullace). The results of the course will be presented at the "Biennale dello spazio pubblico" held in Rome, May 31–June 1, 2019. Several dissertations and degree theses on the same topics have been developed over the last few years.

[9]A survey has been developed among the students hosted in the Newton residence, aiming at knowing their opinion about their quality of life and their availability to take part in activities involving local people. According to Veronica Signorelli's dissertation—entitled "Residenze universitarie: una nuova risorsa sociale," tutor: O. E. Bellini, A.A. 2017/18—117 students out of the 232 interviewed (50.8%) are available to take part in the experimentations. The students come from different nationalities, among which Italy, India, Pakistan, Iran, Turkey, and China. They are equally divided in terms of gender and education. The general opinion of the students regarding the residence is positive, even if they reveal a number of issues with regards to the urban position (distance from the city center and the university structures) and the management of common spaces (lack of cooking areas, noise). Local associations and players are very active on the territory, promoting activities

In 2017, the authors developed a project to take part in the competition Polisocial,[10] which in that year was dedicated to the theme "Periphery." The project had the merit to start a collaboration among departments dedicated to research and technical bodies—"ATE—Area Tecnico Edilizia," "Servizio Residenze"—fostering a better comprehension of the student housing phenomenon in terms of management and financing, on the basis of which to orient the research phase. The project had the endorsement of important institutions operating in the sector, such as the University of Milano—Direzione del Patrimonio Immobiliare, Centro Studi TESIS, RUI Foundation, Legambiente.

The study identifies four areas of intervention, in which social inclusion plays a fundamental and strategic role: 1 (In) social, including activities of learning, education, social cohesion; 2 (In) environment, with actions related to the environment, sustainability, circular economy; 3 (In) sport, considering sport activities as a fundamental part of the student housing experience; 4 (In) science, for contributing to the dissemination of scientific research.

The experimentation is now part of the Off Campus project, a development program financed by Polisocial. The program aims at fostering new forms of field teaching and research, putting into relation the academic organisms and knowledge with the local community's needs.[11] Off Campus are physical structures placed in the city, working as delocalized satellites of the university, able to encourage on-field research and teaching activities, with a specific attention to the characteristics of places, the relationships between university and local reality, the way of living and dwelling in urban territories. The presence of students inside this area represents a big opportunity for the territory, leading to the idea of opening an Off Campus satellite in the Newton residence (Fig. 4).

---

for raising awareness and building citizenship within the local population. Among others, we can mention the network "Non Riservato," fostering initiatives such as "Gallab" or "Quartiere Aperto."

[10]Polisocial is the Politecnico di Milano's social responsibility program, a fundamental part of the university's Third Mission, to promote new multidisciplinary programs for human and social development, increasing the educational opportunities and the chances for dialogue and confrontation among students and researchers. The project submitted to the Polisocial Award, entitled "Polimi (in) Social," has been developed by the following working group: Oscar E. Bellini (Scientific Coordinator), Luisa Collina (Project Manager), Andrea Tartaglia, Gennaro Postiglione, Roberto Rizzi, Francesco Vitola, Maria Teresa Gullace, Ivano Ciceri.

[11]Off Campus "Il cantiere per le periferie" is promoted by Polisocial, the Politecnico di Milano's social responsibility program. The initiative is coordinated by Gabriele Pasqui, Francesca Cognetti, and Ida Castelnuovo. Through this project, for the first time in Italy, the university tries to investigate the double benefit that follows its presence within the urban context: both in terms of didactic methods enhancement—due to the closer relationships between teaching activities and local territories—and opportunities for researching and experimenting activities. The continuing legacy of this activity in the urban contexts represents a starting point for a social and physical requalification of the urban environment. Off Campus has a duration of 3 years and is going to be concentrated in 4 focus areas, corresponding to an equal number of actions and thematic areas: (1) Observatory of Dwelling and Urban Periphery, Abbiati Street—San Siro District; (2) Observatory of Student Housing: Isaac Newton Residence—Gallaratese District; (3) Observatory of Re-Activation of the Municipal Market in Monza Avenue—Nolo District; (4) Dwelling Urban Periphery, Rizzoli Street—Crescenzago District.

Fig. 4 Students of Politecnico di Milano hosted in the "Isaac Newton Student Residence"

An important moment for the research took place on May 16, 2019, during the conference "Living and Dwelling University. A critical view of student housing in Italy," promoted by the ABC Department with the scientific involvement of the Dastu Department, ATE—Area Tecnico Edilizia, and Sevizio Residenze of the Politecnico di Milano.

The national conference was aimed at developing a critical balance of the law 338/2000 and the following procedures, focusing on the new role of student housing as a driving factor for the renewal of academic training courses, for attracting private and public investments to build and manage new structures, for experimenting new methods and procedures in architectural project, for fostering innovative and interactive practices involving students and local population.

The conference represented an important moment for favoring a dialogue among stakeholders, professionals, architects, political representatives, and academical researchers, which will follow a publication of the proceedings. Furthermore, the conference was an opportunity for launching the "Observatory of student housing of the Politecnico di Milano," with the purpose of monitoring the student housing situation in Lombardy, strengthening competences and skills for the management, design, administration, and governance of the structures.

4 Student Housing as a Community Hub

The research carried out and the open perspectives clearly demonstrate the potential of student housing as a privileged field for the construction of Community hubs able to provide spaces and furniture to local people as well as social support to the population by young students with high educational profile and specific linguistic, technical, and digital skills.

Community hubs are public spaces able to bring together community agencies and neighborhood groups, offering a range of activities, programs, and services referred to the specific needs of the local population. They encourage social gatherings, improving the use of public spaces, embracing multiple services under one roof. Among the others, Community hubs can include health services, education, and employment amenities, childcare and sports facilities, social, cultural, and recreational spaces (Bagnoli et al. 2019). Community hubs foster the integration of local population, helping to put in relation people who speak the same language, with similar cultural backgrounds (Sousa 2013; Brotsky et al. 2019).

This gives the interpretation of student housing a double meaning, considering it on the one hand as "hardware"—a physical place able to provide innovative spaces and facilities to citizens—on the other hand as "software"—a social environment able to interact with the multicultural tendencies of a contemporary metropolis. Hardware and software become the new tools for generating integration, cohesion, inclusion and new human and social capital.

In conclusion, the research has opened an innovative interpretation of student housing, as a strategic field for promoting sociocultural regeneration of urban environments, triggering virtuous interactions among citizens—in particular among the more vulnerable groups such as the elderly, differently abled, children without access to a decent education, immigrants, and second generations of immigrant families—and fostering accountability in students, favoring their empowerment in urban life and their involvement in active citizenship.

References

Abidin, N. Z., Najib, N. U. M., & Yusof, N. A. (2011). Student residential satisfaction in research universities. *Journal of Facilities Management, 9*(3), 200–212.

Agnoli, M. S. (2010). *Spazi, identità, relazioni. Indagine sulla convivenza multiculturale nelle residenze universitarie*. Milano: Franco Angeli.

Bagnoli, L., Bartocci, A., & Borlini, M. M. (2019). *Obiettivo Periferico. Visioni e previsioni sul futuro della periferia urbana*. Milano: StreetLib.

Bellini, O. E. (2015). *Student housing_1. Atlante ragionato della residenza universitaria contemporanea*. Santarcangelo di Romagna: Maggioli.

Bellini, O. E. (2019a). *Student housing_2. Il progetto della residenza universitaria*. Santarcangelo di Romagna: Maggioli [published soon].

Bellini, O. E. (2019b). La residenza universitaria come dispositivo per ri-abitare le relazioni sociali nella periferia. In *La nuova architettura Spazi contemporanei nella città storica, Architettura e Città*. Milano: Di Baio.

Bellini, O. E., & Mocchi, M. (2016). Students: Those animals! The issue of the 'users' in the student housing design. In R. Del Nord, A. Baratta, & C. Piferi (Eds.), *Residenze e servizi per studenti universitari* (pp. 285–296). Florence: TESIS.

Bellini, O. E., Bellintani, S., Ciaramella, A., & Del Gatto, M. L. (2015). *Learning and living. Abitare lo Student Housing*. Milano: Franco Angeli.

Bellini, O. E., Bellintani, S., Ciaramella, A., & Del Gatto, M. L. (2016). Learning and living the student residences a new design beyond the law. In *Proceedings of Giornata internazionale di studi Residenze e servizi per studenti universitari*, Florence (pp. 297–308). http://hdl.handle.net/11311/1012076.

Borlini, B., & Memo, F. (2008). *Il quartiere nella città contemporanea*. Milano: Mondadori.

Bosio, G., Minola, T., Origo, F., & Tomelleri, S. (Eds.). (2018). *Rethinking entrepreneurial human capital: The role of innovation and collaboration*. Berlin: Springer International Publishing.

Brotsky, C., Eisinger, S. M., & Vinokur-Kaplan, D. (2019). *Shared space and the new nonprofit workplace*. Oxford: Oxford University Press.

Ciaramella, A., & Del Gatto, M. L. (2012). Housing universitario di iniziativa privata: scenari di sviluppo e fattori critici di successo. *Techne, Firenze University Press, 4*, 271–279.

Costa, P. (2014). *Valutare l'architettura. Ricerca sociologica e Post Occupancy Evaluation*. Milano: Franco Angeli.

Del Nord, R. (Ed.). (2014). *Il processo attuativo del piano nazionale di interventi per la realizzazione di residenze universitarie*. Firenze: EdiFir.

Downing, K., Ganotice, Jr, & Fraide, A. (Eds.). (2017). *World university rankings and the future of higher education*. USA: IGI Global.

Eikemo, T. A., & Judith Thomsen, J. (2018). Aspects of student housing satisfaction: A quantitative study. *Journal of Housing and the Built Environment, 25*(3), 273–293. https://doi.org/10.1007/s10901-010-9188-3.

Eversley, J. (2019). *Social and community development: An introduction*. Berlin: Red Globe Press, Springer Nature.

Ferrante, T. (2012). *Valutare la qualità percepita. Uno studio pilota per gli hospice*. Milano: Franco Angeli.

Hassan, A. S., Khozaei, F., Ramayah, T., & Surienty, L. (2012). Sense of attachment to place and fulfilled preferences, the mediating role of housing satisfaction. *Property Management, 30*(3), 292–310. https://doi.org/10.1108/02637471211233945.

Kader, S. (2017). Development of student satisfaction survey tool to evaluate living-learning residence hall. In *ARCC 2017 Conference Architecture of Complexity*, Salt Lake City (UT) (pp. 326–335). https://www.brikbase.org/sites/default/files/ARCC2017_Session3B_Kader.pdf.

Khajehzadeh, I., & Brenda, V. (2016). Shared student residential space: A post occupancy evaluation. *Journal of Facilities Management, 14*(2), 102–124. https://doi.org/10.1108/JFM-09-2014-0031.

Laudisa, F. (2013). Le residenze universitarie in Italia. In G. Catalano (Ed.), *Gestire le residenze universitarie. Aspetti metodologici ed esperienze applicative*. Bologna: Il Mulino.

Livi Bacci, M. (2008). *Avanti giovani, alla riscossa. Come uscire dalla crisi giovanile in Italia*. Bologna: Il Mulino.

McBride, Y. (2017). Future of student housing: Meeting emerging student needs. *On the Horizon, 25/2017*(3), 190–196. https://doi.org/10.1108/OTH-05-2017-0026.

Mocchi, M. (2019). Il ruolo dello student housing nella costruzione di nuovi paesaggi urbani. In *La nuova architettura Spazi contemporanei nella città storica, Architettura e Città*. Milano: Di Baio.

Micheli, G. A. (2008). *Dietro ragionevoli scelte*. Per capire I comportamenti dei giovani adulti italiani, Fondazione Giovanni Agnelli, Torino.

Najib, N. M., Yusof, N., & Tabassi, (2014). Living in on-campus student housing: Students' behavioral intentions and students' personal attainments. *Procedia—Social and Behavioral Sciences, 170,* 494–503. https://doi.org/10.1016/j.sbspro.2015.01.052.

Newman, J. (Ed.). (2016). Implementation guidelines to the ISCN-GULF sustainable campus charter. https://www.international-sustainable-campus-network.org/downloads/charter-and-guidelines/443-iscn-gulf-charter-guidelines/file.

Radder, L., & Han, X. (2009). Service quality of on-campus student housing: A South African experience. *International Business & Economics Research Journal, 8*(11), 107–119. https://www.researchgate.net/publication/277566390_Service_Quality_of_On_Campus_Student_Housing_A_South_African_Experience.

Rosina, A., Micheli, G. A., & Mazzucco, S. (2007). "Le difficoltà dei giovani all'uscita dalla casa dei genitori. Un'analisi del rischio", *La Rivista delle Politiche Sociali*, 3(4), Ediesse, Roma, pp. 95-111.

Semi, G. (2015). *Gentrification. Tutte le città come Disneyland?* Bologna: Il Mulino.

Simmel, G. (1995). *L' educazione in quanto vita*. Torino: Il Segnalibro.

Sousa, J. (2013). *Building a co-operative community in public housing. The case of the Aktinson housing co-operative*. Toronto: University of Toronto Press.

PolimiparaRocinha: Environmental Performances and Social Inclusion—A Project for the Favela Rocinha

Gabriele Masera, Massimo Tadi, Carlo Biraghi and Hadi Mohammad Zadeh

Abstract By the middle of the current century, the world's population is projected to grow exponentially, becoming one of the major concerns for the built environment all around the world, where informal settlements are going to grow even faster. This growth will increase the demand for basic infrastructure which is lacking in such contexts. In developing countries, the promotion of urban technologies could contribute immensely to a sustainable development and to population well-being, besides creating interesting economic opportunities. Urban technologies could reduce the environmental impact of cities' development and of urbanized slums renovation, creating employment opportunities for locals and economic opportunities for investment. However, deploying this in slums is a complex and challenging task. This text presents a project based on a multidisciplinary and integrated design methodology for the sustainable regeneration of Rocinha, one of the largest favelas of Rio de Janeiro. The project adopts a systemic approach and foresees the deployment of an urban management system (UMS) able to manage and integrate several urban services including sanitation, energy, mobility, waste, food delivery and cultivation, and the flow of information connected to them, with the aim of reducing the environmental impact while improving the quality of life of citizens. Each of these areas required the development of a specific project that, empowered by the UMS, will allow for the circulation of information between citizens, fostering social inclusion, and raising awareness on the topic of the city's resource management. This project is a demonstration of how minimal but calculated local modification can produce considerable global reaction and ultimately change the system as a whole.

Keywords Favela · Informal settlements · System thinking · Complex adaptive system · Urban management system · Multiscale approach

---

G. Masera (✉) · M. Tadi · C. Biraghi · H. M. Zadeh
Architecture, Built Environment and Construction Engineering—ABC Department, Politecnico di Milano, Milan, Italy
e-mail: gabriele.masera@polimi.it

S. Della Torre et al. (eds.), *Regeneration of the Built Environment from a Circular Economy Perspective*, Research for Development,
https://doi.org/10.1007/978-3-030-33256-3_12

1 Introduction

As the urban population of the world is increasing dramatically, it is predicted that by the year 2050 about 70% of this population will live in informal settlements. While this is an alarming matter for policy makers and urban managers around the world to revise and replan development, it highlights the importance of studying such organizations for scientific communities too.

Depending on the local environment, cultural context, size, and the contextual relationships with the surrounding urban areas, the informal settlements could appear in a variety of shapes and forms. Nonetheless, there are structural features shared among them worldwide. There are innate characteristics such as high population densities, poor infrastructures, and social segregation associated with them which make them much more challenging to manage, and at the same time, there are also surprising peculiarities, like certain environmental behaviors, offered by them to learn from. Working on such human organization can provide valuable opportunities to examine the capacity of today's ability for managing tomorrow's likely threats, on the one hand, and unveil the inherent capacities, on the other hand, of these integral contexts for efficiency in energy consumption.

This text summarizes the morphological studies of the project "PolimiparaRocinha", a 2016 Polisocial winner dedicated to the Favela Rocinha which is the biggest single favela in Brazil. PolimiparaRocinha is an interdisciplinary project coordinated by the Department of Architecture, Built Environment and Construction Engineering (ABC) with the Department of Civil and Environmental Engineering (DICA), the Department of Architecture and Urban Studies (DAStU) and the Department of Energy, and several academic and non-academic partners outside the Politecnico di Milano.

Acknowledging the particularities in all of its aspects, there is no doubt that Rocinha is far from ordinary urban settlement. Its placement in the heart of Rio, along with its practical isolation from it, the semi-independent functional distribution within its boundaries, its strong community-oriented social fabric, its informal organic-like morphology that accommodates an astonishing population density, and the bewildering energy consumption statistic associated with it outlines a complex system of multidimensional urban organisms linked to one another in a profound and occasionally paradoxical way producing a wide variation of situations. Studying such a context demands a synthesis-based approach able to address its profound systemic interconnectedness and occult qualities which are the source of both strengths and weaknesses in Rocinha's performance. The interdisciplinary framework of this project should also be structured around an operative holistic methodology used as the departure and reference point for all the defined projects in different realms and areas.

The core methodological tool for the investigation, evaluation, and project definition used in PolimiparaRocinha is *Integrated Modification Methodology* (IMM). IMM is a procedure encompassing a set of scientific techniques for understanding the systemic structure of urban settlements and proposing modification scenarios to enhance their socioeconomic and environmental performances. It was developed by the IMM Design Lab based in the ABC Department of Politecnico di Milano. Based on system thinking, the main purpose of IMM is to introduce modification scenarios in order to morphologically transform the built environment—in different scales—into ecologically better-performing systems.

2 Integrated Modification Methodology (IMM)

Integrated modification methodology (IMM) is a procedure encompassing an open set of scientific techniques for morphologically analyzing the built environment in a multiscale manner and evaluating its performance in current states or under specific design scenarios (Vahabzadeh Manesh et al. 2011).

In IMM, the built environment is considered a complex adaptive system (CAS) in which the relationships between the parts are highly complicated in a way that a mere local modification starts a chain reaction and ultimately changes the entire system.

According to system theory, the functioning manner of any system is fundamentally directed mostly by the relationship between the parts and depends less on the quality of its individual components (Wächter 2011).

IMM recognizes the built environment as a complex adaptive system (CAS) comprised of numerous subsets and many variables interacting on various levels, various scales, and a diverse set of subcategories. Rendering the CAS's nature, a mere local action accrued in an individual subset will produce a chain reaction within the network of its parts and trigger a process which consequently leads to the global change of the entire system. In other words, system agents adapt themselves in response to the complex network of reactions arisen from individual changes (Vahabzadeh Manesh and Tadi 2013).

The generic morphological subsystems recognized by IMM are namely: *urban built-up*, *urban void*, *types of uses*, and *links* (Tadi et al. 2015). In the first phase, they are being investigated individually, and the structural attributes resulting from their fusion is studied. The former distinctively gives an understanding of the component, and the latter quantifies the relational attributes that as previously explained shapes the functioning manner of the context. These steps are called horizontal investigation and vertical investigation, respectively, and unveil the weakest elements and mechanisms mostly responsible for the current performance. The next phase is to assess this analysis and formulate strategies to modify the system based on design ordering principles (DOP). The phase after that is to test the design scenarios through the same procedures that evaluate the existing situation in order to reach the optimum modification plan. The outcome is locally retrofitted in the last phase, and the achievements in performance improvement are reported.

In PolimiparaRocinha, four main categories of challenges are defined: 1. People engagement, 2. Managing the unbalanced density, 3. Proposing waste management strategies, and 4. Proposing water management. For addressing these issues, five project themes have been identified: 1. Ecosystem services, 2. Food production, 3. Mobility, 4. Energy, and 5. Waste management (Arcidiacono et al. 2017).

The project activities are initiated with IMM phasing in order to provide a modified morphology flexible enough to achieve maximum performances in all the mentioned project themes.

The following is a summary of the IMM intervention on Rocinha.

3 Vertical Investigation

In vertical investigation, the attributes associated with these relationships are to be referred to as key categories. Since the performance of any system is resulted from the relationships between its elements, it is safe to state that vertical investigation is the methodological engine of IMM.

Six key categories have been investigated in Rocinha: Porosity, Proximity, Diversity, Effectiveness, Accessibility, and Interface.

Porosity

Normally, analyzing porosity in IMM encompasses a certain number of concepts including building coverage, density, volume distribution concentration factor, etc., in a comparable manner. However, because the population density in Rocinha is dramatically high, it is almost impossible to carry out a comparative analysis. Density is the only key player in Rocinha, and no realistic modification scenario could be imagined that could abate this staggering statistic (Tadi and Mohammad Zadeh 2017).

Thus, the porosity investigation in PolimiparaRocinha is a comprehensive study of built-up density which with consideration of integrity in social characteristic in the whole favela could also be directly interpreted as population density.

In this analysis, the buildings have been categorized with regard to their heights. Considering the almost uniform size of the building footprints, the porosity investigation here shows the distribution of density in an acceptably accurate way. Although there are limited numbers of buildings that are up to eight stories, the highest typical buildings are four-story buildings. This typology finds its peak primarily in the vicinity of the western section (because of the metro station) and alongside da Gávea street. The volume distribution in the rest of the favela is following a quasi-random pattern (Fig. 1).

Proximity

Proximity is the quality by which an urban area's main uses can be reached by means of non-motorized transportation (mainly walking). The main relationship here is the one between functions and volume/voids. Of course, the street network is also a key factor. In order to analyze proximity, according to its definition, it is fundamental to define the key urban functions and to investigate the way in which the functions influence non-motorized mobility (Tadi et al. 2015).

Fig. 1 Porosity in Rocinha

Considering the playful topography of Rocinha and the limited number of functions, the catchment areas have been considered as circles with a radius of 150 meters. However, these circles have been modified by a morphological limit. This means that they have been located with regard to the functions, and the buildings' footprints have been cut away from them in such a way that they are projected onto the voids (this is obvious because people cannot walk through the actual buildings). It is important to notice that the proximity analysis shows the actual/potential walking flow.

The proximity of Rocinha is regulated by the location of the metro and da Gávea street where there are both relatively more functions and enough void spaces. Because of its adequate width and its physical relationship with da Gávea, the walking flow is continued to R. Nova at the center. Occasionally, there are a number of accessible spots in the southern part for walking where the density is medium and the spaces between buildings are enough to support local functions. These scattered patterns indicate a certain level of functional independence due to the significant distance between these areas and the main proximity core.

Diversity

Similar to the conceptual linkage between open spaces and functions, diversity is about the characteristics of voids influenced by diverging functions. In other words, diversity is the quality of open spaces in giving access to different types of functions (Meurs 2007).

In order to evaluate diversity, IMM as a sustainable-oriented methodology aims at clustering the functions based on travel distances between compatible types of functions. In this regard, if an urban area offers an optimum functional diversity from a social point of view, there is a high chance that an important level of daily needs is met in smaller distances and that helps to avoid unnecessary urban journeys.

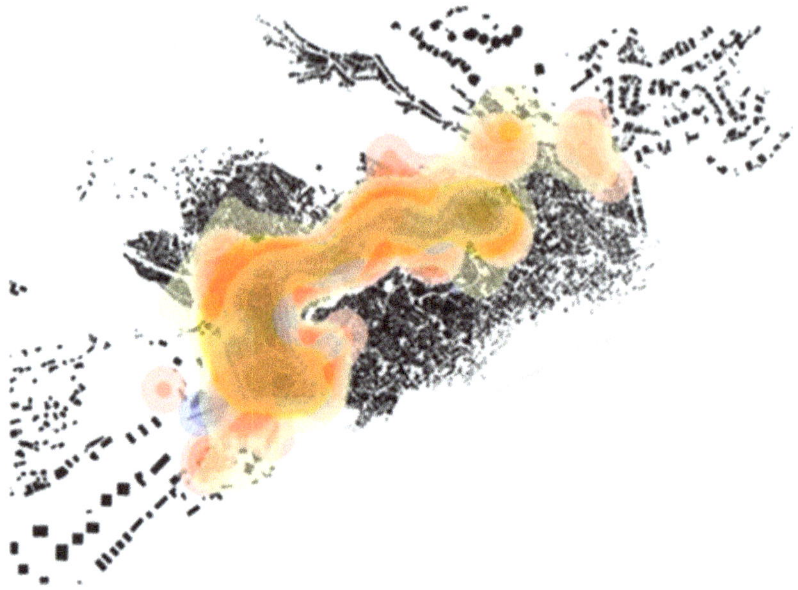

Fig. 2 Diversity in Rocinha

From the social point of view, there are three categories of urban functions: 1. Necessary activities, 2. Optional activities, and 3. Social activities (Olwig 2016).

Because it is impossible to pinpoint social activities and to involve the time patterns in urban trips, IMM modifies the mentioned categories into: 1. Necessary regular activities, 2. Necessary occasional activities, and 3. Optional activities.

As it is shown in the diversity analysis of Rocinha, the most diverse parts are again in the areas near the metro station and da Gávea street (Fig. 2).

Accessibility

Accessibility is the quality of allowing for main functions to be reached via public transportation systems in a certain amount of time. The functional and mobility layers are the boldest urban elements in this key category. To put it simply, the accessibility map illustrates the coverage functions of the public transport stops. The catchment areas are the same as mentioned in effectiveness (Manesh and Tadi 2016).

Because of the Rocinha's simple pattern of functional development around the most accessible areas, it is not shocking that the accessibility analysis is almost identical to the mobility analysis in the horizontal investigation.

Effectiveness

Mobility and built-ups are the two main building blocks at the heart of effectiveness. As one can observe in its name, this key category is about the effectiveness of the public transportation system. Probably, the most solid way to carry out such an analysis is to study the relationship between population density and public transportation stops. This is to show the density that a stop/station can cover in its walkable catchment areas. According to the literature, this catchment area is a circle (projected to open spaces) with a 400 meters radius for bus and tram stops and 800 meters for metro stations (Handy 2005).

Below is the effectiveness analysis of Rocinha with regard to the various mobility configurations existing in the favela.

Interface

IMM interface is evaluated through mean depth calculation and the axial analysis provided by Space Syntax. The axial analysis is a simple iterative computation based on graph theory in which the number of the intersections to reach a certain link is calculated on the basis of all the parts of the street networks. At the end, the links that gain lower depth are the ones which are connected to the system with much higher integrity (Hillier and Iida 2005).

$$D = \frac{\Sigma d \,.\, n}{k - 1}$$

D: mean depth, d: depth, n: number of unit spaces at a specific depth, k: total unit spaces that comprise the system.

The interface analysis vividly illustrates that the street network of Rocinha provides a very low level of connectivity, dictating a low quality of internal movement. It is not surprising that the urban flow is easily interrupted throughout. Interestingly, the parts with low integrity are exactly where criminal groups prefer to arrange their activities. This situation is mainly due to the limitations caused by topography and the irregular pattern of buildings (which itself is an indirect consequence of topography (Fig. 3).

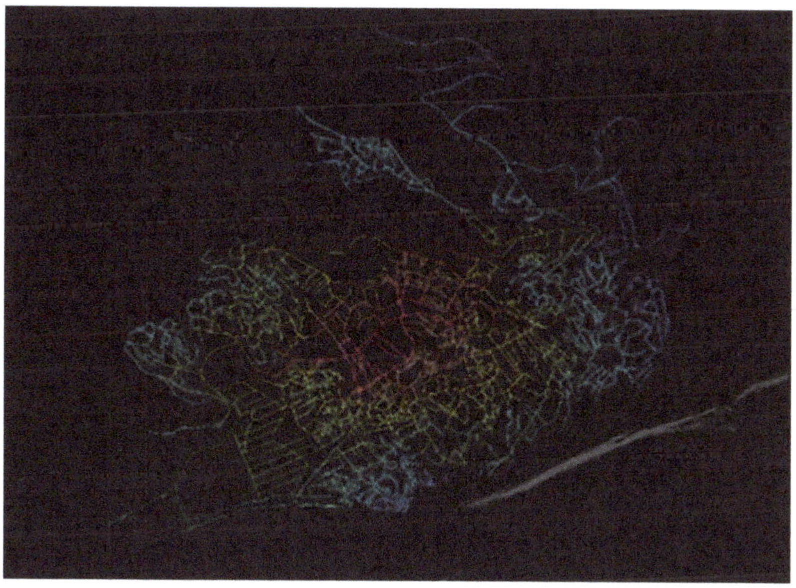

Fig. 3 Interface in Rocinha

4 Proposed Morphological Modification

According to the investigation phase, it is evident that the malfunctioning urban element is the void layer and the most problematic key category is the interface. Rocinha is suffering from not having enough empty spaces to provide sufficient flexibility for urban flow and functional support. On the other hand, the street network is a broken system unable to offer adequate connectivity for smooth movement. However, minor changes can be made to improve the situation and overall functioning of the system.

Accordingly, the initial concept is driven by the idea of providing more open spaces, hence more integrity to the street networks by relocating a small number of low buildings where it is possible and beneficial. A very conceptual change in the interface analysis supports the idea that with a limited local modification, considerable global enhancement can be achieved.

Based on the interface analysis, 21 locations have been identified where the definition of new links resulting from minimum relocation projects could lead to massive global changes in system integration. Accordingly, a total of 108 small buildings—which in comparison with the whole of Rocinha can be safely considered negligible—were predicted to be relocated to the nearest buildings possible. This decision was entirely supported by the local partners of the project including Sorriso dei miei Bimbi which is an educational institute inside Rocinha and is in close contact with the local community. However, due to specific considerations regarding the social fabric of the different zones, it was suggested that the work be initiated in six specific zones (Fig. 4).

Fig. 4 Intervention zones

This systemic modification creates an optimum morphological flexibility in view of proceeding with the project themes. The immediate consequence is to have a better mobility flow that not only makes the area safer, but also allowed to define a locally based bicycle network supported by bike-sharing systems which work in compatibility with the existing public transportation system. In some of the new spaces defined by the relocation project, community gardening and aquaponic projects will be established in order to raise awareness on the value of local food production. These projects are integrated with the ecosystem service to ensure the management of runoff and water conservation and the definition of a smart energy grid for harvesting and managing the renewable sources for energy production and management. Local strategies to use organic waste for producing biogas have also been considered, and new waste management plans in compatibility with local programs have been proposed.

It is crucial to address the totality of the structure made by local projects in the selected zones. These six zones are the locations in which local strategies like the aquaponics, photovoltaic panels, community gardening, sewage system, etc., are placed together to create an integrated system of a prototype network throughout Rocinha. This system has been designed in such a way as to ensure two levels of circularities on two different scales. They form a closed system so that their inflow is provided locally. The food production uses local resources, the solar radiation is harvested on top of the local buildings, and the proposed functions are in compatibility with local needs. However, they are linked together all over the favela with the smart grid centrally managed by an urban management system (UMS). The proposed improvements require the development of a specific project which, empowered by the UMS, allows for the circulation of information between citizens, who become the main actors of the whole system, promoting social inclusion and the sustainable regeneration of the favela. The UMS as a system of computer-aided tools will monitor, control, and optimize the information flows coming from the different sectors improving services for citizens such as street lighting, electrical local urban transportation, food delivery, waste management, goods delivery, etc. In this way, the UMS can, for example, reduce traffic in congested areas, encourage the use of more efficient and ecological transport systems, prevent the frequent blackouts as well as establish citizens' virtuous behavior in terms of waste collection, energy savings, etc. (Fig. 5).

On the Rocinha scale, this system creates a balance between inflow and outflow by allocating the local resources to the overall outflow. Moreover, thanks to the prototypes, a new bicycle network has been designed which connects the intervention zones and other places (where the topography allows) physically. This means that local resources provide global energy storage, public lighting, and overall connectivity. This integrity in the prototype network allows us to move from 21 critical locations to be improved to only 6 intervention zones without sacrificing the totality of the favela; nevertheless, the prototype network provides a capacity of integration with more intervention zones applying the same strategies in the future (Fig. 6).

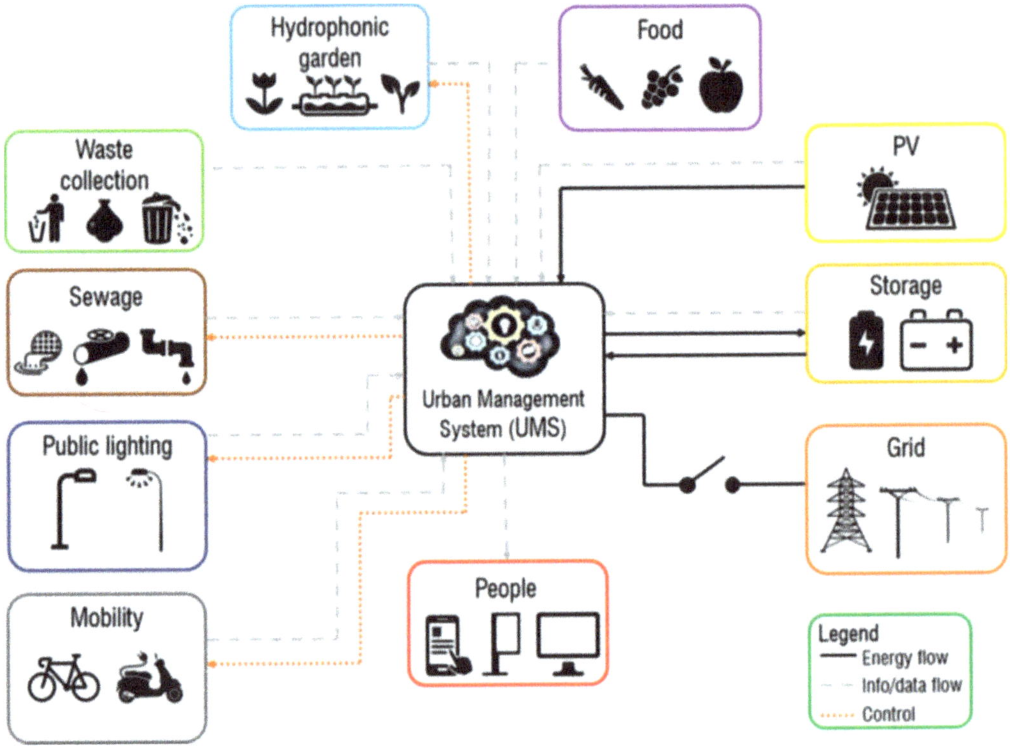

Fig. 5 Urban flow system

5 Conclusion

As was explained previously, the relocation project would enable the other sub-projects to proceed and create maximum unity between them on different scales. Along with creating new urban spaces and connections in local zones which immediately leads to having a smooth urban flow and a greater level of safety, it raises the ranks of other links throughout Rocinha, which become more integrated. The retrofitting phase clearly showed an advancement in numbers. The modification process in a project of this magnitude and the urban mechanisms quantitatively contributed to revealing the hidden links between the structure and performance, which are naturally measured by different indicators. Such an approach not only helped in pinpointing the key issues in Favela Rocinha and making appropriate decisions, but also provided a new diagnosis system which is measurable, objective, and performance-oriented (Fig. 7).

PolimiparaRocinha is a clear demonstration of how systemic local actions integrated with the whole can produce controlled chain reactions to induce changes on the scale of the entire favela. The proposed sub-projects will not only effectively change the different aspects of urban life in the intervention zone for the better but they will also make tangible improvements to the performance of Rocinha as a whole, even in those areas where the project does not reach. The procedure of interventions proposed by PolimiparaRocinha can easily be replicated for the other parts of the

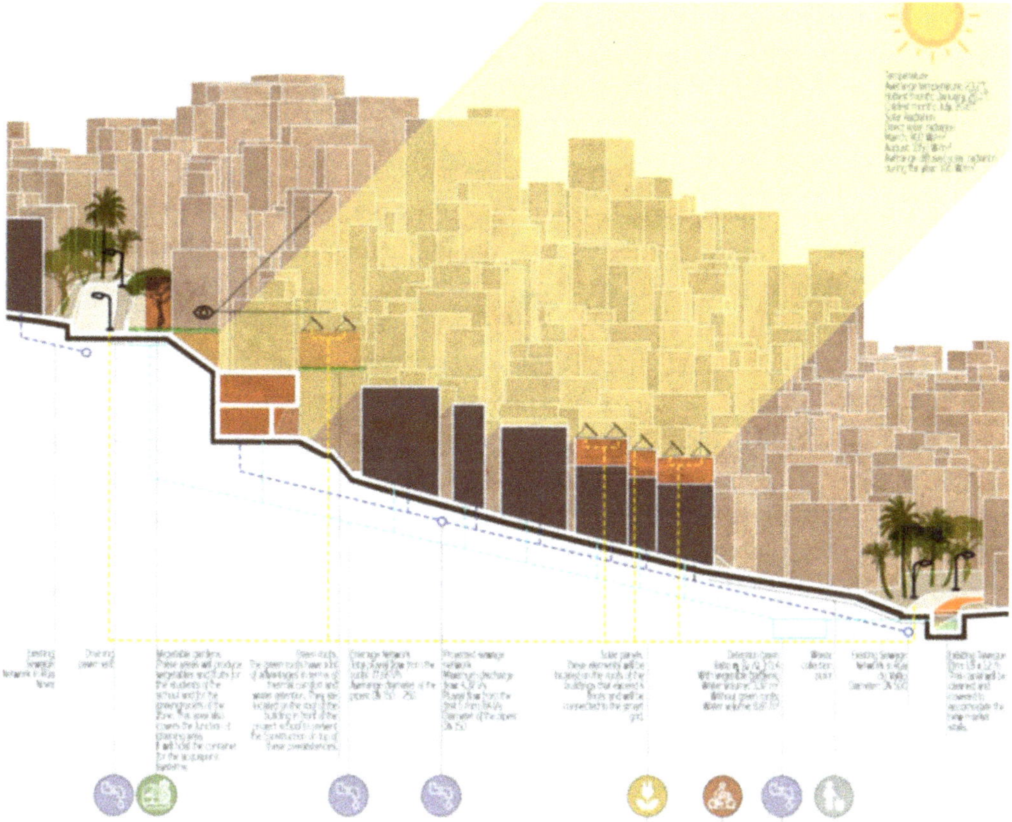

Fig. 6 Local interventions

Fig. 7 Local interface of an intervention zone before (left) and after (right) the intervention

favela and create a high level of integrity which could advance the quality of life and environmental performances therein (Arcidiacono et al. 2017).

The investigation phase highlights the structural blockage in urban flow due to the morphological pattern of Rocinha. Although there were 21 locations in which the morphological modification could create a systemic reaction on a favela-wide scale, an integrated prototype network allowed for the intervention to be applied in only six locations, still activating the same systemic reaction. The UMS designed to control the flow of energy and information is based locally and can include future intervention in Rocinha to integrate this with the whole favela system.

Today, we are facing challenges of unprecedented difficulty such as climate and socioeconomic inequity, which cast a shadow of doubt over our sustainable future. As most of the problems have their roots in cities, sustainability becomes an urban matter. While there should be a collective effort to minimize urban marginalization in future developments, the current problems of these areas should be addressed and effective methods to improve the quality of life within them should be studied. There are indeed favorable traits in the structure of the informal settlements especially in adequate energy consumption which could be learned from.

This project is not the first study proposed to deal with the favela Rocinha or with the informal settlements in general. In most of them, the informal settlements are regarded as a problem to be solved and the efforts were directed to formalize them or to eliminate them from the face of the cities. It is no surprise that they could not relate to the local communities and resulted in producing more conflicts and segregation. In contrast, PolimiparaRocinha is regarding Rocinha as an integral part of the city and a source of opportunity which with a locally based and minimal and systemic set of modifications has the potential to perform better and provide greater opportunities for integration with the rest of the city.

References

Arcidiacono, A. et al. (2017). Environmental Performance and social inclusion: A project for the Rocinha Favela in Rio de Janeiro. *Energy Procedia*.

Handy, S. (2005). Smart growth and the transportation-land use connection: What does the research tell us? *International Regional Science Review*.

Hillier, B., & Iida, S. (2005). Network and psychological effects in urban movement. In *Lecture notes in computer science (including subseries Lecture Notes in Artificial Intelligence and Lecture Notes in Bioinformatics)*.

Manesh, S. V., Tadi, M. (2013). Sustainable morphological transformation via integrated modification methodology (I.M.M): The case study of surfers Paradise District of Gold Coast City, Australia.

Manesh, S. V., & Tadi, M. (2016). A sustainable urban morphology for a greener city. *The International Journal of Architectonic, Spatial, and Environmental Design*.

Meurs, M. (2007). Understanding institutional diversity. *Comparative Economic Studies*.

Olwig, K. R. (2016). Life between buildings: Using public space. *Landscape Journal*.

Tadi, M., & Mohammad Zadeh, M. H. (2017). Urban porosity. A morphological key category for the optimization of the CAS's environmental and energy performances.

Tadi, M., Vahabzadeh Manesh, S., Mohammad Zadeh, M. H., & Zaniol, F. (2015). Transforming urban morphology and environmental perfornances via IMM® the case of Porto Maravilha in Rio de Janeiro. *GSTF Journal of Engineering Technology*.
Vahabzadeh Manesh, S., Tadi, M., & Zanni, F. (2011). Integrated sustainable urban design: Neighbourhood design proceeded by sustainable urban morphology emergence. *WIT Transactions on Ecology and the Environment*.
Wächter, P. (2011). Thinking in systems—A primer. *Environmental Politics*.

Urban Renovation: An Opportunity for Economic Development, Environmental Improvement, and Social Redemption

Paola Caputo, Simone Ferrari and Federica Zagarella

Abstract This study finds its origin within the framework of the EU-cofunded UIA-OpenAgri project, fostering the creation of small and medium enterprises in the agri-food sector, through the lens of circular economy, while also promoting the urban regeneration of a degraded peri-urban area and social inclusion of disadvantaged people. The project is led by the Comune di Milano and involves 16 partners. The ABC Department participates mainly by contributing to energy and environmental evaluations and also by supporting with tools and indicators. The first part concerned the preliminary analysis of the energy uses and potential renewable supply in the area. Within this framework, a preliminary design was included of the building energy retrofit of Cascina Nosedo, an ancient farmhouse. Other parts focus on the assessments of the food chains involved in the agricultural lands which are involved in the project.

Keywords Agri-food · Food chains assessment · Jobs and skills development · UIA-OpenAgri · Rur-urban · Circular economy

1 Introduction

In Europe, over 70% of the total population lives in urban areas, which can reasonably play a key role in pursuing a sustainable development (UIA Web site). In order to provide urban areas with resources to test innovative solutions to the main urban challenges, the European Union (EU) has launched a set of initiatives named 'Urban Innovative Actions' (UIA). Among the challenges faced, a lively debate looks at the strategic role of the agri-food sector in ensuring sustainable urban development. Broadly speaking, the agri-food sector has multidimensional implications on the economy, society, health, and the environment and is interconnected with several sectors in mutual competition for resource exploitation, e.g., fishery, forestry,

P. Caputo (✉) · S. Ferrari · F. Zagarella
Architecture, Built Environment and Construction Engineering—ABC Department, Politecnico di Milano, Milan, Italy
e-mail: paola.caputo@polimi.it

S. Della Torre et al. (eds.), *Regeneration of the Built Environment from a Circular Economy Perspective*, Research for Development,
https://doi.org/10.1007/978-3-030-33256-3_13

energy, and transportation. On a worldwide level, food production is responsible for about 30% of end-use energy, 70% of global freshwater withdrawals, and 22% of greenhouse gas emissions. Given the expected increase in the global food demand, in step with population growth, and the ongoing dietary changes due to cultural and technological attitudes, policies increasingly encourage this sector's transformation, promoting innovative agricultural practices with a reduced use of land, water, fertilizers, and energy (FAO 2017).

In this framework, under the UIA umbrella, the project 'OpenAgri-New Skills for new Jobs in Peri-urban Agriculture' (UIA-OpenAgri Web site) was launched in order to foster the creation of small and medium enterprises (SMEs) in the agri-food sector, while also promoting urban regeneration of a degraded peri-urban area and social inclusion of disadvantaged people. In detail, it promotes: an inclusive, coherent, and reflexive urban-rural food governance system; the development of an infrastructure to reduce the distance between producers and consumers and to boost circular economy; new opportunities for local quality food producers; the challenge for experimenting new forms of entrepreneurship in the agricultural sector and for creating new jobs and skills. At the core of the UIA-OpenAgri project is the creation of an 'Open Innovation Hub on Peri-Urban Agriculture' as a 'living lab' for promoting open innovation on the different dimensions of the initiative involved (entrepreneurial, social, and technological). The hub will be located in a peripheral district of south Milan, an 'urban fringe,' i.e., a peri-urban area between the urban built environment and the nearby rural areas within the surrounding parks ('Parco della Vettabbia' and 'Parco Sud'). The project site includes some existing facilities that play a key role. The ancient farmhouse Cascina Nosedo is expected to be renovated and host new functions for the coordination and promotion of foreseen activities, the agricultural area of Vaiano Valle to host agricultural enterprises; moreover, the close wastewater treatment plant (WWTP) Depuratore Nosedo, managed by Metropolitana Milanese SpA (MM SpA), and other farmhouses are important symbols of the local territory (Fig. 1).

The project involves 16 partners among municipal institutions, universities and research centers, social cooperatives, start-ups, and non-governmental organizations.[1] For its realization, nine work packages (WPs) have been set and the ABC Department is charged with contributing to WP7, 'Environmental modeling and impacts,' by defining and implementating analytical tools for supporting and monitoring the energy and environmental performances of the implemented project. Such analyses are divided into three main phases:

- the preliminary outline of the main energy and environmental figures of the project area (Caputo et al. 2017b), as outlined in Sect. 2;

[1]Municipality of Milan, Milan Chamber of Commerce, Industry, Craft and Agriculture, Fondazione Politecnico di Milano, PTP Science and Technology Park, Milan University—UniMi, Politecnico di Milano—Polimi, Poliedra, La Strada Social Cooperative, Sunugal, IFOA—Training Institute for Enterprises Operators, Mare s.r.l. social enterprise, Food partners SRL, Avanzi SRL, Cineca, Future Food Institute, ImpattoZero SRL.

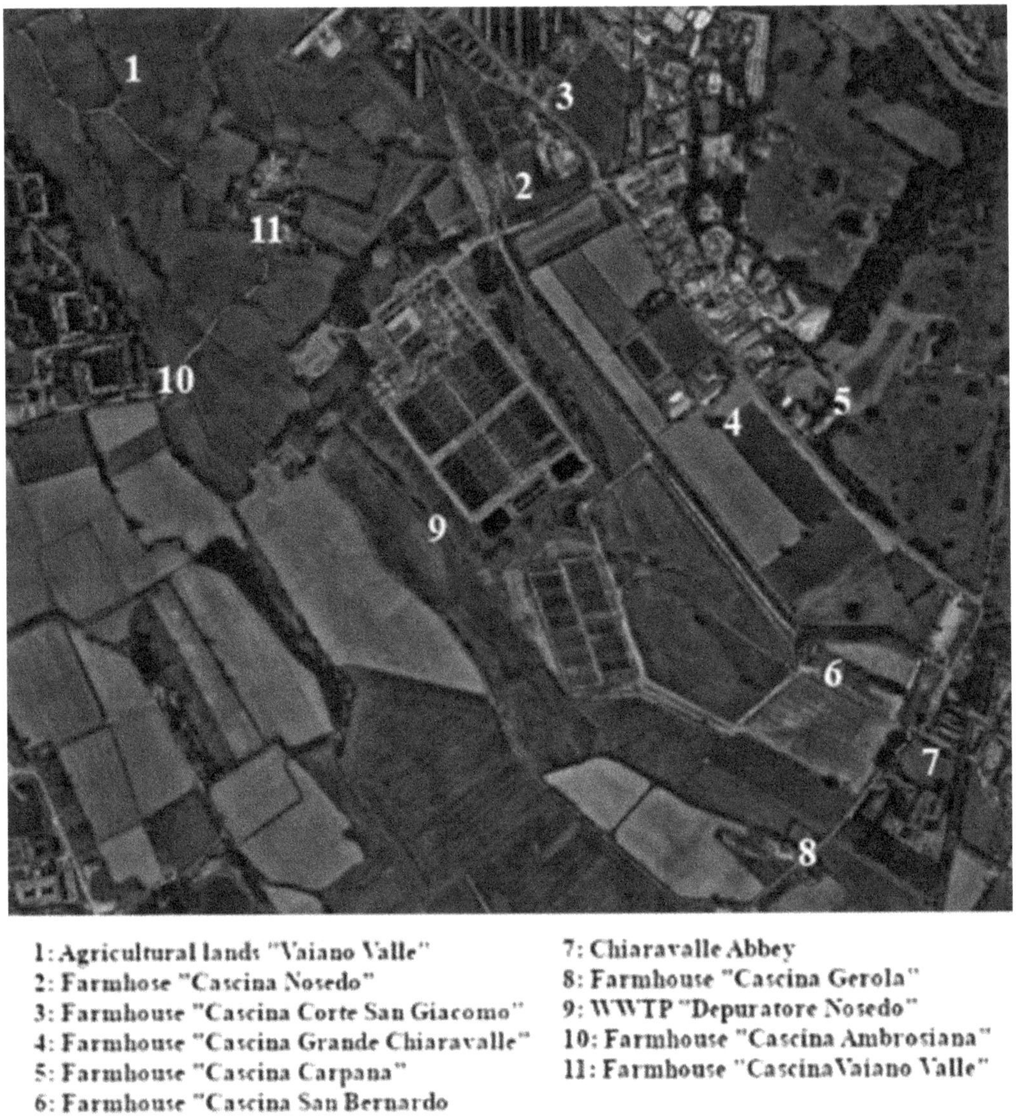

Fig. 1 UIA-OpenAgri project area

- the ongoing evaluations to evaluate the energy consumption and the global warming potential (GWP) of different food chains, as outlined in Sect. 4;
- and the final phase regarding the simulation and representation of different scenarios to provide guidelines for a low energy/carbon and efficient agri-food hub enhancing local resource exploitation and its economic and social effectiveness.

2 Main Energy and Environmental Figures of the Project Area

At the beginning of the project, the area of Cascina Nosedo was investigated in order to define the current performance of the built environment and its relation to the natural one.

The main energy and environmental figures of the project area have been intended for both the demand and the supply sides, as to follow the concept of a metabolic analysis (Caputo et al. 2016), and have been assessed according to three different spatial scales: the urban one, the whole district one (1-km radius around Cascina Nosedo), and the one corresponding to the Cascina Nosedo buildings involved in the project.

An analysis of the district built environment has been accomplished showing that the area encompasses 220 residential buildings, the majority of which was built between 1946 and 1960, and 86 non-residential ones. For those buildings, a statistic evaluation of the energy demand was carried out according to a proven method considering building age, shape, and use category (Caputo and Pasetti 2017), as described in Fig. 2.

Regarding local energy resources, by the first draft investigation, it was calculated that the potential energy production that could be obtained by installing crystalline silicon photovoltaic (PV) panels covering 75% of the residential buildings' rooftops in the district has been estimated as able to cover 80% of the electricity consumption.

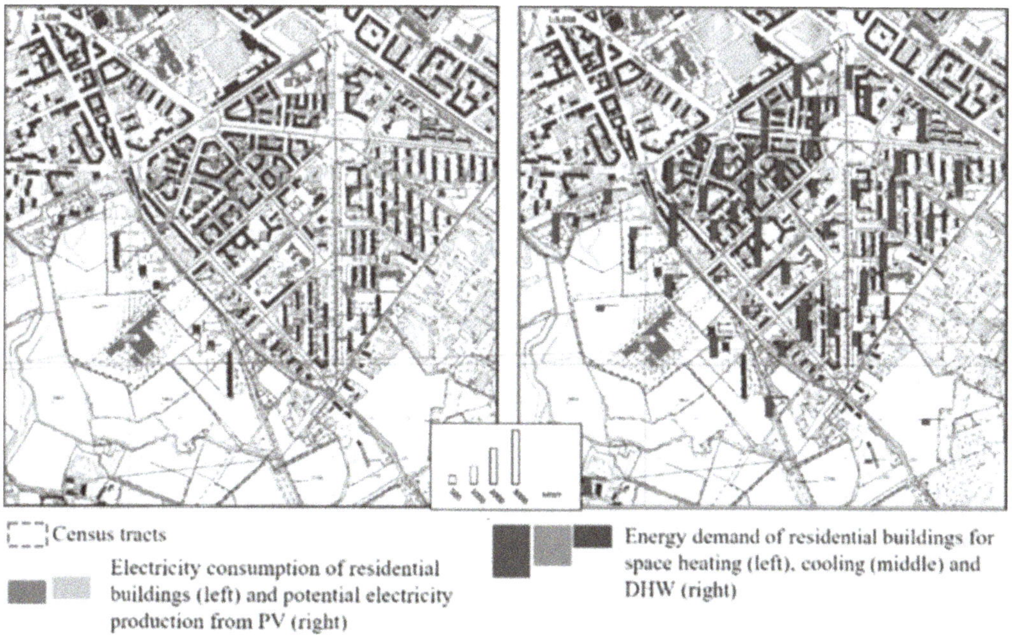

Fig. 2 Main energy figures for the district area

However, the most important local energy source is that relating to the operating WWTP. Despite not being already exploited, the plant treats about 150 million m^3 per year of wastewater that can be considered as a:

- source of heat by waste or treated water;
- source of biogas in the case of anaerobic digestion of the sludge;
- source of power (or heat and power in cogeneration) in the case of biogas use in engine[2];
- source of bio-methane in the case of upgrading of the biogas;
- source of power in the case of PV integration on the components.

Considering only the heating season, about 157 GWh could be made available by the WWTP to heat pumps, and supplying about 79 GWh of electricity, about 236 GWh could be made available as heating for buildings.

Another interesting source of heat could be the sewer collector (SC) located near Cascina Nosedo, since its temperature is generally between 10 and 20 °C, all year round. Considering only the heating season, about 37 GWh could be made available for heat pumps, and suppling about 19 GWh of electricity, about 56 GWh could be made available as heating for buildings.

2.1 Cascina Nosedo Renovation

The ancient farmhouse Cascina Nosedo (its origins date back to 1600 AD) is made up of 11 protected buildings around a courtyard. In the UIA-OpenAgri proposal, two buildings (called B9 and B10 in the following) were foreseen to undergo the energy retrofit (Fig. 3). Hence, to assess the feasibility of implementing energy efficiency measures and of the local RES integration, consistently with the protected buildings constraints, a conservation status survey was carried out to identify the elements and materials to be kept unaltered or restored.

A building retrofit scenario was proposed (Caputo et al. 2018) consisting of the replacement of windows and roofs and the opaque envelope insulation from the outer side. However, based on the Superintendence's opinion, an alternative retrofit solution, regarding the insulation from the inner side of the walls, was defined. Both retrofit scenarios, having 10-cm wood fiber panels and the same thermal transmittance, have been assessed.

A building energy model was developed with the IESVE tool, by adopting hourly data on internal gains, ventilation rates, and domestic hot water (DHW) from the swiss technical workbook SIA 2024 for five thermal zones (kitchen, restaurant, laboratory, expo/conference room, and office).

[2]Sludge anaerobic digestion with Combined Heat and Power (CHP) has been adopted in some WWTPs.

Fig. 3 Cascina Nosedo farmhouse

Then, through dynamic simulations, the energy needs for space heating, space cooling, and DHW as well as the electricity demands for appliances and artificial lights were evaluated.

In terms of annual energy needs (heating and cooling), the simulations accomplished show negligible differences between the two alternatives, while, in terms of thermal power, the external insulation scenario provides a slightly lower peak. Therefore, it can be stated that, by having an intermitting control system regime, serving many adjacent zones that are thermally independent and considering the constraints involved in a protected building retrofit, the internal insulation scenario could be the optimal solution in terms of energy behavior, architectural integration, and feasibility in this particular case of study. Of course, the results obtained are strongly affected by the software calculation method and by the assumptions carried out on the thermal zones functions that could slightly change in the definitive version of the project.

As a further analysis, considering the closed presence of the sewer collector, the possibility of extracting heat through reversible heat pumps (HPs) and exploiting it in the heating/cooling and DHW systems was analyzed. Moreover, an estimate of the potential production from building integrated photovoltaic (BIPV) was accomplished. Considering only B10, the first simulations showed that the south-western pitch presents a potential annual production of 50.7, 47.5, and 31.7 MWh in the case of monocrystalline, polycrystalline, and thin film, respectively (Table 1).

After these elaborations, the project went ahead and the executive design for the renovation of Cascina Nosedo is now in progress. Due to encountered obstacles, the renovation will consist of the refurbishment of the external floor of the whole

Table 1 Results of overall energy evaluations for B9 and B10

Energy service	Thermal energy needs [MWh/y]		HP efficiency[a] [–]	Electricity demand [MWh/y]	Potential electricity production from PVs[b] [MWh/y]
	II	EI			
Heating	32.8	39.9	4.0–5.0	9.1–7.3	
Cooling	36.4	33.7	3.0–4.0	11.7–8.8	
DHW	3.8		3.0–4.0	1.3–1.0	
Lights				46	
Appliances				71.5	
Total				139.6–134.6	50.7

[a]Seasonal performance coefficient for WWHP from (Hepbasli et al. 2014)
[b]PVs previously calculated in the case of monocrystalline technology

complex, the realization of a new dedicated electricity cabin, and the renovation of the ground floor of B10, which is expected to be equipped with reversible air-to-water heat pumps.

3 Energy and Environmental Evaluations of the Food Chains in Vaiano Valle Area

During the progress of the project, the opportunity to include an agricultural area of about 30 ha located in Vaiano Valle was presented. Despite many criticalities relating to the current abusive use, abandonment, environmental degradation, and unavailability of water for irrigation purposes, this challenging condition was integrated since it is appropriate to the implementation of an actual agri-food innovative hub (Fig. 4).

In the frame of the UIA-OpenAgri project, these lands are expected to host agricultural start-ups adopting innovative, sustainable, short, and participated food chains: **'AgriPorto'** is cultivating legumes and cereals intercropped, **'Birra per ilCorvetto'** is cultivating barley for brewing beer, **'City_organic_delivery'** would have cultivated vegetables, **'Narrare il pane'** is cultivating spelt for baking, **'Zappada'** could cultivate vegetables, **'Sinergie AgriCulturali in Vettabbia'** could set a regenerative agroforestry system (Götsch 1996) and **'Officine Agricole Milanesi'** would have integrate auomation and heliciculture.

To provide insights into the energy-envrionmental effects from the UIA-OpenAgri concepts, a set of improved scenarios is defined:

- **Intermediate implementation**: already operating agricultural enterprises (i.e., the ones that have proceeded with crop sowing by 2019) and state of the art of the B10 retrofit;

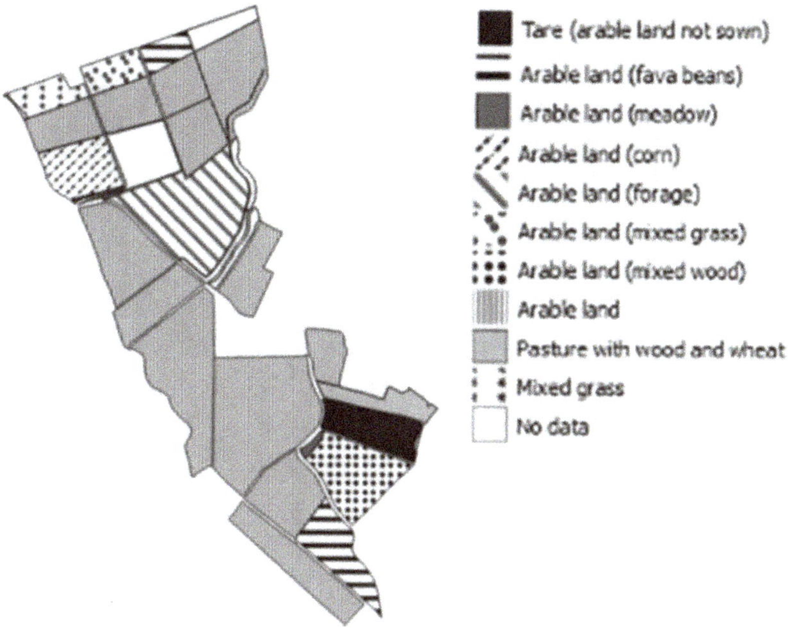

Fig. 4 Vaiano Valle area consistency before the OpenAgri project

- **Design scenario**: all the foreseen agricultural enterprises, considering the current drawbacks of the project (e.g., lack of water) and B10 retrofit;
- **Ideal scenario**: similar to design scenario but with all the needed resources (e.g., water);
- **Optimal scenario**: as ideal scenario but with an optimization of food chain management and all Cascina Nosedo buildings retrofitted.

The different scenarios have been compared to each other and to a 'Scenario Zero', i.e. referring to a different and more impactful agricultural use of the area.

The different food chains implemented in the framework of the project are investigated in order to evaluate the fossil cumulative energy demand (CED) and the global warming potential (GWP) throughout the different steps of the productive chain. To that end, LCA-based methods and tools and the relative datasets are studied, also taking into account the outlines of the previous experiences in local institutional catering (Caputo et al. 2017a).

In the frame of the UIA-OpenAgri project, an assessment of food production and, for some pilot foodchains, of its transformation and distribution are carried out with the additional aim of evaluating the relating environmental impact per equivalent hectare of the area, as to be comparable with other projects.

Potentially, other investigations could focus on: the potential quantity of biomass recovered by pruning urban trees; the needed water flow for land irrigation; the achievable share of organic food produced for the final users.

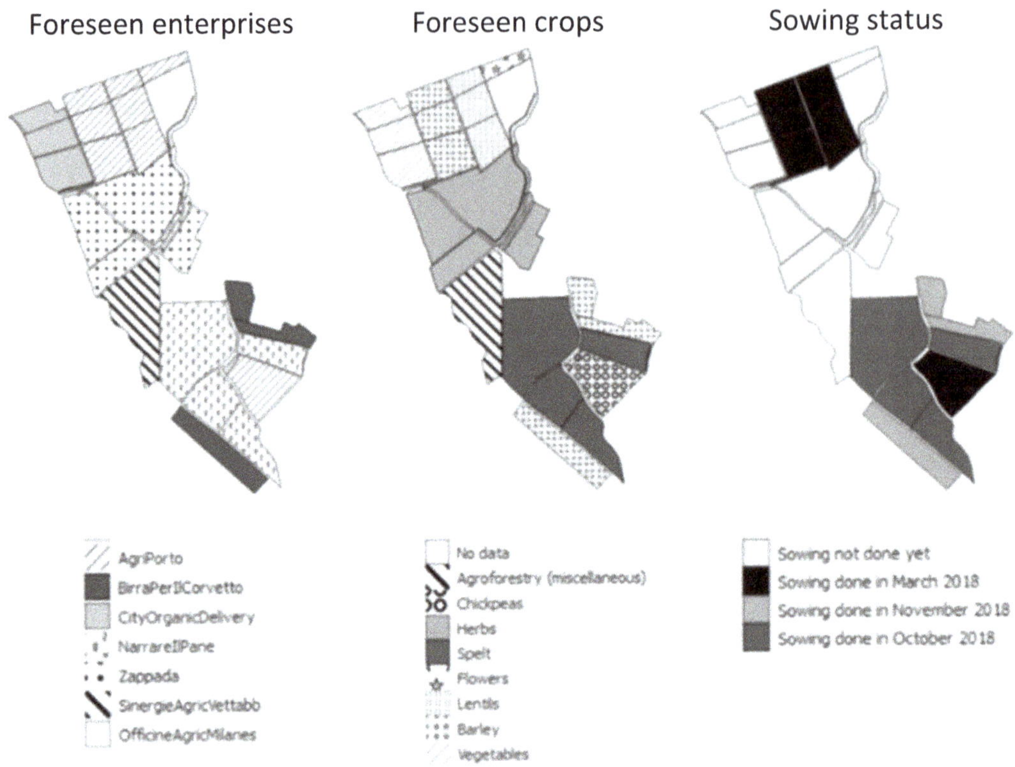

Fig. 5 Agricultural enterprises features

The mentioned evaluations are quite complex because of the data collection[3] from the involved start-ups. The collection of such primary data from the set of agricultural enterprises has been carried out in the period April-July 2019; in case of any lack in primary data, data from the proper technical literature are considered (e.g., Caputo et al. 2017a; Mistretta et al. 2019; Cerutti et al. 2018).

Figure 5 shows the foreseen enterprises, crops, and their sowing status.

4 Conclusions

This chapter introduced the state of progress of the activities of the UIA-OpenAgri project WP7 'Environmental modelling and impacts,' taken on by the present research group at the ABC Department.

The authors believe that this project could be a significant pilot experience of circular economy in rural/urban areas. The idea of enhancing jobs and skills in a compromised area provokes a buildings' renovation project which represents a real opportunity for economic development, environmental improvement, and social

[3]Type and quantity of seeds, fertilizers, pesticides, compost, mulching; fuels and electricity for the machines and for transportation; needed water; type, quality, and quantity of produced food and waste, etc.

redemption through the creation of an innovative food production hub, certainly able to attract other actors and investments at the end of the project. In fact, the UIA-OpenAgri has the merit of regenerating a degraded area, by avoiding further building construction, renovating existing buildings, promoting social inclusion, and mobilizing job resources. The experience is guided by a low carbon and high-efficiency approach aimed at optimizing the global metabolic performance of the area (Caputo et al. 2019). As examples, the following measures are foreseen: reduction of food waste; reuse of waste and materials throughout production, packaging, and commercialization phases; use of organic mulching from pruning plants in place of fertilizers. Furthermore, the project is consistent with the municipal food policy and the accomplished assessments can hopefully provide insights for developing analogous experiences in the territory. From an energy perspective, the whole district is made up of buildings with a high potential for retrofit and RES integration. Accordingly, the WWTP and the sewer collector could produce a significant supply of energy. Furthermore, biomass potential could be considered in the future.

References

Caputo, P., Clementi, M., Ducoli, C., Corsi, S., & Scudo, G. (2017a). Food chain evaluator, a tool for analyzing the impacts and designing scenarios for the institutional catering in Lombardy (Italy). *Journal of Cleaner Production, 140*(2), 1014–1026.

Caputo, P., Ferla, G., Pasetti, G., Cereghetti, N., Saretta, E., & Bonomo, P. (2017b). Deliverable D.7.5.1 First report of main figures of the project—Outline Report of the main energy and environmental figures of the project.

Caputo, P., Ferla, G., & Ferrari, S. (2018). Energy retrofit of rural protected buildings. The case of a new agri-food hub in a peripheral context in Milan. In *13th SDEWES Conference* (pp. 1–11).

Caputo, P., & Pasetti, G. (2017). Boosting the energy renovation rate of the private building stock in Italy: Policies and innovative GIS-based tools. *Sustainable Cities and Society, 34,* 394–404

Caputo, P., Pasetti, G., & Bonomi, M. (2016). Urban metabolism analysis as a support to drive metropolitan development. *Procedia Engineering, 161,* 1588–1595.

Caputo, P., Pasetti, G., & Ferrari, S. (2019). Implementation of an urban efficiency index to comprehend post-metropolitan territories—The case of Greater Milan in Italy. *Sustainable Cities and Society, 48,* 101565.

Cerutti, A. K., Ardente, F., Contu, S., Donno, D., & Beccaro, G. L. (2018). Modelling, assessing, and ranking public procurement options for a climate-friendly catering service. *The International Journal of Life Cycle Assessment, 23*(1), 95–115.

Food and Agriculture Organization of the United Nations (FAO). (2017). Adoption of climate technologies in the agrifood sector ISBN 978-92-5-109704-5.

Götsch, E. (1996). *O renascer da agricultura. Assessoria e Serviços a Projetos em Agricultura Alternativa*. Rio de Janeiro (in Portuguese).

Hepbasli, A., Biyik, E., Ekren, O., Gunerhan, H., & Araz, M. (2014). A key review of wastewater source heat pump (WWSHP) systems. *Energy Conversion and Management, 88,* 700–722.

IESVE https://www.iesve.com/support/userguides. Accessed May 7, 2019.

Mistretta, M., Caputo, P., Cellura, M., & Cusenza, M. A. (2019). Energy and environmental life cycle assessment of an institutional catering service: An Italian case study. *Science of the Total Environment, 657,* 1150–1160.

UIA-OpenAgri https://www.uia-initiative.eu/en/uia-cities/milan. Accessed May 7, 2019.

Urban Innovative Actions (UIA). (2014). https://www.uia-initiative.eu/en/about-us/what-urban-innovative-actions. Accessed May 7, 2019.

Regenerative Urban Space: A Box for Public Space Use

Elisabetta Ginelli, Gianluca Pozzi, Giuditta Lazzati, Davide Pirillo and Giulia Vignati

Abstract The essay addresses the issues of centrality and reactivation of urban public spaces, illustrating the project 'multiplyCITY: container TOOLS.' The project is composed of a system of 'devices' that can be placed in urban or natural contexts and is capable of hosting multiple functions for citizens, even in total energy autonomy. The project was presented and mentioned in the competition 'Volumezero design competition: Unbox 2017: ReThinking Containers,' completed in 2018. It consists of a system of sheltered spaces, modular, and flexible for temporary use. The system is defined by the adoption of principles assumed as design criteria: sustainability, multifunctionality, flexibility, temporariness, and customizable use. Through the combination of guiding principles, the reuse of dismissed shipping containers and the industrialized installation method, it has been possible to propose a TOOL that could be used in policies and actions aimed at urban regeneration. The design proposal has a multifunctional nature and is able to enhance the open space, assuring fast execution times and costs containment during construction, management, and maintenance. This is achievable through the use of dismissed shipping containers, which are reusable and convertible over time through minimal and low-cost interventions, offering more lives to a highly durable object.

Keywords Multifunctional tools · Shipping container · Urban regeneration · OFFGRID · Re-appropriation of public space · Circular economy

1 Cultural Background

The quality of urban spaces is expressed and marked by the environmental/ecological, human/social, structural, and symbolic functions that such spaces may adopt (Stiles 2009).

E. Ginelli (✉) · G. Pozzi · G. Lazzati · D. Pirillo · G. Vignati
Architecture, Built Environment and Construction Engineering—ABC Department, Politecnico di Milano, Milan, Italy
e-mail: elisabetta.ginelli@polimi.it

S. Della Torre et al. (eds.), *Regeneration of the Built Environment from a Circular Economy Perspective*, Research for Development,
https://doi.org/10.1007/978-3-030-33256-3_14

Compared to the planning processes of large city areas fostered by huge investments, the regeneration and the reclamation of abandoned and degraded urban spaces are often hampered by administrations due to the lack of assets. Design solutions based on the recovery, reuse, and recycling of buildings, materials, and components, within the circular economy scenario, for temporary or permanent projects are winning proposals, from both the environmental and the financial point of view (Ginelli et al. 2019).

Furthermore, urban regeneration represents a practice for the development of strategies which can overcome some critical aspects of contemporary cities: 'Innovative experiences carried out within the international context link urban regeneration to the wider governance scenario, pointing out operational behavior and research approaches that do not merely make urban regeneration as a design matter exclusive, but push it out as strategic opportunity for creating a new physical order and new, upgraded, urban performances' (Losasso 2015).

Indeed, urban regeneration is a combined set of urban/building projects and social initiatives that include the redevelopment of the built environment and the reorganization of urban assets. The main goal is the search for urban, environmental, social, and economic quality. Its outcome should be an integrated process for a continuous improvement over time. The keywords are polycentric re-balance, densification, hybridization, participation and inclusion, eco-efficiency of resources treatment, investment efficiency, economic and social enhancement.

Urban public spaces, as open unbuilt areas between buildings, play a strategic role with respect to the future of cities, assuring comfort and environmental preservation.

Nowadays, the theme of public space is extremely relevant since cities, marked by social inequalities and various limits, requires the presence of public spaces as key factors of urban relationship and participatory elements of citizen life. These spaces represent essential goods for comfort and life quality.

We are aware that urban space is considered as *place* (Augé 2009) if it is recognized as a distinctive space, an area full of sociality, participation, and symbolization, a testament of the strong link between social aspects and collective history (Dardi 1992).

The *place* is the balanced combination of space and identity, because it can make history and leave a 'memory' even in temporariness.

We assumed the concept of space, place, aggregation, shared space, network system, time, and strategy as a methodological key for the project. The combinations space/place, sharing/relationship, artificiality/nature, temporary/permanent, connectivity/integration, open/close represent essential reference criteria to design a place where the user belongs to his community.

We therefore propose the use of active and stimulating devices that meet functionality and safety requirements and are capable of triggering interaction between the cultural, social, landscape, environmental, economic, and institutional dimensions of a context: They are an active connection hub. The challenge is to design multi-dimensional and multifunctional spaces.

Indeed, the dynamism of change is representative of place quality. This statement fully explains our project proposal. Multifunctionality is hereby assumed as a mandatory characteristic for the redevelopment of public space. It is used with twofold meanings: multifunctional use of space as the interrelation between functional, social, and morphological possibilities, in which activities can be integrated and coexist simultaneously; multifunctionality over time of the object as its potential and useful transformation, guaranteeing new lives to it.

The activation of regeneration projects through a strategic approach based on a gradual reactivation, on the promotion and active involvement of multiple actors, increases the attractiveness and quality of the urban environment in order to satisfy needs and reach the greatest number of users. The result of these actions enables to 'achieve something greater than the sum of the parts,' determining an increase in the value of the space for the benefit of the community (Stiles 2009). The gradual reactivation allows for an economically feasible action, monitoring the results over time, and an urban regeneration process, replicable in different contexts thanks to its adaptability.

2 The Contemporary City as MultiplyCITY: The Framework

The contemporary city can become an experimental center of progress and creativity, also thanks to the adoption of new drivers for sustainable growth, innovation, creation and dissemination of knowledge and information: These processes tend to benefit greatly from the physical proximity and diversity offered by cities, especially the large ones (Santagata 2009).

Within the recognizable image of the city network of spaces, hierarchies, and connectivity (Lynch 1960), the public space plays a strategic role to foster city vitality, individual fruition and social condensation, becoming a magnetic space admitting aggregation, hosting activities and offering opportunities (Carta spazio pubblico 2009).

Urban open spaces of citizenship nuclei are cornerstones on which to found improvement. They are the starting points to propose a space assuming a sharing and cohesion significance, thus producing a supplementary value based on the relations it establishes between the primary functions (by design) and the complementary functions (already present on the territory) (Ginelli 2015).

The call 'UnBox 2017: ReThinking Containers' announced by Volzero[1] addresses the themes of reuse and recycling through the Realization of architectural works that contribute to the urban regeneration of city public spaces, in a scenario of multiple initiatives concerning the reference framework synthetically illustrated below and particularly the circular economy.

[1] Volzero: a digital platform that deals, through works, with the themes of architecture, design and landscape, promoting competitions aimed at young designers and students (www.volzero.com).

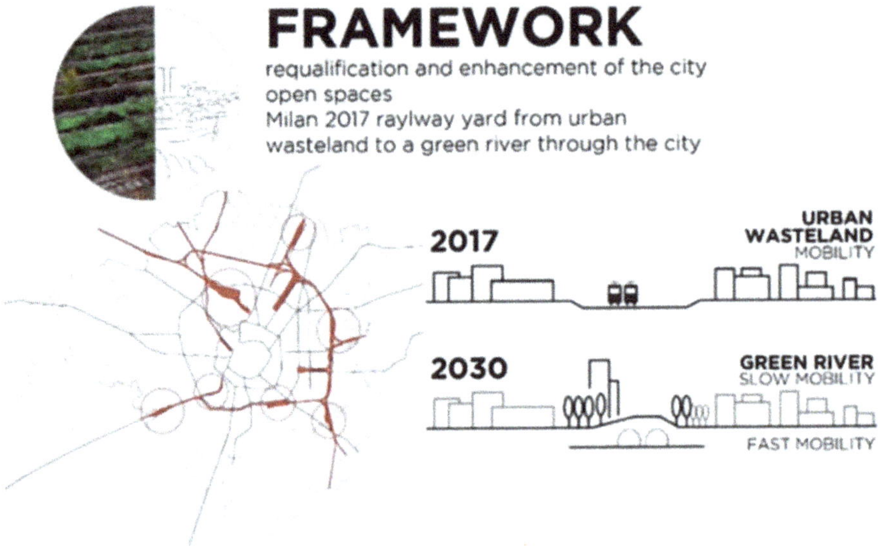

Fig. 1 Project framework: the transformation of Milan's dismissed railway yards

The call focuses on the inventive functionality of shipping containers for the large public by using them to craft space in the public environment, in order to highlight the future of the public space experiencing their new functions thanks to cutting and manufacturing carpentry interventions.

Participants from 57 countries, for a total of 323 proposals, have explored different ways of designing spaces that involve communities with solutions repositionable in every part of the world (Fig. 1).

The contextualization of the project proposal within a specific site, identified in relation to its cultural environment, was one of the evaluation criteria. In a metadesign scale, the presented proposal has been included in the initiative '*Dagli scali, la nuova Città.*' The initiative promotes a strategic vision of Milan in favor of a change in the mobility and image of the city, through the requalification and enhancement of seven dismissed Milan railway yards.[2]

3 Theme and Context

The reconversion of the railway yards is an opportunity to reconnect the suburban areas with the center of Milan. Figure 2 shows the multiplyCITY: container TOOLS placed into Porta Romana railway yard, as compared to the aforementioned seven areas: from an empty urban space to a new attraction center for sports and market.

Within the substantial urban requalification intervention of the dismissed areas, which will be redeveloped into new neighborhoods featuring large greenspots, the

[2]Iniziative organized by Comune di Milano, Regione Lombardia, and Ferrovie dello Stato (http://www.scalimilano.vision/).

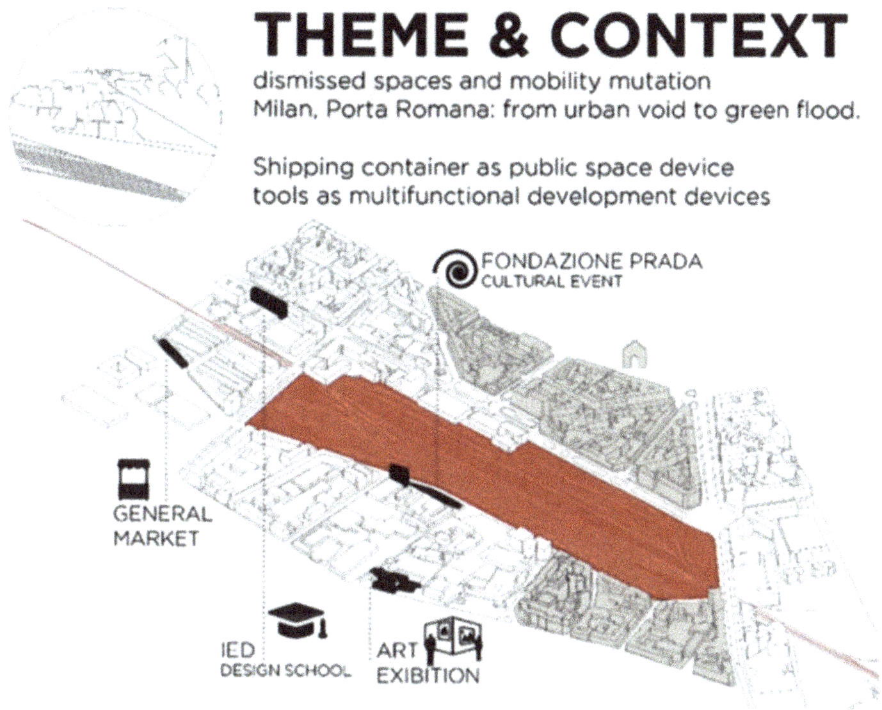

Fig. 2 Context of the project proposal: dismissed space in Porta Romana, Milan

incremental development proposal will start with a first phase aimed at enabling the use of new parks and open spaces offering enough environmental comfort when plants are not completely grown.

The solution triggers a dialogue between the surrounding areas and the designed multifunctional devices for 'public utility,' proposing a replicable model which is flexible to demographic changes and the dynamism of the site.

The developed project proposal supports urban transformation processes within open public spaces. In a logic of incremental development, the project is articulated in three temporal phases corresponding to the most significant moments of the transformation of the context:

- the first phase, following area reconversion operations, corresponds to the re-appropriation of a portion of the open space by citizens; through the project's spatial devices, a limited number of activities—including temporary ones—will be included within the area;
- the next one, a transitory phase toward the proposal's conclusion and the total reopening of the area, entails the introduction of a range of activities through different modular configurations of spatial devices. The identification of the activities with a greater guarantee of success results from the responses recorded during the first phase, which determine the diversification by functionality, user target, and temporality of use of the spaces;

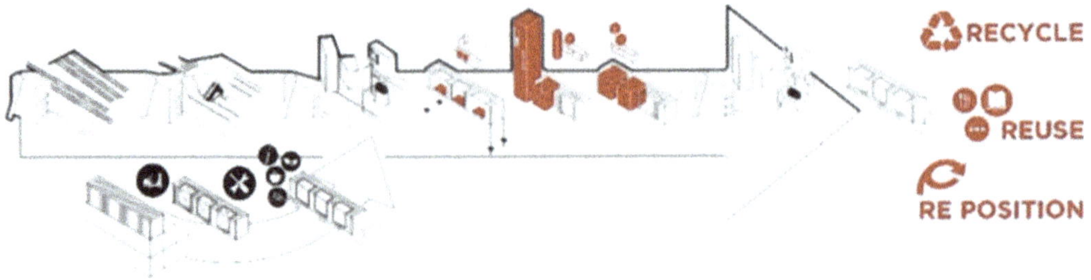

Fig. 3 'multiplyCITY: container TOOLS' main temporal phases according to incremental development

- the third phase corresponds to the total reopening of the area, in which part of the devices has been replaced by permanent structures provided by the area intervention master plan (Fig. 3).

The device can be repositioned and reused to ensure the circularity of the intervention and therefore a second life in another context, due to its possibility of being easily reusable or, in different scenarios, of being recycled or to permit the reusability of its components.

4 Multifunctional Container TOOLS

The application of a circular model for regeneration processes sees the 'Shipping Containers Building' as an urban space resource within a scenario of assets reduction through the reuse of dismissed boxes (saving additional energies and assets for the realization of new spatial objects/modules).

Shipping containers' main purpose is the transportation of goods; this characterizes their realization according to dimensional and material standards, which assure ease of transport, structural strength and global distribution (Kotnik 2008; Kramer 2015). These features, together with modularity, allow for several different conformations that lead to the adoption of design strategies being based on their reuse, through creativity and functionality; a potentiality and an economically viable solution for abandoned spaces, even in a condition of scarce resources.

The project consists of the placement of a spatial device composed, in its basic configuration, by a dismissed 40' HC shipping container (length 12,192 m, width 2,438 m, height 2,896 m). Through carpentry operations on the external cladding sheet, cuts, and openings, it is possible to increase the useful surface and arrange the metal structure. Such interventions allow to introduce further elements, for example canopies obtained from reusing the removed sheet metal, equipment elements for street furniture or the possibility to connect additional shipping containers to increase the usable space. These elements, clamped together in workshops, are called TOOLS and enable the device to react to multiple activities in a multifunctionality logic (Fig. 4).

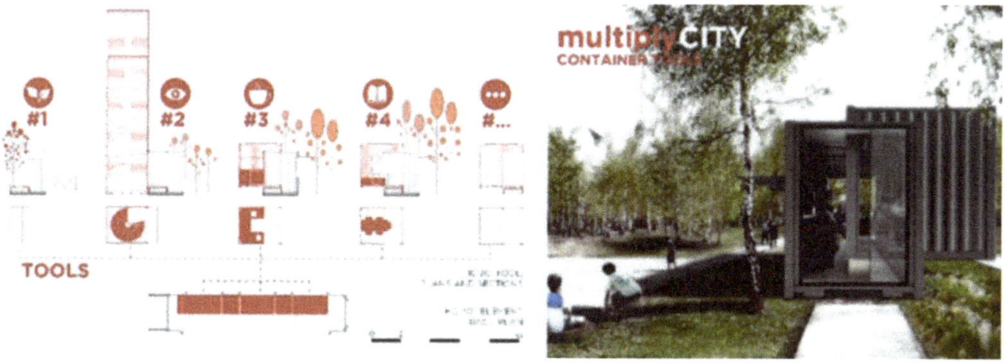

Fig. 4 'multiplyCITY: container TOOLS' multifunctional TOOLS

The TOOLS define a set of reversible solutions. The 40' HC shipping container in its basic configuration includes cutting and opening operations conditioned by two main reasons: not compromising the integrity of the steel structure and allowing the interface between the basic configuration and three models of shipping containers (10' BOX, 20' and 40' HC). The cuts and the openings have the same size as the three types of shipping containers which can be combined to define the multifunctional TOOLS, since structural components and dimensions have been standardized except for the length.

These multifunctional TOOLS enable configuration changes in order to increase the useful life of the spatial device and offer a response to the development of the context, in relation to the needs of the area and the resources available (Fig. 5).

The basic 40' HC shipping container permits different configurations by adding a first element, TOOL ∝, which is an equipped platform. This object is a support for street furniture, similar to a seat allowing the insertion of vases for growing plants, and consists of a technical compartment for lighting the area as well as some charging

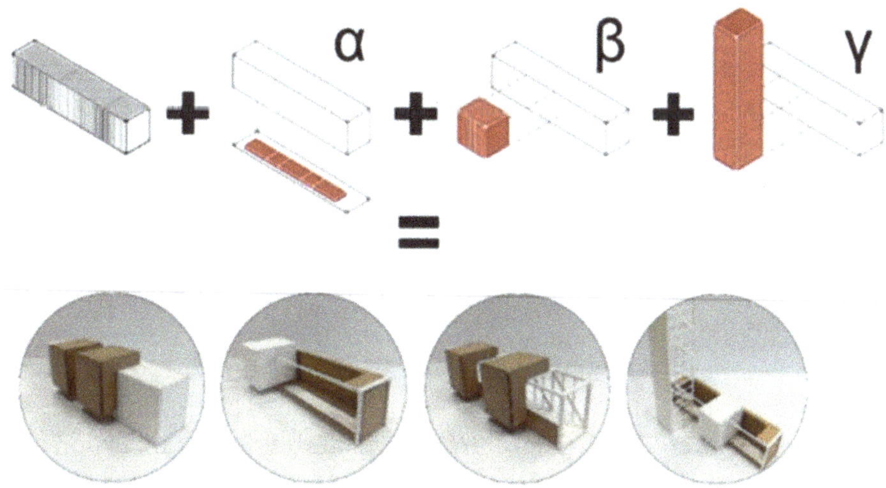

Fig. 5 'multiplyCITY: container TOOLS' multifunctional TOOLS

Fig. 6 'multiplyCITY: container TOOLS' goals of the project proposal

and Wi-Fi points for small electronic devices, if energy self-production systems are set up.

To increase the functional possibilities, the dimensions of the basic spatial device may be increased through the 10' BOX shipping containers, TOOL β, and the 20' or 40' HC shipping container, TOOL γ, here placed vertically. These elements are connected by clamping techniques, in order to facilitate assembly, disassembly, and modification operations and support the reuse of the employed material (Fig. 6).

The TOOLS provide useful services to the community in response to the requirements of flexibility, transformability, recognisability, and energy autonomy. This objective is pursued through the introduction of multifunctional spaces for meetings and exhibitions, as well as for supporting socialization and promoting sport and tourist fruition by hosting further possible functions such as playrooms, info-points with wireless connectivity, and bike-sharing services.

The project has been studied to be self-sufficient from an energetic point of view (i.e., energetic independent) thanks to the adoption of an OFFGRID solution, which makes it completely disconnected from the electricity and gas supply networks. It is powered by renewable sources, directly producing the electricity needed to meet the energy needs (Fig. 7).

Electricity is generated by photovoltaic panels placed on the roof. The produced energy is then accumulated and distributed by the equipped platform, TOOL. Among the various functional configurations, the plant system admits the inclusion of toilets, assuming the presence of water supply network in the area. The addition of data logger and remote management brings out the most performing functions, addressing the

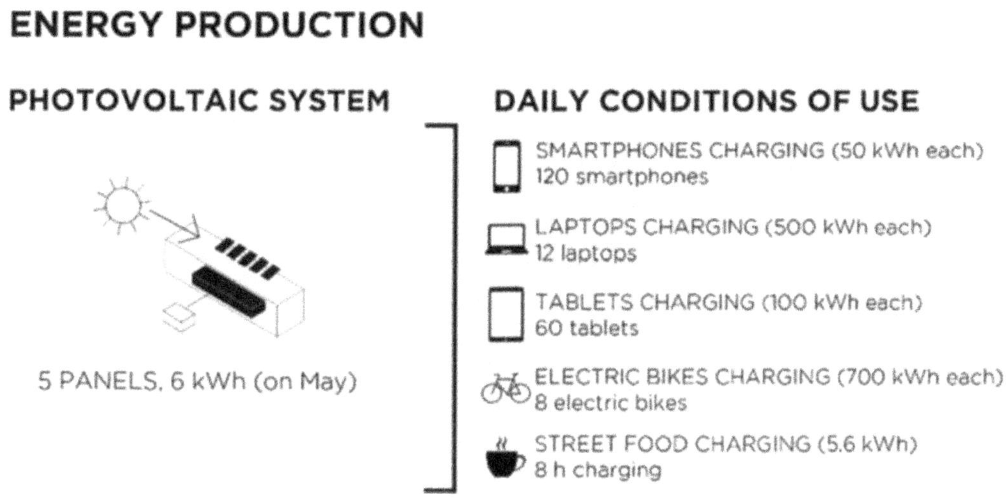

Fig. 7 'multiplyCITY: container TOOLS': possible daily use of the photovoltaic energy system produced

most useful ones. Digital data provide useful information about use frequency and environmental monitoring.

5 Conclusion: Potential and Future Developments

The proposal provides for a multidisciplinary approach (technical, social, environmental, economic, etc.) and, within a smart city scenario, refers/pertains to smart manufacturing and industry 4.0 technologies (Internet of Things, digital fabrication, etc.).

The proposed devices can become a landmark system able to acquire knowledge and to transform the environment, being disposed to adapt to the dynamism of their users while posing a minimal intervention (economic sustainability) and remaining reversible (environmental sustainability). Consistently with the incremental development for urban reactivation (institutional sustainability), it pursues multifunctionality and energy independence objectives.

The devices are able to interact and adjust to the social context in which they are placed, improving it (social sustainability); this goal is achieved through the creation of a relationship system able to expand and to 'contaminate' the urban environment that needs to be revitalized (Fig. 8).

Fig. 8 'multiplyCITY: container TOOLS': TOOL evolution within Porta Romana, Milan and possible insertion in different contexts, i.e., Parco degli acquedotti, Rome

References

Augé, M. (2009). *Nonluoghi. Introduzione a una antropologia della surmodernità*. Milano: Eèuthera. II ed (ed. or. 1992 Non-lieux. Paris: Editions du Seuil).

Dardi, C. (1992). Elogio della piazza. In L. Barbiani (a cura di), *La piazza storica italiana: analisi di un sistema complesso*. Venezia: Marsilio.

Ginelli, E. (a cura). (2015). *L'orditura dello spazio pubblico. Per una città di vicinanze*. Milano: Mimesis.

Ginelli, E., Lazzati, G., Pirillo, D., Pozzi, G., Vignati, G. (2019). Il progetto cHOMgenius: relazioni virtuose fra progetto, prodotti e impresa. in U&C. UNIFICAZIONE E CERTIFICAZIONE 5 2019.

INU Istituto Nazionale di Urbanistica. (2013) Carta dello Spazio Pubblico.

Istituto Nazionale di Urbanistica. (2009). Carta dello Spazio Pubblico, Roma: INU.

Kotnik, J. (2008). *Container architecture*. Barcellona: Links.

Kramer, S. (2015). *The box, architectural solution with container*. Salenstein: Braun Editore DA AGGIUNGERE IN ARTICOLO CHOMGENIUS.

Losasso, M. (2015). Rigenerazione urbana: prospettive di innovazione. in Techne TECHNE 10 2015.

Lynch, K. (1960). *The image of the city*. Cambridge: The MIT Press.

Santagata, W. (2009). *Libro bianco sulla creatività. Per un modello italiano di sviluppo*. Milano: Università Bocconi Editore.

Stiles, R. (a cura di). (2009). Manuale per spazio urbano. Istituto di disegno e architettura del paesaggio. Politecnico di Vienna.

Slow Mobility, Greenways, and Landscape Regeneration. Reusing Milan's Parco Sud Decommissioned Rail Line as a Landscape Cycle Path, 2019

Raffaella Neri and Laura Anna Pezzetti

Abstract This study is part of the EU-GUGLE project FP7 and aims at integrating a demonstration pilot case for the improvement of the efficiency of buildings with experiences of mitigating urban connection system and cycling lines on a district scale along with peri-urban landscape recovery. This is achieved through the correct management of the distributed green areas in order to improve the overall efficiency and the optimization of slow mobility pathways (cycle and pedestrian) in order to reduce the use of cars, while guaranteeing the best conditions of usage (mitigation, shading, resting points and services, safety, etc.), and coherent insertion within the public transport network. The study explores a peri-urban connection system in Milan integrating different kinds of green infrastructure while also analyzing them through specific design solutions. The recovery of a dismissed railway is explored through design for its landscape potential, thus proving the resilience of the city's urban palimpsest.

Keywords Slow mobility · Mitigation paths · Green infrastructure · Decommissioned railway recovery

1 The District's Scale

The research is part of the EU-GUGLE FP7 project for improving existent districts' and buildings' energy efficiency through retrofitting and develops the integration of mitigated urban paths and spaces, reusing existing railway lines and roads while connecting to major district facilities. The scale of the analyzed area allows to reconsider the relationships with public space and territorial transport networks to optimize the transport system by establishing a hierarchy between the different types of paths

Design Group: Raffaellla Neri and Laura Pezzetti, coordinators, with Alessia Cerri, Maria Giulia Atzeni, Heken Kanamirian, Li Kun. Sergio Croce, Marco Prusicki, consultants.

R. Neri (✉) · L. A. Pezzetti
Architecture, Built Environment and Construction Engineering—ABC Department, Politecnico di Milano, Milan, Italy
e-mail: raffaella.neri@polimi.it

S. Della Torre et al. (eds.), *Regeneration of the Built Environment from a Circular Economy Perspective*, Research for Development,
https://doi.org/10.1007/978-3-030-33256-3_15

(pedestrian, cycling, driveways, etc.) and levels of roads (highway, crossing, local, zone 30 km/h, etc.), to realize an effective connection with the public urban mobility systems, and thus to reduce the use of cars in favor of slow mobility systems designed as greenways. Furthermore, slow mobility and greenways aim at ensuring the interconnection of both urban and local services in order to avoid peripheral conditions and guarantee the presence of green and collective urban spaces.

The intervention at district scale is also decisive in ensuring the economic sustainability of existing buildings' energy retrofit interventions. On the other hand, the district scale is also appropriate to explore interventions that reaffirm the urban identity of peri-urban places. The need to ensure the optimization of the existing buildings thus involves the relationship with the city, taking into account both functional integrations (the complementarity between housing and facilities, schools, leisure and commercial activities), urban-scale facilities, and accessibility.

A city is 'smart' if the sustainable renewal of the whole promotes a vision of urban, architectural, and environmental quality that impacts positively on the life quality of its inhabitants, their sense of belonging, and the resulting urban and civil behaviors (ISPRA 2015; XI Rapporto ISPRA 2013; UNHS 2009; RETICULA 2013).

2 The Demonstration Areas and Their Historical Transformation

The demonstration areas of EU-GUGLE belong to a wide urban–rural system in the southeastern region of Milan, between two strategic areas for urban transformation (ATU), Porto di Mare and Rogoredo. The areas are endowed with mixed features ranging from high environmental, heritage and landscape quality, to a segregated district near a new development area.

The municipality of Milan has identified three buildings on which to apply retrofitting initiatives with regard to the research project. These are two residential buildings and a school located in two neighboring but clearly distinct areas: a residential building and a kindergarten in the Rogoredo area, near the transformation site of the Santa Giulia District and two residential buildings belonging to a single unit in the Chiaravalle area.

Although the two areas are relatively close, their characteristics and history show almost opposite developments, transformations, and conditions. The two sites are now separated by several major infrastructures, such as the southern railway that also includes the high-speed line and the junction to the east expressway. They are almost insurmountable infrastructures that highlight the historical division and the factor of isolation from the center and 'consolidated city.' They have developed according to different logics: Chiaravalle preserved its agricultural characteristics, while Rogoredo-Santa Giulia became an industrial site.

The historical transformations of the site explain the present characteristics while providing valuable indications concerning the main criticalities and the possible points of intervention.

The Chiaravalle District, thanks to its isolation, limited development, agricultural nature, many green areas, and the Vettabia Park, does not require significant mitigation issues but lacks adequate and equipped social spaces. The few existing paths are not shaded and do not provide any kind of additional service. Due to the proximity to the ancient Abbey and the agricultural land, the Chiaravalle hamlet is not affected by expansion projects. The north part of district, instead, is part of the ATU Porto di Mare's redevelopment project.

In the perception of its inhabitants, the district suffers from isolation with respect to other parts of the city, laying beyond the railway and lacking urban connection to the road network and public transport system.

The Rogoredo station (suburban railway, high-speed railway line, and underground yellow line) although relatively close is separated by the presence of the expressway that makes the access to the station difficult, limited to a one-lane road. The area has a tourism potential due to the presence of the historical Chiaravalle Abbey and the potential connection to cycling trails and paths leading to the countryside and the Abbeys of the territory (Valle dei Monaci).

Between the village and the Abbey is the abandoned Rogoredo-Poasco railroad track. The project demonstrates the potential of this infrastructure that has been thus far considered as a barrier. At present, the first effect of its dismantling is the elimination of the crossing between the Abbey and the hamlet, which re-establishes better connections and favors the tourism relaunch of the site (Fig. 1).

Fig. 1 Areas of the EU research with the exiting and designed cycle paths

The Rogoredo-Santa Giulia area faces an opposite situation: is an industrial brownfield that has lost the identity of the nucleus that developed around it. It is fenced in by the road interchange system and the railway, which represents a potential but also a problem. The area has captured the interest of an ambitious project for the construction of the new Santa Giulia District (in the area of the former Montedison steelwork company Redaelli, PII 2005, Project N. Foster, P. Caputo partnership), which, left unfinished, failed to renew the identity of the area. A new project is now ongoing.

Urban and social segregation, disorder, heterogeneity, and lack of social spaces and facilities characterize this part of the city, although it enjoys both rail and metropolitan connections (underground yellow line).

3 Integration of Green and Cycling Paths in Milano's Smart Districts

Mitigated and cycling paths form the support structure for 'slow mobility' intercepting and directing consistently the localization of district facilities while assuring new uses of the city and urban relationships. Advanced communities have started to rethink their own development processes, leading to new open strategic options in view of a change in their overall behavior. One of the benefits is a new rising sensibility toward 'slow mobility (Croce et al. 2017).'

The part of the city in which the EU-GUGLE interventions are carried out has therefore emphasized the need to rethink and reorient the slow and cycling mobility not only in a radial direction, connecting the suburbs to the downtown, but also in a circular direction to reconnect districts which are isolated from infrastructures, enhancing their proximity to peri-urban parks and their access to connection hubs (FS Rogoredo station, subways), oting green lines and finding a new use for neglected infrastructures, such as disused railways, provides an opportunity for low carbon travel experiences since reconversion policies promote new uses, arrest decay processes, and re-establish continuity in the environmental system, using existing linear infrastructures. Consequently, the decommissioned railroad recovery has become a focus of redevelopment projects in many European countries. Green lines implementation and Rogoredo-Poasco decommissioned railroad recovery has been assumed by the research and Milan Municipality as a major opportunity to connect with the many ATU (urban transformation areas) and peri-urban projects that so far were not considered in a comprehensive frame of the smart city and low-carbon city concept.

Pedestrian and cycle connections are also means to trigger sustainability processes relating not only to mobility and transportation but also to the subject of a 0-km production chain. The project may connect to other existing projects such as OpenAgri, the 'Open Innovation Hub on Peri-Urban Agriculture,' Sharing Cities, and Lighthouse, which are located in the area.

The project also reconnects the EU-GUGLE-renovated buildings to the new ongoing masterplan of Santa Giulia, extending the connection of mitigated cycling and pedestrian paths to the surrounding areas and the intermodal Rogoredo station. Mitigated and cycling paths form the support structure for 'slow mobility' intercepting and directing consistently the localization of district facilities while assuring new uses of the city and urban relationships (Figs. 2 and 3).

4 The Plan: New 'Green Lines' Combined with Smart City Concepts

The PUM (Milan's Mobility Plan, Osservatorio PUMS—Piano Urbano della Mobilità Sostenibile) establishes the general network and defines priorities. It is developed on a large urban scale, so it is not consistently related to urban transformation projects nor specifically defined on a district scale.

It has been analyzed and integrated by the project concerning the green and cycling paths, introducing a number of modifications in order to connect it consistently to the opportunities emerging from site-specific conditions and smart district concepts. The new cycling paths aim to be innovative green infrastructures, identifying different levels of complexity and smart city concept integration according to each specific urban situation (ISPRA 2010).

The project has provided a set of principles capable of combining holistically the issues relating to 'slow mobility,' to 'green infrastructures' (GI), and to 'urban forestation' (UF), while enhancing their role as 'green social streets' within urban and landscape redevelopment projects. The goal of these principles is to reduce the ecological impacts of urban space fragmentation and support the multifunctional potential of green trails in organizing urban connections and heat island abatement.

In order to achieve these goals, greenways, ecological corridors, and ecological networks need to be planned and constructed within the concept of 'connectivity.'

On the other hand, the aim of the greenway strategy has been related to three ecosystemic services: cutting air pollutants, cutting risks of water outflow, and reducing temperatures.

The masterplan identifies a set of cycling and pedestrian lanes that are connected in a unique network with already existing and planned paths in the new Santa Giulia District. The green streets system consists of a network of shaded streets that connect residential and public buildings in the two parts of the district that are still suffering from isolation and a lack of services and are the focus of *urban oases* that link mitigated parking areas within a 300-m radius and district facilities (especially schools). These lanes are intended as 'green social streets,' intercepting a number of social places, and are endowed with urban oases where different facilities are provided according to their hierarchy (level of the street) and specific urban situation: shade, seating, bio-ponds, water and electricity supply, bike sharing or car sharing,

Fig. 2 Chiaravalle area: plan and sections of the cycle paths

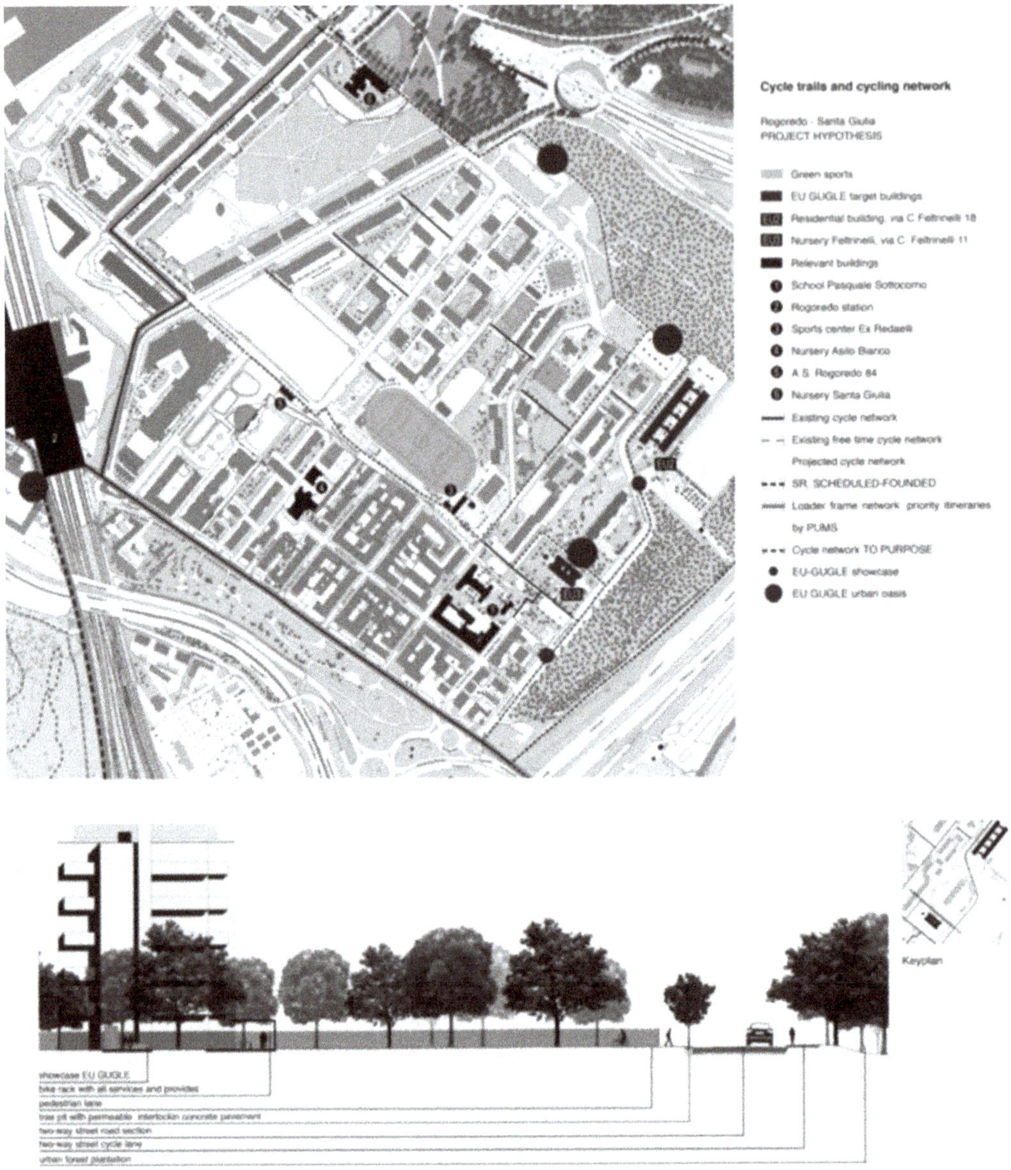

Fig. 3 Rogoredo—Santa Giulia area: plan and cycle paths

interchange with subways and railroads, LED public lighting, ICT platforms, smart parking control, and 'zone 30' areas.

The insertion of new collective places guarantees livability and safety to the routes, privileging green-planted spaces, reorganized and rehabilitated, strengthening the retrofit projects applied to the individual buildings and improving environmental quality and well-being.

In addition to the sequestration of CO_2 by the tree cover, which, however, to be significant cannot be separated from the reduction in its production, the tree structures provide shading and cooling. They also bring social, psychological, hygienic-sanitary, environmental, and energy-related benefits, along with induced labor-related benefits (Bonafè 2006; Morabito et al. 2015).

In addition to mitigating routes and providing shade for resting places, the planned trees provide green bands with the purpose of cooling and mitigating the noise pollution that is present in this area. Specifically, the cycling lanes and the break areas take on different meanings:

- the connection between the different parts and the Rogoredo station, which represents the closest metropolitan public transport hub. As it is significantly close to both areas, yet perceived as distant (especially from Chiaravalle due to the difficulty of access), the protected cycling lane represents the possibility of reconnecting to the center and to other parts of the city;
- the connection of the new routes to a system existing and planned urban cycling lanes, still fragmentary. In this way, the network would allow users to reach central parts of the city of Milan through a safe, secure, and relatively short cycling path, equipped with services and rest areas;
- the connection with external routes on a territorial scale, which concerns leisure activities, the relation with the agricultural countryside to the south and with the historical heritage, Abbeys, farms, hydraulic works, etc. The connection involves also the Forlanini and Lambro Parks. This would favor the development of slow and sustainable tourism, especially at Chiaravalle.

The planned continuity of green areas provided by the green lines and cycling paths allows for better air circulation within the urban and peri-urban districts. In addition to the implementation of the new planned green connections, the ecosystemic complexity of the areas will also be enhanced through a reforestation initiative along the northern tracks of the railroad (Porto di Mare southern area).

In cities, including Milan, the function of rows of trees is usually reduced to the mere shading of the streets. The mitigation of pedestrian areas, cycle paths, and neighborhoods' living spaces becomes a goal to guarantee conditions of thermo-environmental well-being in the urbanized space, a need induced by the urban heat island (UHI) phenomenon. Enhancing the cooling capability through vegetation along green lines and selecting vegetation with a high density of foliage and resistant to water scarcity will help to provide shade for the soil, which will stay moist and fresh for longer. This means to integrate this new conception of infrastructures in the regeneration or development projects for public spaces and an appropriate synergy with the location of district facilities (Comune di Firenze, no date).

5 The Recovery and Landscape Resilience of the Rogoredo-Poasco Decommissioned Railroad

A new crucial role is emerging for the reuse of disused rail lines worldwide. Italy has also proposed a law for the realization of a national network of slow mobility, based on intermodality between biking, walking, leisure trails, and local railways, which promotes green mobility, landscape resilience, physical activity of people, recreation, tourism, and safeguarding of the diffused territorial assets.

The recovery of a 4-km decommissioned railroad as a connection route and landscaping cycling appears to be a priority. It would assure a connection not only between districts, but also to a regional and national cycling system, stitching up a multitude of itineraries that are still fragmented.

The route would join the underground station and the interchange node of Rogoredo, intercepting the crux of the two major areas: the Abbey with the town of Chiaravalle and the large school and sports grounds, i.e., the very civic core of Rogoredo. The systemic potential of this short stretch extend, on the one hand, to the landscape enhancement of the system of the Vettabia valley, Abbeys, farms, parks, and paths to which the neighborhood of Rogoredo, which is today confined to an infrastructural enclave, would connect (Forlanini Park, Vettabia, and South Park).

The 'landscape cycling' project here developed looks to two strategies that are economically sustainable and focus on the resilience of the railway track: its reuse through special bicycles hooked on the rails, along the scenic stretch (from Chiaravalle as far as Nosedo); a cycling path flanked by a system of multipurpose mobile elements (pergolas, pedestals, chairs, small pavilions) along the flat stretch of the urban cycling route (from Chiaravalle to Rogoredo), so as to constitute an equipment in support of multiple initiatives that can take place throughout the year.

At the same time, the green railroad would constitute an effective permanent 'showcase' path of Milan's sustainability agenda, aiming to promote education in sustainable behavior along the cycling path itself. Along the paths, a number of meaningful urban locations are identified that relate to the presence of existing facilities. The design proposes two kinds of showcase components: the larger ones are more complex and integrate panels disseminating EU-GUGLE's good practices to be implemented in a smart city, seating, water supply; the smaller ones are simple as they consist only of replaceable panels. Together they give rhythm and continuity to the 'sustainability' landscape path (Fig. 4).

Fig. 4 Reuse of the decommissioned Poasco-Rogoredo railroad as a cycling trail passing through Chiaravalle

References

Bonafè, G. (2006). *Microclima urbano: impatto dell'urbanizzazione sulle condizioni clima tiche locali e fattori di mitigazione.* Report ARPA 2006 Area Meteorologia Ambientale—Servizio-Idro Meteorologico—ARPA Emilia-Romagna.

Croce, S., Fiori, M., & Poli, T. (2017). *Città resilienti e coperture a verde.* Santarcangelo di Romagna (RN): Maggioli editore.

ISPRA. (2010). *Verso una gestione eco-sistemica delle aree verdi urbane e peri-urbane.*

ISPRA. (2015). *Il consumo del suolo in Italia Relazione annuale Comitato per lo Sviluppo del Verde Pubblico,* Ministero dell'ambiente e della tutela del territorio e del mare, 30 maggio 2015.

Migliori pratiche per la gestione sostenibile delle acque in aree urbane. Linee Guida per unregolamento del verde, Comune di Firenze, Agende 21 locali.

Morarbito, M., et al. (2015). *Urban-hazard risk ana lysis: mapping of heat-related risks in the elderly in major ltalian cities.* PLOS.org.

Planning sustainable cities global report on human Settlements, United Nations Human Settlements Programme, 2009.

RETICULA n. 4/2013 *Climate change, naturalità diffusa e piani ficazione territoriale*

XI Rapporto ISPRA "Qualità dell'ambiente urbano" Edizione 2015.

Standards and Laws

Disegno di legge n. 1734, *Riconversione ecologica delle città e limitazione al consumo di suolo.* Senato della Repubblica - Comunicato alla Presidenza, 23 dicembre 2014.

Disegno di legge n. 2383, *Contenimento del consumo del suolo e riuso del suolo edificato.*

Legge 14 gennaio 2013, n. 10, Norme per lo sviluppo degli spazi verdi urbani (G.U. n. 27 dell'l febbraio 2013).

UNI/PdR 8:2014 Linee guida per lo sviluppo sostenibile degli spazi verdi - Pianificazione, progettazione, realizzazione e manutenzione.

Nature and Mixed Types Architecture for Milano Farini

Adalberto Del Bo, Maria Vittoria Cardinale, Martina Landsberger, Stefano Perego, Giampaolo Turini and Daniele Beacco

Abstract The project presented here, carried out within a research framework on abandoned railways areas in Milano, faces the issues of building an urban part by looking at the future city with particular attention to the themes of living into the relationship with nature. The project, starting from the analysis of the urban role of the area, gives relevance to the main directions built by the city construction and to the north-west direction of the city expansion. A central importance is given to the park as primary element of the urban structure made up by blocks not entirely surrounded by roads fostering a significant internal traffic reduction. The second element concerns the deep research content of building typological natural experiments and the character of originality achieved by further examination carried out on the plan and housing design, with attention also to the solution based on the typological contamination. The park displacement in the plan central area is the decisive event of the project in relation to the urban reference scheme of which persist the main lines and the urban step rhythm, considered the most significant architectural elements along with the twin towers located in north-west. The studies on the patio-houses settlement and on the multi-storey linear building enrich the variety of building forms and characters together with the design of the mosque as element of a multicultural and open new city.

Keywords Nature · Mixed types · Urban composition · Continuity · Tradition

---

A. Del Bo (✉) · M. Landsberger · D. Beacco
Architecture, Built Environment and Construction Engineering—ABC Department, Politecnico di Milano, Milan, Italy
e-mail: Adalberto.delbo@polimi.it

M. V. Cardinale · S. Perego · G. Turini
Milan, Italy

S. Della Torre et al. (eds.), *Regeneration of the Built Environment from a Circular Economy Perspective*, Research for Development,
https://doi.org/10.1007/978-3-030-33256-3_16

1 Introduction

The project presented here, carried out within a research framework on abandoned railway areas in Milano, faces the issue of building an urban part by looking at the future city with particular attention to the themes of living and to the relationship with nature.

An important point concerns the identification of an urban structure made up by blocks not entirely surrounded by roads (located on three sides with the terminals as cul-de-sac) and directly connected to a large park located in a central position as an element of organization and order of the whole plan.[1] The structure behaves with a significant internal traffic reduction and the possibility to reach the park and the public buildings without crossing roads. The structure of the settlement proposed is directly referred to the city idea drawn by Ludwig Hilberseimer, of which the project also offers the characteristic mixed housing typologies (in particular high-rise and low-rise buildings) able to achieve the required density.

The second element concerns the deep research content of building typological nature experiments (about which the next interventions deal) and the character of originality achieved by further examination carried out on the plan and housing design, with attention also to solutions based on typological contamination.

The park displacement in the plan central area is the decisive event of the project in relation to the urban reference scheme of which persist the main lines and the urban step rhythm, considered the most significant architectural elements along with the twin towers located north-west.

In this context, the assumption of the railroad direction as the main reference of the project guidelines in the north is a relief matter: indeed, the directions expressed by the dialectic of the different positions constitute a very important point of the urban project because through them, we tend to express an evaluation on the city and its constituent parts.

In the northern part of the Dergano–Bovisa area, the high level of disorder represents an element of uncertainty that is difficult to use as a reference, while in the south (beyond the railways), the confirmation to the Corso Sempione direction constitutes a substantial adhesion to the prevailing layout of the historical city (Fig. 1).

[1]Adalberto Del Bo, La costruzione di un'idea di piano. La nuova città oltre l'isolato, in La Casa, Milano 2013, a cura di G: Malacarne.

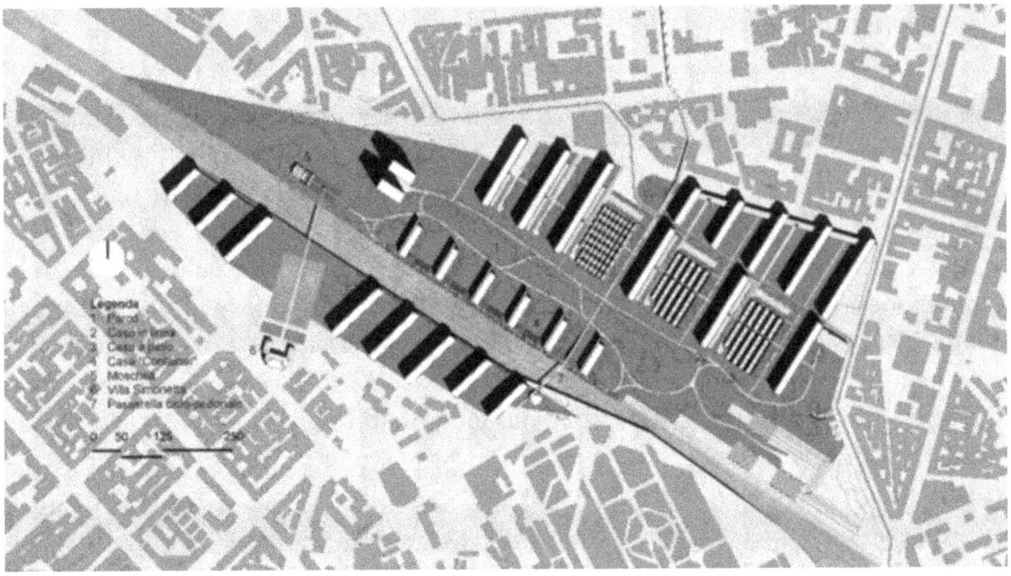

Fig. 1 Milano Farini. Site plan with shadows

2 Patio-house: A Living Type

"The architecture is placed in the space and at the same time encloses it. From this arises a double problem: the control of external and internal space (…)". These words by Ludwig Hilberseimer summarize the meaning of the project by Mies van der Rohe for a three-courtyard house. The project was designed, probably, from 1934. The theme is the development of a sort of single-family home prototype. The design consists of the definition of an enclosure within which the house is freely composed. The enclosure also defines the separation between the internal and private home space and, depending on the possible different locations, the natural or urban outdoor space.

Mies van der Rohe drawings describe the character of the project: an introverted building whose relationship with the outside is realized by a small, but necessary, entrance door; a uniform brick façade and a thin slab covering the interior space which—as we can see in the plan—occupies only a part of the enclosed garden.

Inside the enclosure, the T-shaped plan defines three courts, different in character and size, which establish different relationships with the parts of the house facing inside them. The large living room looks onto the space of nature that is a real walled garden, while the service areas look on the smaller and paved courtyards. In this way, from any point of the covered space it is possible to see the nature of the large green courtyard and the brick wall of the enclosure.

Representing a clear idea of dwelling, Mies, with few elements, defines the character and the size of his home.

Mies van der Rohe does not invent anything but, on the contrary, seeks in the history an analogous example to be repeated not so much for the form as for the validity of the general principle proposed. Probably, his reference is the Roman house in which the direct relationship with the city is denied in favour of the definition of a "different private world".

The Roman domus is, in fact, an introverted house in which the relationship with the urban space is realized only by the necessary entrance door.

The roman house is composed around the open space of the courtyard, an element of representation of the type and a necessary part from the functional point of view. The courtyard, in fact, is the place where the various rooms of the house overlook and from which they take light and air.

As in the Mies project, originally conceived as isolated and then composed to build blocks in the city, the idea of the domus is summed up in the construction of a separation wall between inside and outside. What is important is the representation of an idea of dwelling consisting in showing the "privacy" of the family life as opposed, and alternative, to the public life.

The project of the low houses aims to reinterpret similar historical examples according to new needs and requirements in term of quantity and urban dwelling quality.

In the specific case of the realization of a new urban part, the proposed ensemble of patio houses is defined through a brick wall considered as the element which makes the composition recognizable and measurable.

As proposed by Mies van der Rohe for the three-court houses, the wall surrounds one or more patios faced by individual households. The upper floor façades of the two-storey dwelling entertain long-distance relationship with the park in which the houses are placed. According to this point of view, the wall is that fixed element able to legitimize any formal and typological variation in the construction of the individual houses.

From the typological and morphological point of view, the design envisages the construction of high-density blocks consisting of two-storey row patio houses. According to the orientation and to the relationship with the block, the design suggests two-house types. The wooden structure and the 2.50 height is constant and needed in order to contain building costs and energy wastes, as shown by international legislations.

The first house type is a T-shaped faced south-east. The single-storey T-short side contains a living room overlooking two symmetrical courtyards. The second side, on two floors, consists of three modules of which the central one, with no windows, contains the staircase leading to the sleeping area on the upper floor and to the terrace placed on the roof of the living room below.

The houses are put together to form rows arranged according to the longitudinal direction of the block and facing the storey houses. This ensures both flexibilities in the setting of the house that can be enlarged lengthwise by adding constant modules, as well as a good exposure (south-east) and the cross-ventilation of the building.

A projecting element at the upper level acts as a sunscreen for the lower floor which is almost entirely windowed because of its relationship with the garden and its collective character. Upstairs, the windows are smaller and the projection becomes a small loggia.

In order to arrange the houses to face the park crosswise to the block, the second type of low houses has been designed. The principle of structural flexibility and good orientation remains unchanged also in this case. The solution consists of two-storey row patio houses with south-east exposure. In consideration of the arrangement in the transverse direction of the block, the horizontal distribution of the house is located along the north-west wall, in order to guarantee full flexibility in the event of a possible extension.

The two-house types envisage wood as constructive system, both for the structure and the wall plug. This choice respects the actual requirements of flexibility, cost control, sustainability and speed of construction.

The intention to show the exposed structural system and the plug (the prefabrication system and the modular design allow a dry-stone construction) led to use wood as outer cladding too. The façade of the house is thus formed by a series of slats anchored to a steel structure to build a ventilated wall useful for the purpose of containment energy and durability of the building (Fig. 2).

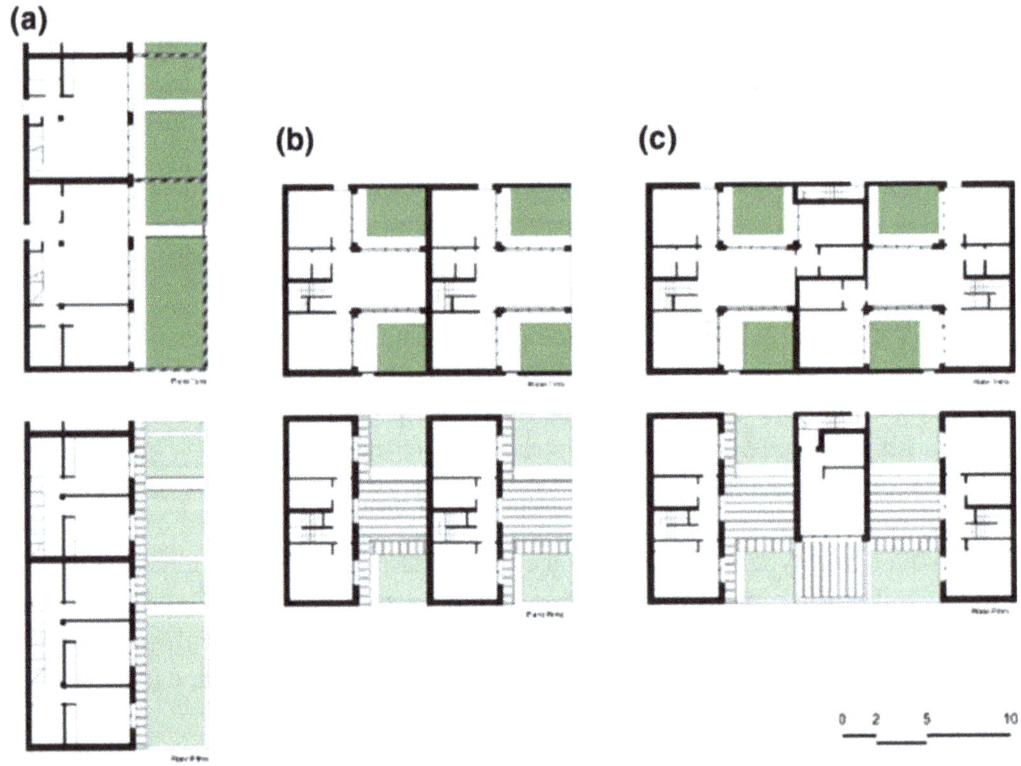

Fig. 2 Milano Farini. Patio-houses

3 Idea and Development of Multi-storey Linear Building

The settlement unit designed for Scalo Farini is defined by two elements: the courtyard house and the multi-storey linear building. Both elements are designed with common aims that can be synthesized under the terms of flexibility and standardization.

The main reference about the building studied here is placed in the townhouses designed by Mies van der Rohe at Lafayette Park in Detroit.

The starting requirement consists of a possible overlapping of the Detroit block townhouses. The aim posed consists to achieve a solution formed by duplex apartments and provided with a corridor at alternate floors.

The interest towards Detroit's townhouses is due to the progress on the typological solution that is represented. It contains the traditional characters of the townhouses although shows an interesting solution about the bedroom distribution at the first floor related to the limits of the living room at the ground floor.

Through an ingenious solution of the façade subdivision in three parts, Mies van der Rohe reached a development of the type starting from the traditional characters of the townhouse.

An analogous solution, in terms of distribution, was studied by Josep Lluís Sert for Casa Bloc, in Barcelona, 1933. Also here, the apartments are duplex served with an internal small stair that leads to the room floor where Sert proposed a similar distributive solution that will adopted by Mies in Detroit but without the same clarity about the relationship with structure, façade partition and space.

This difference in term of measure among the living room and the upper bedrooms, however, is not contained in a clear drawing of the fronts as in the case of Detroit. In fact, in Casa Bloc this problem is masked. The façade of the Casa Bloc is drawn by horizontal strips of the lodges and horizontal windows. But the windows are not related to each room: for three rooms correspond two windows and one of it is placed across two rooms. In the drawing of townhouses, Mies contains the difference within a unified design where the relationship with the steel structure is inseparable to the spatial division of the dwelling.

The design of the multi-storey linear building comes from a philological process because it is based on the original building shape designed by Mies, redrawn through the analysis of the sources as, for example, Mies's Drawings Archives, thanks to the several surveys and the different reconstructions of the original Lafayette Park proposal carried out by our resource unit about this important settlement in the last decade. However, that process is not only concerned with the reproduction of the same building but tends to develop it in a progressive way starting to the clear and not-modifiable aspects of the reference.

The comprehension of the structural system of Lafayette townhouses, reproposed in this project, represents a fundamental passage for correct knowledge. Is necessary refer to two combined homes. The sketch posed on the text side is realized for this necessity.

Mies, on the subdivision in three parts of the fronts, juxtaposed a subdivision in two parts in the main floor where are the living space that is symmetrical on the central wall division. This wall contains, in the extended measure of the stair, two pillars that sustain two beams posed in the longitudinal verse, perpendicularly to that wall.

Each living space measure 18′ width (5.40 m)–36′ (10.80 m) referred to two combined unit. The vertical elements that subdivided into three parts the façade generate three rooms on the first floor. Although, the three-vertical elements support the "C" profile edge beam.

Related to the subdivision into three parts of the front rooms on the first floor taking a suitable size. Those dimensions would not be possible if the subdivisions of the bedrooms were strictly contained into the width of the living room below.

The overlapping of three duplexes (six floors) with 2.50 m storey height on a commercial basement had required a check of the general framework and a reshaping of the structural elements. Distribution is guaranteed by a steel corridor juxtaposed on the north-west side, while on the south-east side, with the same principle, there are lodges to protect the great window of the living and the bedrooms against the sunlight in the summertime. Each part juxtaposed are related to the building structure and have a structural measure of 1.80 m.

3.1 *Students Dwelling. The Container Reuse*

Studying the student dwellings problem, instead, the group had followed a resource way marked by some European and extra-European experiences. Today, the container's reuse represents a vast interesting way of architectural resource to investigate as well shown by many realized example in north Europe.[2]

In Scalo Farini, the project is designed six buildings of which the width is obligated and corresponds to the maximum container standard, 40′ (12.20 m). The second dimension is near 60 m. On this building, in the same way of the buildings describes before, are been juxtaposed the corridor and the loggias. These buildings are posed perpendicularly to the public elevate promenade that defines the edge of the railway (Figs. 3 and 4).

---

[2]An interesting example of container's reuse is Keetwonen, in Amsterdam where, without the aid of any structural system (only particular elements in relation to the contact point of the containers) there are several five-storey buildings with distribution corridors and loggias realized with an autonomous steel structure. The depth corresponds to 12.20 m (40′), height is 2.89 m (9′) and the width is 2.43 m (8′).

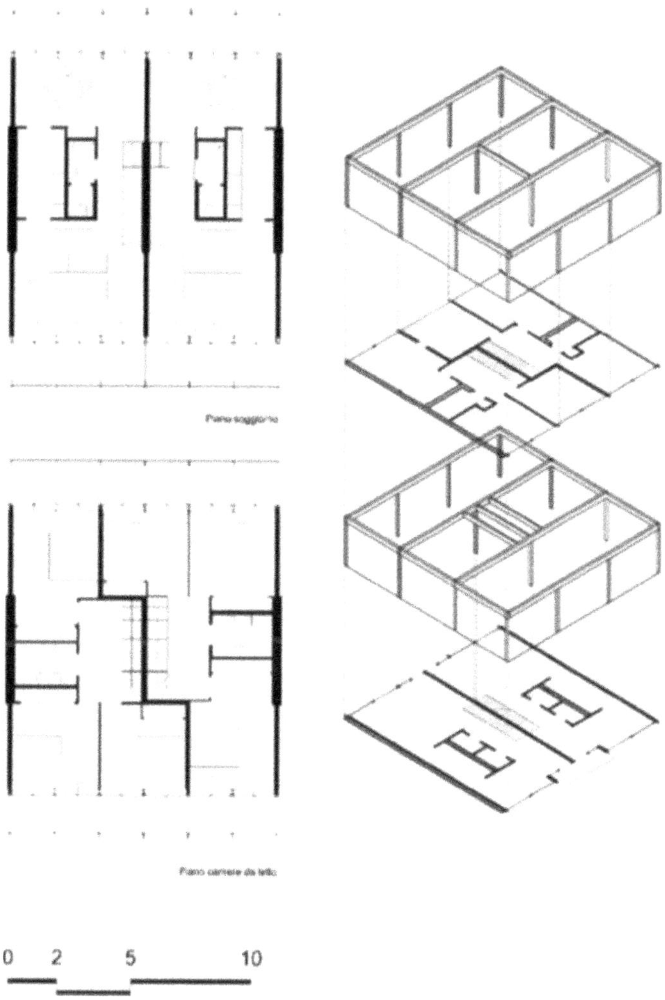

Fig. 3 Milano Farini. Multi-storey building

4 Scalo Farini: Design of a Mosque

Architectural studies regarding the morphological state of a mosque is an essential task that allows understanding of the design and building processes of ancient and contemporary artefacts. In an area where the existing structures dedicated to the Islamic community are sparse, the design of an Islamic holy place must include studies of similar cases from non-Islamic countries (especially in Europe and the USA) where many mosques have been built since the last century. The comparative study between contemporary and ancient mosques creates the opportunity of discovering the morphologically stable state of this place of worship. The religious artefact has to follow the direction of the Qibla (which is the direction of Mecca that houses the Islamic shrine of the Kaaba, towards which devotees must face during prayer) that in the case of the fortuitous rail yard known as Farini, corresponds exactly to the axis of the tracks as well as the reference lines of the new urban blocks.

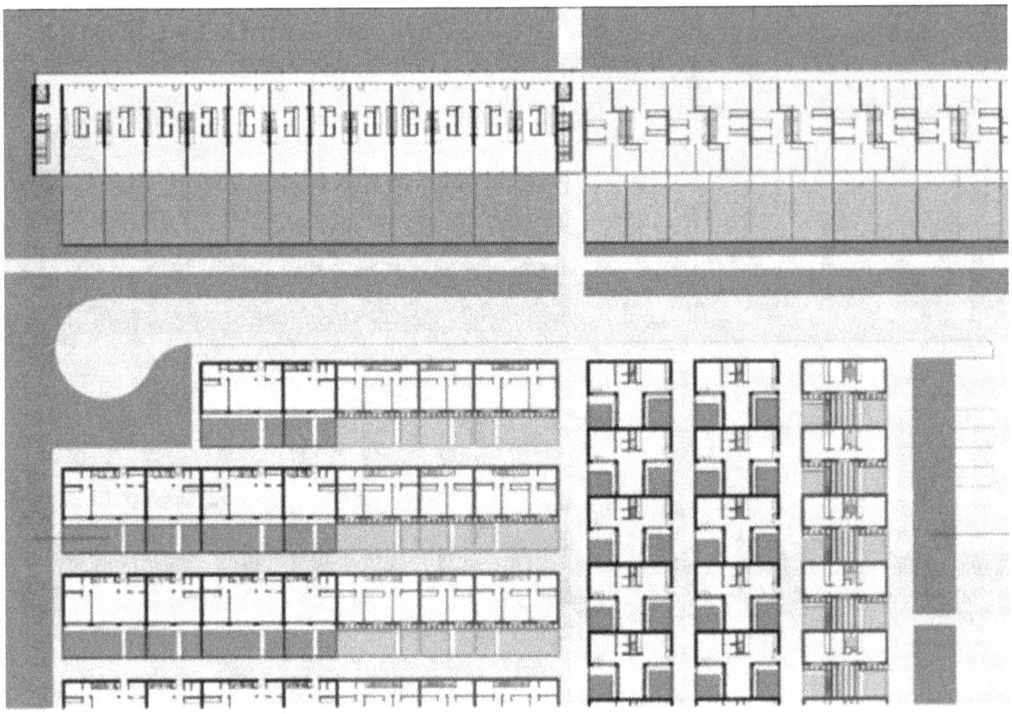

Fig. 4 Milano Farini. Typical floor

The greenery (located in the north-west area of the rail yard) creates a free disposition that makes the mosque similar to a pavilion, as a punctual element within a free and natural surrounding. The mosque has a rectangular plan, which consists of a large courtyard with two-side entrances. Found on both sides of this enclosed open space, it provides access to stores and services which are located in front of the main entrance. This space is arranged to create ablutions at the sides of the rooms (which are divided for men and women) for the necessary purification before prayer. The prayer area (musalla) is a square-shaped space that allows worshipers to be ordered in rows. The hypostyle hall consists of twenty-five pillars, of which a provision of five pillars on each side creates a central row that is used to support the vertical wooden panel that separates women from men in the same room. This space also allows spatial remodulation using portable panels between the pillars which can create confined areas for reading activities and studying.

Villa Simonetta and the mosque are similar in regard to their greenery area, which was designed by duplicating the original geometric pattern of Italian gardens whilst creating new green areas. The geographical and temporal aspects of the geometrical characteristics of the two completely different artefacts are related through the pedestrian path that connects the renaissance house, crosses the railway grounds and intercepts a fountain.

Sustainability and energy conservation of the building is provided by the solar orientation of the openings. This analysis uses the details of these opaque parts and openings due to their inflexible direction towards the holy city of Mecca. The exchange of air and natural cooling is provided by openings found on the cover as well as a combined system of skylights and solar shading. This combined system is adjustable according to the change of seasons and inclination in order to decrease the heat load during the summer and to get extra heat loads during the winter.

Rehabilitation Projects of the Areas of the Decommissioned Barraks in Milan, 2014

Raffaella Neri

Abstract Projects and studies were born from a research and a workshop promoted by the School of Architettura Civile and continued through master thesis and a Convention with the Ministry of Defense. The paper deals with the role that these areas can play in the transformation of peripheral sites through the settlement of new activities and collective places, parks and residential activities, as well as the possibility of recovering existing structures. The chapter includes a selection of projects.

Keywords Barraks · Decommissioned areas · Urban design · Urban composition

Today, the main transformations of historically established systems mostly happen when large areas are decommissioned and become newly available to the city for redevelopment. After the decommissioning of large industrial sites that began in the 1970s and the long process to redevelop them for new programs, other large areas are now becoming available in Milan and in several other cities as the result of structural changes in production, transportation, institutional. The guidelines of urban and territorial plans reflect such changes in ways that generally refer to particular issues and programs: today, the main strategic areas, in Milan and in other Italian and European cities, are rail-road yards and military areas, either already decommissioned or in the process of becoming so. As such, they are the object of a special focus by the master plans that are expected to indicate their future transformation. When important programs that usually occupy large sections of the city's core get relocated, they usually leave behind valuable buildings or architectural complexes. In any case, they are often particularly relevant in terms of location and size as they form large enclaves within the established built fabric between the city core and its suburbs. As large, enclosed areas, set apart and inaccessible, they are still intact and thus can be repurposed for a totally different and surprising new life. Their availability represents an important resource that can potentially redefine, subvert and guide the future life

R. Neri (✉)
Architecture, Built Environment and Construction Engineering—ABC Department, Politecnico di Milano, Milan, Italy
e-mail: raffaella.neri@polimi.it

S. Della Torre et al. (eds.), *Regeneration of the Built Environment from a Circular Economy Perspective*, Research for Development,
https://doi.org/10.1007/978-3-030-33256-3_17

of the neighboring city sections, with an influence that reaches out to farther areas they may be reconnected to.

In 2014, the School of Architettura Civile promoted a workshop about either decommissioned or soon to be decommissioned barracks—considered as strategic areas by the new territorial zoning plan—that was based on the results of an ongoing research started in 2012. This research has revealed extended, complex and rich, due to the multiplicity of issues it tackles, such as the impact of the military settlements' diverse purposes and layouts on the construction of the city; the different and multiple reasons of their location; the settlement and typological features of the barracks as large complexes that incorporate several buildings and large open areas, as reflected by an extended and established literature; how their sites and buildings reflect military life and organization; their building practices and decoration forms; the complex and unexplored connections with other similar situations in Italy and abroad, and so on. While these settlements have general and recurring features, their urban condition is so particular and specific that they are, at the same time, deeply related to the city and its history.

Due to their programs, these are almost invariably very large developments that acquire specific and different features when they expand. During the course of history their large enclosed areas have been relocated within the city for different reasons, and left important traces of their presence in the sites, buildings and conditions they generate all around. These are settlements that influence urban design by establishing or preventing relations between city sections that remain in place even after their decommissioning.

Eleven design groups that include professors, researchers, students and graduate students, and the contribution of several others, have worked on the sites of five decommissioned, or about to be decommissioned, barracks, originally indicated by the territorial zoning plan as areas for urban transformation. These were the barracks of the Milizie district, involved in the long discussion about the relocation of the Brera Academy, the large unbuilt site of the Parade Ground in Baggio a small section of which is occupied by warehouses, the Montello barracks in via Caracciolo, the Mameli barracks in viale Suzzani and finally, the Mercanti barracks in via Rubattino in the Lambrate district.

The projects always consider the areas and the built heritage that will be soon available for their potential in terms of urban transformation and redevelopment, of enhancement of the contexts and their buildings, with the goal of redefining the sites that will become newly available to the city by establishing collective facilities of urban interest, public institutions, open areas and parks, new facilities and community centers, buildings for social activities and programs, by calling for the redevelopment and construction of buildings for special, temporary, protected, collective, emergency housing, and so on. These large strategic areas can guide the transformations of the city and become its new centers, new landmarks that integrate and consolidate the city's collective sites, as public places of urban and territorial relevance that can rarely be found in the city's suburbs.

1 A Regeneration Project for the Military Area in the Baggio District of Milan: A Park and Square for West Milan

Milan has a long history of moving its "piazza d'armi" (military camp and stronghold), but this never-ending saga of "fated moves" (F. Reggiori) is about to be resolved once and for all with the removal of the city's last military camp on via delle Forze Armate. This affair has played a fundamental role in the history of Milan and its architecture, and is also important if one wishes to have a better understanding of the city. The main character in this story is a masterpiece of Milanese Renaissance architecture: the large porticoed enclosure of the Lazzaretto (a lazaretto, i.e. isolation hospital). The site, therefore, poses various complexities which the project resolves by using the architecture of the Lazzaretto as its central point of reference. The main aim of the project is to give shape to the themes posed by the new phase of the area's transformation while respecting its identity and also enabling the site to use the invaluable expanses of space that are an intrinsic part of its character and have been lost to us for so long. This is the key to expressing a new quieter and more cloistral centricity, which is required for an archipelago of separate units that are otherwise unable to express any civilized character (Fig. 1).

Fig. 1 History of the "Piazze d'armi" in Milan; perspective view of the maquette. Design group: M. Prusicki, with P. Cofano, E. Colonna, G. Frassine, M. Cristina Loi, F. Pocaterra, A. Schiavo, A. Drufuca (Mobilità), A. Ferrari (Verde) and C. Bianchi, C. Candia, A. Cova, Q. Lu, E. Solbiati, M. Sundovska, Pupak Tahereh B., G. Tacchini (Ph.D. students) and students of the Scuola di Architettura Civile

2 Asylum. City-Refuge. The Milan Barracks: Replacement, Conservation, Adaptation or Physiological Transformation?

The project takes on board the task of requalifying the civil life of fairly heterogeneous communities, the current and real representation of the other "total institutions" (the prison system, those of education and professional training, health, social security, labor organisations, et cetera) in their direct relations with social society, according to two strategies to be considered interlinked:

- the first for ordinary administration, with the building of a Cité de Refuge aimed at reorganizing activities to curb the hardships and privations of outcasts, the "wretched of the earth" (from the title of Frantz Fanon's 1961 essay);
- the second for extraordinary management, with the establishment of a "Center for Strategic Coordination of the Environment."

In short, we are not talking about "liberating"—emptying ad excludendum—military zones and barracks, but instead about making use of them through compatible activities, reconverting the military arrangement into an internal front—i.e. to the problems of civil society—to redeem through typological devices—Asylums—the segregation regime of "total institutions." Even if the extant building types can be adapted for use as temporary residences, nonetheless the need emerges to conceive functions of social integration, such as training courses at various levels along with social activities (Fig. 2).

Fig. 2 Perspective view of the Baggio decommissioned area. Design group: R. Canella, M. Dezzi Bardeschi, G. Luca Ferreri, L. Monica with L. Bergamaschi, M. Bordin, A. Brusetti, M. Canesi, G. Cattani, S. Cusatelli, G. Fiorese, P. Galbiati, V. Garatti and students of the Scuola di Architettura Civile

3 A Sports Park in Baggio

The project reflects the guidelines of Milan's territorial zoning plan about the activities and quantities that could be developed in the area. The extension of the area and possibility to accommodate new urban collective activities are the conditions that can project the areas as new city centers, and public, open, green locations with common activities and public institutions.

The project proposes it as the site for new urban-scale sports facilities—a new water sports complex and a sports palace fronting on the central green park that, along with its public buildings, acts as the main element of the new development.

The remarkable housing volume planned by the territorial zoning plan is concentrated in few large buildings located in the park and integrated with the necessary district facilities: the housing is laid out to provide a satisfying connection between the buildings and the central free area (Fig. 3).

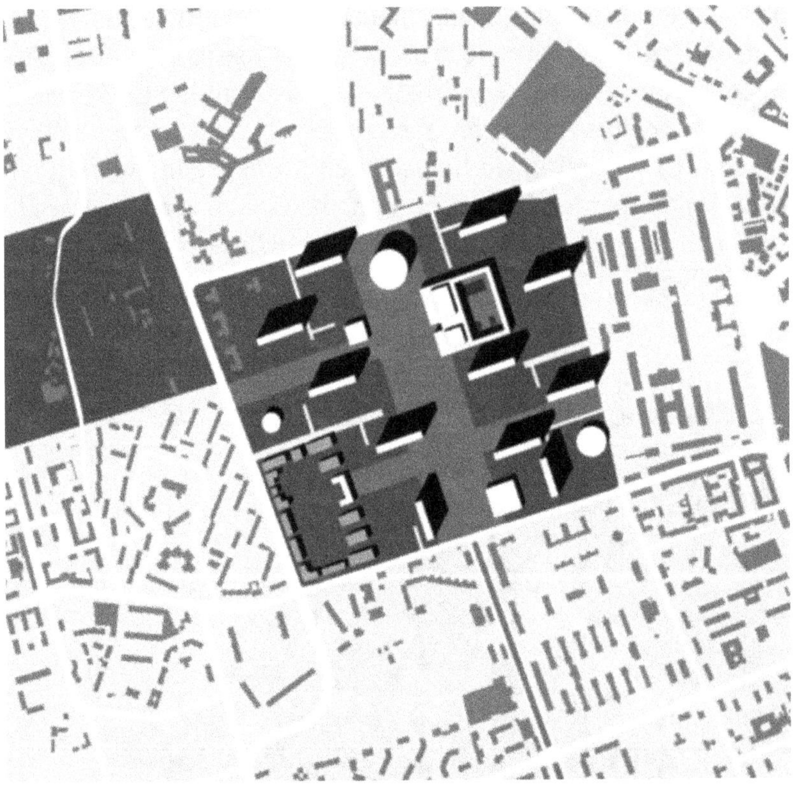

Fig. 3 Masterplan for the Baggio decommissioned area. Design group: R. Neri, T. Monestiroli, I. Boniello with: C. Campanella, E. Garavaglia, G. Guarisco, M. Passerella, F. Zangheri and students of the Scuola di Architettura Civile

4 Montello Barracks, Between via Caracciolo, via Arimondi, via Bertolini, via Amari. Adaptive Reuse for Prison Decongestion Structures, Public Housing and Collective Services

The Montello Barracks, former "Caserma di Cavalleria al Rondò della Cagnola" (Cavalry Barracks of Cagnola Circus), was built between 1910 and 1913 on the boundary of Corso Sempione, historic axis of Milan's expansion toward the northwest, in a segment between the current Piazza Firenze, via Caracciolo, via Arimondi, via Bartolini and via Amari. The ensemble's typology, pavilions type, was recurrent in the later nineteenth century, recommended by the reference handbooks to several large urban facilities (barracks but also hospitals, hospices, nursing homes, markets, expo, etc.). The project aims to answer to several current urban and social emergencies and requirements. In detail, there are provided: structures for the reduction of the prison overcrowding, by means of a housing unit for the semi-detention treatments placed in a new construction toward via Bartolini; some studios and workspaces for training and apprenticeship, obtained reusing the stables and the riding-school building near to via Arimondi; also, public housing and accommodations for students, immigrants, elderly and vulnerable population obtained recovering a large part of the building in via Caracciolo. In the central part of lot, there will be a new compound building, that has an out-of-alignment position against the original complex. This will host an auditorium and other cultural and associative spaces, as well as sports equipment and a public swimming, with adjoining cabins and utilities; while on the short side toward via Amari, a linear building hosts a cafeteria, a library and study rooms (Fig. 4).

Fig. 4 Axonometric view from northeast of the Montello barraks to prison decongestion structures, public houses and collective services. Design group: E. Bordogna, G. Canella, E. Manganaro with: T. Brighenti, F. Costantino, L. Locatelli and students of the Scuola di Architettura Civile

5 A Project for Brera's Academy

The projects deal with the functional re-zoning of the so-called Quartiere delle Milizie, a urban complex composed by several barracks, such as XXIV Maggio's, Magenta's and Carroccio's. Quartiere delle Milizie is located at the west of Parco Sempione, between Giardino Valentino Bompiani and Parco Guido Vergani, in an area that developed in the late eighteenth century. The new urban layout defines a square which, affected by the dramatic nature of the surrounding context, fragments its edges and reveals connections with the existing civic pattern. The project, characterized by variances and cross-references, maintains unaltered the architectural character of XXIV Maggio and Carroccio's barracks. Moreover, it replaces Magenta's barracks with a large building which hosts the board of education of Brera's Academy and defines a new public space where different multi-functional buildings appear (Fig. 5).

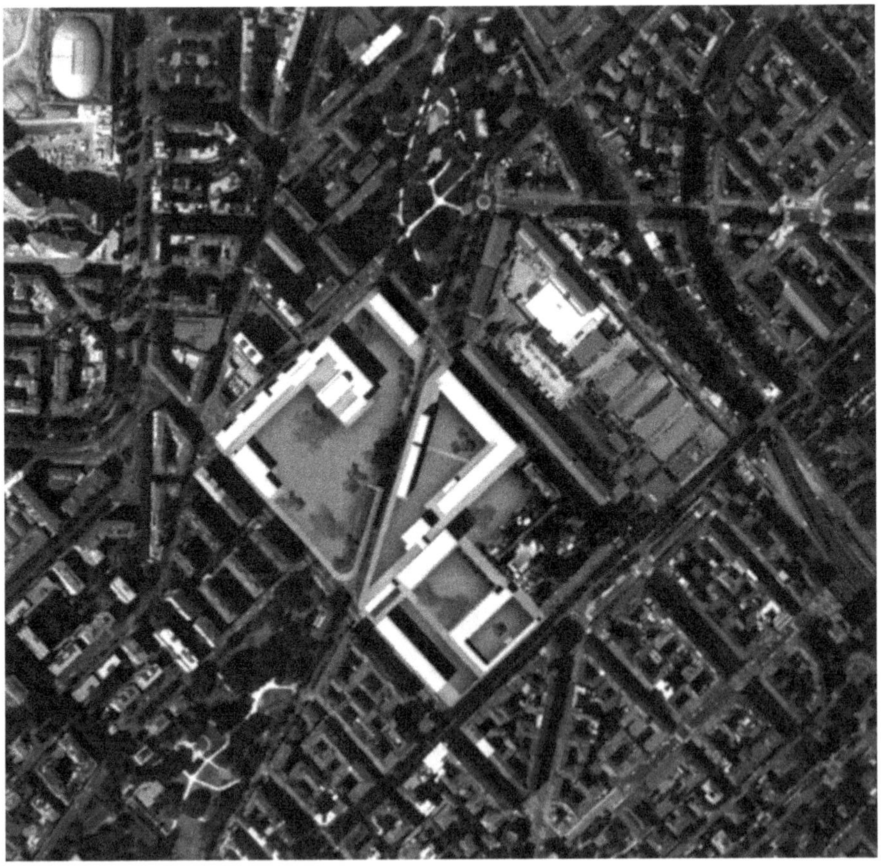

Fig. 5 Masterplan for the "quartiere delle Milizie" area. Design group: R. Bonicalzi, F. Bruno, F. Belloni, E. Miele, V. Petrini with: A. Faniuolo, L. Forti, V. Lattante, L. Spinelli, D. Vallariello and students of the Scuola di Architettura Civile

6 A New Center for Brera: Barrack "XXIV Maggio-Magenta-Carroccio"

The projects start from the assumption of partial or complete displacement of the Brera Academy, reusing the listed buildings of the district "XXIV Maggio-Magenta-Carroccio," taken as ordering elements of the new system of buildings, hinged on the barracks of via Mascheroni.

This barrack is reconstructed according to the design of the late nineteenth century and is divided into three parts: the existing linear building of Via Mascheroni, the building of the "Ex Leva" barracks and the internal central one, originally U-shaped, of which remains only the right-wing. This fragment is freed from the one-story adjunct, which connects it to the slim building along Via Pagano ("Carroccio" barracks), and is reconstructed as it was around the central courtyard. The new rebuilt building completes the existing one, taking from this its volume size, its height, the order of the openings and interrupting itself only at the transverse passage, which is accessible from the entrance gate on the Via Pagano (Fig. 6).

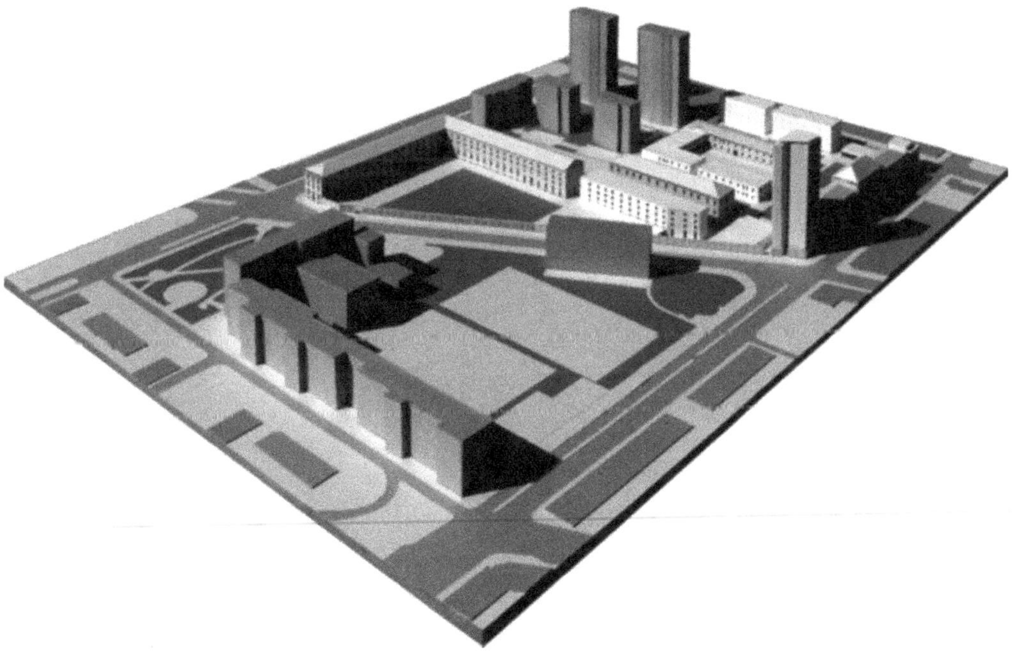

Fig. 6 View of the project for the "quartiere delle Milizie" area. Design group: M. Caja, P. Iarossi, N. Lombardini with M. Foglia, S. Zaroulas nd students of the Scuola di Architettura Civile

7 Former Military Barracks: From Isolated Fortress to Place of Integration

The architecture of the barracks introduces in the city the typical features of military settlements: demarcation and separation from the urban body, introversion of the system of activities, plurality of typological structure. The presence of spatial differences according to several functional diagrams assigns barracks' features to the ones which are distinctive of the city, as it is condensed within the confined horizon of a separate community: that is to say a real "citadel."

The divestment military areas and properties represent a potential system of extraordinary devices able to cope with major social emergencies according to a logic of integrated mobilization of resources. For each of the four former barracks has been identified a priority task capable of positive synergies with other activities and functional systems: for prison decongestion (achieved through alternatives measures to detention): Montello Barracks; for the assistance to the immigrant population: Military Citadel of Baggio; for housing and services for elderly population and students: Mameli and Mercanti Barracks; for affordable housing and utilities: Military Citadel of Baggio (Fig. 7).

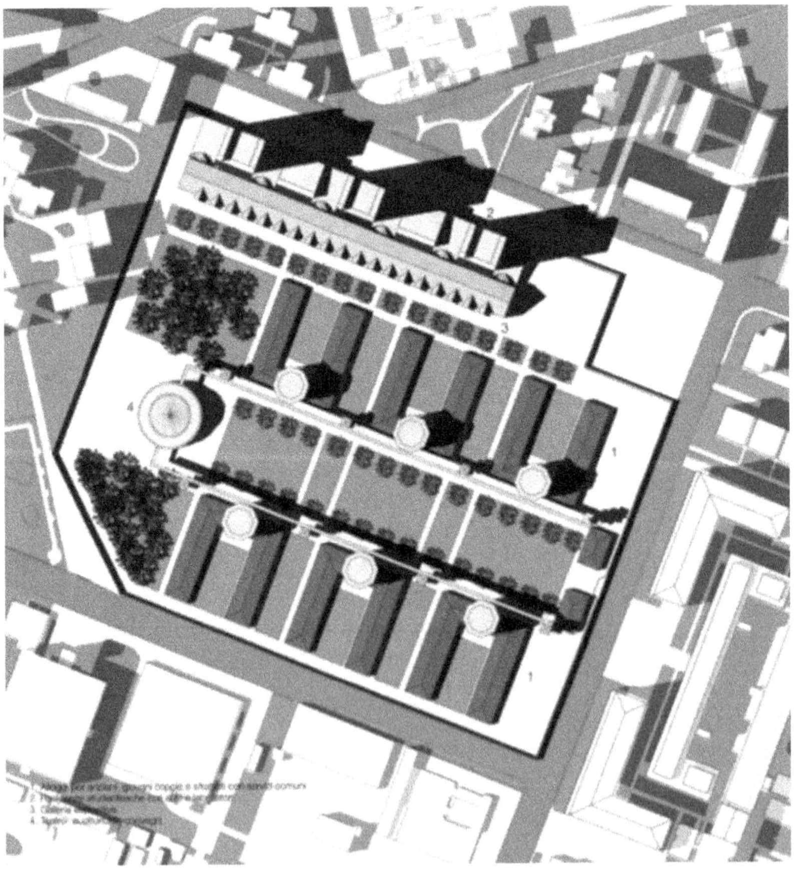

Fig. 7 Masterplan for the "quartiere delle Milizie" area. Design group: P. Bonaretti, M. Biagi, C. Pavesi and students of the Scuola di Architettura Civil

8 A Park for the Temporary Housing in the Mameli Barracks

The Mameli barracks is a wide enclosure over 300 m long; a remarkable building volume is planned in the area as the site for housing and collective facilities. The superintendency intends to preserve most buildings all while allowing for their partial enlargement and adaptation.

The project develops the large central area as a new collective park for the neighborhood, a green open area that extends to create smaller gardens between the buildings as a sort of urban outpost of the northern Park.

Given the layout of the barracks, its proximity with the Bicocca University campus and the presence of several major hospital facilities nearby (Niguarda, CTO, Galeazzi, Bassini), it seems advisable to develop the existing buildings and the new developments as the system of temporary and social housing that the city currently lacks: student housing, hospital-related accommodation, small temporary units, some social housing, along with public and collective facilities to serve the new development and integrate the other developments of the city all around it.

Two buildings for hotel facilities are aligned with the central park; their layout creates a two-level square that defines the system's hub, distributes to the development's open space, the facilities in the hotel buildings and the underground squares, and provides access to the housing. A third tower that becomes the area's boundary to the densely built area to the north accommodates small-sized housing units and social housing (Fig. 8).

Fig. 8 Masterplan for the Mameli decommissioned area. Design group: R. Neri, T. Monestiroli, I. Boniello with: C. Campanella, E. Garavaglia, G. Guarisco, M. Passerella, F. Zangheri and students of the Scuola di Architettura Civile

An Experience of Urban Transformation in Multan-Pakistani Punjab

Adalberto Del Bo, Daniele F. Bignami, Francesco Bruno, Maria Vittoria Cardinale and Stefano Perego

Abstract This publication concerns studies, programmes and designs for the project Sustainable Social Economic and Environmental Revitalization in the historic core of Multan City in Pakistani Punjab developed by several Politecnico di Milano Departments and Fondazione Politecnico di Milano, an institution that cooperates with Politecnico di Milano in the research fields of architecture, engineering and industrial design. The activities are part of the Debt Swap Agreement signed in 2006 between the governments of Italy and Pakistan for development in the social sectors. Besides the extraordinarily valuable architecture of the Walled City of Multan and its dense and hard-working population, there is a physical and environmental condition that is extremely problematic and that may threaten the continuity of life in the historic part of a city, well known for being among the world's most ancient settlements. The social and cultural interest and the academic challenge of a new opportunity to deal with great traditions pushed the researchers to face the urgency and delicacy of a very complex theme. After the analysis, the surveys and the proposals, the Politecnico group completed the first operational phase reorganizing one of the main City Gate Place, building a new open pavilion and restoring a huge public building and the Gate. The last activity, planned and not yet implemented, refers to the Sarafa Bazaar Project, an integrated system for the urban arrangement through infrastructures systems as sewerage, public lighting and shading, new paving and conservation of historic building's façades.

A. Del Bo (✉)
Architecture, Built Environment and Construction Engineering-ABC Department, Politecnico di Milano, Milan, Italy
e-mail: adalberto.delbo@polimi.it

D. F. Bignami
Project Development Department, Fondazione Politecnico di Milano, Milan, Italy

F. Bruno
Milan, Italy

M. V. Cardinale · S. Perego
Milan, Italy

S. Della Torre et al. (eds.), *Regeneration of the Built Environment from a Circular Economy Perspective*, Research for Development,
https://doi.org/10.1007/978-3-030-33256-3_18

Keywords City revitalization · Architecture · Conservation · Cross-cultural cooperation · Walled city

1 Introduction

The project "Sustainable, Social, Economic and Environmental Revitalization in the Historic Core of Multan City" is aimed at promoting socio-economic improvement and protection of historical and environmental heritage in the ancient Walled City of Multan in Pakistan.

The project, developed by Fondazione Politecnico di Milano, in cooperation with several departments of the Politecnico di Milano[1] and in collaboration of few other research institutions,[2] is funded through the debt swap agreement between the Italian Government and the government of the Islamic Republic of Pakistan (PIDSA) and is supported by the Italian Embassy of Islamabad, Ministry of Foreign Affairs and International Cooperation of Italy, Italian Development Cooperation, and Pakistan Ministry of Finance, through its Economical Affair Division, and routed by the Ministry of Housing & Works, during first phase, and by Local Government & Community Development Department—Government of Punjab (LG & CD), for the implementation of the second phase of the project.

Multan is one of the oldest cities in the Asian subcontinent, rich in history and culture, dating back at list 2000 years, but probably founded near 5000 BC and part of Indus Valley Civilization period (Cuneo 1986; Nabi 1983; Page 2008; Raza 1988; Sen 1988). It is located in the Southern Punjab Province in centre of Pakistan. The city is situated at the intersection of major roads linking the North and South of

[1]Polimi Departments: ABC (Architecture, built environment and construction engineering); ex BEST (Built environment science & technology); DASTU (Architecture and urban studies); ex DIAP (Architecture and planning); DICA (Environmental and Civil Engineering); ex DPA (Architectural Design); INDACO (Industrial design arts and communication).

Polimi Workgroup: Christian Amigoni, Francesco Augelli, Daniele Beacco, Irene Bengo, Eleonora Bersani, Daniele F. Bignami, Daniele Bocchiola, Matteo Bogana, Paolo Bonasoni, Maurizio Boriani, Francesco Bruno, Barbara Calvi, Samuele Camolese, Gabriele Candiani, Maria Vittoria Cardinale, Nelly Cattaneo, Daniele Cerizza, Emanuela Colombo, Gabriele Confortola, Alessandro Conti, Giovanni Maria Conti, Paolo Cristofanelli, Giorgio Dalla Via, Enrico De Angelis, Adalberto Del Bo, Elena Dell'Oro, Claudio Di Benedetto, Vincenzo Donato, Dario Guerini Matteo Fiori, Lidia Fiorini, Maria Romana Francolino, Federico Frassy, Rossana Gabaglio, Giuseppe Galloni, Andrea Garzulino, Eugenio Gatti, Mariacristina Giambruno, Marco Gianinetto, Franco Guzzetti, Marco Introini, Ermes Invernizzi, Monica Lancini, Luca Listo, Michele Locatelli, Lorenzo Maffioli, Pieralberto Maianti, Andrea Mainini, Umair Malik, Carlo Manfredi, Andrea Marchesi, Roberta Mastropirro, Maria Teresa Melis,, Rasha Mozil, Vassilis Mpampatsikos, Giorgio Pansa, Riccardo Paolini, Stefano Perego, Davide Pini, Sonia Pistidda, Tiziana Poli, Renato Pugno, Letizia Ronchi, Renzo Rosso, Francesco Rota Nodari, Marco Rusmini, Andrea Soncini, Matteo Tasinato, Alessandra Terenzi, Grazia Tucci, Giorgio Valè, Paolo Vercesi, Gian Pietro Verza, Elisa Vuillermoz, Anna Sara Zanolla.

Scientific Director—Adalberto Del Bo; Project Manager—Daniele F. Bignami; Project Director phase I—Juan Xabier Monjas; Project Director phase II—Francesco Bruno.

[2]Ev-K2-CNR Committee and the University of Florence.

the country (to Lahore and Karachi) and the routes going from East to West. Its geographical position makes Multan a crucial and strategic site in the country (Dutt 2004). As a consequence of the recent process of urbanization, Multan is now the core of a big hinterland of medium towns, large villages and small clusters of shacks.

Starting from this role, the need of crucial interventions to protect the "soul" of Multan was clearly highlighted by Pakistani authorities. Consequently, an urgent action of architectural heritage preservation of the Old Town has been evaluated as necessary, together with the commencement of a cultural and social development process within the Walled City, characterized by high population density, significant problems about energy, water and sanitation and many different commercial activities.

On the basis of available resources (Abu l'Fazl 1596) and of preliminary investigations, the project has been conceived aiming at developing a pilot model in conservation and revitalization of the oldest part of Multan, focused on specific areas and monuments of the Walled City, significant from the historical and symbolic point of view (Dani 2008; Rehman 1997; Hoagh 1978; Marshall 1937; Burckhardt 1985), and able to act as a guide intervention to be transferred in other areas of the Old Town. The main action of the project concerns the conservation of few selected historical buildings and the renewal of a part of the ancient historical centre.

The phase II of "Sustainable, Social, Economic and Environmental Revitalization in the Historic Core of Multan City" has been preceded by a careful and thorough series of studies, including investigations carried out accordingly to the theoretical and practical expertise of Politecnico di Milano, and the tools and the methods developed in its research tradition (Rossi 1966).

In a second step, the studies focused on a specific Walled City pilot area and on individual building characteristics through a specific survey carried out with the active collaboration of students from the Bahauddin Zakariya University of Multan.

With the collaboration of experts in different disciplines all the results, gathered in several publications[3] and delivered by Fondazione Politecnico di Milano to Project Management Unit of the Walled City of Multan, were the fundamentals for the implementing phase of the conservation and the design renovation works within.

Regarding the organisational structure of the project, it is necessary to refer to some general provisions that allowed the planning, structuring and implementing of the different objectives and components. A Project Implementation Committee at the local level headed by the Commissioner—Multan Division—in collaboration with Fondazione Politecnico di Milano ensured that the project could be developed and implemented according to the directives of the Steering Committee.

The project was designed to be managed through a specially created Project Management Unit (PMU) working under LG & CD, with the supervision of a high-level Steering Committee at Provincial level. The PMU closely coordinated the preparatory activities with the different involved line agencies (WASA, MEPCO, SNGPL,

---

[3]Cfr. Del Bo and Bignami (2014), Del Bo and Introini (2013), Augelli et al. (2015).

PTCL[4]). On this regard, the PMU created two structures (Infrastructure Design and Management Group and Project Design and Management Team), which worked independently or jointly depending on the task.

The principal partnership under the project is with Fondazione Politecnico di Milano which provided and still provides the competence and the facilities to develop and coordinate the entire project tasks: guidelines for working drawings, outline plans, consultancy services and supervision aimed at the implementation of the entire activities.

2 The Components of the Project

The Multan Walled City, with an approximated area of 1.2 km^2 and a population of around 127,000, was once the place where all the local arts were born and developed. The traditional arts are still alive in the area particularly in the form of jewellery, blue pottery and embroidery. There are approximately 3500 shops in Hussain Aghai Bazaar, Chowk Bazaar, Haram Bazaar and Sarafa Bazaar; about 1500 shops are pertaining to jewellery and manufacturing facilities and 1000 shops to textile sector. The approximate population associated with this business is almost 15,000 people; most of these people are employed on the shops and are within the poverty line. Therefore, the overall objective of the project was to initiate a sustainable process of social and economic revitalization and to upgrade the physical and environmental quality, through the improvement of livelihoods and living conditions of the residents.

For this reason, and for their characteristic and location inside the Walled City, the choice of the two main project areas—Haram Gate Place and Sarafa Bazaar—has been considered strategic for developing the pilot project as an example of possible future renovation inside the Walled City.

In addition, the selected precincts could enhance a more general touristy promotion by the improvement and conservation of the sites where the revitalized public space could be appreciated by the visitors. All this related to the conservation of the Haram Gate as an architectural heritage to be preserved for the collective citizen memory. Moreover, proposing a technical reorganization of the facilities aimed at the enhancement and the improvement of public space: i.e. enhancement of sewer system, electricity reorganization and urban shading.

A brief description could help in understanding the entity and the complexity of the second phase of the project, including the following components: Haram Gate conservation and Haram Gate Place regeneration, Musafir Khana building restoration, portion of Sarafa Bazaar regeneration and several capacity building activities.

[4]Water and Sanitation Agency, Multan Electric Power Company, Sui Northern Gas Pipelines Limited and Pakistan Telecommunication Company Limited.

In relation to these preliminary objectives, the physical working phase has quite been totally completed, except for the Sarafa Bazaar, for which the working documents have been finalized and the construction site is expected to be opened in few months.

The first project component is the Haram Gate area, one of the most important gateways to the Walled City. Today the precinct is a place of traffic and a starting point of an important tourist route that leads to inner part of the Walled City. The west side of the place, towards Alang Road, has been subject to recent demolitions of a part of the urban texture built on the original site of the ancient city walls. Together with the Gate conservation project, there was the need to act with a plan for the entire reorganization of the place. The Haram Gate Place project, in fact, is strictly connected with the Haram Gate conservation project, with the aim to create a real urban place, in opposition to the current traffic and parking place, as a communitarian site located at the entrance of the Walled City. For this purpose, the project shaped a new sequence of spaces around the Haram Gate: the entire area—between the Circular road and the Gate—has been paved with bricks, a new lighting system has been settled, trees have been planted along the side of the place facing Circular Road, and a new pavilion has been built, on the site of several ruined buildings, to create a sort elevated terrace, covered by a steel and wooden structure, where the inhabitants as well as the tourist, could enjoy a protected space.

The small pavilion refers to the typical elements of the architectural tradition of the great royal gardens: the *diwan* was in fact a resting place in the shade set within a composition of geometries and perspectives.

Compared to the first phase of the project, the pavilion underwent some substantial changes regarding its shape and the materials. In fact, related to the architectural characteristics of the building and the role it plays in the reorganization of the square, its proportions have been revised. It has in fact opted for a plan based on a 3:5 ratio clearly expressed thanks to the adopted structural step. The same ratio was maintained between the short side and the height of the building. The design of the flooring and the choice of materials remained almost unchanged compared to the first proposals. The paving of the square is continuous and made with a brick already used for the inner street inside the Walled City. The edge surface of the pavilion stylobate is made within local white granite with pinkish veins about 30 cm wide.

The development of the project has also led to the revision of some initial choices due to more simplicity of construction and availability of materials. For this reason, the roof of the building, initially designed with triangular section beams that needs a very complex manufacturing, has been redesigned with standardized elements in iron and for the secondary structure in wood. The whole roof was covered in wood with staves about 15 cm wide and painted red as well as the elements of the building. The choice to simplify the design of the elements that make up the pavilion also guaranteed the involvement of local workers from the Multan district.

Related to the relationship with the surrounding space and orientation, the roof has three overhangs on the east, south and west sides, while the north side, towards the toilets, is devoid of them. To increase the shading, a row of trees placed to the south, at the level of the circular road, completes the design of the limit of Haram Gate Place.

The discovery of an ancient well to the east of the pavilion during the excavation activities required a revision of the design of the big steps that connecting the street level to the podium. Thanks to an accurate survey of the discovered well about its dimensions and position, the design of the big steps—made by the same granite used for the pavilion stylobate—was redefined with a centre in the ancient well that today is visible thanks to a glass covering.

The pavilion is a covered construction provided by seats for the waiting and *rendezvous*. This kind of traditional building has been placed along north–south direction, becoming the support of amorphous photovoltaic surfaces, able to produce enough electricity to light its illumination system during the night. To complete the empty area on the north side, created by the demolitions, a services building, is located in front of the new pavilion, provided of public washroom.

For achieving the complete results and make the Gate free from every kind of encroachment—for instance the "crowd" of overhead cables running along the place—preliminary to its conservation works, it was necessary to improve and reorganize all the infrastructure system in the vicinity; i.e. the telecommunication and the electric power distribution infrastructure, the water supply system, the natural gas distribution, the sewage disposal and the storm water drainage systems (Wang et al. 2011), all of them replaced with underground lines.

The Haram Gate project achieved an exemplary conservation intervention in a field which is strategic for a country rich of monuments. The conservation and the strengthening techniques answered to the problems of decay and instability that were causing the serious state of deterioration of the building. The theoretical approaches and the technical solutions provided, in line with the most advanced methods of restoration in the international scenario, allowed to reach an expected result in term of intervention quality.

In accordance to the same considerations, it should be read the second component of the project which has been fulfilled with the completion of the Musafir Khana renovation. The building is an important historical legacy of the inner city of Multan and it is located in a strategic area characterized by several Holy Sites. The symbolic, historic and cultural importance of the Musa Pak complex makes it one of the most significant and representative within the historical core of Multan.

The third component taken into consideration by the Multan Walled City initiative is the Sarafa Bazaar project, the only one among those planned not yet completed, for which, however, all the materials necessary for the working phase have been totally finalized. The relevant portion of the Sarafa Bazaar project extends from Musafir Khana to the North. The bazaar, in accordance with its commercial nature, presents at the ground floor spaces used for shops and on the upper floors are located laboratory and dwellings.

The aim of the project is to bring order to the bazaar through a general arrangement able to represent both the local tradition and the necessary innovation in infrastructures, tourism improvement and energy saving.

Sarafa Bazaar Project provides an integrated system for the urban arrangement through infrastructures; public lighting; shading system; new paving; facades improvements and conservation of historic building's façades.

Sarafa Bazaar Project foresees the restoration of the façades. This kind of process is focused on urban and social problems with the purpose of a new general urban quality. The regeneration of a part of Sarafa Bazaar with a wide re-design project of the historic and recent building's façades wants to face problems as organization of public spaces, accessibility to the Old Town, insufficient lighting, traffic, security, and so on.

The general goal is to improve the life quality of the inhabitants, encouraging the tourism and make the city more attractive for the economic activities. So, the facades and open spaces rehabilitation and the facilities services improvement could have a positive effect on the re-appropriation of the spaces from the inhabitants that could inspire further actions on the interior spaces and the contiguous areas with a general improvement of the life quality. A regenerated space could become more attractive for tourism, producing a general improvement of the local micro economy. The urban rehabilitation requires, even more than the restoration of single monument, an overall program to build a general agreement of ideas and a shared involvement of the resident population.

The fourth and final component provided by the project is to develop a capacity building programme, based on a University networking. Therefore, the execution of the project offered a double opportunity: on the one hand, the collaboration of Italian and Pakistani personnel in the execution of the works, on the other hand, the opportunity to develop new skills in Pakistan in the architectural field. The proposed topics are both related to practical and theoretical aspect concerning the project and related to the architectural and urban planning theories.

The practical modalities and the intervention techniques with which it was possible to achieve the project outcome are in fact closely linked to specific knowledge on the restoration procedures as well as in the survey filed and data collection. Those disciplines are, in cases like this, the tools themselves for the development of the architectural project and its practice, especially in complex areas such as the Islamic city.

In conclusion, as described, the project is an important example of cross-cultural cooperation and collaboration project in the field of urban regeneration and transformation, showing how academic competencies, coordinated by a specialized structure of management of research and knowledge transfer projects can meet ambitious objectives and the challenge of achieving real improvements of delicate, but precious urban context (Figs. 1, 2, 3 and 4).

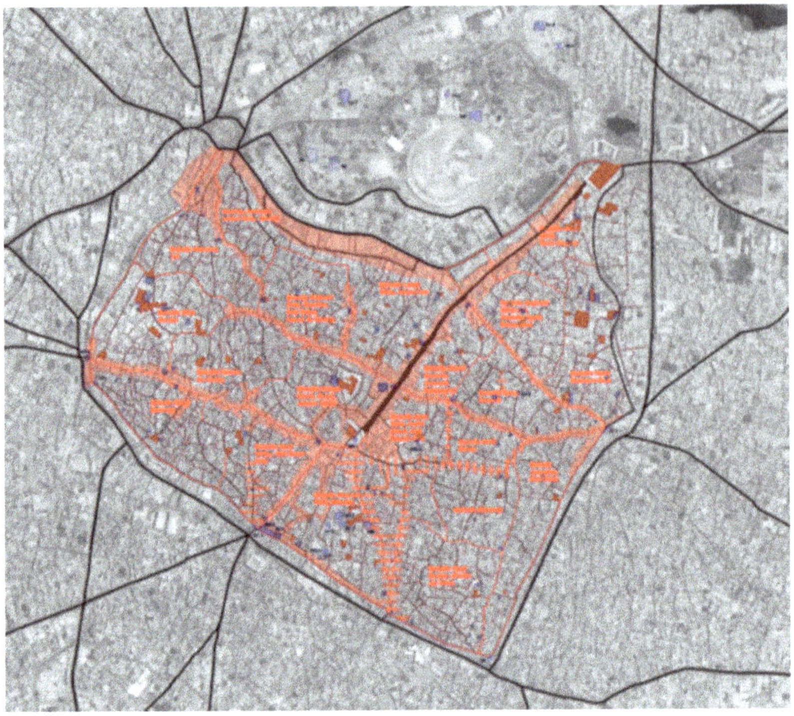

Fig. 1 Walled city of Multan and the Mohalla structure (in red)

Fig. 2 Multan. Pilot area Masterplan

Fig. 3 Multan. Haram Gate after conservation work

Fig. 4 Multan. Haram Gate Place and the New Pavillion

References

Abu l'Fazl. (1596). *Akbarnama* (by H. Beveridge, The Asiatic Society, 2000).

Augelli, F., Giambruno, M. C., Mastropirro, R., & Pistidda, S. (2015). *The walled city of Multan. Guidelines for maintenance, conservation and reuse work*. Firenze: Altralinea. ISBN 978-88-98743-50-6.

Burckhardt, T. (1985). *L'art de l'Islam, Langage et signification*. Arles: ACTES SUD.

Cuneo, P. (1986). *Storia dell'urbanistica—Il mondo islamico*. Bari: Laterza.

Dani, A. H. (2008). *History of Pakistan*. Lahore: Sang-E-Meel Publications.

Del Bo, A., & Bignami, D. F. (Eds.) (2014) *Sustainable social, economic and environmental revitalization in Multan City*. Cham, Heidelberg, New York, Dordrecht, London: Springer International Publishing AG. ISBN 978-3-319-02116-4.

Del Bo, A., & Introini, M. (2013) *Multan, Pakistan. La città murata*. Milano: Silvana Editoriale. EAN: 9788836625628.

Dutt, R. C. (2004). *The civilisation of India*. New Delhi, Chennai: Asian Educational Services.

Hoagh, J. D. (1978). *Architettura islamica*. Milano: Electa Editrice.

Marshall, J. (1937). The monuments of Muslim India. In *Cambridge history of India* (Vol. 3). Cambridge, Dry.

Nabi, K. A. (1983). *Multan history and architecture*. Islamabad: Institute of Islamic History, Culture & Civilization—Islamic University.

Page, J. B. (2008). *Indian Islamic architecture* (G. Michel, Ed.). Leiden, Boston: Brill.

Raza, M. (1988). *Hanif, Multan past & present*. Islamabad: Colorpix

Rehman, A. (1997). *Historic towns of Punjab. Ancient and medieval period*. Rawalpindi, Lahore, Karachi: Ferozons (PVT) Ltd.

Rossi, A. (1966). *The architecture of the city*. Padova: Marsilio Editore.

Sen, S. N. (1988). *Ancient Indian history and civilization*. New Delhi: New Age International.

Wang, S.-Y., Davies, R. E., Huang, W. R., & Gillies, R. R. (2011). Pakistan's two-stage monsoon and links with the recent climate change. *Journal of Geophysical Research, 116*(D16), 27. https://doi.org/10.1029/2011JD015760.

The Transformation of the Great Decommissioned Farini Railroad Yard: The Research for a Modern Housing Settlement

Raffaella Neri and Tomaso Monestiroli

Abstract The paper deals with the theme of the transformation of the large abandoned areas of the city, of their new destination, of the role of parks and gardens in the construction of the modern city, of the research on the housing units settlement principles. The essay collects several projects carried out over time: they are the results of a national PRIN research.

Keywords Railroad yard · Housing · Urban composition · Housing units

1 The First Project, 2009[1]

The Farini railroad yard is an important and strategic site due to its remarkable extension and availability as well as to its now central location within the city, its connection with the transportation network and the proximity of its urban facilities. As such, it is a part of the city that needs to be reconceived and rebuilt. How? Based on which city concept? By building what connections and based on which principles and elements?

From the urban planner's point of view, a preliminary question should be asked when approaching this issue: given the area's high potential, would it be possible to build a new and challenging high-density settlement, a modern development within the nineteenth-century city, without creating yet another suburb—albeit a luxury one, gravitating on the city of Milan—and use it as an opportunity to redesign the built tissue surrounding it? What conditions would lead to such an outcome? And, given that concentration and building density allow for a more limited use of surface, both in the undeveloped areas around the city and at its very core, what does it mean to

[1]Design Group, Antonio Monestiroli, coordinator, with Ilario Boniello, Massimo Ferrari, Stefano Guidarini, Tomaso Monestiroli, Raffaella Neri, Claudia Tinazzi Coll. Marcello Bondavalli, Lorenzo Margiotta, Guido Rivai.

R. Neri (✉) · T. Monestiroli
Architecture, Built Environment and Construction Engineering—ABC Department, Politecnico di Milano, Milan, Italy
e-mail: raffaella.neri@polimi.it

S. Della Torre et al. (eds.), *Regeneration of the Built Environment from a Circular Economy Perspective*, Research for Development,
https://doi.org/10.1007/978-3-030-33256-3_19

promote the development of this area rather than of others, in a context that can only be considered at the territorial scale?

The city administration's decision to consolidate the central core of Milan by developing great building volumes necessarily implies that the new district is adequately connected with the road and public transportation—both road and railway-based—networks, and that these are reviewed and adequately upgraded. In other words, for the new development to become a part of the city, it must be accessible and well connected to the urban and territorial system.

A second important issue that should be considered to prevent the area from becoming a suburb within the city revolves around the activities it will accommodate, which should be different, mixed and above all include urban interest facilities that might contribute to it becoming a new centre open to the city, and would make the site recognizable and the district an identifiable part of the city. The multiplicity of activities reflects the richness and diversity of collective and private spaces. The mission of architecture is to interpret such richness and to create places that convey character and quality.

Starting from such considerations, we have approached the issue of design in order to define several elements including the composition principles that would support the construction of a both coherent and articulated new city sector; the basic housing units and their building types, as different from the old city blocks; the collective places and their character, the connections between buildings and open spaces, the role of green spaces, the relation between facilities and housing, between commercial facilities and other programs.

The tracks and the railroad yard cut through and separated entire sectors of the city which have grown independently and created an interruption in the rings of the Beruto Plan. The building blocks developed from Corso Sempione had to stop against the railway; the so-called Isola district, developed at the east around the old road to Como, had also to be interrupted; other outer districts were developed around the old cores of Dergano, Affori, and Bovisa in the northern direction along the railway and the lines that connect Milan to other destinations. Since the early twentieth century, the city has grown beyond the railway and its continuing role of separating void.

The order and location of the settlement are decided by the railway, the main line connecting Milan to its surroundings. An expressway also runs alongside the tracks and given its interurban character, only has one point of access in the district, a non-pass-through rest area close to the business centre.

The system of road infrastructure is defined by a hierarchical principle, the goal of which is to give coherence to the settlement. The urban and interurban road network runs along the outer borders with two expressways—one alongside the tracks and the other straddling the tracks to unite via Caracciolo and via Lancetti. A new urban road connects the blocks to the south, along the border of the park; the existing perimeter roads define the area and connect it to the neighbouring districts; finally, the inner roads, of different capacity and role, define a regular grid made of 140 metres green squares within which the buildings are located.

The hierarchical order reflected by the roads sorts traffic by destination, directs cross traffic to the expressways, and as a consequence only allows for traffic serving the housing and other local activities into the area itself.

The focal point at the north-west apex of this almost triangular area where the interrupted thoroughfares that articulate the city and its territory still converge is the point from which the settlement can be organized and provided with an internal hierarchy to define and articulate the elements of the new district.

The unique character of the north-west apex of the system is expressed in the plan by the exceptional urban quality of the activities and by the architecture that represents them—a system of office and hotel towers organized around a square that becomes the core of the settlement, completed by a building for cultural activities open to the entire city (museum, auditorium, etc.). The 37- and 29-storey iron and glass towers become the beacon of the new district and of the surrounding territory (Fig. 1).

Fig. 1 Plan of the project

The development is surrounded by green spaces—partly landscaped and planted, partly lawns surrounded by rows of trees—open to public use. The presence of green spaces and the definition of the relation between buildings and open and landscaped spaces is an unavoidable issue in the construction of the modern city. From the relation between city and rural areas to the definition of the character of urban green spaces (parks, gardens, courtyards, or squares), it implies the precise definition of how green areas contribute to the design of a new development, how buildings define open spaces. In more general terms, the main issue is the role of green spaces in the use and composition of places.

The plan concentrates the buildings in a portion of the area in order to create an extended forest-like park which connects the districts separated by the railway. The pedestrian routes and bike lanes in the park establish the relation between the two city sections. Long rows of trees border the thoroughfares that articulate the district, highlight their importance and define the lawns that accommodate the new buildings, and replace the old urban blocks. As defining elements of the new development, the green spaces have different qualities, layouts, and characters based on their relations with the buildings, size, and treatment. The green spaces include the urban ground from which the buildings rise, divided into "rooms" for private housing and collective facilities, as well as the park, gardens, lawns, and rows of trees typical of Lombardy's landscape.

Another hub of collective activities is located in the decommissioned customs across from the main square and accommodates the primary schools and sports facilities, public gyms, and swimming-pools.

The two hubs are connected by a central green thoroughfare that runs alongside the railway tracks and articulates the entire district as a sort of Rambla along which the main commercial and collective facilities are located: a pond, an 18-storey bridge building for studios and workshops, a garden that straddles the tracks and connects the development to the park and the section south of the railway. Other collective and commercial facilities for the district are located on another axis alongside the Rambla.

The definition of housing as made of minimum repeatable units based on the development of a rule and its possible variations are a thread that runs through the history of the city—the development of the block bordered by roads, in ever-changing shapes based on the same principle, guided the construction of cities up until the twentieth century.

Can the block be replaced in the fabric of the modern city? Is it still necessary to define a settlement principle for housing, the most relevant urban element in terms of quantity in the development of the city, as a principle that can match, or at least point to, the diversity of places that was typical of the ancient city?

The housing proposed in the plan looks out onto green spaces, the open courtyards' lawns, the tree-lined roads, and the park. The old enclosed blocks open up and acquire a new character and a green heart—a collective area with different facilities measured by the relation between the houses.

The presence of such facilities introduces a principle of variation that makes the different places recognizable and the courtyards themselves busy and full of life, each with its own characters. Their openness means that the green spaces can be crossed and perceived as even more extended than they are, as well as well connected to the spaces at the centre of the district.

The hierarchical structure of the settlement defines the character of the courtyards based on their specific location—close to the Rambla, or to the roads that run alongside the area and the small squares that accommodate the neighbouring roads, occupied by the pond, fronting the garden, etc.

This settlement principle is reflected in the structure of the housing, the main quality of which is the diversity of frontages. The frontages may have either a full brick enclosure, corresponding to the sleeping areas that look out onto the inner tree-lined roads or a mixed glazed enclosure for the living areas, large light-filled verandas that look out onto the lawn of the courtyards. The 12-storey houses are perpendicular to the district's roads and laid out alternately so as to define basic units built on the system of small and large courtyards.

Special housing units such as the residences for students and senior citizens have a different character due to their particular location, with a double volume and double frontage in correspondence with the lawns and glazed living rooms on both sides.

The buildings that accommodate working activities, such as professional studios and workshops, also introduce variations in terms of location and type, as they are slightly taller and built as bridges straddling the two main roads that define the system. They are organized as large lofts that can be combined for specific requirements and become secondary reference points that measure the distances within the district's regular grid.

Facilities and collective buildings are distributed within the courtyards, along the two main roads. The facilities include mainly commercial activities that can be located below the ground level, or cinemas, theatres, and auditoriums that require no direct lighting and are perceived as large glazed atria on the lawn, large skylights that direct the light, and people in the underground spaces so that the surface can be occupied as much as possible by green spaces.

The distribution of activities in the area is based on the criteria of importance and easy accessibility—the urban museum and auditoriums are in the main square, commercial and catering activities are along the Rambla and the parallel road, recreational activities are close to the pond, kindergartens and primary schools are in more protected courtyards, administrative and health-care facilities define the smaller squares on the area's perimeter, close to the outer districts, cinemas and cultural activities are close to the urban railway stop, the library is in a quiet green area, etc.

2 The Second Project, 2012[2]

The research has been further detailed in a second master plan conceived by Antonio Monestiroli that confirms the first master plan's general layout but proposes blocks and housing units that, while always open and green, develop a possible interior complexity that creates places of different nature, character, and measurement, defined by the relation between different kinds of houses, facilities, and green spaces.

Based on this proposal, we have decided to test the general elements of its principle, to assess its potential, and allowance for variation, as it usually happens with the construction of the city.

We selected the general features, and we considered unassailable and translated them into a master plan, a framework within which many groups could develop their designs: the only constraints we indicated, in order not to compromise the main principles, were the general layout, the grid of open blocks with a central green space, the construction of its borders along the distribution roads, and the coexistence of different housing types (Fig. 2).

Since we consider green space a truly fundamental element in the construction of the modern city and its many collective areas, the core of the block is a park in the master plan we have developed—green squares along with gardens, parks, fields, and places that currently lack a precise identity may be described and defined by the buildings and their connections.

Urban parks have long been traditional places of the city. Milan has the Sempione Park, or the Porta Venezia Gardens, among others, just like Rome, Paris, and Berlin have their own famous parks. As metaphors of the rural areas outside the city walls,

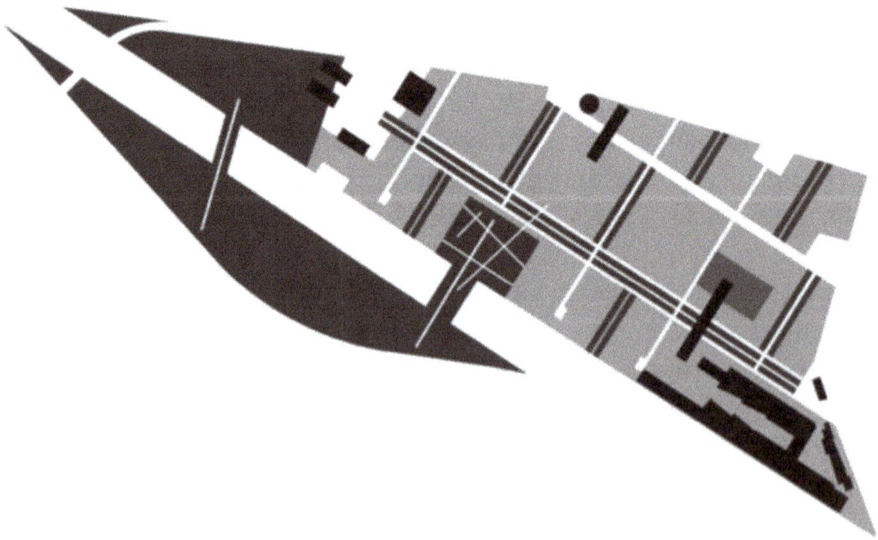

Fig. 2. Structure of the settlement and the public green spaces

[2]See Footnote 1. Design Group, Antonio Monestiroli, coordinator, with Claudia Tinazzi, Fabio Sebastianutti, Luca Cardani.

and destinations for leisure, promenades, hangout, and parks are fully and truly public places that have rightfully become part of the city. In American cities like New York or Chicago, the presence of green areas means higher real estate values: in cities that have no real tradition of squares, large parks are true urban collective spaces, the core of public life. They characterize their districts just like churches used to characterize theirs in the past and qualify the housing that enjoys their view, proximity, and presence.

But can green spaces at a smaller scale, with a different identity and size, characterize the places of housing and even be the *place* of the house?

The second condition we wanted to experiment was the coexistence of different kinds of housing and ways of living and connecting the house with its surroundings in the same block, thus creating different housing environments.

The block may be a mixed unit that includes several building types each developing its own spaces that coexist and interrelate: the courtyard, the aligned house, the tall house, and their complements—the space of the courtyard, the frontage of the aligned house, and the view from the tower. Facilities, workshops, offices, and shops also contribute to the definition of these collective places within the block.

We expect this unit to express both a general principle that is as recognizable as that of the old city and formal features that may change based on the location, requirements, activities it accommodates, and on the buildings it includes, so that each block is different, unique, and identifiable; the city represents a community that is the sum of many different individuals. The only way to transform the "tumult in the whole" into a rich environment is a clear order in the housing models.

3 The Second Project, 2012. First Variation[3]

The project explores a possible variation within the previously established principles of organization of the block and based on the observation of the modern city and the studies on the changing house–street relationship.

In the project, here proposed each block incorporates public urban space—a green space that expands in the combination of the blocks themselves, and is at the same time a place the houses look out onto, a public collective facility, a place of distribution to the buildings and the activities there located, and a place of life for the residents and of facilities open to the city. Being only accessible by pedestrians and bicycles, it is separated from the streets that divide the different blocks and are merely for service and car access to the buildings.

Several separated places, alternated in succession, look out onto the central green area: houses and buildings for collective activities are articulated to provide open courtyards and small squares, also green, and are intentionally conceived to establish

[3]See Footnote 1. Design Group, Raffaella Neri, coordinator, with Federica Cattaneo.

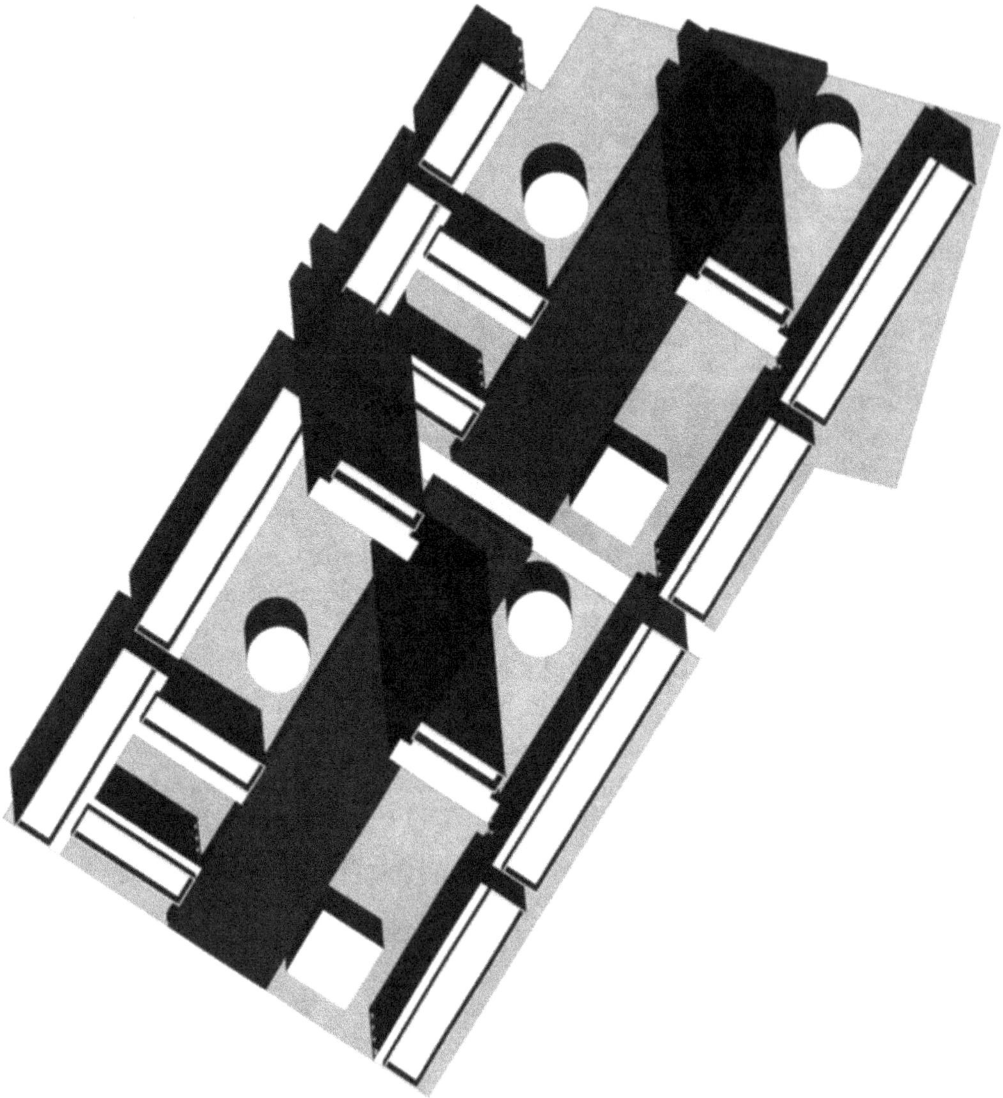

Fig. 3 Housing unit, first variation

a hierarchy of public spaces of different character, a wide range of places, and a variety of views one perceives while walking around the park along its central axis.

The reversed role in terms of public character between the street and the space within the blocks is reflected by a reversal of building solutions and type choices for the house: along the streets the block is defined by low buildings developed towards the interior by porticoes and loggias, with open pathways and passages towards the central green area. The tall houses are located freely within the block, at right angles to the streets, in connection with the park, just like the lower courtyards are open onto the same green area.

This results in a clear definition of outside and inside environment, a separation that in the old city generally kept private and inaccessible space. Here, it simply defines two collective places of different character, with access and distribution roads as purely functional pathways, while the places for housing, once more public as they were in the old city, include parks and gardens.

Every unit includes three types of housing: open courtyard housing, aligned housing, and tall housing that organize different places, each with its own character. The more enclosed and intimate C-shaped courtyards close to the longitudinal streets that run through the settlement and partially border the space inside the block are four-storey high and defined by aligned buildings along the streets and two transversal buildings of the same height. The other open courtyards are wider and typically feature a relation between different buildings—the street-facing aligned building, the tall perpendicular house that defines its measure, and a service building on the third side. The common facilities, also located within the blocks, are mainly built along the two longitudinal streets that run through the entire settlement (Fig. 3).

At a larger scale, the tall houses establish a more expansive landscape: they interact between each other at a distance within each block, are conceived in the general plan of the new settlement, and develop a relationship with the towers planned in the front square of the system as new subjects in the comprehensive design of a city made of separate and hopefully recognizable elements, that in turn is part of the Lombard landscape at a broader scale.

4 The Second Project, 2012. Second Variation[4]

The variation on the initial plan takes the architecture of the buildings as crucial to the composition as a whole. A block that can be walked through and enjoyed by the community, with no streets open to vehicles, onto which the apartments, facilities, and towers all look. The block is delimited by five-storey buildings where the loggia-living rooms of iron and glass look onto the park in the middle of the block. Sleeping areas and facilities of the apartments look onto tree-lined streets while the loggia-living room becomes the new vantage point to observe the city immersed in nature, the central hub of the home, like the loggia of Gardella's Casa al Parco, which looks straight out onto the Sempione Park almost as though to assert exclusive rights to its use.

Towards the city, the walls of the bedrooms, one level higher, constitute the compact, linear street frontage delimiting the block lengthwise. The apartment buildings are interrupted only at points corresponding to the towers inside the block, creating small squares that differ in each case, and provide lateral access to the residential block as well as a path running all the way through it.

The towers are based on the same principle as the apartment buildings, with a distinction in terms of construction and outlay between the sleeping and living areas.

[4]See Footnote 1. Design Group, Tomaso Monestiroli with Claudia Tinazzi, Federica Cattaneo.

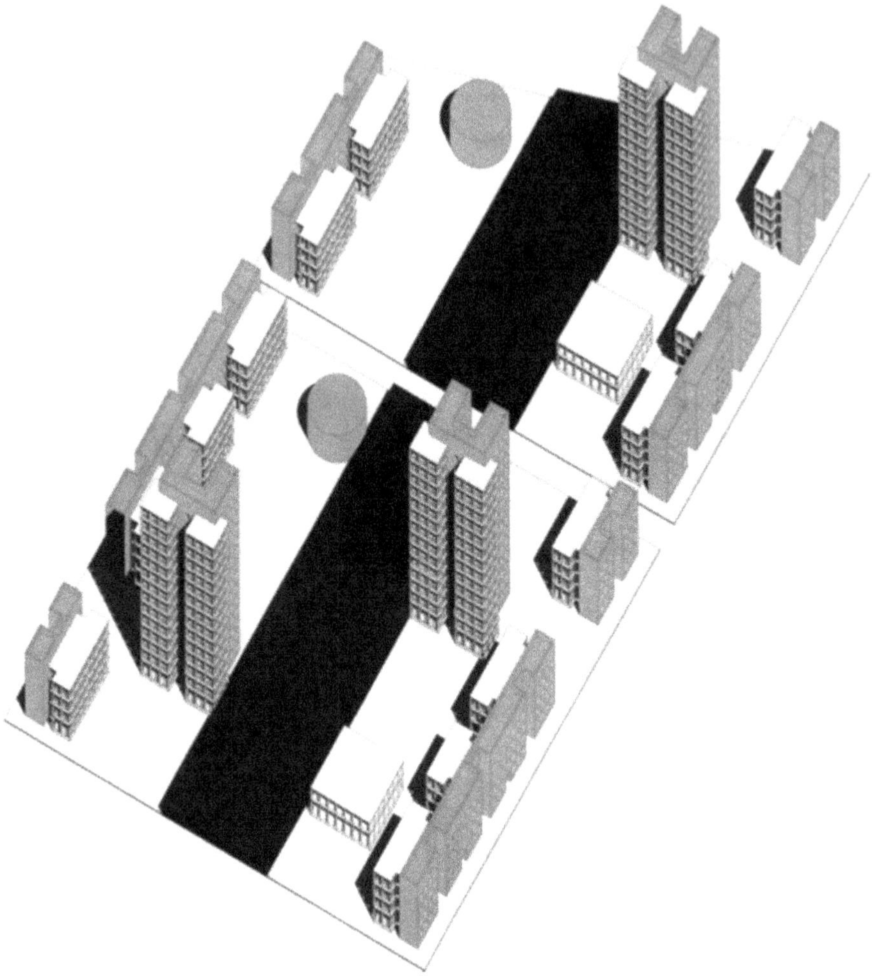

Fig. 4 Housing unit, second variation

The living rooms have full-length windows looking south onto the central avenue and the large public park beyond the railway line. Being 55 metres tall, the towers look out a long way and can be seen from afar, thus making it possible to identify the different relations with the blocks to which they belong and with the city. Perpendicular to the living rooms, the walls of the bedrooms and facilities are oriented east-west. The resulting T-shape encapsulates the importance attached to the view of the city and the natural environment. Located in the green areas of the block after the towers are the collective facilities, which help in turn to develop the relations required for the creation of places of ever increasing complexity and diversity to be discovered and experienced on walking through the block (Fig. 4).

Toward Sustainable Product and Process Innovation in the Construction Sector

Sara Cattaneo, Camilla Lenzi and Alessandra Zanelli

Introduction

This section focuses on the third challenge mentioned in the Introduction, namely the environmental sustainability of the construction sector and the eco-innovation of the transformative processes of the materials incorporated in buildings.

This section intends to deal with the following problematic aspects: a) the innovation of products/systems/components and processes, starting from the reuse and second life of products/materials up to the modification of supply chain relations (life cycle assessment); b) the use of innovative materials, with the aim of promoting the development of structural requalification techniques based on the use of recycled, recyclable and/or easily re-convertible materials in a circular economy perspective.

In particular, the modernization of construction supply chains—according to the methods and procedures with lower impact on the environment—is at the heart of the first chapters. Alternative approaches are taken into consideration for the disposal and virtuous reuse/recycling of building components, with the final objective of experimenting with circular economy approaches also in the field of production of goods and services in the building sector.

The next five chapters in this section propose specific case studies that aim to demonstrate how eco-innovation in the building sector must deal with both the design and strategic dimension as well as the technical-productive dimension.

Different materials/techniques are considered; in particular, Tartaglia and Biolzi et al. propose a different solution to reduce the environmental impact in the production of concrete, while Zanelli et al. propose strategies to be applied in lightweight architecture. Other studies focus on the solutions for the renovation of the exterior walls. In this section, the theme of the durability of the building components appears to be closely correlated with the service life foreseen for the buildings. This connection is not at all obvious in current design approaches, but highlights the no longer delayable need of experimenting and validating new production and management models in the construction field.

Design Strategies and LCA of Alternative Solutions for Resilient, Circular, and Zero-Carbon Urban Regeneration: A Case Study

Andrea Campioli, Elena Mussinelli, Monica Lavagna and Andrea Tartaglia

Abstract This paper analyzes the results and the methods applied to an environmental research activity within a team participating in the C40 reinventing cities call of the Municipality of Milan. The aim was to support the decision-making process in the selection of material, construction, design choices oriented toward the circularity of resources, and the reduction of impacts connected to the greenhouse effect (carbon footprint), through the verification of environmental performances (life-cycle assessment) of alternative solutions and to identify an innovative and efficient environmental model for low carbon buildings.

Keywords Zero carbon development · Life-cycle assessment · Carbon footprint · Circular building · Resilient cities

1 The Scenario

In 2005, the network C40 Cities Climate Leadership Group was established to cope against the growing environmental issues derived by the traditional models of city development. The idea was to form a collaboration among large cities to implement shared policies and common action able to produce a measurable reduction in greenhouse gases (GHG) and in the risks deriving from climate change. Starting with the representatives of eighteen megacities, after only one year the network included 40 cities, giving the name to the network.[1] Nowadays, total affiliated cities are over ninety of which more than 70% have already activated programs and actions to cope

[1] The major activities of the network aim to: "*connect city officials with their peers around the world to help deliver solutions to climate challenges; inspire innovation by show casing the ideas and solutions of leading global cities; advise city peers based on experience with similar projects and policies; influence national and international policy agendas and drive the market by leveraging the collective voice of cities*" (source: https://www.c40.org/networks).

A. Campioli (✉) · E. Mussinelli · M. Lavagna · A. Tartaglia
Architecture, Built Environment and Construction Engineering—ABC Department, Politecnico di Milano, Milan, Italy
e-mail: andrea.campioli@polimi.it

S. Della Torre et al. (eds.), *Regeneration of the Built Environment from a Circular Economy Perspective*, Research for Development,
https://doi.org/10.1007/978-3-030-33256-3_20

with climate change. Inside this scenario in 2018, starting from a former experience, carried out by the Municipality of Paris, 14 cities[2] of the network selected 31 underused sites to be used for an international competition named *Reinventing Cities*. The competition's goal was to involve developers, designers, and environmental experts in the definition of projects of interventions capable of reducing to zero the carbon footprint deriving from the construction/reconstruction and the use of these areas. In fact, the project groups, which would have bought the area in the event of victory, would have been selected with respect to the project's contents of the proposal evaluated in view of the capacity to respond to climate change and to favor the evolution of the territories in which they were located. The organization of the competition provided a set of guidelines that were the same for all the sites. The guidelines addressing the design of a carbon-free project stressed ten elements to be aware of or challenges[3] which would have also been the criteria for the evaluation of the various proposals. The challenges interpreted the issue of carbon footprint and resilience with a truly wide view correctly obliging the groups to work and think in view of a life-cycle approach. The city of Milan participated in identifying five sites of different sizes. The ABC Department was involved as the environmental expert[4] of a group[5] competing for the transformation of the area of via Serio: an area of almost 0.5 ha, property of the Municipality and partially used as a parking lot. The project proposes an innovative residence solution consisting of minimal housing modules, intended for students and young workers.

[2]The cities involved in the call were: Auckland, Chicago, Houston, Madrid, Milano, Montréal, Oslo, Paris, Portland, Reykjavík, Rio de Janeiro, Salvador, San Francisco, and Vancouver.

[3]The ten challenges as defined in the guidelines were: building energy efficiency and a supply of clean energy; sustainable materials management and circular economy; green mobility; resilience and adaptation; new green services for the site and the neighborhood; green growth and smart cities; sustainable water management; biodiversity, urban re-vegetation and agriculture; inclusive actions and community benefits; innovative architecture and urban design.

[4]The research group from the ABC Dept. was composed of: environmental design, urban scale studies and NBS—Elena Mussinelli, Andrea Tartaglia (general coordinator), Giovanni Castaldo, Davide Cerati; environmental performances, LCA and carbon footprint—Andrea Campioli, Monica Lavagna, Tecla Caroli, Anna Dalla Valle, and Serena Giorgi.

[5]The team for the project named Proxima was composed of: promoter—Energa Group S.r.l.; architectural design and coordination—Joseph Di Pasquale Architects S.r.l.; environmental expert—ABC Dept., Politecnico di Milano; engineering—Studio Tecneas, Siemens S.p.A.; technical specialist project consultant—Siemens S.p.A. Building Technologies Division; geology and geothermal energy—Dr Umberto Puppini; fire design—Building S.r.l.s; App interface design—IED—Istituto Europeo di Design S.p.A.; operating/management partner—Dovevivo S.p.A.; graphic representation—arch. Emanuela Sara Cidri; administrative and legal advisor—Bertacco Law Firm; financial management—Prothea S.r.l.; financial intermediaries—Crowdfunding Walliance S.r.l., Fundera S.r.l.; project partners for Sharing mobility—Axpo energy solutions Italia S.p.A.; project partners for environment—LegambienteLombardiaOnlus; project partner for the supply of wooden structures—Rikohišed.o.o.

2 The Environmental Approach

As environmental expert, the research group from the ABC Department had the role of supporting the design process identifying and selecting approaches, tools and solutions able to guarantee the highest environmental performances in the intervention throughout its entire life cycle. Thus, it was a significant opportunity to transfer theoretical models of analysis and evaluation into a real situation carrying out the activity in a continuous confrontation and collaboration with the typical stakeholders that characterize design, construction and management activities in the real estate area.

The aim was to go beyond the state-of-the-art about carbon footprint issue in buildings, adopting, experimenting, and testing innovative solutions. As a starting point, of course, the selected environmental approach took into account elements/indicators that are typically considered in the various environmental certifications with voluntary adhesion present in the Italian market (e.g., ITACA protocol, LEED certification, CasaClima, and Well) paying attention to elements such as user well-being, water and other natural resources management, energy and pollutant consumption, materials, site features, and integration in the context, relations, and mobility systems. All of these issues were addressed in order to reach levels of excellence with respect to the possibilities provided by technologies and indeed by introducing solutions of strong process and product innovation. In addition to this, in the environmental assessment model proposed, the users and their behavior during the use phase were also introduced as fundamental elements both to measure the real impacts of the intervention and to allow, through continuous monitoring and rewarding solutions, the progressive improvement of the "building-human being" system with respect to the issues of environmental sustainability, the use of resources, the response to climate change, quality of life, and the construction of a "resilient community."

Therefore, the final choice was to launch an ambitious challenge in which the environmental values of building interventions, deriving from human being-building interaction, would have been really monitored and verified also during the use phase to support the introduced tools for the correction and continuous improvement of environmental performance. This was done because the measurements made once the buildings are in use normally show a substantial difference between design forecasts in terms of consumption/impact up to 200% (Lehmann et al. 2017). Moreover, the human factor or "human behavior" is normally not considered or assessed in environmental protocols, even if human behavior in energy consumption alone can produce variations with respect to design forecasts of between 10 and 80% (van Dronkelaar et al. 2016).

For this reason, in order to reduce to the minimum the environmental impacts—with the ultimate goal of eliminating any impact over a time span of 50 years, which was the duration defined for the project during the structuring phase of the initiative—a number of specific solutions were introduced in the final project.

In particular, an integrated management system of the two-way relationships between user/building, operator/building, and operator/user was introduced to monitor the performance of the building and living behavior. This was carried out through the sensorized building and typological system, integrated through a suitable software platform. Moreover, living devices are directly linked to each individual user, to their preferences and behavior, which group together short-term functions and technologies that can be implemented during each maintenance/replacement/regeneration intervention with components with a lower environmental impact, thus gradually improving the overall performance of the whole building system (building system as a dynamic reality) during its life cycle. The monitoring system (defined to involve indoor areas, open spaces, and ways of use) is an integral part of the environmental protocol and cannot be eliminated in either the project or during use, as it is also used to define the economic agreements between a property and its housing services manager, and can also be used to control and optimize management costs.

Furthermore, a complete integration between nature-based solutions (NBS) (tree planting, bioswales, rain gardens, green roofs, and green walls) and technical and construction solutions was decided in order to pursue project goals.

3 Life-Cycle Assessment to Support Design Choices

To achieve the objective required by the call for a zero carbon settlement throughout the entire life cycle, in the different phases of the decisional process the design choices were subjected to verification of the carbon footprint, using the LCA methodology (EN 15978:2011).

In the preliminary phase, the research group indicated to the design team on which elements it was important to focus attention, in view of achieving such an ambitious result. The elements that have the greatest role on environmental impacts are the supporting structure of the building (for the huge amount of material used) and the energy aspects (consumption and type of energy carriers used). Hence, the choice of materials for the building's supporting structure and the control of energy aspects (design strategies aimed at reducing consumption, through the use of a high thermal performance envelope, and the installation of systems for energy production from renewable sources) were considered as priorities. With the attention being focused only on thc carbon footprint indicator, therefore of CO_2 equivalent emissions, the only way to compensate for the impacts of materials production and building construction is to use wood (or resources of the renewable plant supply chain), which allow to also include carbon absorption during plant growth into the carbon footprint balance. Several studies demonstrated the GHG emissions reduction achieved by timber structure in buildings (Fouquet et al. 2015; Skullestad et al. 2016). The storage of carbon in the wood can be considered in the balance as an advantage only if it is assumed that at the end of the building's service life the wood is not burnt (waste-to-energy), releasing the CO_2 absorbed during growth back into the atmosphere, but is reused (if still intact) or recycled. Considering that the current chain of chipboard and wood composites is very active, not only in the construction supply chain but also in the furniture supply chain, end-of-life recycling of structural wood is a plausible hypothesis. The project was therefore designed with a predominantly wooden structure, with pillars and floors in X-lam, in line with the design choices aimed at constructive reversibility and the potential reusability or recyclability of the entire construction (circular building).

From the point of view of system choices, to have an advantage in terms of carbon footprint, the choice must necessarily fall on the use of photovoltaic which can produce free energy from the sun. In this case, attention must be placed on effective positioning of the panels with respect to solar exposure so that the production of energy during use compensates for the production impact of the panel and allows for CO_2 gains in terms of avoided impacts compared to the use of other sources.

In the later phases of the project, the contribution of environmental consultancy to project choices focused on more detailed aspects, trying to optimize the carbon footprint of the other parts of the building. The call requires a low-carbon building, compared to a "business as usual" (BAU) building. Consequently, the work setup was based on a comparison among technical solutions and design choices, demonstrating through LCA evaluation the "environmental gains" obtained from the project choices with respect to choices typically implemented in current practice.

The "background" data (EC-JRC 2012), related to the environmental LCI and LCA of building products, were derived from the Environmental Product Declaration (EN 15804:2012) and, only when the EPDs were not available for the specific component, from databases (Ecoinvent, Ökobaudat, Inventory of Carbon and Energy ICE). The choice to use primary data deriving from EPD is linked to the desire to identify low impact products not only by comparing alternative materials but also by selecting products with the lowest environmental impact within the same material compartment. The materials selected have a lower carbon footprint for their recycled content, their production process based on the principles of a circular economy (e.g., industrial ecology) or their plant matrix content (absorbers of CO_2 during the growth of the plant). Transportation was also taken into consideration: for example, in the case of the concrete that constitutes the foundations, a more distant producer was chosen, but which guarantees a concrete with a lower environmental impact in the production process.

After the collection of CO_2 data related to alternative solutions, the assessment considered the highest and lowest values of CO_2eq emissions related to the phases A1–A4 (A1—raw materials supply, A2—transport to the production plant, A3—production, and A4—transport to the building site). For each part of the building considered, a comparison was made among possible materials and alternative producers, selecting the product with the lowest emissions (l.e.) and the product with the highest emissions (h.e.) among those (with EPD) present on the market; therefore, the material with the lowest emissions was selected (if compatible with the high-performance levels required by the project target). The database values were considered as a reference for the average values or assumed as comparison values only for materials without an EPD (Figs. 1 and 2).

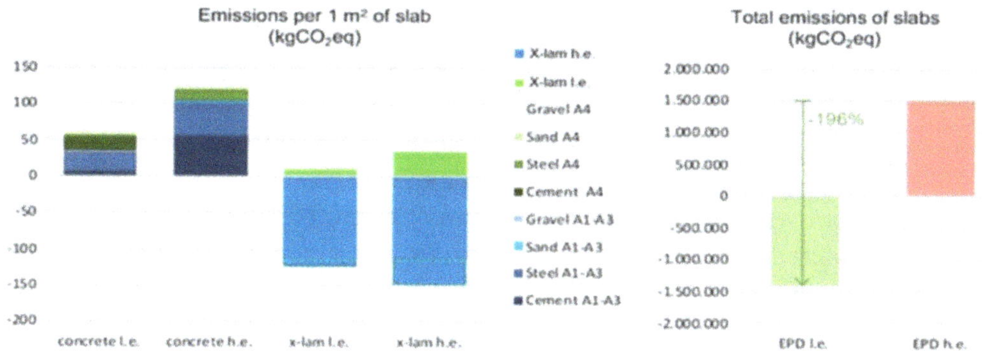

Fig. 1 LCA comparison, relating to 1 m^2 of slab, among lowest emission products and highest emission products, based on EPD data, for different materials (reinforced concrete and X-lam) and LCA comparison between the total impacts (entire buildings) of the project choice (X-lam l.e.) and BAU model (concrete h.e.)

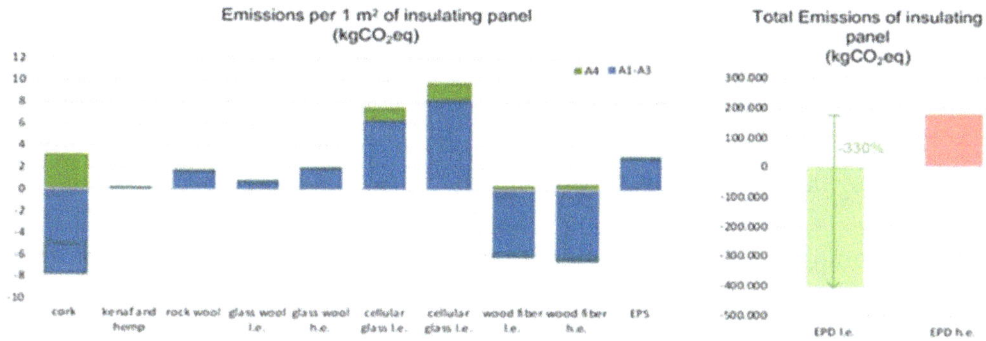

Fig. 2 LCA comparison, relating to 1 m^2 of panel, among lowest emission products and highest emission products, based on EPD data, for different insulating materials and LCA comparison between the total impacts (entire buildings) of the project choice (wood fiber l.e.) and BAU model (EPS for slabs and rockwool for walls h.e.)

After the selection of the lower carbon materials, for each building part (load-bearing structure of foundation, retaining walls and stair core, pillars, beams, slabs, façade cladding, thermal insulation, vertical walls frame, interior covering panels, floor coverings, and window frames), a comparison was made between the design choice and the BAU material choice (assuming the worst design choices among those compared, as a precautionary approach), considering the total quantity of material in the entire intervention, and therefore evaluating the total reduction in emissions achieved by the project.

At the end of this process of assessments and design choices, an overall summary evaluation was carried out relating to the impacts of production and transportation of all the parts of the project, showing the comparison between project choice and BAU. As assumed in the preliminary phase, the supporting structure is the element that has the greatest influence and that determines the greatest environmental advantage.

With regard to the use phase, the energy consumptions assumed for the project are based on a water–water heat pump with geothermal probes, characterized by a COP

= 4 and electrically powered. The electricity is supplied via photovoltaic panels of 2037 m^2, installed on site. In this case, the production of photovoltaic energy exceeds the requirements. For BAU model, the consumptions considered are related to the minimum mandatory requirement (so higher than the ones achieved by the project) and are connected to a heating system with a methane gas condensation boiler and a cooling system with an air–water heat pump characterized by a COP = 2.8 and electrically powered. The production of electricity connected to photovoltaic panels of 243 m^2, corresponding to the minimum surface area required by the Region of Lombardy, covers only a minimal part of the need for electricity, making it necessary to obtain energy from the electrical grid. As a result, there is a significant reduction in the impacts of the project. The calculation compares the impacts of the project, considering the production impact of the photovoltaic panels and two cycles of the photovoltaic panels replaced during the building life, and the impact of the BAU model, considering the electrical (national electricity mix) and thermal (methane) energy consumed (Figs. 3 and 4).

It should be pointed out that the environmental advantage achieved in the use phase, thanks to energy-saving strategies and the installation of plants for production from renewable sources, is considerably greater than those achieved in the production phase. In fact, in conventional buildings, high consumption (even in compliance with the current regulations on energy efficiency), and the use of fossil fuels (also for the production of electricity) determine considerable environmental impacts. At the same time, it must be emphasized that, in the future, when the legislation on zero-energy building will be applied and it will become common practice to construct low consumption buildings with integrated systems for the production of energy from renewable sources, the impacts related to the production of materials (embodied carbon and embodied energy) will become increasingly important elements.

With regard to the maintenance phase, the replacement cycles of bathrooms and kitchens were considered. To facilitate maintenance operations, the project team

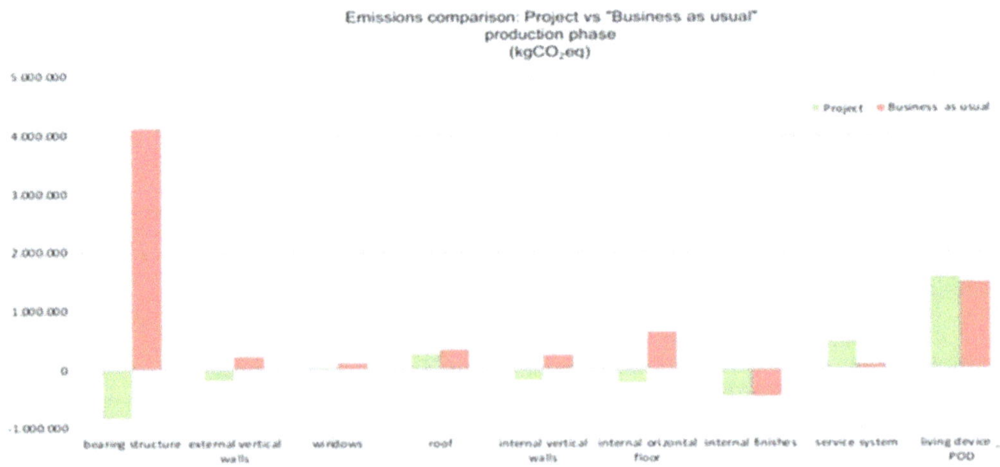

Fig. 3 LCA comparison, relating to the buildings as a whole and relating to production phase, between the design choice (green) and the BAU model (red), for each building part

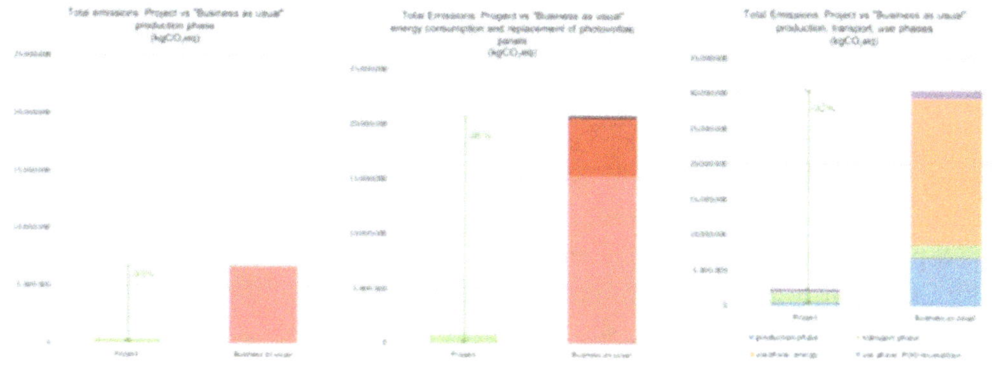

Fig. 4 LCA comparison relating to the buildings as a whole between the design choice (green) and the BAU model (red): to the left relating to the production phase of building materials, in the center relating to the use phase and systems production, and to the right relating to the entire life cycle

designed an innovative POD solution, such as reversible prefabricated cells, which can be disassembled, brought to the factory, "re-manufactured" and reassembled, reducing waste material and replacements, in view of a circular building perspective. The calculation accounted for the disassemblable POD in the project model and the traditional replacement of the systems in the BAU model. In the case of the POD, a deep-renovation maintenance cycle is planned every 20 years and, considering a useful life of 50 years, two renovation cycles are considered. During that operation, the load-bearing structure of the PODs is recovered by 100 and 50% of the materials and components subject to the renovation could be recovered. In the BAU case, it was considered that 100% of the materials and components subject to renewal would be replaced.

Contrary to what was expected, in this case, the environmental advantage obtained, although present, is small, since the structure of the POD (which ultimately is an "additional" element) significantly affects the carbon footprint (production impact of the steel frame). An in-depth analysis of the structural design of the POD, in order to optimize and reduce the amount of material used, could demonstrate a more advantageous environmental balance of the POD disassembly solution.

In the end, the reduction of CO_2eq emissions of the entire intervention was calculated, comparing two models: a project model and a BAU model. In the evaluation of the entire life cycle, the phases of production A1–A3, transport to building site A4, use B6 (energy consumption) and replacement B4 were considered. The construction phases and the end-of-life phase were not considered, both because these phases typically have a reduced incidence, about 2–4% (Lavagna et al. 2018), and because in this particular project, the use of dry construction techniques allows for the fact that the impacts of the construction site both during construction and demolition are reduced (mechanical assembly activities only) and at the end of their life, most of the building materials can be reused or recycled as the building is completely reversible. The results obtained point out the virtuousness of the design choices that were made considering the CO_2eq emissions on different scales: from the material to the product, from the subsystem to the building.

Finally, all the benefits—such as direct sequestration of CO_2 and reduction of GHGs—deriving from the use of NBS were calculated in terms of CO_2eq. using values from the scientific literature and databases (database Qualiviva; CNT 2010; IPCC 2007; McPherson et al. 2006) and I-Tree Eco software (V.6).

All the adopted solutions—detailed and careful selection of construction (materials and supply model), management model, maintenance solutions and NBS—have made it possible to contain the impact of a building over 50 years to approximately 1.6 kg CO_2eq/m^2 per year. To compensate this value, a forestry intervention on an area of fewer than 2 ha would be sufficient.

4 Critical Aspects and Future Developments

The experience of a real participation alongside a project team and in response to a call from a public body was definitely positive, because it shows a virtuous case of promotion of sustainability aspects by a public administration, which therefore urges the project team to consider the environmental aspects and leads to the involvement of environmental consultants in an effectively integrated way from the first phases of the project, in order to be able to achieve the ambitious goal required. However, it is also necessary to highlight the aspects that remain critical in this type of experience. In particular, the fact of having chosen a single environmental indicator (the carbon footprint), considered a priority in the international debate (Rockström et al. 2017), risks orienting the design choices in a direction that is not entirely sustainable.

As mentioned above, in order to reduce the carbon footprint of a building, the necessary choice is to use large amounts of wood in its construction. Some researchers show that a cross-laminated timber building gives the lowest life-cycle carbon emission while a beam-and-column building gives the highest life-cycle emission (Doodo et al. 2014). Although it might seem counterintuitive, the increasing of quantities in the case of wood, therefore abounding rather than optimizing, decreases the carbon footprint, since it increases the quantity of stored CO_2 that becomes a minus in the environmental balance. However, by using more material unnecessarily, the project brings about a disadvantage compared to all the other environmental impact indicators (only in the case of the carbon footprint is there the possibility of having the minus sign in phases A1–A3 raw materials supply-transport to the production plant manufacturing).

Moreover, although different methodological choices and assumptions can lead to opposite conclusions, there is no consensus on the assessment of biogenic carbon in LCA. Incorrect biogenic carbon assessments could lead to inefficient or counterproductive strategies, as well as missed opportunities (Breton et al. 2018). There is a need for a government mandate for improved data quality and for support for the development of a transparent and simplified methodology (De Wolf et al. 2017). Therefore, making environmental choices by considering a single indicator is likely to indicate a constructive solution with respect to a single environmental theme, without considering the impacts related to other aspects (energy consumption, acidification, human toxicity, and soil consumption). For example, the wood supply chain is critical with respect to land use and acidification issues.

Hence, the actions promoted by public administrations should reconcile the need for a simplified approach (also for checking the results obtained by the project) with a complete environmental approach, which requires a systemic capability to control environmental impacts in their complexity.

References

Breton, C., Blanchet, P., Amor, B., Beauregard, R., & Chang, W. S. (2018). Assessing the climate change impacts of biogenic carbon in buildings: A critical review of two main dynamic approaches. *Sustainability, 10*(6), 2020.

CNT. (2010). *The value of green infrastructure. A guide to recognizing its economic, environmental and social benefits*. Center for Neighborhood Technology.

De Wolf, C., Pomponi, F., Moncaster, A. (2017). Measuring embodied carbon dioxide equivalent of buildings: A review and critique of current industry practice. *Energy and Building, 140*, 68–80.

Dodoo, A., Gustavsson, L., & Sathre, R. (2014). Lifecycle carbon implications of conventional and low-energy multi-storey timber building systems. *Energy and Building, 82*, 194–210.

EC-JRC. (2012). *The international reference Life cycle data system (ILCD) handbook. Towards more sustainable production and consumption for a resource efficient Europe*. European Commission, Joint Research Centre, Luxembourg

EN 15804:2012 Sustainability of construction works. Environmental product declarations. Core rules for the product category of construction products.

EN 15978:2011 Sustainability of construction works. Assessment of environmental performance of buildings. Calculation method.

Fouquet, M., Levasseur, A., Margni, M., Lebert, A., Lasvaux, S., Souyri, B., et al. (2015). Methodological challenges and developments in LCA of low energy buildings: Application to biogenic carbon and global warming assessment. *Building and Environment, 90*, 51–59.

IPCC. (2007). Climate change 2007: Mitigation. In B. Metz, O. R. Davidson, P. R. Bosch, R. Dave, L. A. Meyer (Eds.), *Contribution of working group III to the fourth assessment report of the Intergovernmental Panel on Climate Change*. Cambridge University Press

Lavagna, M., Baldassarri, C., Campioli, A., Giorgi, S., Dalla Valle, A., Castellani, V., et al. (2018). Benchmarks for environmental impact of housing in Europe: Definition of archetypes and LCA of the residential building stock. *Building and Environment, 145*, 260–275.

Lehmann, U., Khouryb, J., & Patel, M. K. (2017). Actual energy performance of student housing: Case study, benchmarking and performance gap analysis. *Energy Procedia, 122*, 163–168.

McPherson, E. G., Simpson, J. R., Peper, P. J., Maco, S. E., Gardner, S. L., Cozad, S. K., et al. (2006). *Midwest community tree guide. Benefits, costs, and strategic planting*. Create space Independent Publishing.

Rockström, J., Gaffney, O., Rogelj, J., Meinshausen, M., Nakicenovic, N., & Schellnhuber, H. J. (2017). A roadmap for rapid decarbonisation. *Science, 355*, 1269–2127.

Skullestad, J. L., Bohne, R. A., & Lohne, J. (2016). High-rise timber buildings as a climate change mitigation measure: A comparative LCA of structural system alternatives. *Energy Procedia, 96*, 112–123.

Van Dronkelaar, C., Dowson, M., Burman, E., Spataru, C., & Mumovic, D. (2016). A review of the energy performance gap and its underlying causes in non-domestic buildings. *Frontiers in Mechanical Engineering, 1*, 1–14.

Circular Economy and Recycling of Pre-consumer Scraps in the Construction Sector. Cross-Sectoral Exchange Strategies for the Production of Eco-Innovative Building Products

Marco Migliore, Ilaria Oberti and Cinzia Talamo

Abstract The chapter reports the results of a research entitled "Ri-scarto", conducted with the contribution of the "Fratelli Confalonieri" Foundation of Milan. The research investigates the conditions that can facilitate the cross-sectoral exchange (various manufacturing sectors-construction sector) of pre-consumer by-products and scraps, that can be used and/or recycled for making building products. The research proposes the framework of a cross-sectoral virtual marketplace, where the different stakeholders (manufacturers, possible users of by-products and scraps, industrial process planners, public administrators, etc.), organised in a network, can identify, locate and exchange available reusable waste.

Keywords Circular economy · Waste · By-products · Pre-consumer scraps · Sustainable production · Construction sector and innovative building materials

1 Introduction

Reducing the production of waste through prevention, recycling and reuse is one of the sub-targets present within "Responsible consumption and production", the twelfth of the 17 Sustainable Development Goals of Agenda 2030 (UN United Nations 2015); it also represents one of the basic strategies at the core of the many measures and guidelines of the European Commission (EC European Commission 2014, 2015, 2010) supporting the circular economy (MacArthur Foundation 2015a). The circular economy (MacArthur Foundation 2010, 2015b) perspective leads us to attribute to by-products and recyclable wastes the potential of virtuous generator of

M. Migliore (✉)
Milan, Italy
e-mail: marco.migliore@polimi.it

I. Oberti · C. Talamo
Architecture, Built Environment and Construction Engineering—ABC Department, Politecnico di Milano, Milan, Italy

S. Della Torre et al. (eds.), *Regeneration of the Built Environment from a Circular Economy Perspective*, Research for Development,
https://doi.org/10.1007/978-3-030-33256-3_21

new markets, capable of activating new skills and entrepreneurship and innovating the production processes according to the circular economy perspective (strategies downstream of production and consumption) (Lacy and Rutqvist 2015). At this aim, the different stages of the life cycle of the products should be made interdependent and permeable, in order to facilitate the exchange of materials, information and knowledge between the various production sectors. This implies a change of paradigms-involving culture, information and production processes-in the direction of a strategy focused on recognising the economic potential of recyclable waste and the possible involvement of a plurality of subjects: the companies extracting raw materials, the manufacturers processing raw materials; the designers and manufacturers of products; the designers and manufacturers of complex systems (buildings, consumer goods, equipment, etc.); the managers of the use phase (maintenance and upgrades); consumers/users; the managers of demolition/disassembly processes; the designers and the manufacturers of secondary raw materials and recycled products. This is a very complex scenario, in which stakeholders, belonging to different sectors and disciplines, interact on both a strategic and operational level and exchange information and materials.

2 Circular Economy Approaches for the Construction Sector

If the construction sector is considered, many questions arise, connected both with the areas and ways of application of the circular economy and with the roles of the many operators involved, such as:

- how to reconfigure existing building products and/or design new ones in order to reduce waste and/or characterise scrap and by-products, so that they can be applicable, as recyclable for other sectors;
- how to reconfigure existing building products and/or design new ones in order to use scrap and by-products from other sectors, thereby lowering production costs and increasing the environmental value of buildings;
- how to design the building systems for disassembling parts for reuse/recycling;
- how to assess and communicate the environmental quality of building products involved in recycling processes.

Considering circular economy, these and other issues open up to multiple perspectives of innovation for the construction sector and to new market segments involving the need for new skills, related to various stakeholders, for example:

- the manufacturers of building materials and components, that may offer recyclable waste that can become secondary raw materials for other sectors;
- the construction firms, that may offer recyclable waste that can become secondary raw materials for other sectors;

- the manufacturers of building materials and components, that may become the receiver of recyclable waste from other sectors;
- the designers of buildings, that may orient this market and can guide environmental quality strategies;
- the environmental certifiers, that may support the demand and the supply of recycled materials by highlighting the environmental parameters (and the related data) involved in the assessment procedures.

Actually, all these stakeholders share a double field of interest, defined by the "The Waste Framework Directive 2008/98/EC" (EC European Commission 2008) recently emended by the Directive 2018/851 (EC European Commission 2018): on the one hand, by-products[1] and on the other hand, certain specified wastes, that can reach an "end-of-waste status[2]", that is able to cease to be waste[3] when they have undergone a recovery, including recycling, operation. Working in a circular economy perspective (Charter 2019) implies, therefore, developing all those actions, skills, knowledge and information that allow us to:

- recognise and enhance the possibilities for by-products and secondary raw materials markets;
- orientate design and production in order to decrease the percentage of waste;
- characterise and improve the knowledge and traceability of by-products and secondary raw materials;
- analyse what, coming from the production and the usage processes, is commonly considered scrap in order to recognise and select the parts of it that might have a new use (recyclable waste) in comparison with the parts to be eliminated for being conclusively deemed discardable;
- create and characterise new supply chains based on recycling activities;
- support recycling chains[4] through information and sensitisation campaign.

---

[1] A substance or object, resulting from a production process, the primary aim of which is not the production of that item, is a by-products if: (a) further use of the substance or object is certain; (b) the substance or object can be used directly without any further processing other than normal industrial practice; (c) the substance or object is produced as an integral part of a production process and (d) further use is lawful, i.e. the substance or object fulfils all relevant product, environmental and health protection requirements for the specific use and will not lead to overall adverse environmental or human health impacts (EC European Commission 2008).

[2] The conditions for the end-of-waste status are: (a) the substance or object is commonly used for specific purposes; (b) a market or demand exists for such a substance or object; (c) the substance or object fulfils the technical requirements for the specific purposes and meets the existing legislation and standards applicable to products and (d) the use of the substance or object will not lead to overall adverse environmental or human health impacts (EC European Commission 2008).

[3] A substance or object which the holder discards or intends or is required to discard (EC European Commission 2008).

[4] On the issues of overcoming barriers when launching a waste market, see the interesting study from the European Topic Centre on Sustainable Consumption and Production: ETC/SCP Working Paper No 5/2013, Approaches to using waste as a resource: Lessons learnt from UK experiences, 2013.

3 Construction Sector's Demand and Manufacturing Sectors' Supply: A Research Proposal for a Cross-Sectoral Platform

In order to apply to the construction sector the possible actions, related to circular economy approaches, a research, funded by a "Fratelli Confalonieri Foundation" fellowship, has been developed starting from 2017. The research, named "Ri-scarto", starts from some basic assumptions:

- building products are highly cross-sectoral (according to the Italian ANCE[5] report, 31 of the 36 economic sectors are suppliers of construction sector, that buys goods and services from more than 88% of the economic sectors);
- by-products and pre-consumer scraps, coming from various manufacturing sectors, can represent important sources of secondary materials, useful for reducing the high environmental impacts[6] of the construction sector, due to the intensive use of raw materials and to the generation of huge amounts of waste (C&D waste)[7];
- by-products and pre-consumer scraps, coming from manufacturing sectors, are easy to be located, characterised, forecasted, quantified, are concentrated in the site of their production and represent, if well-known, a potential supply for recycling processes oriented to the production of building products;
- information can play an important role where cross-sectoral platforms can support and strengthen the dialogue between the construction sector demand for secondary materials and the manufacturing sectors supply of by-products and pre-consumer scraps.

On the basis of these assumptions, the research has developed two parts:

- a first part dealing with an investigation of experimental cases of successful matching between the construction sector's demand for recycled products and the manufacturing sectors' supply of by-products and pre-consumer scraps recycled for building products. The output of this part is a database of cases regarding products and processes, that can be analysed and compared according to various reading keys in order to share practices and highlight trends;

[5]ANCE, The construction industry: structure, sectoral interdependencies and economic growth, in italian "L'industria delle costruzioni: struttura, interdipendenze settoriali e crescita economica", 2015.

[6]UNEP (United Nations Environment Program Environment for Development) reports, in one of his study (UNEP-United Nations Environment Program Environment for Development 2018), that buildings use around 40% of the world's energy, 25% of global water, 40% of global resources, and emit about 1/3 of greenhouse gas emissions and are responsible for around 50% by weight of waste.

[7]Every year, the European construction sector produces about 820 million tonnes of C&D waste, which represents 46% of the total amount of waste generated (Gálvez-Martos et al. 2018). The typical composition of C&D waste shows that a percentage up to 85% is characterized by concrete, ceramics and masonry, although it can be heterogeneous depending the specific origin and it can contain large amounts of plasterboard and wood.

- a second part dealing with a study about the conditions for the development of a cross-sectoral virtual marketplace, where the different stakeholders (manufacturers, possible users of by-products and scraps, industrial process planners, public administrators, etc.), organised in a network, can identify, locate and exchange available by-products and pre-consumer scraps. The output of this part is the proposal of a framework of a cross-sectoral platform that can allow various stakeholders to share information and create trades.

4 The Database of Best Practice

In order to outline the practices, the experimentations and the trends in the field of applied research, the study has investigated the European funded researches, related to recycling and secondary resources. The examined projects are those supported by: the LIFE Programme[8] (EEC European Economic Community 1992), the CIP programme[9] (EU European Union 2006) and some Horizon 2020 (EC European Commissions 2011, b, c) initiatives.

In particular, focusing on the LIFE Programme projects allows to highlight both the European research strategies towards innovations in products and processes, involved in recycling (De la Paz 2014), and the trends of various manufacturing sectors towards the market generated by circular economy. In economic terms, the EU support to the programme has grown exponentially, from the 400 million euro of the first loan to the EUR 5.450 million in funds provided for 2021–2027. This is the sign of the success achieved by the initiative and the quality of the results produced by the more than 4.700 projects funded so far. Besides, LIFE Programme allocates to the area “environment and resource efficiency” more than the 30% of the total budget, showing a great interest in manufacturing initiatives that can improve the efficient use of raw materials, prevention of waste and production of secondary materials. Considering the year 2017, for this area of the LIFE programme, we have witnessed a 15% increase in projects funded, reaching a final amount of more than

[8]From 1992, the LIFE is the EU’s funding instrument for the environment. The general objective of LIFE is to contribute to the implementation, updating and development of EU environmental policy and legislation by co-financing pilot or demonstration projects characterised by European added value. For the period 201420, the fifth version of the LIFE programme for the environment and climate action establishes the EU’s main funding framework for environmental and climate change policy. The programme provides action grants for pilot and demonstration projects to develop, test and demonstrate policy or management approaches. It also covers the development and demonstration of innovative technologies, implementation, monitoring and evaluation of EU environmental policy and law, as well as best practices and solutions. The European Commission is particularly looking for technologies and solutions that are ready to be implemented in close-to-market conditions, at industrial or commercial scale, during the project duration. See: https://ec.europa.eu/easme/en/section/life/life-environment-sub-programme.

[9]The Competitiveness and Innovation Framework Programme (CIP) supports SMEs in innovation activities (including eco-innovation), provides better access to finance and delivers business support services in the Regions.

EUR 80 million of contribution over a budget of over EUR 160 million. With regard to the nationality of the applicants, Italy and Spain have broken the record for the number of funded projects. Considering the 2014–2016 triennium, more than 50% of the projects financed were Italian and Spanish. Focusing on the issue of waste, 582 projects have been revealed during the 1992 and 2019 period. Within these, approximately 45% of the total selected projects concern recycling, reduction and use of waste, and more than 20% refer to waste from the industrial sector, from the C&D sector and the management of dangerous waste.

In the research, in order to monitor and compare the projects regarding cross-sectoral exchange of by-products and recyclable scraps between manufacturing sectors and construction sector and to identify possible trends in innovation, a database that can integrate the basic database, managed by the LIFE programme[10] or others, has been developed (Fig. 1). The database collects the following information: type of the project (LIFE, CIP, etc.); code of the project; year of start; country; NACE code of applicants; type of applicant (public/private research centres, universities, local/regional authorities, international companies, big companies, SM enterprises, cooperatives, etc.); type of potential partners involved (development agencies, inter-governmental bodies, international enterprises, large enterprises, local authorities, mix enterprises, NGO foundations, national authorities, park-reserve authorities, professional organizations, public enterprises, regional authorities, research institutions, SMEs, training centres and universities); name of the project; type of proposed innovation (new production process, innovative production process, new product with recycled content, innovative product with recycled content, services); target

Fig. 1 Main categories of keys adopted for the database: characteristics of the companies involved (economic sectors), type of waste, type of innovation, type of activity carried out on scraps/waste

[10]See: http://ec.europa.eu/environment/life/project/Projects/index.cfm.

goals of the project (defined by the applicants); typology of activities conducted on scrap/waste (reduction, recycling, elimination); budget of the project (euro); EU contribution (%); sector of destination of the project; NACE code of destination sector; type of building product deriving from the project (according to the omniclass_21 system); type of technical element of product deriving from project (according to the classification of UNI 8290 standard); specific treated scraps/waste; code CER code of the treated scraps/waste; description of the CER code; positive impacts of the project (e.g. reduction of CO_2 emissions, reduce of energy consumption, etc.); progress of the project. At present, the selected and analysed projects are about 100 (considered period from 2004 to 2016). The database, that is periodically updated, allows to compare, according to a set of reading keys, the selected experiences and to highlight some features: referring attention to NACE economic activities, emerges that one of the sectors with more fundings assignments is that relating to the ceramic industry. Compared to the examined projects, around 40% refers to initiatives that involve the ceramic industry, the types of innovations implemented refer both to product innovations and process innovations, and in all of them there is a reduction and/or elimination of the waste, which is reintroduced into the process. The reasons that justify this trend are different: this sector has the possibility of being able to introduce very heterogeneous materials in the mixture (deriving from recycling and recovery) without compromising the final performance of the product; there is a great availability of secondary raw materials that can be used for this purpose, aggregates (Gálvez-Martos et al. 2018) and other types of scraps/waste (WEEE, sludge, etc.); and finally the positive impacts deriving from these process and product innovation are far-reaching (reduction of natural resources consumption, etc.). Depending on the type of secondary raw material, the quantity that can be introduced in the production mixture is variable, therefore it is not possible to define a univocal trend, but it is necessary to observe projects.[11]

It emerges, in a widespread way, that when the scraps can be reduced to powder, losing main characteristics, they can be reintroduced in many production processes such as those related to the production of: thermal insulation (25%),[12] mortar and concrete (5%) (Awoyera et al. 2018), artificial stone, etc. This apparently could represent a not efficient innovation, because it represent a downcycling process, but we must consider that often the recovered material is already poor material, that could not recover value if not in this way.

Analyzing the beneficiaries of LIFE funding, it is possible to highlight the significant amount of small- and medium-sized firms (Fig. 2).

Finally, considering the most widespread types of innovation (Fetsis 2017), it emerges that most of the projects involve improvement of existing production process. There

[11]For further details see the projects: LIFE05 ENV/E/000301, LIFE10 ENV/IT/000419, LIFE11 ENV/IT/000036, LIFE12 ENV/IT/000678, 12 LIFE12 ENV/IT/000436.

[12]For further details see the projects: LIFE05 ENV/DK/000158, LIFE06 ENV/D/000471, LIFE12 ENV/ES/000079, LIFE07 ENV/IT/000361, LIFE13 ENV/IT/001225.

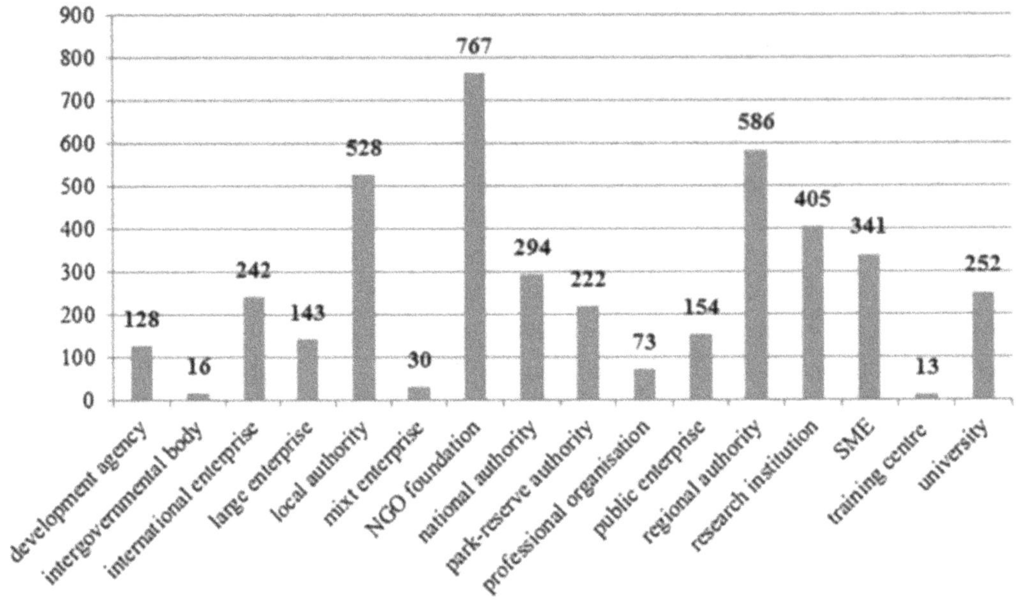

Fig. 2 Distribution by type of beneficiary of the projects (data extracted and processed from the LIFE projects database, period 1992–2019)

are very few cases in which new production processes are activated for the realisation of a new product.

5 A Virtual Marketplace for by-Products and Pre-consumer Recyclable Scraps

The objective of the second part of the research is to define the characteristics of the structure and the operating procedures of an inter-sectoral information platform (Web-based), designed to match supply and possible demand of by-products and pre-consumer recyclable scraps in order to create a virtual marketplace. The platform, according to its characteristics and structure, might have different applications: to be delivered to third parties for the development of Web applications; to be proposed for its operational evolution through participation in competitive research projects; to be a tool for activating clusters and/or industrial symbiosis networks. To this end, the research primarily has identified information sets, capable of describing various types of by-products and scraps, coming from many manufacturing sectors, in relation to different characteristics (chemical, physical, morphological–dimensional, embodied energy, in terms of the environmental impact of the equivalent CO_2 emitted, etc.). The purpose is to stimulate various operators for the collection of unified and unambiguous data and to facilitate, through a shared knowledge, the identification of possible alternative uses of by-products and scraps for the construction industry.

The structure and the contents of the platform are based on:

- a taxonomy of by-products and scraps, which are codified and classified on the basis of the economic activities they come from (according to the CER catalogue);
- a set of information related to the characteristics of the codified by-products and scraps and to the parameters useful for the environmental and economic assessment of scenarios for reuse/recycling;
- a supply/demand relationship matrix, able to correlate the taxonomy of by-products and scraps and the different classes of technical elements of the building system, in order to identify the possible construction products (materials, semi-finished products, components, systems) that can be manufactured by using entirely or partially by-product and/or pre-consumer scraps;
- the definition of a geo-referencing GIS tool, useful for mapping amounts of by-products and pre-consumer scraps, available in defined geographical areas. The GIS tools can be useful also for supporting the creation of local hubs, necessary for the collection, separation, storage, management and distribution of by-products and pre-consumers scraps, to be processed for becoming secondary raw materials or directly be used in the construction sector.

6 Conclusions

Circular economy orients to operate in a virtuous way, trying to progressively minimise waste non-recyclable because considered useless, superfluous or not convenient for new uses (Webster 2017). The aim is to pursue the "end-of-waste" status, trying to identify areas of convenience (not only economic but also environmental and social), through actions such as:

- searching for, recognising, defining, inventing a use, and a specific purpose for waste. In this sense, it is important to activate some strategies. Firstly, we must promote project activities capable, on the basis of availability of information on the characteristics of recyclable waste and semi-finished products, of pursuing innovations both by developing new products and by defining new characterisations of existing products. Secondly, we must sustain the practices of inter-sectoral "dialogue" in order to widen the view both on the characteristics, the quantity and origin of different types of waste and on the possible fields of use and of the possible markets;
- recognising supply and demand in relation to possible uses and thus, designing market scenarios. Recognising the demand means on one hand having previously defined the possible purposes of reusable portions of waste. On the other hand it means having evaluated and possibly quantified the potentially interested subjects, in terms of both consumers and manufacturers, taking into consideration these purposes. Recognising the supply means mapping, tracking and characterising waste. Designing market scenarios involves identifying the conditions for meeting supply and demand implementing information support to make the manufacturing feasible using cost/profit analysis, supported by economic and environmental indicators;

- identifying the characteristics of the waste. As long as waste represents an "opaque" material from an information point of view, it is very difficult to activate matchmaking processes between supply and demand. The characterisation of the waste is very important to understand opportunities and barriers for their usage, to verify the absence of any problems linked to regulatory requirements and to develop environmental assessments. The characteristics may regard not only the material properties, but also other aspects such as, for example, in the case of "standard" waste, the size, shape, and, for locally defined situations (for example, production districts, production centres, etc.), the amount of waste produced in specif periods (e.g. months, semesters, years);
- monitoring the flows of waste (quantity, characteristics and location) in order to determine the potential supply.

Finally, the role of information seems to be essential (in terms of the contents and methods of treatment and exchange) in order to activate and support the processes necessary for the development of a possible market and to make usable materials by reaching the "end-of-waste" status. These goals must be considered also in relation to the fact that, by 2020, the preparation for reuse, recycling and other types of material recovery, (including backfilling operations using waste to substitute other materials), waste from non-hazardous construction and demolition, excluding the material in its natural state (as defined under item 17 05 04 of the European list of waste), must increase at least 70% in terms of overall weight, according to the European guidelines.

References

Awoyera, P. O., Ndambuki, J. M., Akinmusuru, J. O., & Omole, D. O. (2018). Characterization of ceramic waste aggregate concrete. *HBRC Journal, 14,* 282–287.

Charter, M. (2019). *Designing for the circular economy*. New York: Routledge.

De la Paz, C. (2014). EU LIFE programme: Contributing to waste management in Europe for over 20 years. *Waste Management, 34*(3), 571–572.

EC European Commission (2008). Directive 2008/98/EC of the European Parliament and of the council of 19 November 2008 on waste and repealing certain directives.

EC European Commissions (2010). COM(2010)2020 communication from the commission to the European Parliament, the council, the European economic and social committee and the committee of the regions—a strategy for smart, sustainable and inclusive growth, Brussels, March 2010.

EC European Commissions (2011a). COM(2011)21, communication from the commission to the European Parliament, the council, the European economic and social committee and the committee of the regions—a resource-efficient Europe—flagship initiative under the Europe 2020 strategy, Brussels, January 2011.

EC European Commissions (2011b). COM(2011)899, communication from the commission to the European Parliament, the council, the European economic and social committee and the committee of the regions—innovation for sustainable future. The eco-innovation action plan (Eco-AP), Brussels.

EC European Commission (2011c). COM(2011)808, communication from the commission to the European Parliament, the council, the European economic and social committee and the committee of the regions. Horizon 2020—The Framework Programme for Research and Innovation, Brussels.

EC European Commission (2014). COM 2014-398 final, communication from the commission to the European Parliament, the council, the European economic and social committee and the committee of the regions "Towards a circular economy: A zero waste programme for Europe", 02.07.2014 Bruxelles.

EC European Commission (2015). COM 2015-614 final, communication from the commission to the European Parliament, the council, the European economic and social committee and the committee of the regions "Closing the loop—an EU action plan for the circular economy", 02.12.2015 Bruxelles.

EC European Commission (2018). Directive 2018/851 of the European Parliament and of the council of 30 May 2018 amending directive 2008/98/EC waste.

EEC European Economic Community (1992), Council Regulation No 1973/92 of 21 May 1992 establishing a financial instrument for the environment (LIFE), Brussels.

EU European Union (2006). Decision no 1639/2006/EC of the European Parliament and of the council of 24 October 2006 establishing a competitiveness and innovation framework programme (2007–2013), Brussels.

Fetsis, P. (2017). The LIFE programme—over 20 years improving sustainability in the built environment in the EU. *Procedia Environmental Sciences, 38,* 913–918.

Gálvez-Martos, J. L., Styles, D., Schoenberger, H., & Zeschmar-Lahle, B. (2018). Construction and demolition waste best management practice in Europe. *Resources, Conservation and Recycling, 136*, 166–178.

Lacy, P., & Rutqvist, J. (2015). *Waste to wealth: The circular economy advantage*. Basingstoke (UK): Palgrave Macmillan.

MacArthur Foundation (2010). The circular economy concept, regenerative economy. https://www.ellenmacarthurfoundation.org/circular-economy/concept.

MacArthur Foundation (2015a). Growth Within: a circular economy vision for a competitive Europe. https://www.ellenmacarthurfoundation.org/publications/growth-within-a-circular-economy-vision-for-a-competitive-europe.

MacArthur Foundation (2015b). Towards a circular economy: business rationale for an accelerated transition. https://www.ellenmacarthurfoundation.org/assets/downloads/TCE_Ellen-MacArthur-Foundation-9-Dec-2015.pdf.

UN United Nations (2015). Transforming our world: the 2030 Agenda for Sustainable Development.

UNEP—United Nations Environment Program Environment for Development (2018). 2018 global status report. Towards a zero-emission, efficient and resilient buildings and construction sector.

Webster, K. (2017). *The circular economy: A wealth of flows*. Cowes (UK): Ellen MacArthur Foundation Publishing.

Re-Using Waste as Secondary Raw Material to Enhance Performances of Concrete Components in Reducing Environmental Impacts

Andrea Tartaglia

Abstract This essay outlines the circular economy in the construction sector starting from the study entitled "Ethical concrete" in which techniques for the reuse of glass collection waste have been experimented to reduce the impacts of concrete products and improve their performances. In particular, the non-reusable waste derived by the separated collection of glass can find in the urban sector and in concrete production an interesting opportunity for application as a secondary raw material.

Keywords Secondary raw material · Foam glass · Environmental impacts · Production and waste management

1 Environmental Issues and the Building Sector

Over the last two decades, issues such as climate change, environmental degradation, sustainable use of the resources, economic development and urban resilience have become more and more strictly connected topics in global, European and national politics. On this subject are focused many development strategies, research funding programs, global and local initiatives. Many solutions find a convergence in the model of the so-called circular economy.[1] Moreover, a better use and reuse of resources, the reduction of emission during the productive processes and of the carbon footprint of products is fundamental to support the necessary transition to a climate-neutral

[1] For the European Commission the circular economy is an economy in which "*the value of products, materials and resources is maintained in the economy for as long as possible, and the generation of waste minimized, is an essential contribution to the EU's efforts to develop a sustainable, low carbon, resource efficient and competitive economy. Such transition is the opportunity to transform our economy and generate new and sustainable competitive advantages for Europe*" (European Commission 2015).

A. Tartaglia (✉)
Architecture, Built Environment and Construction Engineering—ABC Department, Politecnico di Milano, Milan, Italy
e-mail: andrea.tartaglia@polimi.it

S. Della Torre et al. (eds.), *Regeneration of the Built Environment from a Circular Economy Perspective*, Research for Development,
https://doi.org/10.1007/978-3-030-33256-3_22

economy. In this sense, the role of the building sector and all the related industrial activities is fundamental to perceive this ambitious goal.

From the point of view of environmental impact and energy demand, many significant advancements have been made with regards to construction: especially, the new NZEB construction (nearly zero energy building) and passive houses are goals that, even if with significant design efforts and frequent financial issues, can already be obtained using products and solutions on the market. So, it is undeniable that nowadays the weakest phases in building processes are the construction and the end of life phases.

In this sense, there have also been numerous initiatives, including of a legislative nature, aimed at encouraging the reduction of consumption and impacts related to the construction of buildings. An example is the minimal environmental criteria (MEC)[2] which are compulsory in the public market and define the minimal environmental standards for design solutions, products and services throughout the life cycle, taking into account current market availability. For the construction activities, among many specific requests, there is a more general indication that at least 15% of the weight of all materials used for a building must be guaranteed to be recycled material.

In fact, waste management is a central issue in the proper use of resources. According to EU data construction activities alone produce almost 900 million tons of waste per year out of a total production (household rubbish, manufacturing wastes, etc.) in Europe of 3 billion tons every year (European Commission 2010).

Regarding household rubbish, the separate waste collection has certainly been an important improvement, but it still presents multiple critical issues with respect to the real recyclability of all the materials collected. For example, in Italy in 2017 glass collection produced non-reusable waste for about 250 kilo tons (VVAA 2018).

2 Scenario of the Research

This scenario and the studies developed by Enrico Bernardo (Materials Engineering Department of Università degli Studi di Padova) in the field of glass-based materials was the foundation on which the study entitled "Ethical concrete" was conceived with the aim of exploring the possibility of using waste products deriving from the differentiated collection of glass in the production processes of concrete products. The study was funded by a call for research and development by the Tuscany Region[3] to a group of three companies operating in the sectors involved (separate collection

[2]The MEC (in Italian *Criteri Ambientali Minimi—CAM*) involve multiple activities and sectors in addition to construction, for example, electronic office equipment; interior furnishings; street furniture; social aspects in public procurement; incontinence aids; paper; printer cartridges; public lighting; cleaning and hygiene products; urban waste; collective catering and foodstuffs; sanitation for hospital facilities; energy services for buildings; textiles; vehicles; public green. The MEC are constantly updated and those related to building and design has been updated in 2017. The updated list and its contents are published on the Website of the competent Ministry.

[3]Bando Unico R&S 2012—Regione Toscana.

and treatment of waste and production of concrete products). In particular, the team included: Unibloc s.r.l. (operating in the sector of concrete vibro-compressed components, responsible for the research was arch. Riccardo Cecconi) as group leader and supported by Assobeton; S.A.M. Engineering S.p.A. (construction company also operating in the production of prefabricated concrete panels, responsible for the research was engineer Tiberio Pochini); La RevetVetri s.r.l. (operating in the separate collection of urban waste, responsible for the research was engineer Massimo Ravagnani); DiDA—Dipartimento di Architettura of Università degli Studi di Firenze (scientific partner, responsible for the research was Alessandro Ubertazzi with Benedetta Terenzi); ABC department—Architecture, Built environment and Construction Engineering of Politecnico di Milano (scientific partner, responsible for the research was Andrea Tartaglia).

The idea was to transform a waste normally disposed of in landfills into a "new" raw material. Moreover, the reuse for construction components had to be conceived by verifying its environmental compatibility, technical feasibility and economic sustainability.

The first step was therefore to identify how and in what to "transform" the waste from glass recycling. Thanks to the support from Enrico Bernardo and the alternative production processes designed by him, the use of the waste for the production of foam glass was identified as the best solution[4] (Table 1). This is a product already widely used in the construction sector in Northern Europe especially as an aggregate in concrete mixtures. The significant advantages related to the processes proposed by the "Ethical concrete" study are primarily:

- The use of waste and not of new resources and components saving the use of a huge amount of non-renewable resources;
- A production process that requires lower temperatures compared to the typical process that starts from new raw materials, this means a reduction in the quantity of energy involved in production;
- The normal presence of organic elements in the waste that allows the activation of the foaming process without the use of additives, with a further advantage over the use of resources.

[4]To obtain this result "*several alternatives have been tested for the waste glass processing in order to achieve an adequate glass sand that can undergo the necessary heat treatment to obtain foam glass. As a consequence of this effort, a virtuous circle has started with the ambitious goal of giving dignity to a new material from a waste product which currently is simply disposed of in dumps. A series of samples with slightly different physical–chemical characteristics have been produced with tests run by the researchers, according to the procedures used in the thermal process to obtain the material set by prof. Bernardo. By comparing the different properties of the foam glass samples obtained, the partners of this project have identified as the most interesting material, according to the set goals, the one with the best ratio between compressive strength and density, therefore, with the best specific resistance. This is because the aggregates are not particularly light but significantly resistant in comparison to the ones currently on the market* (Terenzi 2013: 110–122). *From the chemical perspective, it has been observed that the organic material, naturally present in the waste used, is alone enough to foam the glass without the help of additional agents which, otherwise, would have to be added to the mixture*" (Tartaglia and Terenzi 2016).

Table 1 Results of laboratory tests referred to the different alternatives considered for the foam process. The composition of the samples of glass waste was intentionally varied with different additives and subjected to diversified heat treatments in order to favour their optimal and homogeneous foaming

Sample		Apparent density	Compressive strength	Specific strength
Composition	Heat treatment	g/cm^3	Mpa	(N mm)/g
Glass waste + 1.2% MnO_2 + 1.5% SS + H_2O	850C 10 min	1.093	5.82	5324
Glass waste + 1.2% MnO_2 + 1.5% SS + H_2O	875C 10 min	0.736	4.643	6306
Glass waste + 1.2% MnO_2 + 1.5% SS + H_2O	900C 10 min	0.56	2.415	4313
Glass waste + 1% $CaSO_4$ + 3% SS + H_2O	850C 30 min	0.506	1.524	3012
Glass waste + 1% $CaSO_4$ + 3% SS + H_2O	900C 10 min	0.764	5.974	7816
Glass waste + 1.2% MnO_2 + 3% SS + 3% $C_3H_8O_3$ + H_2O	850C 10 min	0.74	4.751	6418
Glass waste + 1.2% MnO_2 + 3% SS + 1.5% $C_3H_8O_3$ + H_2O	875C 10 min	0.987	4.77	4830
Glass waste + 1.2% MnO_2 + 3% SS + 1.5% $C_3H_8O_3$ + H_2O	900C 10 min	0.848	4.007	4724
Glass waste + 1.2% MnO_2 + 3% SS + 1.5% $C_3H_8O_3$ + H_2O	950C 10 min	0.862	5.084	5901
Glass waste + 1% C + 1.5% SS + H_2O	900C 10 min	1.19	5.318	4461
Glass waste + 1% C + 1.5% SS + H_2O	900C 10 min	1.14	5.294	4630

Source Enrico Bernardo—Università di Padova

In particular, the thermal sintering process for the production of expanded glass has proved to be the most suitable with respect to the objectives and also the most efficient both in terms of costs and impact.

3 Applications for Building Sector

The second step of the study was the application of this "new" second raw material in products for building construction and the verification of the performance of such components.

Foam glass is a material that finds large application as light aggregates for concrete products. Because the foam glass pieces that derive from waste had lower compressive strength values than those of the foam glass obtained from pure glass, the decision was made to test the usability in lightweight concrete components (lightweight vibro-compressed concrete blocks and prefabricated panels to be used for example as vertical partition elements or vertical closing elements in buildings for industrial, commercial use and other civil constructions) which normally do not require high structural performance.

The goal was to produce components able to guarantee the requested mechanical standard but with lower thermal conductivity and weight. For this reason, a careful regulatory analysis has been carried out in order to set the minimum required performance for blocks and panels which, subsequently, have been compared with the market demands and the performances offered by the elements normally on the market.

The prototypes of the blocks were realized in the production plant of Unibloc s.r.l. using an optimal geometry[5] that would allow both the construction of a lightweight concrete block with commonly used aggregates (e.g. expanded clay), and the use of the expanded glass obtained in the experimental phase from the glass dust coming from the waste.

Instead, the prototypes of the panels were produced by the laboratories of S.A.M. Engineering S.p.A., equipped with a production control system (F.P.C.) certified by Bureau Veritas Italia for the production of elements with CE marking.

The prototypes, both the blocs and the panels, had aesthetic characteristics absolutely akin to the corresponding products of current productions but they showed significant differences in terms of performance.

In the case of blocks, following a refinement and sorting process of the geometries of the block and of the aggregates in foam glass from waste it was possible to obtain a reduction of the mass of about 25%, passing, with comparable performances, from a concrete lightened with expanded clay block with a mass net volume of 1000 kg/m^2

[5]For the definition of the optimal geometry and a comparison of the results obtained from the test geometries, the thermal values (conductivity) defined in the UNI EN 1745 standard were used; the cavities of the block were evaluated according to the procedure indicated in EN ISO 6946 and each cavity was considered as an average having its own thermal resistance, from which the conductivity in relation to the thickness was calculated.

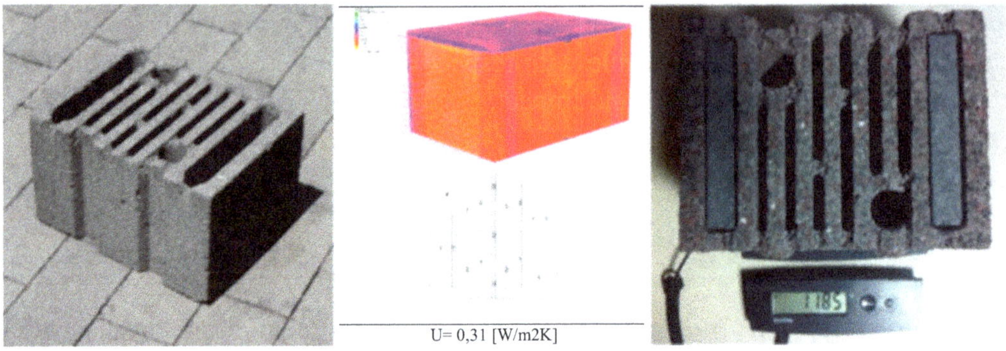

Fig. 1 Images of a prototype block realized by Unibloc s.r.l. with aggregates of foam glass from waste and verification of characteristics. *Source* Unibloc s.r.l.

to a concrete block lightened with foamed glass with a net density of 750 kg/m^2. A significant result, because one of the aims of the study was to not only work on the issue of sustainability of the products but also on their performances (Fig. 1). In this case, the analysis demonstrated that with light aggregates from recycled material it was possible to improve the thermal performance of concrete products with a significant parallel reduction in volume mass and without a drastic reduction in resistance.

In the case of prefabricated panels, the experimentation was carried out with two types that are part of the current production of the company, characterized by different total thickness and insulation but both made with class C32/40 concrete. The first type was made with two outer concrete layers (5 cm thickness each) and in the centre 10 cm of polystyrene as insulating material for a total thick of 20 cm thick. The second was differentiated by a greater thickness of the insulation (two polystyrene panels 5 + 9 cm interposed) which brought the total thickness to 24 cm.

In both cases, the two outer layers were joined together around the perimeter and internally with ribs or connectors.

The casting process was the same as traditional panels: preparation of the formworks to the required dimensions and treatment with disarming of the surfaces in contact with the concrete; installation of metal reinforcements, and spacers to ensure the correct iron cover and of special inserts (for the thermal cut and for lifting and moving the panels); concrete casting for the outer layer of the panel; spreading and the vibration of the first external layer; compacting of the castings; installation of polystyrene insulation for the thermal cutting layer and that for polystyrene intermediate lightening; completion of the reinforcement of the inner layer of the panels; final casting and levelling of the layer that would constitute the internal part of the panel.

The drying process was natural, and a difference was pointed out between the normally used concrete and that realized with foam glass. After twenty-four hours the first reached a characteristic resistance Rckj25 N/mm^2, instead the second reached an average Rckj of 15–17 N/mm^2. Instead, after 28 days, the results were in line with what was expected based on the mix design tests (Table 2). In particular, the breaking

Table 2 Summary of the average resistances obtained and comparison with the concrete normally used in the production of panels by S.A.M. Engineering S.p.A

Aggregates	Weight cube 15 × 15 × 15	Concrete density (kg/m^3)	Compressive strength at 24 h (kg/cm^2)	Compressive strength at 7 days (kg/cm^2)	Compressive strength at 28 days (kg/cm^2)
Mixed	6.7	1985	165	265	385
Foam glass	5.85	1730	160	250	360

Source S.A.M. Engineering S.p.A.

strength of the element with aggregates deriving from the waste was slightly lower (5/6%) compared to traditional ones, but with a reduction in the total weight of the order of 12/14%.

4 Conclusions

> Building products made with the new type of foam glass allows for the pursuit of new levels of sustainability. A sustainability that can be defined as "active", as it adds value to glass waste without further treatment, with a consequent reduction in the carbon dioxide emissions of the final product. It also presents the same ease of recycling in the process of disposal (…) Moreover, there would also be a "passive" sustainability derived from the energy efficiency of buildings and the comfort of the environments resulting from the use of the expanded glass aggregates derived from recycling, as demonstrated by tests performed on prototypes during the "Ethic Concrete" study. (Tartaglia et al. 2016: 220)

Furthermore, from the first in-depth analyses about the realization of an industrial production process, it emerged that glass foam from waste could potentially have a final cost that is more than 20% lower than that of the material currently on the market derived from new non-recycled glass.

The process and product innovation—related to the possible reuse in the building sector of up to 250,000 tons per year of glass waste (currently to be land filled)—would reduce the use of non-renewable raw materials derived from quarry extraction (with the related environmental and landscape problems), would decrease energy consumption in production processes, would improve the performance of a number of products widely used in the construction sector (better energy performance and load reduction) with a consequent improvement in building performance, would diminish process and material/product costs and would create new production chains and new entrepreneurial opportunities.

In this sense, the "Ethical concrete" study highlights a significant opportunity for the realization of a true circular economy, through the transformation of an environmental criticality into an economic opportunity with significant correlated environmental benefits.

References

European Commission. (2010). Being wise with waste: The EU's approach to waste management. Publications Office of the European Union.

European Commission. (2015). Communication from the commission to the European Parliament, the council, the European economic and social committee and the committee of the regions. Closing the loop—an EU action plan for the circular economy. COM/2015/0614 final.

Tartaglia, A., & Terenzi, B. (2016). From a waste to a secondary material: Going towards a more sustainable architecture. *SMC—Sustainable Mediterranean Construction, 4*(2016), 65–69.

Tartaglia, A., Terenzi, B., Ubertazzi, A., Cecconi, R., & Ronchetti, A. (2016). Ethic concrete. Environmental impact reduction and enhancement of mechanical and thermal performances of building components in concrete re-using waste. *Italian Concrete Days, 2016,* 212–220.

Terenzi, B. (2013). Il Calcestruzzo etico. Edizioni Centro Studi Valle Imagna.

VVAA (2018). L'Italia del Riciclo2018. Fondazione per lo sviluppo sostenibile, FISE UNICIRCU-LAR, Unione Imprese Economia Circolare.

Bio-Based Materials for the Italian Construction Industry: Buildings as Carbon Sponges

Olga Beatrice Carcassi, Enrico De Angelis, Giuliana Iannaccone, Laura Elisabetta Malighetti, Gabriele Masera and Francesco Pittau

Abstract This work brings together some recent research and results activities aiming at investigating the environmental benefits of using bio-based materials for the construction and refurbishment of residential buildings. The positive environmental effects of wood and other biogenic materials replacing other, more important, conventional ones, analysed through the application of Life Cycle Assessment methods, are here reported. Moreover, the investigated strategies for Carbon Capture and Storage (CCS) are here discussed, to evaluate the potential of carbon uptake of fast-growing biogenic materials when used as insulation systems. The results show the effectiveness of bio-based materials in contributing to the mitigation strategies of the impacts due to climate change.

Keywords Bio-based materials · Timber · Construction industry · Carbon storage · Life cycle assessment · Building retrofitting

1 Introduction

The construction sector plays a decisive role in the achievement of the European targets for the reduction of energy consumption (40% of the total primary energy consumption) and carbon emissions (39% of fossil-related emissions). With this aim, European and, consequently, Italian standards mainly addressed the decrease of the environmental impact during the use phase through the reduction of the demand for operating energy (European Commission 2010; Sartori and Hestnes 2007). As a consequence, the energy performance of buildings has been improved, mitigating the environmental impact deriving from the operation phase, but the importance of the other life cycle stages has increased because of the higher material input (Blengini

O. B. Carcassi (✉) · E. De Angelis · G. Iannaccone · L. E. Malighetti · G. Masera
Architecture, Built Environment and Construction Engineering—ABC Department, Politecnico di Milano, Milan, Italy
e-mail: olgabeatrice.carcassi@polimi.it

F. Pittau
Department of Civil, Environmental and Geomatic Engineering, Institute of Construction & Infrastructure Management—BAUG IBI, ETH Zürich, Zürich, Switzerland

S. Della Torre et al. (eds.), *Regeneration of the Built Environment from a Circular Economy Perspective*, Research for Development,
https://doi.org/10.1007/978-3-030-33256-3_23

and Di Carlo 2010; Lavagna et al. 2018). As a matter of fact, the fossil carbon emitted by manufacturing of materials and construction might significantly affect the carbon saving from operational energy (Rovers 2014). The building material selection strongly affects the overall environmental impact of a building, especially the selection of the materials for the structural frame and the building envelope (i.e. basement, exterior walls and roof) on which the former has a major influence (Pal et al. 2017; Paleari et al. 2016).

The following work presents the results of some studies conducted with the aim of assessing the benefits, from the point of view of environmental impact, deriving from the use of bio-based materials as an alternative to conventional building materials for both new and existing buildings undergoing major renovations.

2 Timber in the Italian Construction Industry

The consumption of forest products has increased in all European regions in the last 20 years, partly supported by public policies which encouraged the use of wood in the construction and renovation sector through the implementation of energy efficiency policies (Martín Vallejo 2015).

Reduced times for construction, combined with high-performance expectations, increased the interest towards prefabricated construction systems. Among these, wood-based preassembled components are those accounting for the largest growth in the Italian market, with approximately 2.8% of the housing assets and 8.5% of the total building stock (Pittau et al. 2016). The picture provided by Centro Studi FederlegnoArredo in their report 'Rapporto case ed edifici in legno' suggests a countertrend with respect to the total amount of investments in the construction industry: starting from 2010, more than 3,000 timber buildings have been built, 89% of which are residential (Gardino 2015). Between 2006 and 2010, the number of wooden houses rose fivefold and increased by 50% within 2015, while the use of other construction materials decreased by 40% between 2006 and 2010 and has increased of 30% within 2015. Italy is the fourth European player in the wooden building sector, overcoming countries with an ancient timber construction tradition such as Austria, Finland, France and the Netherlands. The highest concentration of timber construction industries is in Lombardy, followed by Veneto, Emilia Romagna and Trentino Alto Adige.

The benefits in using preassembled timber components for building constructions are manifold: the manufacturing costs can be significantly decreased by the seriality and modularity of the production, while the rapidity of assembly ensures a short duration of the onsite construction, without decreasing the structural stiffness and the thermo-acoustic performances. Moreover, generally, prefabricated construction technologies allow the optimization of the manufacturing process, as well as decreasing fossil-carbon emissions during material processing and assembly.

Modular timber constructions, especially if based on massive wooden elements (e.g. plywood, LVL panels, cross-laminated timber (CLT), etc.), also allow the storage of a large amount of carbon into the structure (roughly 50% of the mass) (Villa et al. 2012).

The use of these construction technologies can provide several positive benefits both in new buildings and in the refurbishment and retrofit of existing ones.

2.1 *Timber in New Buildings*

With respect to other structural traditional materials, e.g. concrete, the use of wood for construction generally results in lower energy intensity and fossil-carbon emission (Gustavsson and Sathre 2006). Moreover, the Italian market is rapidly changing due to a renewed interest in wood-based products and their outstanding mechanical properties. Italian market is also supported by industries that, following this new environmental trend, try to reach a local production by concentrating manufacturing, as far as possible, in their own country. Since timber-framed panels are a valid prefabricated solution, their request for new construction has been constantly increasing in the last ten years (Confindustria 2018).

For the production of wooden products, energy for drying, cutting, drilling and planning is the only resource used: in this scenario, the energy balance for a wooden building becomes particularly sustainable.

The results of a Life Cycle Assessment (LCA), from-cradle-to-gate, of a CLT panel produced in Italy supported this thesis. This stimulates the exploitation of wood and forests to create regenerative building products which promote a sustainable management of the natural environment (Villa et al. 2012).

2.1.1 ˙CO_2–Wood in Carbon Efficient Construction

'Wood in carbon efficient construction' was a research project, coordinated by Aalto University, focused on the demonstration of the positive effects on climate of using wood in construction. The findings are the result of a large transnational European research project involving twenty organizations from five countries: Austria, Finland, Germany, Italy and Sweden. Even if the current normative policy framework in these emerging matters is still under development, the findings of ˙CO_2 scientifically prove that there are convincing advantages and potentials for using wood in construction to mitigate climate change, whereas the forests are managed so as to maintain or increase forest carbon stocks (Fig. 1).

The research filled in some knowledge gaps by applying advanced methods for determining the carbon footprint of wooden buildings during their full life cycles. A carbon footprint analysis of wooden buildings is more complex than that of many other products, due to the dynamics of forest growth and the variety of byproducts generated. From a life cycle perspective, the environmental impact of wood is strongly dependent on the management of forest and end-of-life (EoL) scenarios. In LCA, assuming the forest system and the use of residues and related benefits as

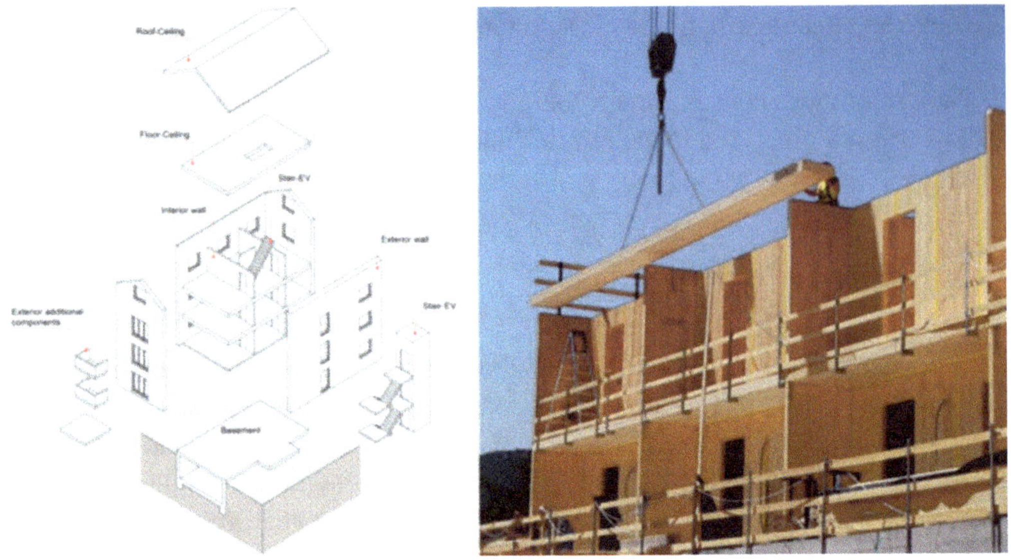

Fig. 1 An Italian case-study in the CO_2 project: Progetto CASE L'Aquila (Luigi Fragola & Partners, Studio Legnopiù srl). Axonometric view (left); onsite CLT assembly (right)

separated systems allows to make wood building and timber products comparable to alternative building materials, i.e. as concrete, steel, etc.

A long-term sustainable forest management as well as an efficient use of primary resources from premium quality (e.g. laminated wood, plywood, timber frame construction) is fundamental conditions to achieve sustainability goals.

In the early design process of timber construction, the deconstruction, reuse and recycling of the products has to be considered too. Besides the results of LCA, other aspects should be considered as relevant to the choice of bio-based products for buildings: reduced operational complexity, total prefabrication with reduced production complexity, integration, lightness, energy efficiency, good seismic and fire performances, easy assembly and disassembly on site, etc. (Kuittinen et al. 2013).

2.2 *Timber for Existing Buildings*

The renovation and the energy retrofit of existing buildings is becoming a fundamental task for the construction sector in next future. According to recent market surveys, in Europe, nowadays roughly 50% of economic activities of the construction sector are strictly related to refurbishment (Juan et al. 2009).

The energy improvement of the building stock realized in the last 50 years, mostly represented by poorly insulated buildings with obsolete heating systems, is an urgent mission in order to meet the goal of a significant reduction of greenhouse gas (GHG) emissions and energy consumption. In the EU, the building sector is responsible for roughly 40% of the total primary energy consumption, 63% of which depends on the residential sector alone (Eurostat 2016).

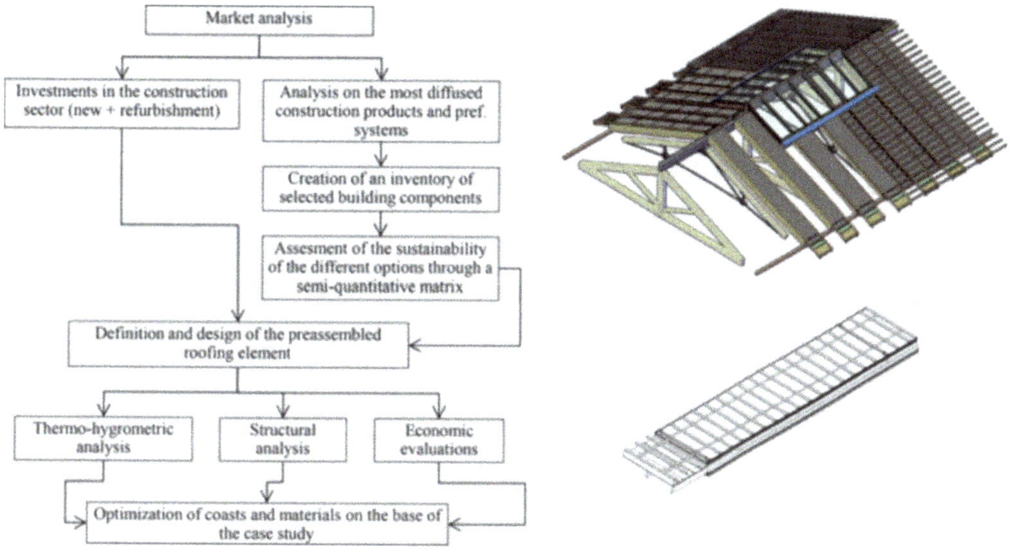

Fig. 2 Structure of the working activities for the development of the preassembled roofing component (left). Substitution of an existing roof with the HABITAT preassembled timber panels (top right) and a single module of HABITAT panel (bottom right)

Considering the EU target of reduction of energy consumption (−20% by 2020 and −27% by 2030), the retrofit of existing façades is an urgent issue that should be solved rapidly in order to reduce the energy need from buildings, increase the indoor comfort and the aesthetics of the facades, that very often requires a deep renovation (Passer et al. 2016; Meijer et al. 2009).

Prefabricated elements are a valid solution to accelerate the renovation process at a large scale, since the duration of onsite installation is faster compared to traditional construction solutions and the integration of all components facilitates quality control during the offsite assembly with a reduced risk of performance failure during the service life (Ramage et al. 2017). Timber-based prefabricated solutions for envelope retrofitting add incremental benefits at different levels, as demonstrated in the following examples.

2.2.1 Habitat

The habitat research project aimed at the development of a prefabricated panel for roof renovation, made of a timber structure with a high content of recycled material. The modular panels were designed to be produced by underprivileged employees of social cooperatives (type B, according to the Italian regulations) located in northern Italy. The component is the final result of a consulting activity for a consortium of social cooperatives (Consorzio Consolida) funded by Fondazione della Provincia di Lecco Onlus.

The methodology for the development of the prefabricated building component was structured in different working steps, as shown schematically in Fig. 2 on the left.

The work included the different analyses for the definition of the main characteristics of the preassembled building component, based on the market potential and the needs and constraints of the social cooperatives, main partners of the research project.

In the first phase, a survey of the most common building products with a high recycled content commonly used in building renovations was carried out in order to provide recommendations for the following design steps. For each selected product, the environmental sustainability and economic costs were investigated on the bases of a semi-quantitative evaluation matrix, which took into account the following four categories (Pittau et al. 2017):

A. Supply chain—which includes the distance of the manufacturing process (from raw materials extraction to final production), the annual amount of production and the annual variability;
B. Sustainability—which includes the amount of recycled materials used for production, the share of material which can be recycled at the end of life (EOL), the embodied energy for extraction and manufacturing and the energy need for product disposal at the EoL;
C. Economic cost—which includes the cost of material supply and the cost of production, divided into automation of production, time needed for a complete production cycle (from transportation to manufacturing to packaging), cost related to the manufacturing area and cost related to the storage;
D. Usage—which includes the physical characteristics, divided into durability, vapour permeability, safety; the reversibility of use, the adaptability to refurbishment and, finally, the innovation value. Based on the results of the evaluation matrix, the concept design of the technical element was implemented: a wood-based composite panel with a high recycled content to be installed on the existing structures (Fig. 2 on the right).

The project demonstrated that, if the dimension and shape of the panels are optimized, the use of an advanced prefabrication system for the renovation of the existing roof is a competitive choice, with a cost which is very close to the cost of a traditional construction system. Moreover, both the quality and reliability of the renovation can significantly increase, since a better control of the whole building process is ensured at every single stage, from manufacturing to post-construction.

3 Bio-Based Materials for Insulation: The Building Envelope as a Carbon Sponge

Considering the increasing social emphasis on environmental issues, waste disposal and the depletion of raw materials, bio-based materials constitute a promising alternative to those obtained from fossil carbon. Fast-growing biogenic materials, e.g. straw or hemp shives, are highly promising alternatives for insulation, since their thermal conductivity is generally low, and they can be locally available (Garas et al. 2009). Moreover, the use of by-products of the food industry, like straw in particular, is highly beneficial from an environmental prospective, since it can be considered as a by-product of the food industry. Thus, no land competition issues are expected if straw is largely used as construction material in replacement of conventional non-biogenic materials. Actually, straw can be considered mostly as a waste, since only 7% of the total production is sold as product—mainly as animal litter—and its use in construction is a valuable contribute which allows to close the cycle and decrease the production intensity of construction materials and the depletion of virgin resources (Eurostat 2017).

During their growth, biogenic materials uptake carbon dioxide through photosynthesis, with a percentage that generally can be assumed as 50% of the dry mass. Contrarily to timber, which takes longer to be fully regenerated in the forest after harvesting, straw requires much less time to be regenerated since after just some months, the vegetal mass harvested can be fully regenerated in the cropland. This fast regeneration leads to a higher regenerative capacity since the biogenic CO_2 that will be released after the EoL of the building will be fully compensated by the CO_2 absorbed in the crop (Levasseur et al. 2012; Guest et al. 2013).

It is estimated that up to 150 Mt of CO_2 can be stored in existing facades in Italy (Ballarini et al. 2014). Thus, building facades can be seen as Carbon Capture and Storage (CCS) systems when the carbon is effectively massively stored in biogenic products (structural elements, but especially insulation) and fast captured in crops. This CCS system, if largely used in construction, can give a significant contribution to mitigate climate change and achieve the Paris Agreement objectives.

3.1 Evaluation of Carbon Uptake Benefits Through a Dynamic Life Cycle Assessment (DLCA)

In the next decades, a large share of residential buildings in the EU-28 is expected to be renovated, and a large amount of insulation materials will be produced. But, when the primary energy requirements of the buildings are reduced after retrofitting, the contribution to carbon emissions due the production of insulation materials increases. The objective of this study, developed together with the chair of Sustainable Construction of ETH Zurich, was to assess the contribution to climate change mitigation of carbon storage potential in different biogenic insulation alternatives when used for the energy retrofitting of existing facades. Five alternative construction solutions for the renovation of the exterior walls were taken as reference: I-joint frame with pressed straw (STR), preassembled frame with injected hempcrete (HCF), timber frame (TIF), hempcrete blocks (HCB) and expanded polystyrene for external thermal insulation composite system (EPS).

In particular, in order to properly consider the amount of carbon stored in products, a dynamic life cycle assessment (DLCA) was introduced to verify the contribution of different bio-based materials on the radiative forcing over time, which contributes to restore the radiative balance of the Earth.

In fact, the lack of time dependence and the treatment of the biogenic CO_2 are critical aspects in LCA and carbon footprint calculations, whereas the dynamic LCA calculation model proposed by Levasseur et al. (Levasseur et al. 2010) allows to take into account carbon uptake and GHG emissions over time. The instantaneous radiative forcing and consequently the dynamic GWP (GWPdyn), were calculated for each wall alternative and for the three disposal scenario (DS) through a DLCA calculation model (Pittau et al. 2019). The values are shown in Fig. 3.

The results show that only bio-based materials with a very fast regrowth, e.g. straw, have an effective potential in removing carbon from the air in a very short time and can contribute to achieve the Paris Agreement goals by 2050.

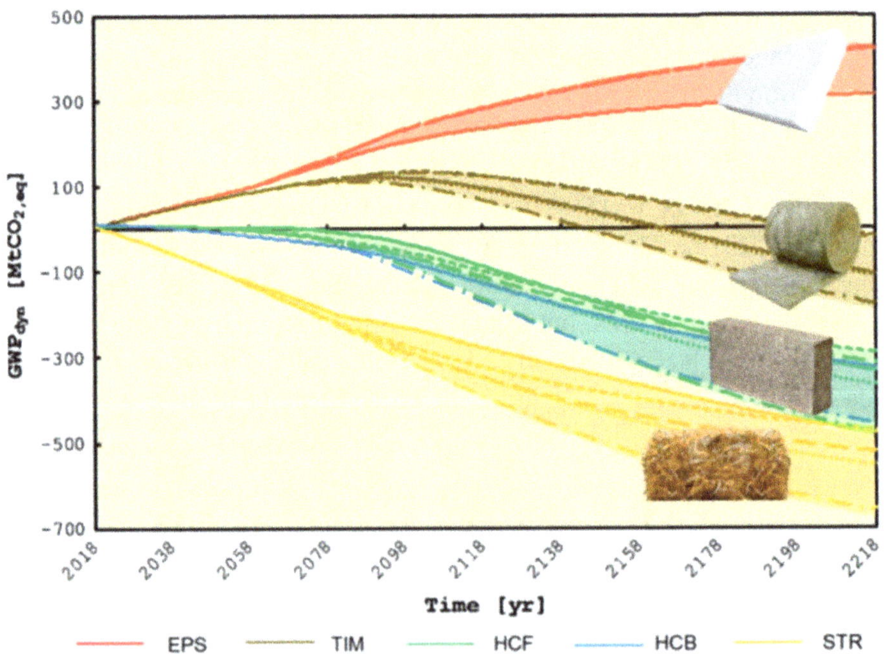

Fig. 3 Scenarios of carbon mitigation of the construction sector due to the renovation of the European residential building stock

4 Conclusion

Achieving the decarbonization targets by 2050 as set by the European Union requires the adoption of several measures. The only reduction of primary energy requirements for both new and existing building is not effective, as the contribution of the production of insulation materials to carbon emissions increases.

A viable strategy could be the introduction of carbon capture and storage systems so to benefit from the long-term carbon storage in the building stock.

The combination of prefabrication with sustainable bio-based building materials, if extended on a large scale, could offer several benefits at different levels.

While the sustainability of wood as a building material is a complex issue, as its environmental impact is strongly related to forest management and end-of-life scenarios, fast-growing bio-based materials are a valuable alternative to insulate the buildings, as the biogenic carbon can be stored in the built environment for a relatively long time. However, this benefit is irrelevant when compared to the total emissions deriving from the use of existing buildings. Therefore, in order to accelerate the transition and meet the carbon budget limits required by 2050, it is necessary to increase the renovation rate of buildings in Europe. In fact, only with a drastic acceleration of the energy renovation of buildings, it would be possible to generate a significant benefit due to the carbon storage in the building stock.

References

Ballarini, I., Corgnati, S. P., & Corrado, V. (2014). Use of reference buildings to assess the energy saving potentials of the residential building stock: The experience of TABULA project. *Energy Policy, 68,* 273–284. https://doi.org/10.1016/j.enpol.2014.01.027.

Blengini, Gian Andrea, & Di Carlo, Tiziana. (2010). The changing role of life cycle phases, subsystems and materials in the LCA of low energy buildings. *Energy and Buildings, 42*(6), 869–880. https://doi.org/10.1016/j.enbuild.2009.12.009.

Confindustria. (2018). IL SETTORE DELL'INDUSTRIA DEL LEGNO NEI TERRITORI DI LECCO E SONDRIO.

European Commission. (2010). Directive 2010/31/EU. *Official Journal of the European Union,* 13–35.

Eurostat. 2017. Main Annual Crop Statistic.

Garas, G, Allam, M., & Dessuky, R. E. (2009). Straw bale construction as an economic environmental building alternative—a case study. *Journal of Engineering and Applied Sciences, 4*(9), 54–59. https://www.scopus.com/inward/record.uri?eid=2-s2.0-78650023657&partnerID=40&md5=05a84deba2193e23490e891f68179986.

Gardino, P. (2015). Il Mercato Italiano Delle Case in Legno Nel 2010.

Guest, G., Bright, R. M., Cherubini, F., & Strømman, A. H. (2013). Consistent quantification of climate impacts due to biogenic carbon storage across a range of bio-product systems. *Environmental Impact Assessment Review, 43*(November), 21–30. https://doi.org/10.1016/j.eiar.2013.05.002.

Gustavsson, Leif, & Sathre, Roger. (2006). Variability in energy and carbon dioxide balances of wood and concrete building materials. *Building and Environment, 41,* 940–951. https://doi.org/10.1016/j.buildenv.2005.04.008.

Juan, Yi K., Perng, Yeng Horng, Castro-Lacouture, Daniel, & Kuo Sheng, Lu. (2009). Housing refurbishment contractors selection based on a hybrid fuzzy-QFD approach. *Automation in Construction, 18*(2), 139–144. https://doi.org/10.1016/j.autcon.2008.06.001.

Kuittinen, M., Alice, L., & Gerhard, W. (2013). Wood in carbon efficient construction. Tools, methods and applications. *Wood in Carbon Efficient Construction. Tools, Methods and Applications*, 78–150. http://issuu.com/eco2book/docs/eco2_book.

Lavagna, M., & Serenella, S. (2018) Impatti Ambientali LCA Del Patrimonio Residenziale Europeo e Scenari Di Prevenzione, 291–98. https://doi.org/10.13128/Techne-22113.

Levasseur, A., Lesage, P., Margni, M., & Samson, R. (2012). Biogenic carbon and temporary storage addressed with dynamic life cycle assessment. *Journal of Industrial Ecology, 17*(1), 117–128. https://doi.org/10.1111/j.1530-9290.2012.00503.x.

Levasseur, A., Pascal L., Manuele M., Louise D., & Réjean, S. (2010). Considering time in LCA: Dynamic LCA and its application to global warming impact assessments. *Environmetal, Science & Technology*, *44*. https://doi.org/10.1021/es9030003.

Martín, V., & Myriàm. (2015). State of Europe's forests 2015. *State of Europe's forests 2015*. Madrid.

Meijer, Frits, Itard, Laure, & Sunikka-Blank, Minna. (2009). Comparing European residential building stocks: Performance, renovation and policy opportunities. *Building Research and Information, 37*(5–6), 533–551. https://doi.org/10.1080/09613210903189376.

Eurostat. (2016). Final energy consumption by sector. Online at:https://ec.europa.eu/eurostat/databrowser/view/ten00124/default/table?lang=en. Accessed 24 October 2019

Pal, S. K., Takano, A., Alanne, K., Palonen, M., & Siren, K. (2017). A multi-objective life cycle approach for optimal building design: A case study in finnish context. *Journal of Cleaner Production, 143,* 1021–1035. https://doi.org/10.1016/j.jclepro.2016.12.018.

Paleari, Michele, Lavagna, Monica, & Campioli, Andrea. (2016). The assessment of the relevance of building components and life phases for the environmental profile of nearly zero-energy buildings: Life cycle assessment of a multifamily building in Italy. *International Journal of Life Cycle Assessment, 21*(12), 1667–1690. https://doi.org/10.1007/s11367-016-1133-6.

Passer, A., Ouellet-Plamondon, C., Kenneally, P., John, V., & Habert, G. (2016). The impact of future scenarios on building refurbishment strategies towards plus energy buildings. *Energy and Buildings, 124,* 153–163. https://doi.org/10.1016/j.enbuild.2016.04.008.

Pittau, F., Malighetti, L. E., Masera, G., & Lannaccone, G. (2016). A new modular preassembled timber panel for the energy retrofit of the housing stock. In *WCTE 2016—World Conference on Timber Engineering*.

Pittau, F., Lumia, G., Heeren, N., Iannaccone, G., & Habert, G. (2019). Retrofit as a carbon sink: The carbon storage potentials of the EU housing stock. *Journal of Cleaner Production, 214*(March), 365–376. https://doi.org/10.1016/j.jclepro.2018.12.304.

Pittau, F., Malighetti, L. E., Iannaccone, G., & Masera, G. (2017). Prefabrication as large-scale efficient strategy for the energy retrofit of the housing stock: An Italian case study. *Procedia Engineering, 180,* 1160–1169. https://doi.org/10.1016/j.proeng.2017.04.276.

Ramage, M. H., Henry, B., Marta, B.-W., George, F., Thomas, R., Darshil, U. S., et al. (2017). The wood from the trees: The use of timber in construction. *Renewable and Sustainable Energy Reviews, 68,* 333–359. https://doi.org/10.1016/j.rser.2016.09.107.

Rovers, R. (2014). Zero-energy and beyond: A paradigm shift in assessment. *Buildings, 5*(1), 1–13. https://doi.org/10.3390/buildings5010001.

Sartori, I., & Hestnes, A. G. (2007). Energy use in the life cycle of conventional and low-energy buildings: A review article. *Energy and Buildings, 39*(3), 249–257. https://doi.org/10.1016/j.enbuild.2006.07.001.

Villa, N., Pittau, F., De Angelis, E., Iannaccone, G., Dotelli, G., & Zampori, L. (2012). Wood products for the italian construction industry—an LCA-based sustainability evaluation. *Proceeding of WCTE, 2012*(5), 609–613.

Sustainable Concretes for Structural Applications

Luigi Biolzi, Sara Cattaneo, Gianluca Guerrini and Vahid Afroughsabet

Abstract For the production of a high-performance concrete (HPC) matrix, a large amount of binder is normally used. The production of ordinary Portland cement (OPC) as the binder of concrete accounts for 7% of CO_2 emission, which has notable environmental impacts, and subsequently results in unsustainable concrete. The aim of the present study was to investigate the effect of replacing OPC with calcium sulfoaluminate cement (CSA) or ground granulated blast-furnace slag (GGBS) as sustainable binders on the engineering properties of HPC. Additionally, the effect of introducing double hooked-end (DHE) steel fibers at a fiber volume fraction of 1% on the properties of HPC was assessed. The compressive strength, splitting tensile strength, flexural strength, and modulus of elasticity of HPC were evaluated. Moreover, a scanning electron microscopy (SEM) method was used to study the microstructure of the concretes. The results indicate that the replacement of OPC with CSA cement results in an improvement in the mechanical properties of HPC particularly at later ages of curing, while combination CSA cement with OPC and GGBS in the binary and ternary systems degrades the concrete's strengths. The addition of 1% DHE steel fibers significantly increased the engineering properties of concrete. The results show that the bond between a cement matrix and steel fibers has been enhanced due to the expansive behavior of CSA cement. The SEM observation also shows the significant influence of CSA cement on the microstructure of concrete by forming a rich amount of ettringite which subsequently results in an improvement in the properties of concrete.

L. Biolzi · S. Cattaneo (✉)
Architecture, Built Environment and Construction Engineering—ABC Department, Politecnico di Milano, Milan, Italy
e-mail: sara.cattaneo@polimi.it

G. Guerrini
Milan, Italy

V. Afroughsabet
Department of Civil Engineering, University of Toronto, Toronto, Canada

S. Della Torre et al. (eds.), *Regeneration of the Built Environment from a Circular Economy Perspective*, Research for Development,
https://doi.org/10.1007/978-3-030-33256-3_24

Keywords High-performance concrete · Calcium sulfoaluminate cement (CSA) · Granulated blast-furnace slag (GGBS) · Double hooked-end steel fibers · Mechanical properties · SEM observation

1 Introduction

Portland cement concrete is the most widely used human-made material on the planet; around 25 billion metric tons are produced globally each year (Celik et al. 2014). Recently, the demand for using high-performance concrete (HPC) has widely increased throughout the world. As is commonly known, for the production of an HPC matrix, a large amount of binder is normally used. Even though the reasons for concrete's dominance are diverse, the massive production and consumption cycle of concrete have a significant environmental impact, making the concrete industry unsustainable. Currently, Portland cement concrete production accounts for around 7% of carbon dioxide (CO_2) emissions annually. Most of the emissions are attributable to the production of ordinary Portland cement (OPC) clinker. The current approach to overcome this problem is through the reducing clinker factor and through replacing OPC with supplementary cementitious materials such as fly ash, slag, silica fume, and natural pozzolan (Gartner & Hirao 2015). However, due to growing field experience and increasing demand for those materials, there is an essential need to develop concrete made with a new kind of cement such as calcium aluminate cements (CAC), calcium sulfoaluminate cement (CSA), alkali-activated binders, and supersulfated cements (Juenger et al. 2011). Recently, CSA cement gained an increased attention due to its lower amount of CO_2 emission as compared to that of OPC (Gartner 2004). It is reported that the CO_2 emissions may drop by up to 35% if OPC is replaced with CSA cement (Berger et al. 2013). Additionally, concretes fabricated with CSA cement can result in an increased sulfate resistance, high impermeability and chemical resistance and a low chance for alkali–silica reactions (Tang et al. 2015).

Several benefits of HPC compared to conventional concretes have significantly increased its use in different structural applications. However, the brittleness of HPC is higher with respect to the normal-strength concrete due to the higher strength, which subsequently increases the vulnerability of HPC to the initiation and propagation of cracks of different sizes within the concrete body (Savino et al. 2018). The addition of discrete fibers in concrete is recognized as a suitable solution to overcome this weakness and develop materials with enhanced tensile strength, flexural strength, toughness, and thermal shock strength (Sanal et al. 2016; Afroughsabet et al. 2016, 2018; Cattaneo and Biolzi 2010; Simões et al. 2017). This study was aimed at analyzing the effects of CSA cement and DHE steel fibers on the engineering properties of HPC. Compressive strength, splitting tensile strength, flexural strength, modulus of elasticity, and microstructural observations were performed in order to evaluate the properties of concrete at different curing ages. The findings of this research are highly promising and show that the simultaneous use of CSA cement and DHE steel fibers can significantly increase the engineering properties of HPC.

2 Materials and Methods

To explore the effects of CSA cement, GBBS and DHE steel fibers on the engineering properties of concrete, eight different concrete mixes were developed in this study. The concrete mixes included concretes containing 100% OPC and 100% CSA, 50% OPC and 50% CSA, 25% OPC with 50% CSA and 25% GBBS without and with 1% DHE steel fibers. To assess the effect of curing age on the strength of concrete, the compressive strength tests were conducted at the ages of 1, 7, 28, and 56 days. Additionally, the splitting tensile tests were performed at 7, 28, and 56 days. All the other features of the concretes were evaluated at 28 days.

2.1 Materials

The binder materials used in this study were ASTM Type I Portland cement; CSA produced by Italcementi Group and ground granulated blast-furnace slag. Both natural sand, with a 2.9 fineness modulus, and crushed gravel, with a nominal maximum size of 19 mm, were used as the aggregates at a volume fraction of 50%. To achieve the desired workability in different concrete mixes, a Driver Care 10-Sika, was used as a superplasticizer. Additionally, in CSA cement-based concretes, tartaric acid was used as a retarder to increase the setting time of those mixes. Double hooked-end (DHE) steel fibers with a 60-mm length and an aspect ratio of 65 were employed in this study.

2.2 Concrete Mixtures and Mixing Procedure

The water-binder ratio was maintained at 0.35 and the water amount was 157 l for all mixtures. A pan mixer was used for the preparation of all the mixes. Prior to adding the raw materials, the surface of the pan mixer was cleaned with a wet towel to avoid the absorption of aggregates moisture by the mixer. The mixing procedure, which was designed by trial, was chosen as follows: initially, the fine aggregate and cement were mixed for one minute. Afterward, approximately half of the water including SP was introduced into the mixer; the ingredients were further mixed for two minutes. The saturated surface dry (SSD) coarse aggregates and remaining mixing water were then introduced and the mixing was continued for another 5 min. To fabricate uniform fiber-reinforced concrete, discrete fibers were added gradually to the rotating mixer and were mixed for an additional 5 min in order to obtain a homogenous concrete mix. Details of mix proportions and the results of a slump test are summarized in Table 1. The content of SP in that table is given as a percentage of the total mass of the binder. To determine the workability of fresh concrete, slump tests were performed as per ASTM C143 (2010) during the preparation of the concrete mixes.

Table 1 Mix-design

Mixture	Binder			Aggregate		Fiber	Superplasticizer		Slump
ID	OPC	CSA	Slag	Fine	Coarse	DHE	DC10	Tartaric	
	(kg/m^3)					(%)	(%)		(cm)
OPC	450	–	–	905	895	–	1.0	–	21
OPC-DHE	450	–	–	892	882	1	1.2	–	21
CSA	–	450	–	901	891	–	1.2	0.2	20
CSA-DHE	–	450	–	888	878	1	1.4	0.2	19
OPC50-CSA50	225	225	–	903	893	–	1.3	0.2	22
OPC50-CSA50-DHE	225	225	–	890	880	1	1.5	0.2	20
OPC25-CSA50-SL25	112	225	112	895	885	–	1.5	0.2	23
OPC25-CSA50-SL25-DHE	112	225	112	881	872	1	1.7	0.2	23

The specimens were molded with different dimensions that matched the requirements of their standard tests. The samples were covered with a wet plastic sheet to prevent them from dripping water in the first 24 h of curing. Then, the concrete specimens were demolded and immersed in lime-saturated water at 23 °C until reaching their testing ages. For each test, three samples were prepared, and the average value is reported as the final result.

2.3 Testing Methods

Compressive and splitting tensile strength tests were performed using a 3000-KN universal compression machine in accordance with ASTM C39 (2003) and ASTM C496 (2011), respectively. Cubic specimens 100 mm in size were used to determine the compressive strength, whereas cylindrical specimens with a diameter of 100 mm and a height of 200 mm were used to evaluate the splitting tensile strength of the concrete. The flexural strength tests were carried out as per EN 14651 (2007) on prismatic beams with dimensions of 150 × 150 × 600 mm. The modulus of elasticity tests was conducted on the cylindrical specimens with dimensions of 100 × 200 mm as per ASTM C469 (2014). To study the microstructure of concrete made with different types of binders, several images were taken from the fracture surface of concrete specimens by using scanning electron microscopy (SEM) method.

3 Results and Discussion

3.1 Consistency

The consistency of the different mixes developed in this study was evaluated by a slump test, and the results are shown in Table 1. The slump values of the concrete varied between 19 and 23 cm.

A minimum of 1% superplasticizer was required to adjust the consistency of concrete. Higher content of superplasticizer was used in CSA-based and in blended concretes compared to that of OPC to obtain an almost similar slump value. This can be explained by the fineness of CSA and a GBBS particle size that is lower compared to that of OPC. Furthermore, the fast rate of CSA cement hydration and its high demand of water to generate ettringite are other reasons that necessitate the addition of greater amounts of superplasticizer. The results further indicate that the incorporation of steel fibers had a negative influence on the properties of fresh concrete. The long steel fibers and aggregates interlock in the body of concrete and lead to a reduction in the slump value. To attain the same consistency in the concretes with and without fibers, the content of the superplasticizer was slightly increased.

3.2 Compressive Strength

The compressive strength results of different mixes at curing ages of 1, 7, 28, and 56 days are shown in Fig. 1.

The compressive strength of concretes containing CSA cement is significantly lower after 1 day compared to that of the OPC mix. This reduction at an early age can be explained by the presence of the retarder in the CSA concrete that postponed the formation of ettringite, and subsequently reduced the strength of the concrete. The full replacement of OPC with CSA cement led to a reduction in compressive strength of 55% after 1 day, while its strength at 7 days was slightly higher than that of the OPC concrete. It was also observed that the compressive strength of the CSA mix was increased by 10% and 12% after 28 days and 56 days, respectively, compared to that of the OPC concrete. The compressive strength of the concrete containing 50% OPC and 50% CSA cement was lower than that of the reference OPC concrete at all the curing ages considered in this study (reduction of 42%, 32%, 21%, and 13% at 1, 7, 28, and 56 days of curing, respectively, compared to those of the OPC concrete). Similar to CSA concrete mix, the significant amount of strength reduction after 1 day is attributed to the presence of the retarder. However, the compressive strength has been increased at later ages as a result of the formation of ettringite (ye'elimite hydration) and also the hydration of alite and belite which are the main components of OPC. The lowest compressive strength at day 1 was achieved by the CSA-blend mix containing three types of binders (i.e., OPC25-CSA50-SL25 mix). However, compared to OPC concrete; the concrete compressive strength reduction is limited by aging (of about 80%, 28%, 15%, and 9% at 1, 7, 28, and 56 days of curing, respectively). Introducing GGBS can result in an increase in the cohesiveness of the cementitious matrix, which reduces the formation of micro-cracks leading to an increased strength of concrete. Moreover, GGBS fills the capillary pores of the cement matrix and consequently improves the properties of the interfacial transition zone (ITZ), while the observed strength reduction at an early age (1 day) can be attributed to the lower hydration rate of concretes incorporating GGBS, which has

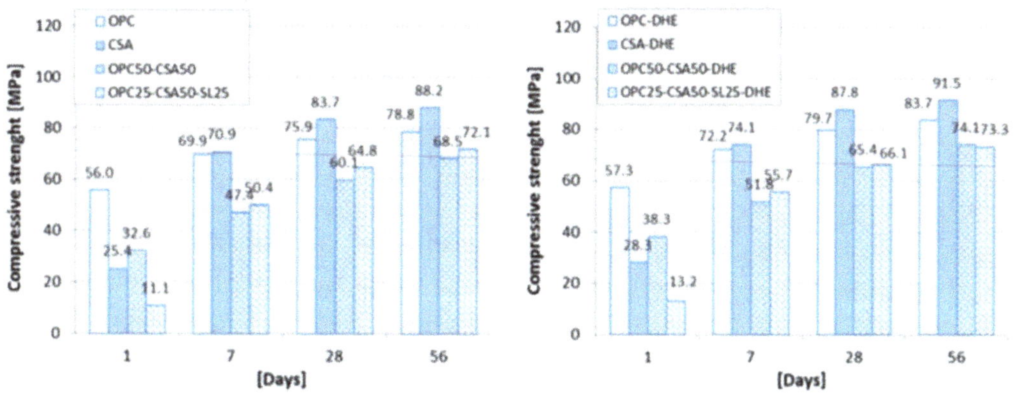

Fig. 1 Compressive strength

been well documented in the literature (Celik et al. 2014). Concretes with steel fibers exhibited the same trend with a slight increase in compressive strength.

3.3 Splitting Tensile Strength

The splitting tensile strength results of different concrete mixes at curing ages of 7, 28, and 56 days are shown in Fig. 2. The full replacement of OPC with CSA cement resulted in a slight reduction after 7 days, while after 28 and 56 splitting strength increased (11%) with respect to OPC.

The strength reduction at 7 days can be attributed to the presence of the retarder which delayed the ettringite formation. However, at later ages of curing, a rich amount of ettringite was formed as a result of ye'elimite hydration, which consequently caused an improvement in the strength of concrete. The results further indicate that a combination of OPC and CSA cements at equal percentage of 50% led to a reduction in the splitting tensile strength of concrete at all curing ages considered in this study. For instance, the splitting tensile strength of the OPC50-CSA50 concrete reduced by 18%, 22%, and 19% at 7, 28, and 56 days, respectively, compared to those of OPC. The incorporation of slag in OPC-CSA concrete led to an improvement in the splitting tensile strength, while its strength is lower compared to that of the reference OPC concrete. This increased strength can be attributed to the formation of additional C–S–H gel, particularly at later ages which is the main strength-contributing compound. Moreover, as observed for compressive strength, slag also fills in the capillary pores and improves the features of ITZ and microstructures of the cement matrix. It was noticed that the best performing mix was the CSA concrete which attained a 56-day splitting tensile strength of 4.77 MPa, while the lowest strength was gained by the OPC50-CSA50 concrete with strength of 3.47 MPa. The results of fiber-reinforced concrete indicate that the addition of 1% DHE steel fibers can significantly increase the splitting tensile strength of concrete. For instance, the splitting

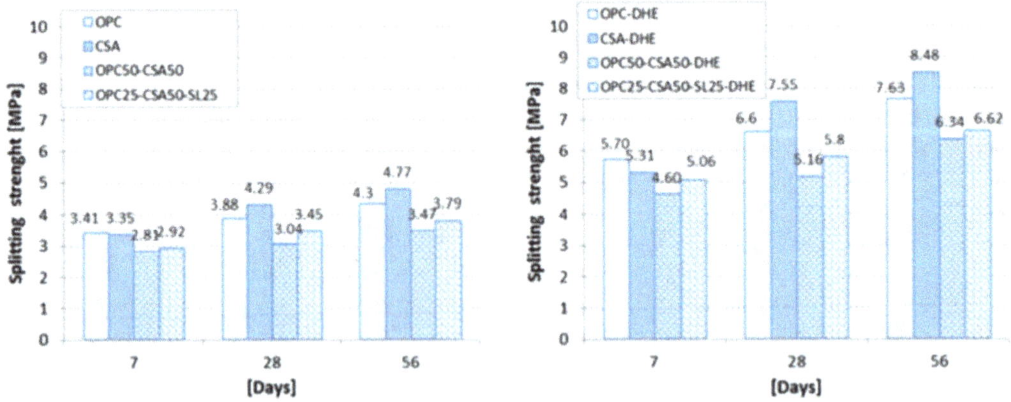

Fig. 2 Splitting tensile strength

tensile strength of OPC-DHE1 concrete mix increased by 67%, 70%, and 77% at 7, 28, and 56 days of curing, respectively, compared to those of OPC concrete. This improvement is attributed to the high tensile strength, elastic modulus, and effective anchoring mechanism of DHE steel fibers, which restrained the extension of macro-cracks in concrete (Afroughsabet et al. 2016). It was also observed that the simultaneous use of CSA cement and steel fibers was very effective in enhancing the splitting tensile strength of concrete, and the best performing mix was attained in the CSA-DHE concrete mix. The splitting tensile strength of the aforementioned mix was increased by 57%, 95%, and 97% at 7, 28, and 56 days of curing, respectively, compared to those of OPC concrete. This improvement can be attributed to a more effective bond between the steel fibers and the CSA cement matrix due to self-stressing that resulted from the expansive behavior of CSA cement. The effect of curing age on the improvement of splitting tensile strength is relatively higher in FRC compared to plain concrete. For instance, the splitting tensile strength of CSA-DHE mix was increased by 42% and 60% at 28 and 56 days compared to its 7-day strength, respectively, while the increase was 28% and 42% for CSA concrete, respectively.

3.4 Modulus of Elasticity

The 28-day modulus of elasticity of different concrete mixes is shown in Fig. 3. The results indicate that the cement type had a significant influence on the modulus of elasticity of the concrete. The full replacement of OPC with CSA cement caused an

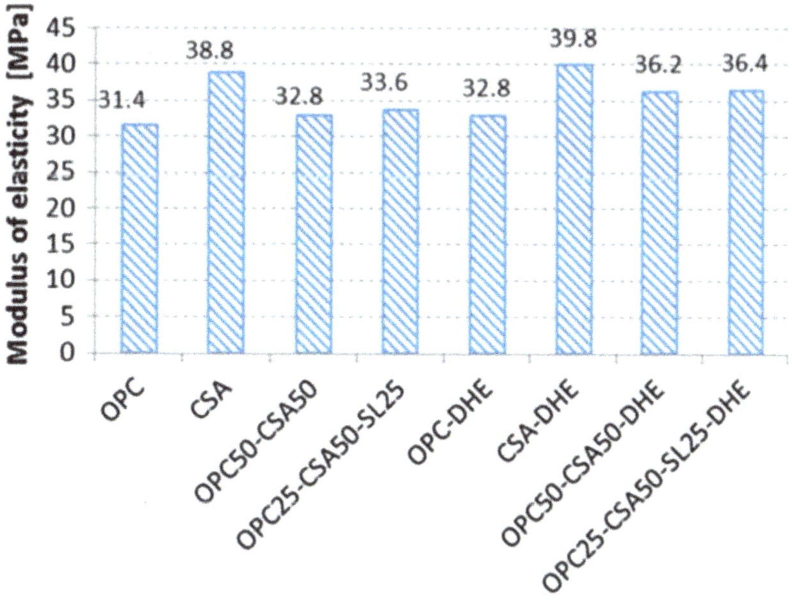

Fig. 3 28-days modulus of elasticity

increase of 24% in the 28-day modulus of elasticity. This increase can be explained by the ability of CSA cement to densify the microstructure of the cement matrix and improve the characteristics of ITZ, which consequently lead to an enhancement in the modulus of elasticity of concrete.

The combination of OPC and CSA cements at equal percentages of 50% led to a slight increase in the modulus of elasticity.

Additionally, the substitution of a portion of OPC with slag in CSA-blend concrete mix resulted in an increase of 7% compared to that of OPC. The lowest modulus of elasticity was attained by the mix containing 100% OPC, while the best performing mix was the CSA mix, which attained a modulus of elasticity of 38.8 GPa.

The modulus of elasticity of OPC, CSA, OPC50-CSA50, and OPC25-CSA50-SL25 concrete mixes containing 1% DHE steel fibers were 4%, 3%, 10%, and 8% higher than those of the corresponding mixes without fibers, respectively. This result suggests that the addition of steel fibers with higher elastic modulus compared to that of the cement matrix can improve the modulus of elasticity of concrete.

3.5 *Flexural Behavior*

The diagram of the 28-day load-CMOD for different concrete mixes is shown in Fig. 4. The behavior of concretes without fibers was almost linear up to the maximum load, followed by a steeper descending branch up to failure point, and then the beam specimens split into two separated parts. The results indicate that the full replacement of OPC with CSA cement resulted in an increase of 20% in the maximum flexural load of concrete. Similar to the splitting tensile strength results, the rich

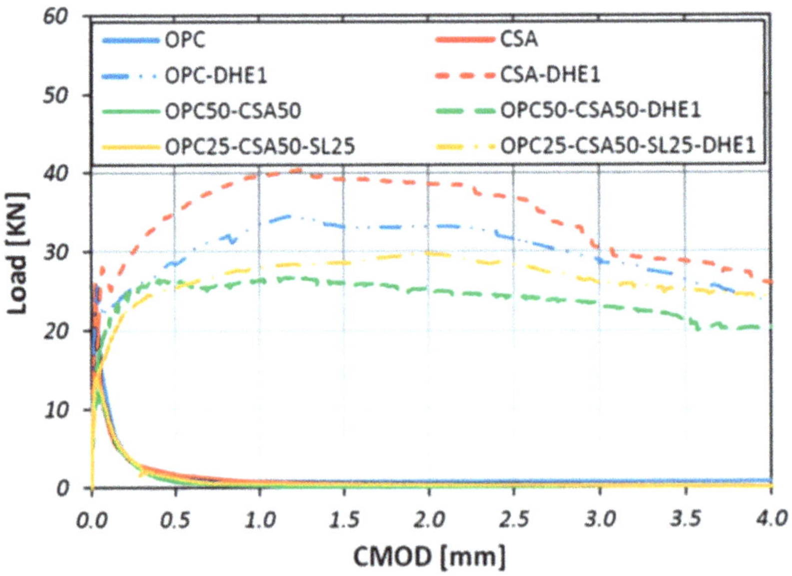

Fig. 4 Flexural load-CMOD curves

amount of ettringite in this mix that was produced by hydration of ye'elimite, which is the main component of CSA cement, is the main reason for this improvement. It was also observed that the flexural strength of CSA-blend mixes was lower compared to that of the OPC mix. For instance, the flexural strength of OPC50-CSA50 and OPC25-CSA50-SL25 mixes were 44 and 35% lower than that of the reference OPC mix. As can be seen, the replacement of OPC with 25% of slag caused an improvement in the flexural strength compared to that of the OPC50-CSA50 concrete. This improvement can be attributed to the formation of additional C–S–H gel which is the main strength-contributing compound as a result of the reaction between slag and calcium hydroxide. Moreover, slag may fill in the capillary pores and improve the features of transition zones and microstructures of the cement matrix.

On the other hand, the results of fiber-reinforced concretes illustrate that the addition of fibers remarkably improved the post-cracking behavior of FRC with an extensive cracking process between first crack load and peak load. It was noticed that the addition of 1% DHE steel fibers changed the behavior of concrete and a deflection-hardening performance was observed in all mixes reinforced with steel fibers. In these concrete mixes, once the first crack occurred, the fibers bridging the crack resisted the load and prevented further crack propagation. The excellent performance of these mixes can be attributed to the ability of DHE steel fibers to carry the load after matrix cracks until further cracks form. Figure 4 shows that the best performance was observed with the mix where OPC was fully replaced with CSA cement and reinforced with 1% steel fiber (i.e., CSA-DHE). The flexural strength of this mix increased by 87% and 55% as compared to that of the OPC and CSA concrete, respectively. The expansive behavior of CSA cement can lead to a better bond between the cement matrix and steel fibers, which subsequently led to an increase in the flexural strength of concrete. The results further show that the flexural strength of OPC, CSA, OPC50-CSA50, and OPC25-CSA50-SL25 mixes containing 1% DHE steel fibers was increased by 60%, 55%, 120%, and 113%, respectively, as compared to that of their corresponding mixes without fibers. As it can be observed in the graph, the inclusion of steel fibers had the most influence on the flexural strength of concrete where CSA cement was used in blend mixes. As previously mentioned, the expansive behavior of CSA-blend mixes may lead to a better bond between the cement matrix and steel fibers as a result of self-stressing, which subsequently leads to an increase in the flexural strength of concrete.

3.6 SEM Observation

To study the microstructural properties of concretes fabricated with different binders, an SEM method was used and images of the fracture surface are shown in Fig. 5. As one can observe, the hydration products of OPC concrete consist of a featureless gel of C–S–H, ettringite crystals with a needle-like shape, and calcium hydroxide (CH) crystals with a plate-like shape. The results indicate that the content of calcium hydroxide is relatively higher than that of the ettringite. Additionally, it can

Fig. 5 SEM images: **a** OPC **b** CSA concrete

be seen that the length of ettringite crystals developed in OPC concrete varied from 1 to 3 μm. Moreover, there are pores in the surface of the cement matrix that can adversely affect the durability properties of concrete. Figure 8b shows the hydration products of CSA cement-based concrete, which mainly consist of prismatic ettringite crystals of different sizes. This type of ettringite crystals causes an improvement in the mechanical properties of concrete and also leads to the dimensional stability of cement (Arjunan et al. 1999).

4 Conclusions

The following conclusions can be drawn from the experimental results: the slump values of all concretes considered in this study varied from 19 to 23 cm. However, a greater dosage of superplasticizer was used in CSA cement-based concretes to achieve a similar consistency to that of the OPC mixes. The addition of steel fibers adversely affects the consistency of concrete. The full replacement of OPC with CSA cement results in an increase in the mechanical properties of concrete particularly at later ages. This can be attributed to the formation of a rich amount of ettringite crystals which, due to the interlocking effect, improve the mechanical properties of concrete. The results also indicate that the strength evolutions of CSA cement-based concretes are higher compared to those of OPC mixes. The addition of 1% DHE steel fibers in concrete significantly increases the mechanical properties of concrete, especially the splitting tensile and flexural strengths of concrete. For instance, the splitting tensile and flexural strengths of the OPC-DHE1 mix after 28 days were increased by 70 and 61% over those of the OPC mix. These increases for the CSA-DHE1 mix compared to those of the CSA mix were 76 and 55%. Moreover, the addition of 1% DHE steel fibers in concrete results in a deflection-hardening behavior. The SEM results indicate that the hydration products of OPC concrete mix are mainly consist for portlandite, while prismatic ettringite crystals are the main products of CSA cement-based concrete.

References

Afroughsabet, V., Biolzi, L., & Ozbakkaloglu, T. (2016). High-performance fiber-reinforced concrete: a review. *Journal of materials science, 51*(14), 6517–6551.

Afroughsabet, V., Biolzi, L., & Monteiro, P. J. (2018). The effect of steel and polypropylene fibers on the chloride diffusivity and drying shrinkage of high-strength concrete. *Composites Part B Engineering, 139,* 84–96.

Arjunan, P., Silsbee, M. R., & Roy, D. M. (1999). Sulfoaluminate-belite cement from low-calcium fly ash and sulfur-rich and other industrial by-products. *Cement and Concrete Research, 29*(8), 1305–1311.

ASTM, C 39. (2003). Standard test method for compressive strength of cylindrical concrete specimens.

ASTM, C 143. (2010). Standard test method for slump of hydraulic-cement concrete.

ASTM, C 496. (2011). Standard Test Method for Splitting Tensile Strength of Cylindrical Concrete Specimen.

ASTM, C 469. (2014). Standard test method for static modulus of elasticity and Poisson's ratio of concrete in compression.

Berger, S., Aouad, G., Coumes, C. C. D., Le Bescop, P., & Damidot, D. (2013). Leaching of calcium sulfoaluminate cement pastes by water at regulated pH and temperature: experimental investigation and modeling. *Cement and Concrete Research, 53,* 211–220.

Cattaneo, S., & Biolzi, L. (2010). Assessment of thermal damage in hybrid fiber-reinforced concrete. *ASCE Journal of Materials in Civil Engineering, 22*(9), 836–845.

Celik, K., Meral, C., Mancio, M., Mehta, P. K., & Monteiro, P. J. M. (2014). A comparative study of self-consolidating concretes incorporating high-volume natural pozzolan or high-volume fly ash. *Construction and Building Materials, 67,* 14–19.

EN 14651. (2007). Test method for metallic fibre concrete-measuring the flexural tensile strength (limit of proportionality (LOP), residual).

Gartner, E. (2004). Industrially interesting approaches to "low-CO_2" cements. *Cement and Concrete Research, 34*(9), 1489–1498.

Gartner, E., & Hirao, H. (2015). A review of alternative approaches to the reduction of CO_2 emissions associated with the manufacture of the binder phase in concrete. *Cement and Concrete Research, 78,* 126–142.

Juenger, M. C. G., Winnefeld, F., Provis, J. L., & Ideker, J. H. (2011). Advances in alternative cementitious binders. *Cement and Concrete Research, 41*(12), 1232–1243.

Şanal, İ., Özyurt, N., & Hosseini, A. (2016). Characterization of hardened state behavior of self -compacting fiber-reinforced cementitious composites (SC-FRCC's) with different beam sizes and fiber types. *Composites Part B Engineering, 105,* 30–45.

Savino, V., Lanzoni, L., Tarantino, A. M., & Viviani, M. (2018). Simple and effective models to predict the compressive and tensile strength of HPFRC as the steel fiber content and type changes. *Composites Part B Engineering, 137,* 153–162.

Simões, T., Octávio, C., Valença, J., Costa, H., Dias-da-Costa, D., & Júlio, E. (2017). Influence of concrete strength and steel fibre geometry on the fibre/matrix interface. *Composites Part B Engineering, 122,* 156–164.

Tang, S. W., Zhu, H. G., Li, Z. J., Chen, E., & Shao, H. Y. (2015). Hydration stage identification and phase transformation of calcium sulfoaluminate cement at early age. *Construction and Building Materials, 75,* 11–18.

Closing the Loops in Textile Architecture: Innovative Strategies and Limits of Introducing Biopolymers in Membrane Structures

Alessandra Zanelli, Carol Monticelli and Salvatore Viscuso

Abstract Biopolymers have been increasingly introduced in some application sectors, such as food packaging, fashion, and design objects, while the typical technical textiles for architecture remain polymeric composites, based on the use of non-renewable resources. In lightweight construction and textile architecture, the introduction of novel materials requires a long process of verification of their performances, in order to guarantee the safety levels required by building standards. The paper aims to focus on potentiality and constrains to the application of more eco-friendly coated textiles, woven, and non-woven membranes in architecture. The paper proposes a couple of strategies and best practices to be applied in lightweight architecture: (1) creating fabrics from recycled fibers, on the one hand, and (2) acting on the coating with biopolymers, on the other hand. Eventually, the paper focuses on some recent experimental research led by the authors at the ABC Department, on the environmental assessment of ultra-lightweight materials, based on the LCA methodology.

Keywords Biopolymers · Technical textiles · Lightweight architecture · Eco-efficiency

1 Textile Industry in a Sustainable Bio-economy

The textile industry in Europe over the last ten years has shown distinctive development trends for the general textile and leather goods sector and its specific technical textiles subdivision (ExportPlanning 2018). Beside almost imperceptible improvements of the main textile sector, consistent European competitiveness appears in the production of "technical textiles," created by high-tech value-added supply chains, such as automotive, geo-textiles, medical, architecture, furniture, and technical clothing sectors (Fig. 1). The world production of woven and non-woven

A. Zanelli (✉) · C. Monticelli · S. Viscuso
Architecture, Built Environment and Construction Engineering—ABC Department, Politecnico di Milano, Milan, Italy
e-mail: alessandra.zanelli@polimi.it

S. Della Torre et al. (eds.), *Regeneration of the Built Environment from a Circular Economy Perspective*, Research for Development,
https://doi.org/10.1007/978-3-030-33256-3_25

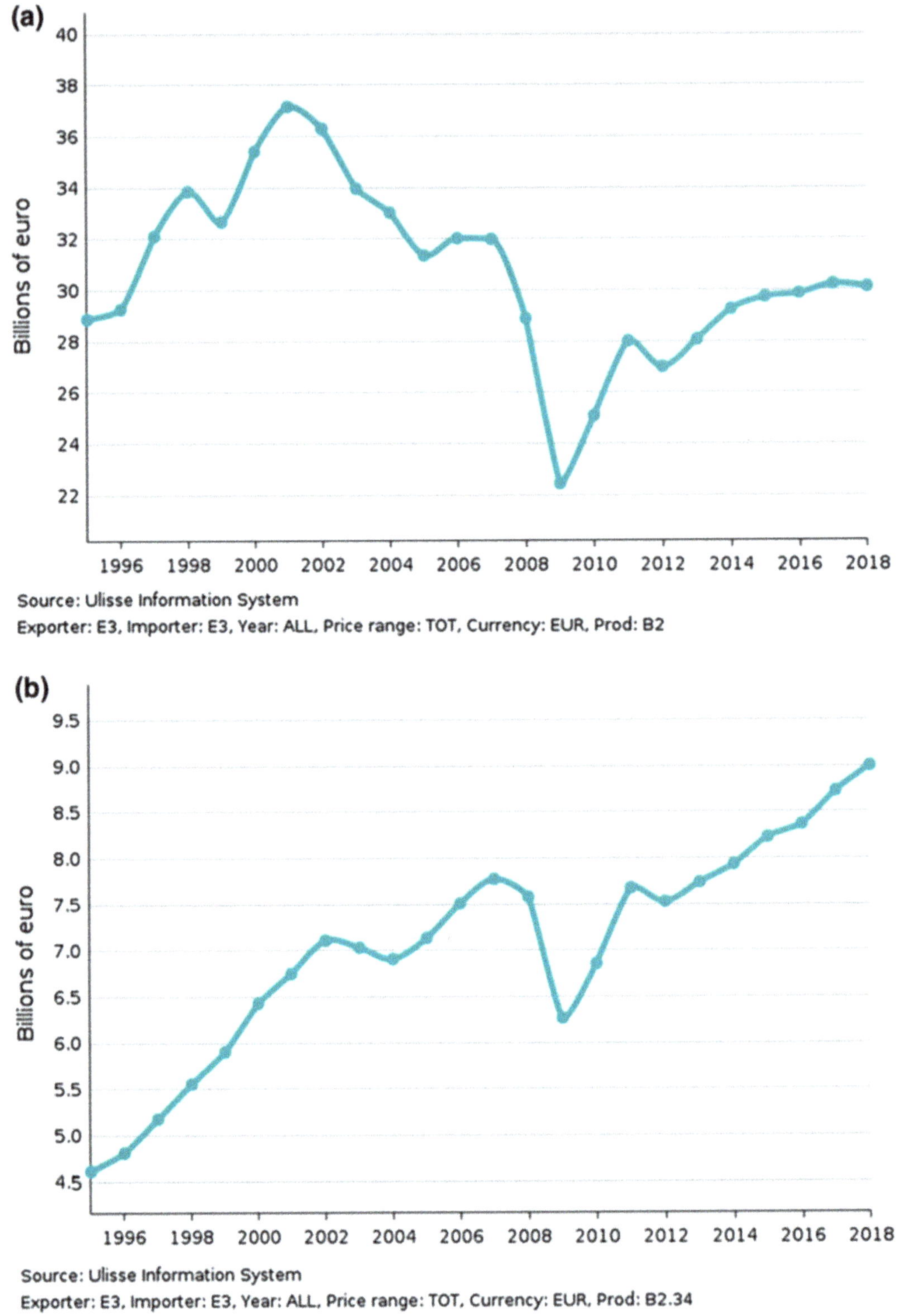

Fig. 1 Production trends of the sector of fabric and leather goods (a, left) and its segment of technical textiles (b, right). *Source* ExportPlanning (2018)

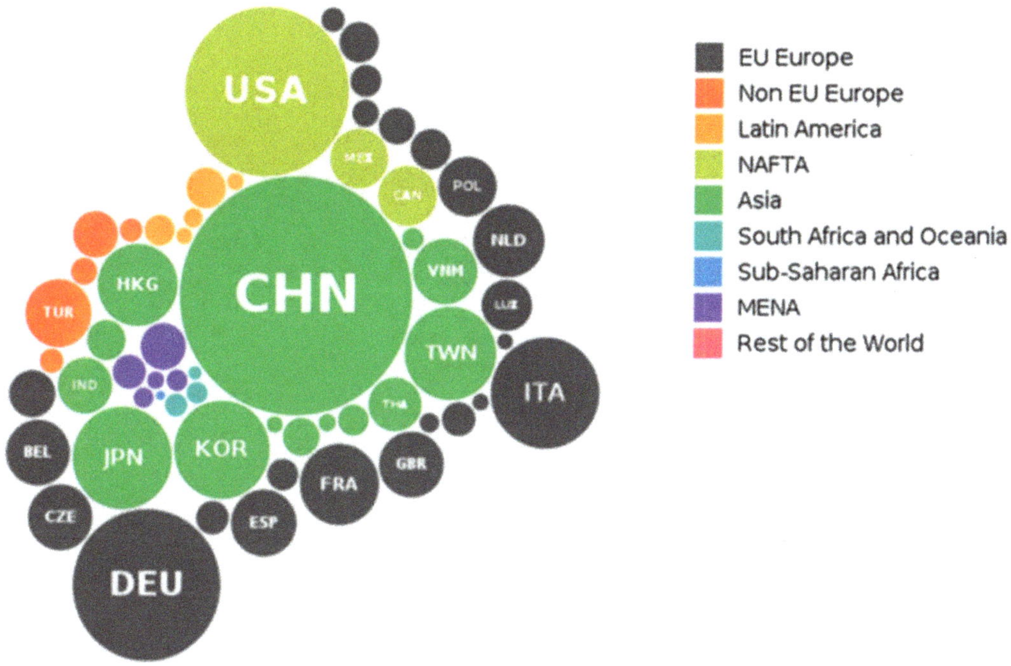

Fig. 2 World production of woven and non-woven fabrics for technical uses, year 2018. *Source* ExportPlanning (2018)

fabrics for technical uses is increasingly over 62 billions of Euros in 2018 where, besides China (14.6 billions) and USA (7.3 billions), in Europe, Germany (5.9 billions), and Italy (3.2 billions) are the most competitive countries (Fig. 2). The abovementioned technical textiles field aggregates the non-woven textiles (43%), a wide range of impregnated, coated, or resin-based fabrics (23.3%) useful for the textile architecture, and another significant variety of products and semi-finished technical textiles (15.6%), while yarns, tapes, and labels for various industrial application cover the rest 18.1% of the cake (ExportPlanning 2018). Furthermore, a clustered area led by Germany and Italy appears the most competitive in Europe for the production of both of impregnated, coated, or resin-based fabrics (Fig. 3a) and other textile products and semi-finished technical textiles (Fig. 3b).

Impregnated, coated, or resin-based fabrics and polymeric foils (TPU, PVC, PTFE) for textile architecture and membrane structures represent surely a niche segment of whole textile market; nevertheless, their impact seems to be as much meaningful and valuable as it deals with the well-being of the final users, and with the long-lasting, performative and non-toxicity requirements at the same time.

Looking at the textile manufacturing sector as a whole, it is also clear that environmental sustainability is still a challenge to be faced and closing the loops thanks to the activation of the virtuous 5 Rs processes[1] is still a dream to be built in the near future (Fig. 4). According to the estimation of European Commission, the EU textile

[1] Environmentalists all over the world profess 5 Rs in ensuring the reduction in solid waste pollution. These are Reduce, Re-use, Recycle, Replace or Remanufacture, and Recover.

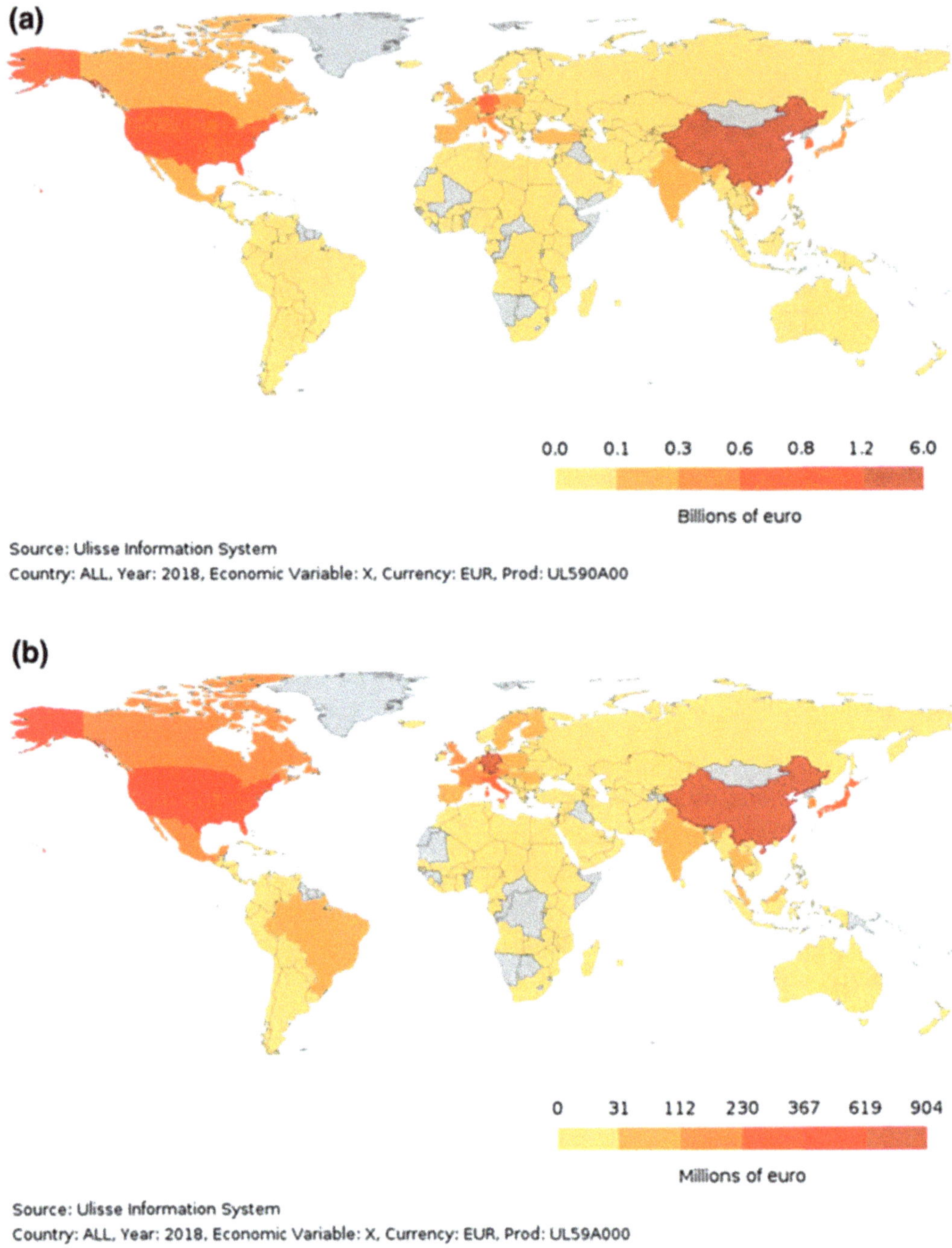

Fig. 3 Competitive position of Germany and Italy in the world production of technical textiles (a, left) and textile products for technical uses (b, right), year: 2018. *Source* ExportPlanning (2018)

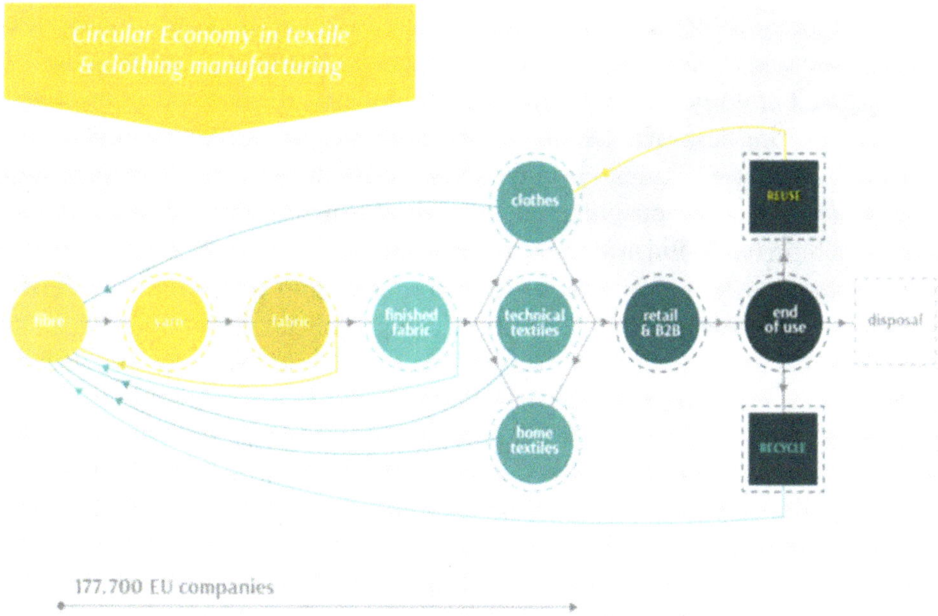

Fig. 4 Forecast scheme on how to make the European textile and apparel manufacturing sector circular. Currently, it is made of 177.700 companies, 99% of which are SMEs and all are involved in the production segment indicated by the arrow below (EURATEX 2019)

industry generates around 16 million tonnes of waste per year, most of which end up in landfills or incinerators. The quantity of clothes bought in the EU per person has incredibly doubled in a few decades, and now we buy an average of 13 kg of new clothes every year of which less than 1% is recycled in new clothing, while only that 13% of recycled textile materials go to other industries for use in lower-value applications such as insulation, mattress fillings, which are no longer recycled after use. The consumer use also has a large environmental footprint, due to the water, energy, and chemicals used in washing, tumble drying, and ironing, as well as micro-plastics shed into the environment (Euratex 2019; SAPEA, Science Advice for Policy by European Academies 2019).

Since 2018, United Nations Economic Commission for Europe has been working to the traceability for sustainable value chains in the textile sector, aiming to ensure that textiles are separately reusable/recyclable in all states by the 2025 at the latest (UNECE 2017).

2 Bio-terminology for Textiles and Polymers Raw Materials

With reference of Europe, more 60% of raw materials of woven and non-woven textiles are synthetic matters, made of fossil fuels and non-biodegradable, while the other 40% refers to natural fibers, although it must not be assumed that the latter's manufacturing processes are automatically "bio." It is well known that the bio-cotton can drastically reduce the environmental impact of conventional cotton, nevertheless the share of sustainable cotton increased from 6% in 2012 to 19% in 2017. Derived from cellulose filaments made of dissolved wood pulp or other starches are covering less of 10% of the fibers utilized in the textile sector. Most of the raw materials used in textile industry are still polymers made of petroleum. A biopolymer includes various materials of natural origin, such as wood, cellulose, chitosan, and chitin (Chiellini et al. 2001). Thanks to the fast advances in the synthesis of renewable raw materials (surplus or waste products from agriculture or foresting) within sustainable processes via fermentation, using a special mix of microorganisms and bacteria—a wider number of biopolymers can be created. Most of them are not degradable or compostable, and thus, only few of them are really closing the loops. As with conventional plastics, biopolymers are available in many grades and with widely varying properties, which depend on the application. A clear distinction between bio-based and fossil-based plastics on one hand, and biodegradable on the other hand has been done by many scientists (Niaounakis 2015), nevertheless the list of each family of plastics truly compatible with the bio-economy is going to be updated, and hopefully implemented, in the near future. The crucial difference between fossil-based polymers and biodegradable ones is that the first family is resistant to degradation, while the latter, also named oxo-degradable polymers, can be decomposed by microorganisms in a measurable rate, which depends from three main factors—light, water, and oxygen—and increases with time, while only few are compostable, that is they degrade in a specific environment, yielding H_2O, CO_2, biomass, and inorganic compounds, without leaving visual or toxic residue into the soil (Ashter 2016).

In conclusion, the bio-prefix also applicable to biodegradable synthetic polymers can be misleading as this category can lead to advantages at the end of life when compared to the plastics produced so far, but still remains unsustainable in the cradle, as they use non-renewable resources. Only natural polymers—biodegradable and bio-based biopolymers—promise a high level of eco-compatibility; they are much less of all the other polymers on the market, and several studies on the potentialities of the renewable feedstock, such as plants, animals, or microorganisms are ongoing. Innovative technologies start to emerge, enabling recycling textiles into virgin fibers, as in the case of: Infinited Fiber (Infinited Fiber Company 2019); Re.Verso™ spinning (Nuova Fratelli Boretti 2018); and Raytent™ production (Giovanardi 2019). Nowadays, the greatest challenge is to succeed on the one hand in reducing the quantity of fossil-based textiles, and, on the other hand, to guarantee that finishing treatment—able to confer specific functionalities and technical uses—are also drastically re-developed toward the use of natural alternatives and energy-saving separation processes at the end of life.

3 Textile Architecture Today

Textile architecture and its textile-based construction technology are characterized by the low weight of the embedded materials: around 0.2–0.5 kg/m^2 for transparent fluorpolymer systems up to 0.5–2 kg/m^2 for multilayer textile membrane systems, working in extreme loading condition. Fibers and polymer granulates should be combined in different ways, with the aim to create custom-made materials for textile architecture (Table 1). Nevertheless, this wide potentiality has not yet fully exploited by designers. As much as 90% of membrane structures are made of a limited range of flexible products, as PVC/Polyester, PTFE/Glass, Silicon/Glass, ePTFE (Tenara®) or ETFE foils. The last ten years achievements have shown countless improvements in the ultra-lightweight construction, in terms of: (a) effectiveness and life-span durability of flexible materials; (b) the improvement of construction details and site-specific installation procedures; and (c) the hybridization of this younger building technology with the traditional ones, answering for various functionalities. Textile materials for architecture seem more and more reliable and durable, either used in the form of a flexible membrane, suitably coated, as well as soft formwork of rigid concrete-based (i.e., textile beton) or resin shells (i.e., GFRP), and both for temporary and permanent

Table 1 Fabrics and composite materials available for architectural use. The finished products are related to their production chain (in brown). Performances can be improved by the adding an optional treatment to the semi-finished product (drawing by the authors)

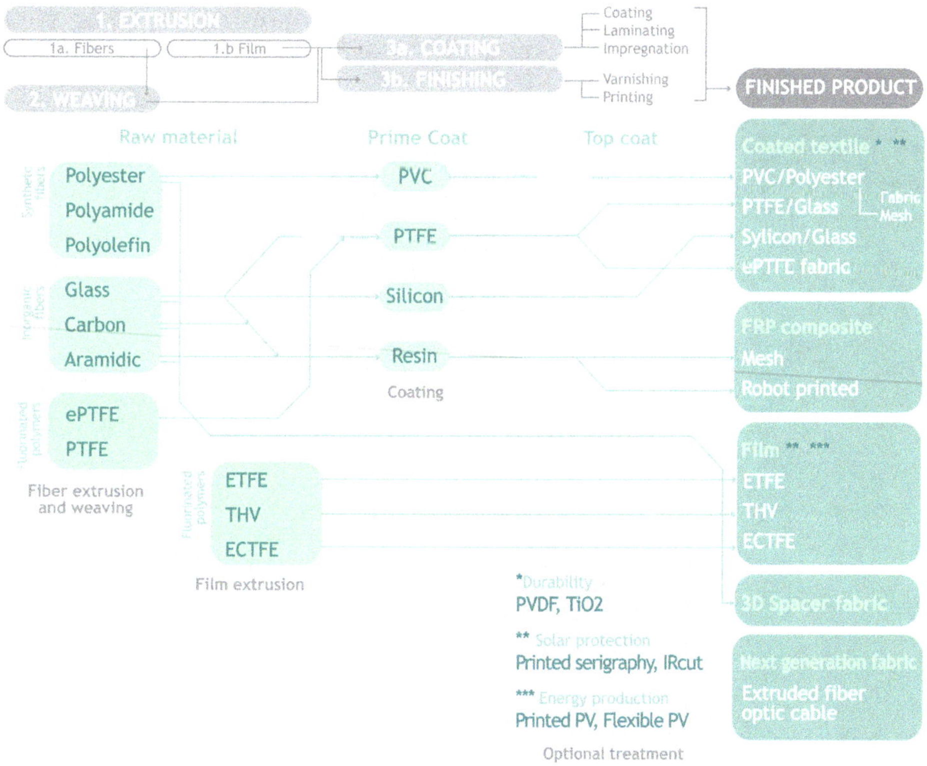

construction. Despite this, the specific sector of textiles and polymers still has a low market penetration in the wider predominant building components sector. In this scenario, innovation occurs more often led by novel designs and structural concepts at the macro-scale (building level) than by looking at the eco-sustainability of the textiles and polymers at the micro-scale (matter level).

After this decade of advances, harmonizing the local regulatory standards (Mollaert et al. 2016), and sharing knowledge through networks[2] and multidisciplinary research projects,[3] urgent open issues under scientists responsibility are: (1) a fairer and environmentally conscious design-driven innovation path; (2) the designers' lack of in-depth knowledge on membranes and foils; and (3) the gap between the increasing interest in innovative designs and the limited number of experimental testing laboratories.

4 A Research-Integrated Design Methodology, Enabling Biotechnologies in Textile Architecture

Since 2015, the multidisciplinary research laboratory TEXTILESHUB (TH Lab) at Politecnico di Milano has been carrying out, in a complementary and mutually reinforcing manner, design consultancies, educational exercises, and experimental scientific campaigns. The common goal of these theoretical and practical activities is assessing the applicability of novel natural/synthetic flexible materials, making progress in the creative and innovative use of ultra-lightweight building systems. Thanks to the different skills available at TH Lab (Table 2), its activity ranges from

Table 2 Interrelation of competences and activities carried out by the multidisciplinary Research Laboratory, with the aim to manage of the whole design to construction process of textile architecture (drawing by the authors)

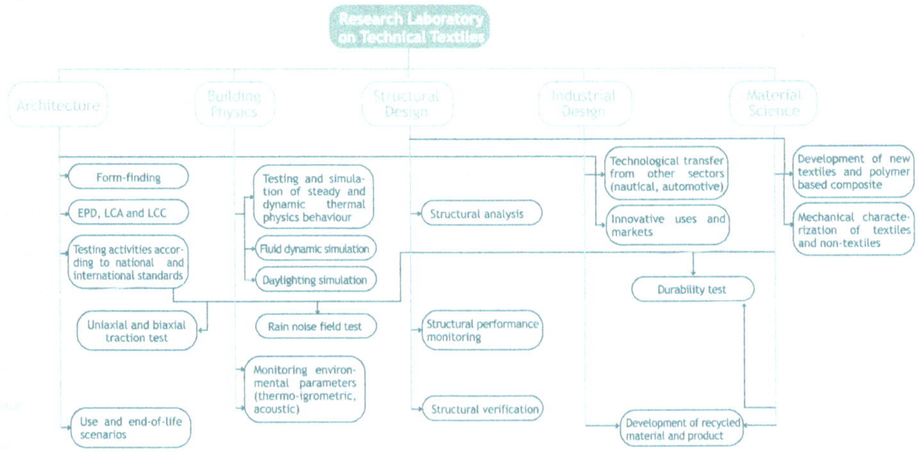

[2]TensiNet in Europe and Latin America; IFAI in USA, IASS around the world.

[3]Contex-T FP6 pr. (2006); COSTActions TU1303, CA17107; Innochain Project (2018).

testing mechanical and optical behavior to measuring performances of membranes and composites. TH Lab also gives service to firms and manufacturers: From 2017, it is an accredited laboratory for uniaxial and biaxial tensile tests, under the signatory of ILAC mutual recognition agreements (Services Accredia 2019). Welding and sewing machines are there available for the researchers' prototyping activities.

The authors, who are members of TH Lab, adopt the methodological approach of architectural technology, which is essentially a systemic design approach applied to the built environment and in a multi-scale perspective, where the material choice plays a crucial role throughout the whole design process—in relation to the requirements and environmental constraints—and it strengthens the specialized disciplines—materials engineering, chemistry, building physics—to drive the innovation into the building sector (Meadows and Wright 2008).

We assume that textile-based membrane architecture is characterized by a medium-low degree of innovation as shown in respective workflows at top and bottom of Table 3. Thanks to a research-integrated and iterative design approach, and an involvement of fabrics/foils producers and manufacturers during the whole design process, innovative loops can appear at multiple levels (the scheme center, Table 3). Nowadays, architects and designers need to cope with a full predictive control of the design-to-construction process. Through this data-driven methodology—in which experimental data constitute the input (i.e., breaking strength, elongation, tensile strength) needed to compute a reliable performance-based design—the TH Lab works as fruitful and disruptive bridging between different expertise at multiple scale. This iterative workflow of *designing-prototyping-testing-scaling up* is closely linked with the material characterizations of membrane and foil.

Due to this multidisciplinary and measure-centered research methodology, a set of novel bio-based coatings and natural fibers might be experimentally tested and validated at laboratory scale, foreseeing the real production. For example, the transfer of some bio-cellulosic products developed for the medical and packaging sectors might drive the innovation also in textile architecture. A first research path experimentally evaluating novel bio-based textiles should be focus on the stiffness, through five main steps: (a) the scope and the scale of the innovation through a concept design

Table 3 Multidisciplinary research path cross-linked to an experimental design process might pull innovation in textile architecture (drawing by the authors)

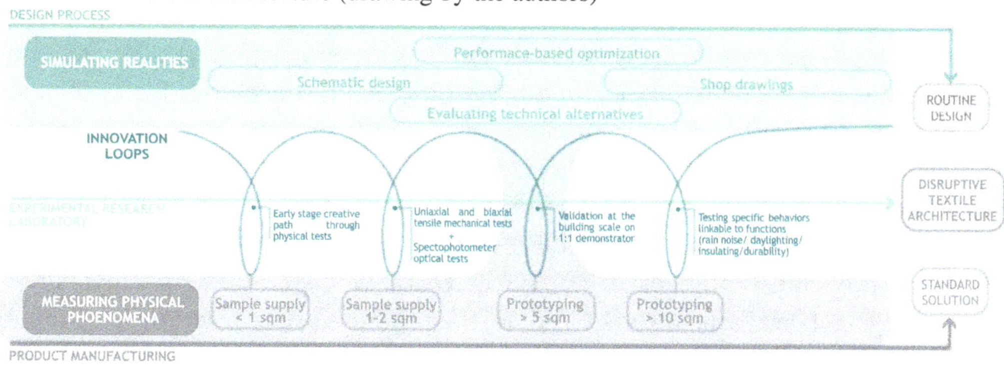

(form-finding); (b) the material characterization through the mechanical testing and continuous cross-validation of finite element modeling (FEM) tools; (c) physical testing the new materials' durability; (d) scaling up the investigation at the architectural concept, through FEM, life cycle assessment and thermal analysis; and (e) finalize shop drawings and real-scale demonstrators.

5 Life Cycle Assessment for Textiles: Comparing the Eco-Efficiency of Bio-based and Fossil-Based Fabrics

In the product and process development of more eco-friendly coated textiles, or a woven or non-woven membrane for architectural application, a double verification of their eco-efficiency (matter level) and environmental performances (building level) is in parallel needed. The LC analysis phase, as appears in Table 2, can provide an early stage evaluation of environmental impacts of a novel design concept and/or a material choice assumption. At that stage, a comparative LCA allows, on one hand, to check the environmental impacts generated during the production of alternative materials, on the other hand, to deepen the eco-profile's incidence of different technical solutions. A building level LCA investigation takes into account the efficiency of the whole system, the efficacy of the foreseeing construction procedures, the structural and thermo-physic and acoustic performances, as well as the costs. In the road map of the eco-efficiency of textiles for architecture, different stakeholders can be associated to the life cycle steps, above all: the chemical industry and the producers of polymeric/bio-based/biodegradable yarns and fabrics, on one side, and the supply companies of tailoring and assembly of the membrane components for the architecture to the other.

The considered scientific sources on the environmental impact assessment of textile and finishing industries clearly show that the investigation of the environmental impacts of the textile industry for clothing, furniture cladding and internal architecture has been started some decades ago, while the interest of the environmental burden of coated membranes and films for architecture starts recently. In general, literature surveys and other LCA studies on textiles show that most of the available process data are still not fully readable and clearly outliers. At the material's production level, TU Delft provided an up-to-date insight into the environmental burden of cotton, polyester, nylon, acryl, and elastane-based textiles (Van der Velden et al. 2014). The Institute of Textiles at Hong Kong Polytechnic developed a way to quantify and rank the ecological sustainability of textile fibers, such as organic cotton, flax, viscose, polyester, polypropylene, acrylic, and nylon (Smith and Barker 1995). The eco-efficiency of textile wet processing in Finland was also studied, as a part of drafting the Best Available Technique Reference documents for the European IPPC Bureau (Bidoki and Wittlinger 2010). Since 2004, Swedish Chalmers University of Technology has been focusing on LCA of textile products used for furniture wrapping (Subramanian et al. 2012), contributing at the adaptation of the LCA methodology to the textile sector specificities, and identifying the basis for a simplified evaluation tool, useful for textile companies. The EU COST Action 628 tried to define the best available technology (BAT) of textile processing and eventually suggested criteria for ISO (Type III) Environmental Product Declaration (EPD) standards (Kalliala and Talvenmaa 2000). In the field of textile architecture, the authors, as leaders of the *Sustainability and LCA* working group of a European project focused on the sustainability improvement of structural textiles (COST Action TU1303 2017), are working on the development of EPDs of membranes and foils, as well as defining their data quality requirements, transferable into Product Category Rules (PCR) documents. Furthermore, a significant eco-design approach for textile architecture can pass from the definition of brief design principles for weight reduction and the efficient of form-structure membrane skins (Monticelli and Zanelli 2019). The TAN group's authors collaborated with EU-funded EASEE project, assessing the environmental impacts of various textile finishing layers for inner walls, considering to cover an area of 3 m^2 as functional unit (Masera et al. 2017). A wide range of textile-based wallpapers and other less flexible finishing solution was then analyzed. Basing on this documented comparison between nature-based and fossil-based textiles (Table 4), the complexity of the LCA approach clearly tends to increase if we do not only look at the production of a new bio-textile—compared to a fossil-based one—but we want to measure its eco-efficiency throughout its service time and final disposal. This comparative LCA needs to: (a) identify key parameters and phases in the whole life cycle aiming to an improvement of the ecological efficiency of the product; (b) optimize the life cycle stage in relation to various disposal scenarios (recycling, incineration, landfill); and (c) carry out an life cycle costing (LCC) evaluation to identify the main cost contributions of the new bio-based textiles and find ways to optimize them.

6 Conclusion

The essay started from the methodological assumption that today it is relevant more than ever for designers to experiment with the matter—and its performance—of the architecture, from the early stages of the creative process. Possible knowledge gaps and innovation lacks that limit the spread of bio-based materials and sustainable circular processes in textiles architecture might be urgently overcome. In this specific building segment, due to the peculiarity of its short and effective from design-to-construction value chain—novel concepts of green products and processes would involve as much as designers, producers, and manufacturers, which should work in parallel, with an high level of exchange of information and cross-verification along the whole iterative process. The presumption that the environmental benefit of a specific material may simply be associated with its natural origin is especially dangerous in the textile architecture field, where textile-based composites and polymeric fabrics are still predominant. This is why the authors stated the need of overlapping quantitative and qualitative tools for assessing the environmental sustainability, referring to life cycle assessment methodology. Eventually, the TH Lab research-integrated

Table 4 Different textile inner finishing layers–LCA results

Impact category	Cotton textile 360 g	Kenaf textile 350 g	Polyester textile 400 g	PVC textile 380 g
Abiotic depletion (kg Sb eq)	0.0115	0.0014	0.0051	0.00461
Acidification (kg SO_2 eq)	0.0183	0.0016	0.0020	0.0041
Eutrophication (kg PO_4—eq)	0.0038	0.0013	0.0010	0.0007
Global warming GWP100 (kg CO_2 eq)	1.9302	0.2393	0.7110	0.6800
Ozone layer depletion (ODP) (kg CFC-11 eq)	0.000000041	0.000000011	0.000000092	0.000000027
Human toxicity (kg 1,4-DB eq)	0.7634	0.1077	0.6625	0.3969
Freshwater aquatic ecotox (kg 1,4-DB eq)	0.9811	0.1042	0.1582	0.1206
Marine aquatic ecotoxicity (kg 1,4-DB eq)	915.9794	210.4671	333.6373	234.1596
Terrestrial ecotoxicity (kg 1,4-DB eq)	0.0739	0.00056	0.0022	0.0038
Photochemical oxidation (kg C_2H_4 eq)	0.0006	0.000043	0.00017	0.00019
Non-renewable, fossil (MJ eq)	20.6502	3.8076	12.0287	10.1658

design approach and its focus on LCA of textiles were presented, together with a comparative study of the environmental impacts of fuel-based and nature-based fabrics, used as finishing layer of a wallpaper in interior architecture.

References

Ashter, S. A. (2016). Introduction to bioplastics engineering. *Plastic Design Library Handbook Series, Elsevier Ltd.* https://doi.org/10.1016/B978-0-323-39396-6.00011-7.

Bidoki, S. M., & Wittlinger, R. (2010). Environmental and economical acceptance of polyviniyl chloride (PVC) coating agent. *Journal of Cleaner Production, 18,* 219–225.

Chiellini, et al. (2001). (Eds.), *Biorelated polymers: Sustainable polymer science and technology*. Kluwer Academic Plenum Publishers.

COST ACTION TU1303. (2013–2017). *Novel structural skins—improving sustainability and efficiency through new structural textile materials and designs*. http://www.novelstructuralskins.eu.

ExportPlanning. (2018). Ulisse information system. http://www.exportplanning.com/analytics/png/.

EURATEX, The European Apparel and Textile Confederation. (2019). Prospering in the circular economy. Available at https://euratex.eu/wp-content/uploads/2019/01/EURATEX_CE_policy_brief_LR.pdf.

Giovanardi. (2019). Raytent: Recycled acrylic yarns, Italy. Available at https://www.raytent.it/home.

Infinited Fiber Company. (2019). Finland. Available at https://infinitedfiber.com.

Innochain Project. (2018). CITA, School of Architecture, Copenhagen. http://innochain.net/about/.

Kalliala, E., & Talvenmaa, P. (2000). Environmental profile of textile wet processing in Finland—Tampere University of Technology, Finland. *Journal of Cleaner Production, 8*(2000), 143–154.

Masera, G., Ghazi, W. K., Stahl, T., Brunner, S., Galliano, R., Monticelli, C., et al. (2017). Development of a super-insulating, aerogel-based textile wallpaper for the indoor energy retrofit of existing residential buildings. *Procedia Engineering, 180,* 1139–1149. https://doi.org/10.1016/j.proeng.2017.04.274.

Meadows, D. H., & Wright, D. (2008). *Thinking in systems.* Chelsea Green Publisher.

Mollaert, M., Dimova, S., Pinto, A., & Denton, S. (Eds.). (2016). *Prospect for European guidance for the structural design of tensile membrane structures. Support to the implementation, harmonization and further development of the Eurocodes*. JRC Science Hub, European Union. https://doi.org/10.2788/967746.

Monticelli, C., & Zanelli, A. (2019). Eco-design principles for a preliminary eco-efficiency assessment in the design phase: Application on membrane envelopes. In Zanelli et. al. (Eds.), *TS19 Proceedings* (pp. 280–291). Politecnico di Milano, June 3–5, 2019. https://doi.org/10.30448/ts2019.3245.41.

Niaounakis, M. (2015). *Biopolymers: Applications and trends.* Oxford: Elsevier.

Nuova Fratelli Boretti. (2018). Filatura C4 and Re.Verso™. http://www.filaturac4.it/progetto-re-verso/.

SAPEA, Science Advice for Policy by European Academies. (2019). *A scienti c perspective on microplastics in nature and society.* Berlin: SAPEA. https://doi.org/10.26356/microplastics.

Services Accredia. (2019). *Accreditation certificate of Politecnico di Milano—Interdepartmental Laboratory TEXTILES HUB, Testing Laboratory 1275 G.* www.services.accredia.it, http://pa.sinal.it/283012.pdf.

Smith, G. G., & Barker, R. H. (1995). Life cycle analysis of a polyester garment. *Resources, Conservation and Recycling, 14,* 233 249.

Subramanian, S. M., Hu, J. Y., & Mok, P. Y. (2012). Quantification of environmental impact and ecological sustainability for textile fibres. *Ecological Indicators, 13,* 66–74.

UNECE. (2017). *TEXTILE4SDG12: Transparency in textile value chains in relation to the environmental, social and human health impacts of parts, components and production processes.* United Nations. https://www.unece.org/fileadmin/DAM/trade/Publications/ECE-TRADE-439E-TEXTILE4SDG12.pdf.

Van der Velden, N. M., Patel, M. K., & Vogtländer, J. G. (2014). LCA benchmarking study on textiles made of cotton, polyester, nylon, acryl, or elastane. *The International Journal of Life Cycle Assessment, 19*(2), 331–356.

Performance Over Time and Durability Assessment of External Thermal Insulation Systems with Artificial Stone Cladding

Sonia Lupica Spagnolo and Bruno Daniotti

Abstract The contribution describes an experimental programme on durability assessment using the accelerated ageing of an outer wall component consisting of plasterboard support, an external thermal insulation composite system (ETICS) in polystyrene and a cladding that was realised half with natural stone and the other half with cast stone. The sample was placed in front of the climatic chamber by means of a special frame, in the so-called door configuration. During the accelerated ageing, this sample was simultaneously monitored over time using temperatures probes and flowmeter tests in order to evaluate the decay of the thermal performance over time. The experimental research was conducted with the aim of assessing the decay in thermal performance of an ETICS covered with artificial stone, comparing it with a similar stratigraphy but with a natural stone cladding.

Keywords Artificial stone · ETICS · Service life · Durability · Accelerated ageing

1 Introduction

European economies depend on natural resources, but if current patterns of resource use are maintained in Europe, environmental degradation and depletion of natural resources will continue. The issue has also a global dimension (European Commission 2005). That is why, artificial stones adoption can contribute in reducing the negative environmental impacts generated by the use of natural resources.

Stones used for cladding are exposed to environmental weathering, which is responsible for alterations in their microstructure (e.g. open porosity, pore size distribution, chemical-mineralogical composition of the phases, etc.), that, in turn, results in a modification of physical and mechanical properties (Franzoni et al. 2013).

The main material which is the subject of accelerated ageing is artificial stone made by means of a suitable Portland cement mix, lightweight aggregates and

S. Lupica Spagnolo (✉) · B. Daniotti
Architecture, Built Environment and Construction Engineering—ABC Department, Politecnico di Milano, Milan, Italy
e-mail: sonia.lupica@polimi.it

S. Della Torre et al. (eds.), *Regeneration of the Built Environment from a Circular Economy Perspective*, Research for Development,
https://doi.org/10.1007/978-3-030-33256-3_26

colours based on permanent mineral oxides. Different research activities have been undertaken on artificial stones (Fatiguso et al. 2013; Martínez-Martínez et al. 2013; Morillas et al. 2015; Stefanidou et al. 2015).

The catalogue of this product provides 32 different types of cast stone, inside of which different types of shapes are reproduced using suitable moulds, in order to replicate the same aesthetic effect given by the natural stone in the most realistic manner possible.

Depending on the desired effect, the artificial stone can be laid with or without joints and the product for grouting (a two-component lightened mortar) is available in five different colours and in two granulometries (fine-grained, 0/3 mm, or coarse-grained, 3/8 mm) (Table 1).

This artificial stone was used as a finishing layer for the thermal insulation system that was created using EPS 8-cm-thick panels, glued onto a plasterboard support by means of specific fibrate cement-based adhesive, also used as a filler on two layers to allow for the positioning of the 160 g/m^2 glass fibre alkali-resistant mesh; to allow comparison with the natural stone use, the same stratigraphy was realised with a natural stone coating, and the sample placed at the door of a climatic chamber was divided into two portions: one was coated with artificial stone and the other one with natural stone.

Table 1 Technical specifications of the artificial stone cladding

Feature	Value
Density (in accordance with ASTM C567-14)	1200 kg/m^3
Surface mass (depending on the texture and the presence or absence of the joint in the installation)	From 35 to 50 kg/m^2
Medium thickness	5 cm
Fire-resistance type	M0
Colour stabilising time	2/6 months
Moisture absorption (according to UBC 15-5)	Between 12 and 22%
Absorption during immersion (according to EN 14617-1:2013)	
– After 1 h	7.6%
– After 8 h	12.5%
– After 24 h	14.4%
Water vapour permeability (average stone μ)	26.4
Thermal resistance (according to ASTM C177-13)	0.16 K m^2/W
Thermal conductivity (according to UNI EN 12667:2002)	0.1866 W/mK (indicative)
Compressive strength (according to EN 14617-15:2005)	21.6 MPa
Flexural strength (according to EN 14617-2:2016)	3.7 MPa
Flexural strength after freezing–thawing (according to EN 14617-5:2012)	3.2 MPa

2 Experimental Layout Definition

The evaluation of the decay in thermal performance was conducted by means of relative comparison of the temperatures profiles and flowmeter measurements performed at time zero and after two accelerated ageing cycles. The test sample was placed at the "door configuration" of the climatic chamber: thanks to this configuration, it was possible to simulate the actual behaviour of the sample as the enclosure element between an internal environment (that of the same laboratory) and an external environment (the one imposed inside the climatic chamber). With this in mind, it was decided to perform a sampling that would be appropriately placed in front of the compartment of the climatic chamber, constituting the closing element (hence the "door configuration" designation).

To achieve so, according to the stratigraphy for monitoring the test sample, the size of the sample together with the correct positioning of the temperature sensors and the flowmeter was organised; in the sample, some probes were also positioned in the internal layers in order to verify the thermo-hygrometric profiles of the entire stratigraphy.

The accelerated ageing was programmed in such a way to be able to monitor the thermal properties of two tested coating types over time:

- natural stone ("NAT" type);
- artificial stone ("ART" type).

The accelerated ageing cycle is structured, as shown in Table 2, in two sub-cycles: winter and summer. This cycle was designed based on years of research on thermal insulation systems in the climate context of northern Italy, considering the average frequency of critical events of winter freezing–thawing and summer heat shock on a statistical basis (Daniotti et al. 2008).

Table 2 Specifications of the adopted accelerated ageing cycle

Sub-cycle	Phase	Air temperature (°C)	RH (%)	Phase duration (min)	Included transitory duration (h)	Repetition	Total duration (h)
Winter	Rain	5 ± 1	100	60	6	**10**	60
	Freeze	−20 ± 1	–	90			
	Winter heat	30 ± 1	50 ± 1	60			
Summer (thermal shock)	Dry heat	80 ± 1	15 ± 1	60	3	**25**	75
	Rain	20 ± 1	100	60			

2.1 Description of the "Winter" Sub-cycle

1. Rain phase (60 min): the test samples were sprayed with water to simulate a rainy event. The air inside the climatic chamber was kept at a constant temperature of 5 °C.
2. Freeze phase (duration 90 min): the air temperature inside the compartment containing the wet test samples was cooled to −20 °C and subsequently kept constant at that value.
3. "Hot winter" phase (duration 60 min): the temperature and the air humidity are kept constant, respectively, at 30 °C and 50% for a duration of 60 min.

2.2 Description of the "Summer" Sub-cycle

1. Dry heat (duration 60 min): the temperature and humidity were kept constant, respectively, at 80 °C and at 15% for a duration of 60 min.
2. Rain phase (60 min): the test samples were evenly sprayed with water to simulate a rainy event. The air inside the climatic chamber was kept at a constant temperature of 20 °C.

The accelerated ageing cycle consisted of ten repetitions of the winter sub-cycle, followed by 25 repetitions of the summer sub-cycle. This ageing cycle was repeated twice.

The expected time steps were therefore as follows:

t_0 = after drying of the sample, before the accelerated ageing;
t_1 = after one accelerated ageing cycle;
t_2 = after two accelerated ageing cycles.

3 Characterisation Tests and Analysis of the Degradation Over Time

For the "door configuration" sample, 3-time monitoring steps were carried out with the following characterisation tests and degradation analysis:

- photographic survey;
- measuring thermal resistance according to ISO 9869-1:2014;
- continuous measurement of heat flow in the flowing section;
- continuous measurements of temperature for analysis of the temperature profiles in the cross section (by placing four surface probes and four interstitial probes on the sample combined with environmental temperature probes).

As above stated, the stratigraphy for this sample is common to both portions until the second coating of the insulating layer. This "pre-coating" stratigraphy is as follows:

- plasterboard support with 15 mm thickness;
- 8-cm EPS panels, glued onto the substrate by means of plasterboard with specific fibrate cement-based glue for application of the adhesive (or smoothing) for coating systems;
- first EPS panel coating layer always with fibrate glue;
- 160 g/m^2 alkali-resistant fibreglass mesh;
- second coating layer always with fibrate adhesive, similar to the one used as an adhesive and for the first coating layer.

The two portions of the sample, differentiated by the type of coating from this point onwards, have the following additional layers:

for the PART COVERED WITH ARTIFICIAL STONE (for brevity called "ART")

- first coating with cement-based glue and natural hydraulic lime;
- glass fibre mesh with anti-alkaline primer weighing 315 g/m^2;
- second coating always with cement-based glue and natural hydraulic lime;
- cast stone, jointed (for the drying of any potential glue) with a two-component lightened mortar.

for the PART COVERED WITH NATURAL STONE (for brevity called "NAT")

- one-component Portland cement-based adhesive and synthetic resins with high elasticity;
- natural stone, jointed (for drying any potential glue) with traditional mortar.

4 Preparation of the Experimental Set-Up

The previously described cycle specifications were translated into operating plans for programming of the climate chamber in compliance with the necessary precedence.

In the testing phase of the set cycles in the operational plans, the actual duration of the same cycle was measured, including transients, lasted about 135 h.

After having programmed the climatic chamber, tested the individual phases of the cycle and measured the necessary transitional times, it was possible to prepare a realistic experimental plan that also takes into account the appropriate manual operations involved between one ageing cycle and another.

To allow placing the test sample in front of the climatic chamber, an ad hoc structure made and fixed above the carriage of the door of the climatic chamber was realised and installed. This steel structure allows the placement of a sample with a maximum size of 106 × 106 cm.

Fig. 1 Temperature probe positioning

The specimen was made in accordance with the stratigraphy and the dimensions above indicated. Between the two coating sections, an acetic silicone separation joint was applied. This material was also used for fixing the plasterboard to the containment frame.

The probes to measure the temperature were placed on the following interfaces:

- Pos 1—exposed surface of the plasterboard (lab side);
- Pos 2—interstitial plasterboard surface, before laying the glue of the EPS;
- Pos 3—pre-bonding coating surface, which corresponds:
  - for the "NAT" part, to the surface after the second coating of the EPS;
  - for the "ART" part, to the surface after the second coating;
- Pos 4—exposed surface of the cladding (climatic chamber side), in correspondence with the surface's centre of gravity on the coating ashlar (Fig. 1).

These temperature probes were placed and then fixed by means of mastic along the electrical cable, in order to prevent the probe from moving when performing the sample or the experimental test. The cables were then positioned vertically along with the sample and passed through the slots and the plastic pipes arranged in the lower part of the sample itself.

During the construction of the sample, it was taken into account that the two surface coating side probes needed to be placed in the centre of gravity of the surface of an ashlar. Therefore, as the other temperature probes (surface probe plasterboard side and probes to lose in the flowing section) must be aligned with these through the flowing section, the precise position of the superficial probes applied on the coating was preliminarily determined even before sampling began.

Prior to the positioning of the sample in front of the climatic chamber, a visual inspection of the surface and a photographic survey at time zero were carried out.

4.1 Specimen Positioning in Front of the Climatic Chamber

The test sample packaged was carried inside the laboratory and fixed inside the appropriate steel frame, which was previously anchored onto the closing carriage of the climatic chamber (Fig. 2).

In order to ease transportation and monitoring activities, a cart was placed in front of the climatic chamber, and the sample was realised within this steel frame.

After placing the sample in front the climatic chamber, both of the flowmeter probes and the surface temperature probes (internal and external) were fixed down,

Fig. 2 Views of "door" sample in front of the climatic chamber before the sensor wiring

and the connection of these to the datalogger was made to allow for the continuous acquisition of data.

For this sample, the continuous measurement of temperatures and heat flows along the cross section was performed, keeping the stationary conditions of 5 °C and 50% RH inside the climatic chamber (Fig. 3).

Fig. 3 Sample view in front of the climatic chamber and sensor wiring

4.2 Exposure of Test Samples to Accelerated Ageing Cycles

After having carried out the characterisation survey at time zero, the sample was exposed to the designed accelerated ageing cycles: as envisaged in the preliminary stage and in the preparation of the experimental set-up, the sample was subjected to two cycles of accelerated ageing in a climatic chamber, each consisting of ten repetitions of the winter sub-cycle (rain followed by a freezing phase at −20 °C, then by a warm winter phase at 30 °C) and 25 repetitions of the thermal shock summer sub-cycle (dry heat at 80 °C followed by rain).

At each time step, the climatic chamber was opened, the photographic survey was carried out on the surface of the test sample and the colorimetric measurement was taken in order to verify any variations in colour. Moreover, the flowmeter trend was constantly monitored, as well as the profile of the flowing section temperatures during the accelerated ageing.

5 Results

The surface temperature on the cast stone showed smaller variations in absolute values than the natural stone, demonstrating the fact that the thermal conductivity of the artificial stone was less than the natural stone one. This means that when the outside temperature drops, the surface temperature of the cast stone decreases less than the natural stone, and conversely, when the outside temperature rises, the surface of the artificial stone is not as hot as the natural stone.

This evidence is attributable to the fact that the thermal conductivity of the cast stone is smaller than the natural stone; this is a characteristic that causes the surface temperature variations to be smaller in the artificial stone compared to the ones that are found in the natural stone. This is regardless of the fact that the adhesive mortar used for the joints of the cast section itself has thermal properties better than the in the mortar used for natural stone.

Through flowmeter measures, moreover, it was possible to determine the trend of the thermal resistance over time, comparing the initial values detected on two of the sample sections at the door with the measured values as a result of the two steps of accelerated ageing in the laboratory.

For the measurement of thermal resistance, the method of progressive averages described in ISO 9869-1:2014 was used. Considered as 100 the initial value detected at time zero for both types of coating at the door of the sample, the following trend of the performance decay over time is showed in the following figure.

From the following graph, it is clear that after a decay in thermal resistance of the same amount of both the sample portions (mainly due to the increase of moisture content associated with exposure to rain), at time "t_2", both parts demonstrated mitigation of the initial performance decay. Of the two, the section coated with cast stone showed better thermal behaviour as a result of the accelerated ageing (Fig. 4).

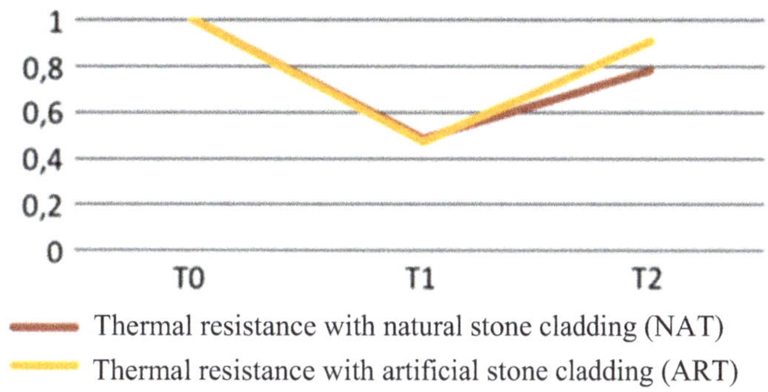

Fig. 4 Trend percentage of thermal resistances in the sample at the door (the curve relating to the coated section with artificial stone is in yellow and the one in brown is with natural stone)

Specifically, with respect to the thermal resistance value before the accelerated ageing:

- t_1 in both solutions show a halving of the thermal resistance;
- at t_2, the thermal resistance of the section of the natural stone showed a decrease of approximately 22%, while that of the artificial stone section decreased by approximately 9% (and therefore a performance decay of around 13% less than natural stone).

6 Concluding Remarks

Following the described accelerated ageing, the experimentation above described showed that:

- considering only the physical degradation, both the natural stone cladding and the artificial stone cladding did not reveal cracks in the stone, delamination or any mechanical type effects;
- the cast stone cladding performed, at time zero and as a result of accelerated ageing cycles, a better thermal behaviour than the natural stone; specifically, the artificial stone cladding shows a lower thermal conductivity, and after two accelerated ageing cycles, a decay in thermal resistance by approximately 13% less than the of natural stone;
- the presence of the stone coating generally involved a thermal shock mitigation effect;
- it is advisable to carry out colorimetric measurements on single-stone blocks in order to precisely evaluate the colorimetric variations of the coated surfaces; eventually, considering how the moisture content has an impact on the component's thermal behaviour and taking into account the porosity of the coating materials, it is also advisable to assess the progress of thermo-hygrometric behaviour over time through simulations with the appropriate "Heat and Moisture Transfer" calculation software.

Acknowledgements The research programme was carried out in collaboration with Geopietra S.r.l.

References

Daniotti, B., Lupica Spagnolo, S., & Paolini, R. (2008). Climatic data analysis to define accelerated ageing for reference service life evaluation. In *11DBMC International Conference on Durability of Building Materials and Components*, (May).

European Commission. (2005). COM (2005) 670 Thematic Strategy on the sustainable use for natural resources.

Fatiguso, F., et al. (2013). Investigation and conservation of artificial stone facades of the early XX century: A case study. *Construction and Building Materials, 41,* 26–36.

Franzoni, E., et al. (2013). Artificial weathering of stone by heating. *Journal of Cultural Heritage, 14*(3 SUPPL), 85–93. Elsevier Masson SAS.

Martínez-Martínez, J., et al. (2013). Non-linear decay of building stones during freeze-thaw weathering processes. *Construction and Building Materials, 38,* 443–454.

Morillas, H., et al. (2015). Nature and origin of white efflorescence on bricks, artificial stones, and joint mortars of modern houses evaluated by portable Raman spectroscopy and laboratory analyses. *Spectrochimica Acta—Part A: Molecular and Biomolecular Spectroscopy, 136*(PB), 1195–1203.

Stefanidou, M., Pachta, V., & Papayianni, I. (2015). Design and testing of artificial stone for the restoration of stone elements in monuments and historic buildings. *Construction and Building Materials, 93,* 957–965. Elsevier Ltd.

Standards

ISO 9869-1:2014 Thermal insulation—Building elements—In-situ measurement of thermal resistance and thermal transmittance heat flowmeter method.

ASTM C567-14 Standard Test Method for Determining Density of Structural Lightweight Concrete

ASTM C177-13 Standard Test Method for Steady-State Heat Flux Measurements and Thermal Transmission Properties by Means of the Guarded-Hot-Plate Apparatus

EN 14617-1:2013 Agglomerated stone—Test methods—Part 1: Determination of apparent density and water absorption

EN 14617-2:2016 Agglomerated stone—Test methods—Part 2: Determination of flexural strength (bending)

EN 14617-5:2012 Agglomerated stone—Test methods—Part 5: Determination of freeze and thaw resistance

EN 14617-15:2005 Agglomerated stone—Test methods—Part 15: Determination of compressive strength

UNI EN 12667:2002 Prestazione termica dei materiali e dei prodotti per edilizia—Determinazione della resistenza termica con il metodo della piastra calda con anello di guardia e con il metodo del termoflussimetro—Prodotti con alta e media resistenza termica [Thermal performance of building materials and products—Determination of thermal resistance by means of guarded hot plate and heat flow meter methods—Products of high and medium thermal resistance]

Multi-scale Approaches for Enhancing Building Performances

Sara Cattaneo, Camilla Lenzi and Alessandra Zanelli

Introduction

What performance can we guarantee if we consider an existing building? And how long can we guarantee a certain level of performance, both in existing buildings and in new ones? This section focuses on the challenge of analysis, simulation and performance control both during the design phases of a new building and during the service life of the building.

The issue of performance control is often reduced to the problem of saving energy resources and consequently optimizing the construction and management costs of the buildings. A more extensive consideration of performative design, in all the phases of the design process, starting from the conception of the building, to the optimization of its architectural volumetric form, as well as of its urban footprint, will have to be increasingly taken into consideration in a perspective of multi-level, economic, environmental and social sustainability.

This section intends to address in particular the following issues: a) multi-scalar strategies (from building to city) for mitigating the effects of climate change, improving local metabolism, improving environmental conditions, promoting energy efficiency practices, integration of locally available resources and the deployment of smart buildings, systems and networks; and b) actions to improve the built environment and public space aimed at reducing health risk factors (individual and collective) and promoting its quality in environmental and social terms including the design, construction, use, maintenance and disposal of buildings.

Circular Economy and Regeneration of Building Stock: Policy Improvements, Stakeholder Networking and Life Cycle Tools

Serena Giorgi, Monica Lavagna and Andrea Campioli

Abstract This chapter shows the results of a study carried out on the application of circular economy principles throughout the building stock regeneration process, highlighting the challenges, the opportunities and several key themes for future research. The methodology of research is based on a literature review and on-field investigation through direct interviews with operators and stakeholders of the building value chain, on a European level. At first, the chapter shows the importance of applying the circular economy concept to the built environment and the crucial role of the building level. After that, the chapter looks into the parallel issue of the current necessity to renovate a large part of existing buildings. Consequently, the opportunities and the challenges in linking the circular economy to building stock regeneration are discussed. Secondly, the chapter identifies the strategies to support the transition towards a sustainable circular building regeneration process, identifying the policy improvements necessary to promote circular strategies during the building process, the strategic partnership useful to activate profitable and sustainable circular business, and the environmental and economic life-cycle assessment tools for supporting decisions and for verifying that the implementation of circular strategies is actually sustainable from an economic and environmental life cycle point of view.

Keywords Life cycle sustainability · Stakeholders · Building process · CDW management · Business models

1 Introduction

«Anyone who believes that exponential growth can go on forever in a finite world is either a madman or an economist» said K. Boulding in 1966 (Boulding 1966), in order to introduce a necessary change in the relationship between economy and

S. Giorgi (✉) · M. Lavagna · A. Campioli
Architecture, Built Environment and Construction Engineering—ABC Department, Politecnico di Milano, Milan, Italy
e-mail: serena.giorgi@polimi.it

S. Della Torre et al. (eds.), *Regeneration of the Built Environment from a Circular Economy Perspective*, Research for Development,
https://doi.org/10.1007/978-3-030-33256-3_27

environment. After Boulding, many others (Georgescu-Roegen; Costanza; Daly; Commoner) have discussed this connection, gradually influencing the policy framework. The argument is still open and all economic sectors are still working to find a solution to decouple economic growth from its environmental impacts (UNEP 2011). Since 2014, European policies have promoted, as part of green economy objectives, the transition towards a circular economy, which focuses on the importance of activating virtuous strategies such as reuse and recycling in order to reduce the quantity of raw materials extracted, and reduce the quantity of waste (European Commission 2014, 2015).

The construction sector is identified as a 'priority area' to transform the current linear economy towards a circular economy. In fact, the construction sector is the main sector that produces waste, representing 33.5% of the total waste generated by all economic activities (Eurostat 2016), and one of the main causes of resource consumption. Moreover, the construction sector is crucial because it provides 18 million direct jobs and contributes to about 9% of the EU's GDP (European Commission 2018). Thus, current studies are looking for solutions to apply the circular economy concept to the built environment.

At the same time, the necessary regeneration of European building stock represents a challenge that can also be an important opportunity to apply circular economy to the built environment. The renovation of buildings could be a favourable circumstance to change the decision-making process, promoting the maintenance and life prolongation of existing buildings, and to change the material/waste flows, promoting the conservation of resources through reuse and recycling. In order to activate an actually sustainable circular economy, it is fundamental to assess the sustainability of the new practices towards circularity, within a life cycle perspective. Therefore, the introduction of life cycle tools to verify the level of sustainability during the building process is, now more than ever, crucial: if the building process has to change to achieve a circular process, it is important to change it in an effective and sustainable way.

There are a lot of challenges, especially because buildings are complex systems in a continuous state of change: they are constituted by various elements, with different lifespan and functions, and the building process involves a lot of stakeholders (Fig. 1).

2 The Circular Economy in the Built Environment

The holistic concept of circular economy in the built environment can be declined at three levels. According to Pomponi and Moncaster (2017): on a macro-level, regarding a system of cities or urban agglomerates, on a meso-level, which considers the buildings' scale, and on a micro-level, focusing on the material dimension.

The *macro-level* is discussed by many studies (e.g. Prendeville et al. 2018) which apply the circular economy principle on an urban level through the 'urban mining approach', considering the systemic management of anthropogenic resources stocked

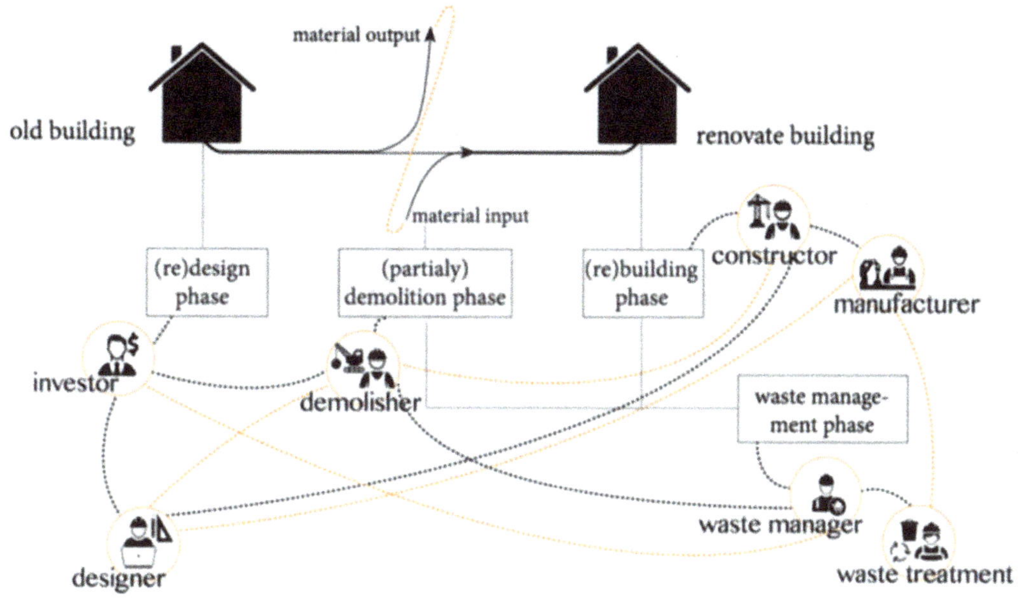

Fig. 1 Changing the building renovation process and stakeholders' relationships towards a circular building renovation process. The orange lines represent the links that have to be enabled in a circular building process

in the urban site, such as materials, waste, water and energy flows. The micro-level is also discussed in a significant number of studies (e.g. Smol et al. 2015), particularly when it comes to considering the exchange of by-products and waste between different industrial sectors (industrial symbiosis) in order to produce new products with recycled components (e.g. to use ash and sludge from purification processes for producing construction products). Hence, the *micro-level* is linked with an intersectoral approach based on the concept of the eco-industrial park and industrial ecology developed in the early Nineties.

The application of the circular economy on a *meso-level* (Pomponi and Moncaster 2017) is yet to be investigated in depth. There are studies (e.g. Cheshire 2016; Geldermans 2016) that give an impulse to the application of circular economy principles at the building level, considering 'buildings as material banks'. In general, there are a number of principles which strongly characterize the circular economy at the building level. These principles are classifiable in three main groups: design process aimed at adaptability and reversibility; resource/waste management aimed at reuse and recycling; business models aimed at extending life and value of products while also changing the concept of ownership. Waste prevention through the extension of the building life, product durability, maintenance, repair, reuse, must be the first goal for an efficient and effective use of resources.

Therefore, research about the circular economy at the building level is fundamental because of the lack of studies in comparison to the micro and macro levels, and because it is a link between these other two levels: circular requirements (e.g. exchange and use of reused/recycled materials) at building level can activate circular practices on an urban level and with regards to materials' composition. To do this, it is important to understand how the entire current building process (the design process, the construction process, the management process and the demolition process) has to change, within practices and relationships, towards a circular building process. It is necessary to involve all stakeholders in the research, in order to understand their relationships, their needs, their requirements and the decision-making steps. It is necessity to rethink the building according to a life cycle approach, considering the environmental impact at every stage of the life cycle: extraction of raw materials, manufacturing, transportation, construction, use, maintenance, recycling and disposal at the end of life.

The prospect requires an improvement in knowledge, skills and relationships between the member of the supply chain, and the inclusion, from the early design stage, of new operators (Campioli et al. 2018).

3 Opportunities and Challenges in Building Stock Regeneration

The European Commission proposed, in 2012, an action plan called 'Construction 2020', in order to assign a number of challenges to the construction sector to be completed by 2020. This action plan (European Commission 2012) highlights the great potential of the renovation of existing buildings and infrastructure maintenance to achieve the later objectives for 2050, with regards to decarbonization and resource conservation. In fact, the European building stock is in particular need of renovation: 50% of residential building stock (which represents 76% of the entire building stock) was built before the 1970 when the energy efficiency regulation did not exist. Only 19% of residential buildings were built after 1990, hence, after the EPBD 2002/91 and the following EPBD 2010/31 (Lavagna et al. 2018).

European policies have introduced more attention on land use, identifying soil sealing as one of the main causes of soil degradation (European Commission 2006). Over the last decade, attention on soil conservation led to the avoidance of the urban sprawl phenomenon, and to the possibility of building on green-field decreased. Consequently, the regeneration intervention of brown-field increased, in order to preserve the soil. In Italy, in 2015, CRESME shows the increase of renovation of existing buildings (+3.5%) in comparison with the new construction buildings (+1.6%).

This context proposes an interesting trial field for the application of circular economy principles. The circular economy approach can limit waste landfills and avoid extraction of raw materials, giving more value to the existing building and avoiding demolition waste increasing the longevity of buildings' subsystems and elements. It is possible to open a new cycle for the unavoidable waste generated by demolition parts of buildings as secondary resources within the construction sector to produce new materials aiming at upcycling. During the renovation process, the construction of new parts for the existing building can be designed and completed with disassembly solutions, using materials that are reusable and recyclable, without toxic or hazardous materials. Moreover, in this perspective construction techniques can also be improved, avoiding the construction waste caused by incorrect operation (e.g. design error, site operation, materials scraps) which can be avoided with a BIM design, which enhances communication, increases efficiency and reduces errors (Osmani 2011).

Despite these opportunities, there are also a number of challenges to address, because in the building process the circular strategies are hardly applied on heterogeneous and long processes with dynamic relationships of different operators related to each other in a discontinuous manner.

Currently, the transition towards a sustainable circular renovation of building stock is still thwarted by political and economic barriers along with a lack of awareness. In the next paragraph, the study illustrates the main obstacles to overcome and provides strategies to support the transition towards a sustainable circular regeneration, through the identification of: (i) policy improvement, (ii) strategic partnerships for circular networks, (iii) environmental and economic life-cycle assessment tools to support the decision-making process.

4 Strategies Towards a Sustainable Circular Building Regeneration Process

In order to identify the obstacles and strategies for the transition towards a circular economy, the study carried out an in-depth analysis, through interviews with stakeholders regarding the building renovation process: the current material and information flows, the relationships among the operators and stakeholders and the tools used during the process. This analysis is useful to understand the current practices, design and management choices when a building has to be regenerated, in order to identify the critical points and necessary changes.

4.1 Policy Improvements

After the publication of the 'European Construction 2020 strategy' and the other European communication which promotes circular economy in the construction sector (European Commission 2014, 2015), it is possible to say that the policies regarding circular economy at European and National levels, are mainly promoting actions that deal with the management of CDW, recycling activities and waste logistics. The other aspects of circular economy on a building level, such as design approach and circular business models, are not yet promoted by policies.

The 'EU Construction and Demolition Waste Management Protocol' (2016), and the 'Guidelines for the waste audits before demolition and renovation works of buildings' (2018) are the primary actions which are part of the Circular Economy Package presented by the European Commission in 2015. These initiatives act on the improvement of waste identification, through a better separation and collection, waste logistics, through better traceability of the waste stream, waste processing, through an efficient recycling process, and quality management, through the introduction of quality labelling and certification.

Analysing the current CDW management of European countries (Giorgi et al. 2018), the first obstacle to a sustainable waste flow management is the lack of a database for monitoring CDW quantities and the confusion regarding who should control and monitor waste management. In Italy, for example, the legislation (d.lgs.152/2006) provides several exemptions from the obligation to declare the quantity of waste generated by the construction and demolition process, as in the case of a medium-size building process. Consequently, the real-waste flow remains unknown. The lack of monitoring also concerns the extraction of materials: there is no official data available on the extraction of construction minerals (such as sand and gravel), even if the extraction of construction minerals represents a large share of total material extraction (UNEP 2016). Moreover, if the materials flow does not change, becoming more efficient and effective, the material consumption in the construction sector is expected to further increase in future (Fishman et al. 2016).

The Member States that present the highest level of CDW recovery, show the introduction of laws banning landfills (such as in Belgium and Netherlands) or high taxes on landfills (such as in the UK) (Resource Efficient Use of Mixed Wastes 2017). These measures have increased the recycling process, mainly through downcycling. Instead, within circular economy, it is important to activate upcycling and reuse processes; however, there are still barriers for the activation of such effective circular practices.

Through direct interviews with stakeholders of the building value chain (Giorgi et al. 2019) the obstacles of upcycling and reuse were successfully identified. The reason that thwarts the activation of a sustainable circular practice at the building level is the lack of expert operators able to disassemble, and of space to store the materials to be reused. These gaps lead to high costs in human labour and difficulties in logistics. However, the main obstacle concerns the legislative framework and responsibility. Nowadays, the legislative framework does not enable the certification of the quality and durability of a reused material, because there is a lack of data and knowledge of the history of the material itself. Consequently, even if it is possible to use reused/recycled materials, designers and constructor companies prefer to use new ones only, because they are responsible for the material quality used to build a building.

More ambitious legislation is necessary to promote the reuse/upcycling of materials. First of all, it is important to improve market demand for secondary materials, also for the construction industry, through the application of laws which ban the extraction of raw materials (e.g. to forbid the opening of new quarries). Secondly, public building renovation should be the exemplary intervention for introducing circular practices throughout the entire process; hence, the development of green public procurement with ambitious requirements (e.g. with regards to the reuse of building parts and elements, the reversible design approach and the use of recycled/recyclable materials) is necessary.

The introduction of economic incentives is fundamental to overcome the economic barriers: for instance, for building renovations that use reused/reusable materials or recycled/recyclable materials; which base the design phase on strategies for disassembly, using BIM tools and off-site construction technics to avoid construction waste; which use life cycle tools to assess the sustainability of the project solutions chosen. Finally, it is important to upgrade the sustainability rating system with new criteria useful for assessing the potential of the project with respect to the themes of a circular economy.

4.2 Relationships Throughout the Building Renovation Value Chain and Circular Business Models

Building renovation is accomplished via a long and complex process, conducted by a lot of operators with different roles and relationships. Sometimes operators are not in contact with one another and the information flow is interrupted during the process. Also, crucial decisions are made by different operators in different moments of the process: for example, the investor decides the type of intervention and the sustainability target to achieve; the designer can decide how to obtain the target, the materials and technical solution; the demolisher decides the demolition techniques (selective demolition or deconstruction); the demolition-yard organization and the management and destination of material/waste. This fragmentary process is one of the obstacles to an easy application of circular economy at the building level.

The analysis of relationships along the value chain shows that the value of materials stocked in the building is completely unknown by the investors; consequently, they are not interested to know the destination (landfill or recovery) of the materials deriving from a renovation process. Also, the designer, most of the time, during the building renovation design process, does not take into account the material quantity output in order to consider the possibility of reusing or recycling it. The pre-demolition audit could be an existing instrument useful to improve the cooperation and communication among designers, demolition companies and waste managers; however, this instrument is not commonly used. Improvement and specificity during the procedure are necessary in order to boost the instrument as a decision-making process and avoid demolition waste. Moreover, designers tie the difficulties in designing a reversible building to a lack of available easily disassembled products on the market. It is necessary to open up a dialogue between designers and producers in order to develop technological solutions to build a building based on a design for disassembly and adaptability.

In order to activate circular strategies, a change in relationships among the stakeholders of the building value chain, is necessary.

Consequently, it is very important to support the operators' network, in activating circularity during the building process, also by using BIM software, to improve the cooperation from the early stage of the process. Moreover, it is important to identify competences and new operators, in order to accomplish the disassembly and remanufacturing phase, to trace the material flows, to improve the collection and to exchange second-life materials, towards a reuse/remanufacturing materials value chain. At the same time, it is important to define the space to store and collect all material quantities (big or small) destined to a second-life.

The promotion of circular business models that shift ownership from user to producer can be useful to overcome the difficulties of relationships among the stakeholders and the problems concerning responsibility and adding new professional figures in the product/service value chain, for example, introducing warranties or third-party figures that play an "insurance" role for the reused material.

4.3 Life Cycle Tools as a Decision-Making Support

The analysis of the state of the art (Giorgi et al. 2017; Geissdoerfer et al. 2017) concerning the application of the life cycle tools within scientific articles, shows that, at the moment, the combination of the circular economy and life cycle tools is still very lacking. Moreover, the link between circular economy and sustainability is not yet clear in the literature (Blomsma and Brennan 2017). Circular economy strategies should aim at safeguarding resources in all life stages of a product/service, encouraging reuse and upcycling with sustainability verification, through the application of life cycle tools for an environmental and economic benefit assessment.

It is, therefore, necessary to evaluate the sustainability of circularity strategies through instruments that are recognized, such as the methodologies involving life-cycle assessment and life cycle cost, which are the ISO-standardized methodologies used to quantify the real benefit, avoiding burden-shifting among different life-cycle phases.

These fundamental assessments must be introduced during the decision-making phases of the regeneration process, from the end of life management of the existing building to the renovation planning phase. Specifically, the design phase is crucial for assessing the environmental impact and market opportunities with the life-cycle approach. The use of life cycle tools, for example, can highlight the benefits of renovation rather than total demolition, and of a reversible building instead of a traditional one. In this way, it is possible to avoid unnecessary upstream waste and maximize the value and sustainable use of materials. Another important phase during the entire process is the waste management phase when, thanks to a previous environmental and economic life-cycle assessment, it is possible to decide the more effective choice when it comes to material waste destination, which can, for example, involve reuse, recycling or landfill disposal.

In this perspective, it is essential to disseminate the environmental sustainability information of the product, promoting, for example, the use of existing certification, such as EPD, or defining a certification that indicates the sustainability of a specific circular strategy (such as reuse, remanufacturing and recycling) considering the entire process (e.g. including the impacts due to transport and the entire logistics required for the circular strategy). However, in this case, not only are policies necessary in order to favour the use of life cycle tools in the building renovation process, but also awareness and knowledge among the stakeholders regarding the sustainability must be encouraged.

5 Conclusion

The chapter discusses the opportunities to link circular economy and the process of building stock regeneration, in order to activate sustainable strategies which can avoid the generation of construction and demolition waste and the consumption of raw materials. In order to achieve the transition towards a sustainable circular renovation building process, a change in policies, relationships and tools is necessary. Regarding policies, future research needs to identify the reasonable differences in price between landfill, raw materials and secondary materials in order to encourage reuse and upcycling process; the achievable but ambitious targets to add to green public procurement to encourage circular practices, and future increasing targets; the economic incentives to promote the design for disassembly and the use of secondary materials. Regarding the relationships, future research needs to identify the best network process among operators in order to activate circular strategies, such as reuse and remanufacturing; what type of agreement or win-win solution can be activated among clients and material producers/suppliers in order to activate take-back strategies or circular business models based on leasing; moreover, the research needs to identify how to train and educate expert operators/advisers on monitoring and optimizing material flows, and accomplishing disassemble projects (in parallel, the mechanics technologies needed to aid human labour should be developed). Finally, regarding the tools, the research needs to define specific tools (while also implementing the existing ones, such as the pre-demolition audit) which can help the decision-making process to shift towards circular strategies with the support of LCA and LCC, in order to achieve only sustainable strategies, identifying the specific decision-step and operators which need the support of sustainable tools.

The application of circular economy through the building renovation process opens operators up to the necessity to identify and train specific expert operators/advisors who can help current operators directly involved during the building renovation process in deciding upon circularity and sustainability.

The challenges are many, however, just by working on all three prospects it can be possible to activate a sustainable circular economy in the built environment, and definitely contribute to sustainability goals.

References

Blomsma, F., & Brennan, G. (2017). The emergence of circular economy. A new framing around prolonging resource productivity. *Journal of Industrial Ecology, 21*(3), 603–614.

Boulding, K. E. (1966). The economics of the coming spaceship earth. In H. Jarrett (Ed.), *Environmental quality in a growing economy* (pp. 3–14). Baltimore: Resources for the Future/Johns Hopkins University Press.

Campioli, A., Dalla Valle, A., Ganassali, S., & Giorgi, S. (2018). Designing the life cycle of materials: new trends in environmental perspective. *Techne Journal of Technology for Architecture and Environment, 16,* 86–95.

Cheshire, D. (2016). *Building revolutions: Applying the circular economy to the built environment.* RIBA Publishing.

European Commission 231. (2006). *Thematic strategy for soil protection.* Bruxelles.

European Commission. (2012). COM 433 Strategy for the sustainable competitiveness of the construction sector and its enterprises. Brussels.

European Commission. (2014). COM 398 Towards a circular economy: A zero waste programme for Europe. Brussels.

European Commission. (2015). COM 614 Closing the loop. An EU action plan for the Circular Economy. Brussels.

European Commission. (2018). *Growth, construction.* Available at https://ec.europa.eu/growth/sectors/construction. Accessed May 10, 2019.

Eurostat. (2016). Key figures on Europe 161–164.

Fishman, T., Schandl, H., & Tanikawa, H. (2016). Stochastic analysis and forecasts of the patterns of speed, acceleration, and levels of material stock accumulation in society. *Environmental Science and Technology, 50,* 3729–3737.

Geissdoerfer, M., Savaget, P., Bocken, N. M. P., & Hultink, E. J. (2017). The circular economy: A new sustainability paradigm? *Journal of Cleaner Production, 143,* 757–768.

Geldermans, R. J. (2016). Design for change and circularity—Accommodating circular material & product flows in construction. *Energy Procedia, 96,* 301–311.

Giorgi, S., Lavagna, M., & Campioli, A. (2017). Economia circolare, gestione dei rifiuti e life cycle thinking: fondamenti, interpretazioni e analisi dello stato dell'arte. *Ingegneria dell'Ambiente, 3*(4), 241–254.

Giorgi, S., Lavagna, M., & Campioli, A. (2018). Guidelines for effective and sustainable recycling of construction and demolition waste. In E. Benetto, K. Gericke, & M. Guiton (Eds.), *Designing sustainable technologies, products and policies—From science to innovation.* Berlin: Springer.

Giorgi, S., Lavagna, M., & Campioli, A. (2019). Circular economy and regeneration of building stock in the Italian context: Policies, partnership and tools. In *IOP Conference Series: Earth and Environmental Science*.

Lavagna, M., Baldassarri, C., Campioli, A., Giorgi, S., Dalla Valle, A., Castellani, V., et al. (2018). Benchmarks for environmental impact of housing in Europe: Definition of archetypes and LCA of the residential building stock. *Building and Environment, 145,* 260–275.

Osmani, M. (2011). *The potential use of BIM to aid construction waste minimalisation.* Available at: https://dspace.lboro.ac.uk/2134/9198.

Pomponi, F., & Moncaster, A. (2017). Circular economy for the built environment: A research framework. *Journal of Cleaner Production, 143,* 710–718.

Prendeville, S., Cherimb, E., & Bocken, N. (2018). Circular cities: Mapping six cities in transition. *Environmental Innovation and Societal Transitions, 26,* 171–194.

Resource Efficient Use of Mixed Wastes. (2017). *Improving management of construction and demolition waste Final report*. European Commission B-1049 Brussels.

Smol, M., Kulczycka, J., Henclik, A., Gorazda, K., & Wzorek, Z. (2015). The possible use of sewage sludge ash (SSA) in the construction industry as a way towards a circular economy. *Journal of Cleaner Production, 95,* 45–54.

UNEP. (2011). *Decoupling natural resource use and environmental impact from economic growth.* Paris: UNEP DTIE.

UNEP. (2016). *Global material flows and resource productivity.*

Re-NetTA. Re-Manufacturing Networks for Tertiary Architectures

Cinzia Talamo, Monica Lavagna, Carol Monticelli, Nazly Atta, Serena Giorgi and Salvatore Viscuso

Abstract The paper introduces the on-going project Re-NetTA, which contributes to apply circular economy in the building sector, focusing on tertiary sector building components, characterized by rapid obsolescence and temporary uses. The Re-NetTA project identifies re-manufacturing and reuse networks and processes as tools to reduce the generation of waste deriving from renewals/transformations carried out on short-term cycles, applying Life Cycle Management and sustainable business models. The goal is to maintain over time the value of the environmental and economic resources, integrated into manufactured products, once they have been removed from buildings, extending their useful life and their usability with the least possible consumption of other materials and energy and with the maximum containment of emissions into the environment. At first, the paper shows how circular economy can be applied to the built environment, according to literature. Secondly, the problem of waste coming from renewal interventions, carried out on short-term cycles of the tertiary sector, is discussed on quantitative data. Consequently, the aims of the research and the methodology, based on an interdisciplinary approach, are introduced. Finally, the research output is pointed out, highlighting the related economic, environmental, and social impacts.

Keywords Circular economy · Re-manufacturing · Built environment · Stakeholder networking · Circular business models · Life cycle approach

1 Introduction

European Commission (2015) identifies the construction sector as a fundamental driver-sector for the activation of circular economy. According to the statistical data in EU-28, the main field that produces waste is construction sector, contributing to 33.5% of the total waste generated by all economic activities and households

C. Talamo (✉) · M. Lavagna · C. Monticelli · N. Atta · S. Giorgi · S. Viscuso
Architecture, Built Environment and Construction Engineering—ABC Department, Politecnico di Milano, Milan, Italy
e-mail: cinzia.talamo@polimi.it

S. Della Torre et al. (eds.), *Regeneration of the Built Environment from a Circular Economy Perspective*, Research for Development,
https://doi.org/10.1007/978-3-030-33256-3_28

in 2014 in the EU-28 (Eurostat 2016). Moreover, the construction sector gives a lot of opportunities in job creation (currently, it provides 18 million direct jobs), contributing to about the 9% of the EU's GDP (European Commission 2018).

From 2015, the efforts to apply circular economy in the construction sector are increasing. However, currently, the circular strategy, more promoted and applied, regards waste management toward recycling (Giorgi et al. 2017). A lot of European Projects (e.g., HISER PROJECT, Resource Efficient Use of Mixed Waste, DEMOCLES, ENCORT) and particularly Life Project (e.g., LIFE-PSLOOP Polystyrene Loop; CDW recycling Innovative solution for the separation of construction and demolition waste) investigate specific recycling strategies (inter-sectoral or within the construction sector) of construction and demolition waste (Talamo and Migliore 2017). Moreover, the largest number of recycling case studies in the construction sector regards downcycling process (such as recycling of inert as road substrate). Instead, from a sustainable circular economy point of view, it is important to consider more valuable strategies that aim to avoid the generation of waste in upstream, encouraging reuse practices and the life cycle extension of products.

Ellen MacArthur Foundation and CE100 network (2016) suggest the six actions, within the "ReSOLVE framework" (regenerate, share, optimize, loop, virtualise, exchange), to guide the transition toward a circular economy in the built environment highlighting the objective of keeping resources into the cycles, creating new uses for materials. This approach can open up new scenarios of a building materials market and it has the potential for developing business model innovations. Other research works (Cheshire 2016; Durmisevic 2018) consider the "Design for Disassembly" as a valuable design strategy in order to encourage reuse processes at the end of the product service life.

Starting from this background, the research Re-NetTA, funded by Fondazione CARIPLO for the period 2019–2021, aims to define new organizational and operational models and new business strategies necessary to launch circular and regenerative economy processes based on re-manufacturing and involving the construction and the manufacturing sectors. The research focuses on buildings for the tertiary sector, usually characterized by quick cycles of renewal and reconfiguration, with the aim of creating the organizational and business conditions to make buildings "components banks" in a circular economy perspective.

2 From Waste to Resources: Short-Term Components from Tertiary Sector and Temporary Use

Some parts of the building have a long service life, while other parts and components have a short service life, requiring frequent replacement cycles and thus becoming potential waste, even though they still have good residual performances. BAMB report (Peters et al. 2017) indicates how often the different categories of products

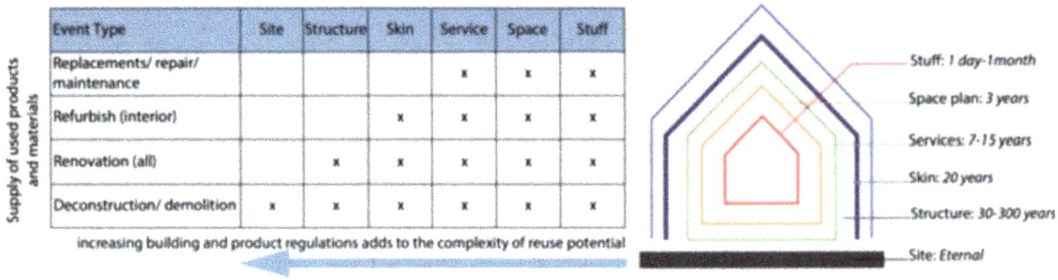

Fig. 1 Frequency of availability of building/product supply by event. *Source* BAMB 2017 (on the left), and Stewart Brand's 6 S's from "How Buildings Learn" (on the right)

need a replacement, in relation to the different interventions types (Fig. 1). The categories of products are based on the six S's system of building from Brand (1994) theory, which identifies the lifespan of each category. This analysis shows that Stuff (furniture, appliances, objects), Space plan (division of space, interior partition) and Services (HVAC systems and moving parts like elevators) not only have a short lifespan, but also, for each type of intervention (demolition, total renovation, interior renovation, and small upgrades and maintenance), they are always substituted. Starting from these issues, the research Re-NetTA investigates the potential second life or the extension of the life of products, characterized by short-term service life. The research focuses on short-term components with a service life lower than 15 years (interiors, services, equipment, furnishings, and fittings), which frequently became potential waste that can be converted into new resources.

These interventions are more frequent in tertiary buildings, especially during the activity of buying and selling. In fact, there is a direct relationship between the number of trades and the number of internal components/fittings renewals due to the accelerated obsolescence, caused by the change of the owners and, therefore, by a change of their needs and requests.

The data from the Rapporto Immobiliare (2017) shows that the share percentage of stocks bought and sold, in a given period, of buildings destined for offices and shops reaches a maximum peak in Lombardy. According to this report, the Real Estate units of the office type, in 2016, are 643,629 in Italy. Among the regions, Lombardy emerges with 140,229 units (which represent 21.8% of the national stock). Regarding the sales volumes of offices, Lombardy alone accounts for more than a quarter of the national exchanges (28.4% of the total number of transition). For the Real Estate units of the shop type also, Lombardy has the greatest presence of shops: 367,862 units of 2,549,924 Italian units, covering a share of stores of 14.4%. As regards the sales and purchases of shops, Lombardy—which alone represents almost 1/5 of the national market—shows a + 13.9% rise in the market in 2016 compared to 2015. Moreover, the report of Cresme (2016) shows how in the city of Milan the amount of buildings available for lease is preponderant (74.6% of the total management properties offered) and increasing (+10.6% in the period 2014–2015).

Accelerated obsolescence of internal components/fittings is also typical in the exhibition and fair field. These activities entail a huge amount of internal fittings and dry disassembled solutions, characterized by high obsolescence, requiring frequent interventions of disassembling/renewal/transformation. The report of Regione Lombardia (2016) shows that Lombardy is the first Italian region for exhibition activities, with over 600,000 m^2 of gross covered surfaces. The regional offer of exhibition spaces is concentrated in Milan (62% of the overall availability of covered spaces).

The presence in Lombardy of a substantial vast tertiary building stock, characterized by subject to frequent renewals/transformations, due to accelerated obsolescence, generates increasing quantities of materials and components—often dry-assembled—still embodying high added value.

Starting from these data, the research considers the specific field of the tertiary sector and "temporary use," that generates a great amount of waste, in the Lombardy Region.

3 Actions to Close the Cycle: Re-Manufacturing and ReUse Business Models

For closing the loop of materials/components, strategies of reuse, repurpose, reconditioning, re-manufacturing, and recycling are encouraged (Fig. 2). According to the standard BS 8887:2:2009 (2009), the reuse is the operation through which a product is put back into use for the same purpose at its end of life, while the repurpose considers a new utilization of a product in a new role that differs from the original purpose

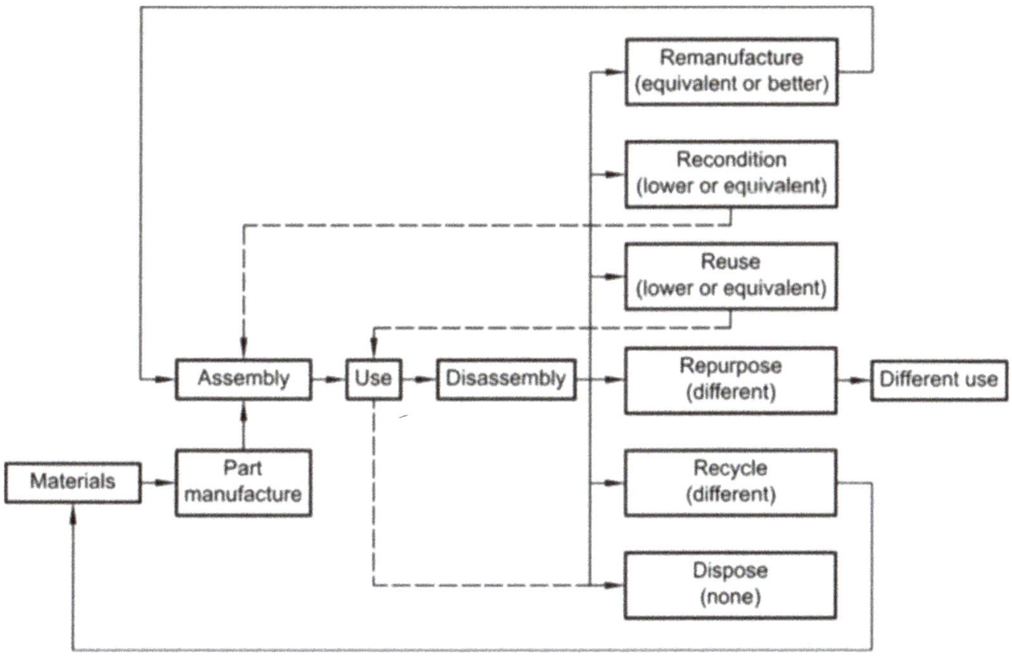

Fig. 2 Product lifecycle. *Source* BSBS 8887-2:2009. The likely change in warranty level compared to original product is given in parentheses

it was designed to perform. Reconditioning regards the return of a used product to a satisfactory working condition, by rebuilding or repairing its major components (with a possible inferior performance, so the warranty is generally less than the new ones). Instead, re-manufacturing is the operation through which a used product returns at least to its original performance with a warranty that is equivalent to or better than that of the newly manufactured product. Recycling regards the process by which the waste is transformed into a secondary material for performing the original purpose or other purposes. Hence, in terms of value, according to the standard BS 8887:2:2009, re-manufacturing is the only process that returns a product characterized by the same, or higher, value than the original product.

Currently, in the built environment, only the movable parts of buildings such as furniture, chairs, desks, shelves are sometimes re-manufactured. Pursuing the circular economy objectives, the Center for Remanufacturing and Reusefounded the European Remanufacturing Network (2016) for academic research in order to encourage industrial re-manufacturing processes (Fig. 3) and business models in different sectors (aerospace, automotive, electronics, machinery, marine, rail).

The development of effective business models may boost re-manufacturing and reuse processes in the tertiary building sector (Osterwalder and Pigneur 2010). In a circular business model, the value creation depends on meeting a new demand for products, after their use, and on the utilization of the economic value retained within them (Linder and Williander 2017).

The deployment of the paradigm of the circular business model in the construction sector requires a profound change in actors' behaviors, in order to pursue the "downside" of ownership. New collaborative business models may allow the "access to" instead of the "ownership of" products, increasing the capacity utilization and thus the efficiency of the deployed resources. Relevant examples from this point of view are provided by other sectors that are now applying the principles of the so-called sharing economy (e.g., Arena et al. 2017) sustainable product–service systems (S.PSS).

A S.PSS is "an offer/business model providing an integrated mix of products and services that are together able to fulfil a particular customer demand ("unit of satisfaction"), based on innovative interactions between the stakeholders of the value production system (satisfaction system), where the ownership of the product/s and/or its life cycle responsibilities remain in the hands of the provider/s" (Vezzoli et al.

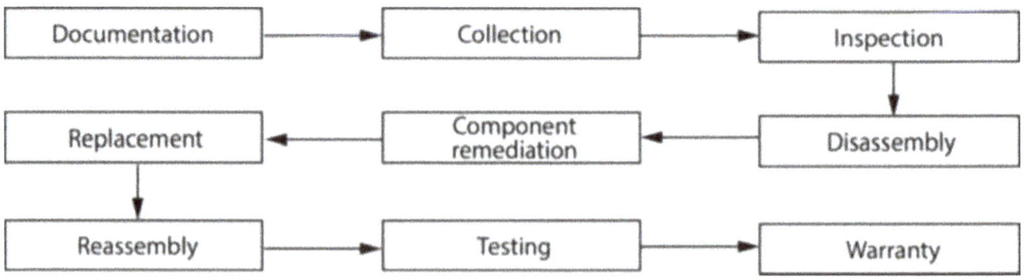

Fig. 3 A generic re-manufacturing process. *Source* ERN (2016)

2014). The S.PSS models are based on radical innovations, not so much on technological ones, but more on new interactions/partnerships between the stakeholders of a particular satisfaction production chain (life cycle/s).

This new vision is closely related to the Life Cycle Management (LCM): a comprehensive analysis along with a change of the processes related to the product life cycle is necessary for sustainable development. Life Cycle Assessment (LCA) and Life Cycle Cost (LCC) are the supporting tools for decision-making, assessing the environmental and economic impacts of strategies (Lavagna 2008; Monticelli 2013).

The research (Fig. 4) transfers successful business models and S.PSS models applied in other sectors to the construction sector, in order to improve the competitiveness of various categories of stakeholders in Lombardy (e.g., small-medium manufacturing companies, FM services providers, etc.) by creating network relationships among operators. Moreover, the research applies the Life Cycle Thinking, using LCA and LCC as supporting tools during the Life Cycle Design (LCD) of new models, rules, and procedures to support innovative Life Cycle Management (LCM).

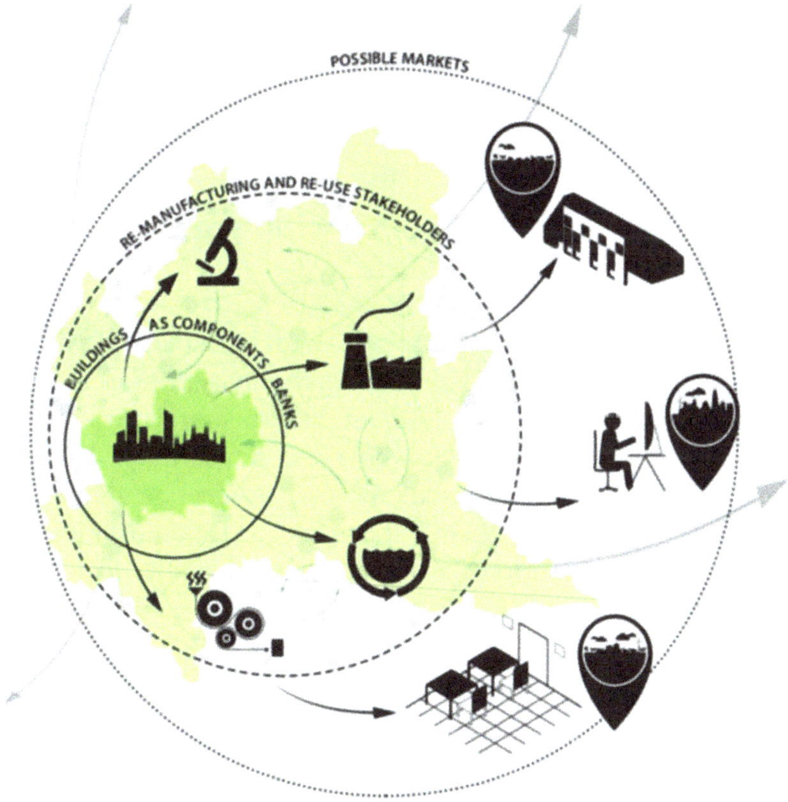

Fig. 4 Multi-scalar vision of the project. *Source* Re-NetTA Project

4 Methodology

In order to define process innovations (in terms of new relationships between stakeholders, new supply chain networks, new methods of construction-use-disassembly and new organizational, operative and business models) related to re-manufacturing and reuse in the context of the transformation/renewal of buildings for the tertiary sector (offices, accommodation facilities, exhibition facilities, retail, temporary shops), the project follows a structured methodological approach characterized by cross-sectoral collaboration and cross-fertilization, starting from the skills and knowledge that characterize three Disciplinary Scientific Sectors DSS) (*Technology of Architecture and Building construction*; *Management and Industrial Engineering*; *Industrial Design and Communication*) and the European Research Council (ERC) sector *Sustainable Design and Eco-design*.

The research is developed according to five phases, namely (Table 1):

- Phase 1. Best practices of Re-* (use, manufacturing) and transferable key criteria to the construction sector
- Phase 2. Field test and stakeholders' identification
- Phase 3. Framework of models, rules, and procedures for re-manufacturing of building components
- Phase 4. Pilot Network for Re-manufacturing and validation
- Phase 5. Management and dissemination

In particular, Table 1 shows the articulation of the research in these phases, highlighting their tasks and actions.

In each stage of the research, both DSS and ERC disciplines collaborate, firstly, adopting methods appropriate to each discipline and, secondarily, fertilizing them in a continuous discussion between the different disciplinary approaches. The outputs of each phase are shared among the different disciplinary approaches through the continuous cross-fertilization during the whole research duration. The research also involves crucial stakeholders (Real estate owners, designers, building components manufactures, construction firms, facility managers, SMEs associations, demolition companies, users, etc.) in order to deepen specific issues and validate the outputs of the project.

5 Framework of Models, Rules and Procedures for Re-Manufacturing and Reuse of Building Components

The final outcome of the research is a framework of models, rules, and procedures for re-manufacturing and reuse of building components, articulated in:

- Definition of the most suitable applications of "re-hierarchy" (re-manufacturing, recondition, repurpose, reuse, and repair) categories to the construction sector;

Table 1 Articulation in phases of Re-NetTA methodology

Phase	Title	Action planned and tasks	Outputs
1	Best practices of Re-* (use, manufacturing) and transferable key criteria to the construction sector	– Definition of the national and international state of art of re-manufacturing practices within industrial and construction sectors and analysis of relevant projects – Identification of sustainable product–service systems (S.PSS) and business models in re-manufacturing practices of other sectors (e.g., automotive, electronics, etc.) transferable to the construction sector – Survey of "design for disassembly" cases in the construction sector	– Definition of re-manufacturing categories to the construction sector – Key criteria for re-manufacturing (design rules, identification keys) and first set of guidelines – Definition of levers for the launch of successful re-manufacturing processes from an economic and environmental point of view
2	Field test and stakeholders' identification	• Activation of contacts with existing re-manufacturing networks, also operating in other sectors sample analysis at the Lombard level of: – entrepreneurial and re-manufacturing potential – potential of facility management suppliers and construction companies to be involved – potential market of buyers – components with greater aptitude for being remanufactured	In relation to different functions (exhibition spaces, commercial, etc.), definition of representative samples to be observed in order to identify methods of intervention in relation to technical elements (finishes, floors, ceilings, external skin, windows frames)

(continued)

Table 1 (continued)

Phase	Title	Action planned and tasks	Outputs
3	Framework of models, rules, and procedures for the re-manufacturing of building components	– Verification of the applicability of the operational, organizational, and business criteria resulting from the multi-sectorial analysis (Phase 1 output) through: transfer from design to construction of S.PSS and business models practices – Definition of a new set of re-rules (redesign; re-manufacturing; reuse) specifically referring to the tertiary buildings and for short-life and dry-assembled components – Verification of the applicability of the rules through the Delphi method with a panel of multidisciplinary experts	– Rules (organizational, procedural, etc.) to support the re-manufacturing processes – Assembly, disassembly and processing procedures – Quality procedures and standards, methods for defining the characteristics of components – Methods for exchanging materials and products – Methods for sharing information, communication protocols, etc. – LC-based indicators to define environmentally and economically effective strategies
4	Pilot network for re-manufacturing and validation	– Creation of a multi-sectorial network of re-manufacturing through the networking of six categories of operators dealing with: facility management; disassembly and recovery of materials and components; re-manufacturing; commercialization of new types of re-manufactured building products; and end users – Simulations and tests of the results of Phase 2, Phase 3, and Phase 4 – SWOT analysis of the network – Project monitoring and optimization	– Modeling of network relationships in relation to the six defined categories of operators – Identification of the engagement level of individual stakeholders on the development of circular processes – Recognition of barriers and opportunities – Recognition of the value of the levers in the activation of the network – Rules of replicability
5	Management and dissemination	– Management of cross-collaboration among academic and professional fields – Dissemination (conferences, publications, training courses, social media, etc.)	– Specific program for professional training for new profiles of young artisans in the re-manufacturing field

- Definition of key criteria for re-manufacturing: criteria for the design of components "to be re-manufactured"; interpretative keys to understand the re-manufacturing attitude of a component to be disassembled and re-manufactured; obstacles/barriers (e.g., legislative) and levers (e.g., guarantee conditions, certified environmental value, economic value);
- Definition, through a multi-sectorial analysis, of: organizational conditions; criteria for the start of re-manufacturing processes; levers for the launch of successful re-manufacturing processes from an economic and environmental point of view; economic, environmental, and social benefits to be used as levers for the start-up of re-manufacturing processes.
- Definition of rules to support the re-manufacturing processes: relationship rules (organizational, procedural, etc.); assembly, disassembly, and processing procedures in relation to various technical elements (interior walls, finishes, floors, ceilings, external skin, windows frames); quality procedures, standards, and methods for defining the characteristics of components easy to be re-manufactured; methods for exchanging materials and products; methods for sharing information and communication protocols; procedures of application of LC-based indicators aiming at identifying the environmentally and economically more effective strategies to be adopted in re-manufacturing processes (e.g. definition of the maximum advantageous physical distance between disassembly site and remanufacturer).

For what concerns the impacts of the project—able to meet the strategies characterizing the circular economy approach—it is possible to mention:

- *Economic impacts*
  - Extending the economic value of building components over time
  - Increasing the opportunity to access to incentive or participate in public tendering in the construction sector
  - Improving competitiveness through environmental certification schemes (Green Building Rating Systems)
- *Environmental impacts*
  - Product life optimization (use extension and intensification)
  - Reduction of environmental flows and impacts related to the extension of the service life of building components
  - Reduction of downcycling and promotion of revalorisation
  - Minimization of the materials toxicity through dry assembly
  - Environmental value of embodied impacts (embodied energy, embodied carbon, and others)
- *Social impacts*
  - Identification of possible new markets of "regenerated products" (e.g., social housing)

  - Identification of new job opportunities for young people with high-level skills (in the fields of: technical design, eco-design, management, and communication) or with low grade of studies (e.g., artisans)

- *Impacts on policies*
  - Identification of possible framework barriers, obstacles, and conditions (regulation and standards) to overcome and adoption of effective action plans to reduce barriers
  - Identification of incentives and promotion of policies
  - Improvement of circular criteria in Green Building Rating Systems and in environmental certification, toward "circular products/service."

Lastly, the project stimulates the development of the local economic system by creating new cross-sectoral processes and relationships, as well as possibilities for new skills and jobs, and by improving the innovation capacity, competitiveness, and growth of SMEs in meeting the challenges of new potential markets.

References

Arena, M., Azzone, G., & Bengo, I. (2017). Traditional and innovative vehicle-sharing models. In S. Savaresi & A. Colorni (Eds.), *Electric vehicle sharing services for smarter cities*. Springer, Research for Development.

Brand, S. (1994). *How buildings learn: What happens after they're built*. USA: Penguin.

Cheshire, D. (2016). *Building revolutions. Applying the circular economy to the built environment*. New Castel: RIBA Publishing.

Cresme Ricerche S.p.A. (2016). *Osservatorio sull'offerta di Immobili ad uso ufficio a Milano*.

Durmisevic, E. (2018). *WP3 reversible building design. Reversible building design guidelines. BAMB Report*. Available at https://www.bamb2020.eu/wp-content/uploads/2018/12/Reversible-Building-Design-guidelines-and-protocol.pdf.

Ellen MacArthur Foundation and CE100. (2016). *Circularity in the built environment: Case studies*. Available at https://www.ellenmacarthurfoundation.org/assets/downloads/Built-Env-Co.Project.pdf.

ERN. (2016). *Map of remanufacturing product design landscape*.

European Commission. (2015). *Closing the loop—An EU action plan for the Circular Economy, COM 614*.

European Commission. (2018). *Growth, construction*. Available at https://ec.europa.eu/growth/sectors/construction.

Eurostat. (2016). *Key figures on Europe* (pp. 161–164). Belgium.

Giorgi, S., Lavagna, M., & Campioli, A. (2017). Economia Circolare, Gestione dei rifiuti e Life Cycle Thinking. Fondamenti, interpretazioni e analisi dello stato dell'arte. *Ingegneria dell'Ambiente, 4*(3), 245–254.

Lavagna, M. (2008). *Life cycle assessment in edilizia*. Milano: Hoepli.

Linder, M., & Williander, M. (2017). Circular business model innovation: Inherent uncertainties. *Business Strategy and the Environment, 26*, 182–196.

Monticelli, C. (2013).*Life cycle design in architettura. Progetto e Valutazione di Impatto Ambientale dalla Materia all'Edificio*. Maggioli, Santarcangelo di Romagna.

Osservatorio del Mercato Immobiliare. (2017). *Rapporto Immobiliare 2017. Immobili a destinazione terziaria, commerciale e produttiva*. Pubblicazioni OMI.

Osterwalder, A., & Pigneur, Y. (2010). *Business model generation*. Lausanne: Osterwalder & Pigneur.

Peters, M., Ribeiro, A., Oseyran, J., & Wang, K. (2017). *Buildings as material banks and the need for innovative Business Models, BAMB report*. Available at https://www.bamb2020.eu/wp-content/uploads/2017/11/BAMB_Business-Models_20171114_extract.pdf.

Regione Lombardia. (2016). *Sintesi del Rapporto "L'Attività Fieristica in Lombardia"—n.14/2001–2016*. Available at http://www.regione.lombardia.it/wps/wcm/connect/dbd5fb88-a06c-4481-9a7d-2fde64c61914/Sintesi_Lombardia_2016.pdf?MOD=AJPERES&CACHEID=dbd5fb88-a06c-4481-9a7d-2fde64c61914.

Talamo, C., & Migliore, M. (2017). *Le utilità dell'inutile. Economia circolare e strategie di riciclo dei rifiuti pre-consumo nel settore edilizio*. Maggioli.

Vezzoli, C., Kohtala, C., & Srinivasan, A. (2014). *Product-service system design for sustainability*. Sheffield: Greenleaf Publishing.

Standards and Laws

British Standard 8887-2:2009. (2009). *Design for manufacture, assembly, disassembly and end-of-life processing (MADE). Terms and definitions.*

Reusing Built Heritage. Design for the Sharing Economy

Roberto Bolici, Giusi Leali and Silvia Mirandola

Abstract In the last years, the construction sector has seen a greater number of building interventions on existing assets rather than the realization of new buildings. The enhancement of urban property assets can become an opportunity both for efficient and effective building management and for the offer of innovative public and private services on the territory. With this approach, based on sustainable urban regeneration, the enhancement could be intended in many different ways such as recovery, maintenance, and reuse of abandoned or underutilized buildings. This phenomenon, present in general in building assets as a whole, is more evident in the management of the public ones. The reuse of these buildings acts as an answer to a change in the needs of the community regarding welfare, culture, and work, generating a new economic, social, and environmental value. In relation to their innovative features, the new functions related to the real dimensions of sharing are emerging, and with them a new approach to the project. The increase in these new kinds of sharing and the insufficient knowledge about design and management of the relative "box" have allowed for the development of the study entitled "Enhancement of abandoned or underutilized assets. Design for coworking." The main goal of the study was to define, within the logic of environmental technology design, the key points of this framework. This was possible thanks to the collection of data which was useful to increase the knowledge regarding the design of these places within abandoned or underutilized buildings and their management.

Keywords Coworking · Urban regeneration · Sharing economy

R. Bolici (✉)
Architecture, Built Environment and Construction Engineering—ABC Department, Politecnico di Milano, Milan, Italy
e-mail: roberto.bolici@polimi.it

G. Leali · S. Mirandola
Milan, Italy

S. Della Torre et al. (eds.), *Regeneration of the Built Environment from a Circular Economy Perspective*, Research for Development,
https://doi.org/10.1007/978-3-030-33256-3_29

1 Introduction

The Europe 2020 Strategy of the European Union has assigned a fundamental role to cohesion policies in the socioeconomic development of the territory. The implementation of these policies requires the enhancement of a more efficient and competitive economy that is more attentive to environmental issues, including in terms of building recovery and land consumption (sustainable growth); support for employment, especially youth employment, to foster social and territorial cohesion (inclusive growth), and finally, the development of a knowledge and innovation economy (smart growth).

Strategies necessary for achieving these objectives are the optimal use of resources and financial opportunities in key economic sectors and the structuring of an integrated and coordinated approach to interventions. The synergic activation of these elements offers new opportunities for businesses and the community, boosts local development, strengthens coordination between community, national, and sectoral policies and broadly facilitates the process of territorial cohesion also through the 'activation of a partnership between local and regional actors, social partners and civil society'.

Within the scenario envisaged by the European Union, the issue of social inclusion, as a way of favoring a better and full integration of the individual within the social and economic context in which they live, is brought back, in addition to the sphere of welfare, to labor policies. For the community, employment is an indispensable prerogative for accessibility to the services and opportunities created by economic growth, in fact, through processes of inclusion and reduction of social hardship, it becomes both a recipient of interventions or services and an active agent of economic development, social life, and the well-being of a territory.

The international economic crisis characterizing the last decade has brought to the forefront the problem of unemployment, especially youth unemployment. A possible way of looking into this issue is the activation of multilateral and innovative collaborations, involving public administration, social parties, educational institutions, communities, and young people (International Labor Office 2012), for the construction of projects that facilitate youth entrepreneurship, which represents an opportunity for local businesses that can draw innovative elements from this, starting from the skills of young professionals and incorporating them into their companies.

The sustainable growth promoted by the European Union is also implemented through rational use of resources and finds in the theme of urban regeneration and therefore the reuse of real estate a wide context of experimentation.

The theme of urban regeneration in a sustainable way represents a priority aspect in the development policies of cities as it offers, on the one hand, the opportunity to trigger architectural, environmental, energy, and social redevelopment processes of urban centers, starting from the reuse of already existing real estate assets. On the other hand, there can be important social and economic consequences from the transformation of degraded urban areas into real catalysts for creativity and innovation. The recovery and strategic management of the abandoned heritage can significantly influence the entire "urban context due to its location in central and valuable areas and to the possible historical and artistic value, thus constituting a precious resource, not only in immediate monetary terms, but also as an element of requalification and growth for large portions of the urban fabric which could increase their value and become attractive for investment" (Baiani and Cangelli 2012).

In this scenario, the enhancement of the underutilized or disused public heritage, implemented through the reuse of that which is built, in addition to being an opportunity in economic terms and rationalization of the expenditure of local administrations, represents an opportunity to experiment regeneration interventions in urban centers. By investing in aspects such as technological innovation and environmental design, this real estate asset is the cornerstone on which to structure a broader strategy to rethink the entire city through the definition of a new network of spaces within consolidated urban fabrics and of alternative functions to those now acquired over time (Ottone et al. 2012).

By this logic, the local administrations are defining new destinations of use for the high quantity of underused or abandoned buildings to give them new value (Manzo 2007) and to respond to the changing needs of the collectivity in terms of welfare, culture, and work. With respect to the panel of possible new destinations, and in line with European labor policies, the functions connected to the performance of "collaborative" work activities linked to a sharing economy emerge due to their innovative nature. The collaborative economy does not propose "merely a new consumption model, but also an alternative way to move (carsharing), to lend (crowdfunding), to work (coworking), to learn, to travel, to be together, to eat and therefore to live" (Maineri 2013).

The "containers" of the collaborative economy therefore provide, on the one hand, a response to the need of public administration to assign a new functions and to make assets that are disposed of or underutilized their own. On the other hand, they offer emerging professionals the opportunity to use their skills in innovative work spaces that allow them to "incubate" their ideas by putting them in a system with those of others and then being able to propose them in a more competitive way to the "outside." The positive effects, following the activation of these containers for the collaborative economy, are also to be sought in the "talent gardens" provided to local companies, capable of encouraging the innovation in socioeconomic terms of the territory.

2 Collaborative Economy Platforms. Analysis and Study of a Growing Phenomenon

The growing increase in collaborative work[1] and the lack of knowledge in planning and management aspects have stimulated the development of the study entitled "Valorisation of abandoned or underutilized real estate assets. Design for coworking[2]" (Bolici et al. 2015). The study, starting from the recognition of a wide and detailed reading of the national panorama of the sharing economy spaces and in particular of those for coworking, allowed us to extend and put systematic design and management indications in order to structure a design concept—with a management that is declinable in relation to the peculiarities of the different contexts (Fig. 1).

Currently in Italy, there is a constant increase in places where it is possible to work together, collaborating and creating a community that uses the same environment: these spaces can be identified with those for coworking, talent gardens, and Fab labs. The term coworking does not only define a physical space but refers to a real style of work-oriented toward sharing an environment, which, however, leaves users with the possibility of developing independent activities. In the talent gardens, in addition to sharing spaces and services, new ideas are formulated for the development of economic activities capable of evolving into start-ups and projects. Finally, the philosophy at the heart of Fab labs is the sharing of ideas and the promotion of sustainable technological development in order to bring innovation and technological knowledge to the territory in which the laboratory operates.

To present a cross section of the containers for a collaborative economy present at national level, the study involved a desk analysis of the dedicated platforms and of the sector literature and of questionnaires given to the space managers; the survey embraced 422 case studies, collected in a database.

84% of the spaces analyzed were coworking, demonstrating that within the national territory, this platform is the one that best responds to market demands, anticipating lower start-up costs compared to the infrastructure of spaces that must support a Fab lab and not requesting specific managerial skills, which typical of a talent garden. The geographical distribution has shown that 65% of the collaborative economy has developed in the northern part of the national territory; specifically for coworking spaces, a high concentration was recorded in the Lombardy region (over 30% of the total), particularly in the Milan area and in its hinterland.

Given the importance in quantitative terms of coworking spaces, the research has looked closer into this new working reality from the point of view of inclusion in the local settlement system, of the location within a given architectural typology, of the type of building intervention, of the surface, of user capacity, of the functions present within the containers, and of the management models. The analysis showed that the placement of the spaces in relation to the context sees a greater presence in

[1] As noted by the "1st Annual Global Coworking Survey" conducted by Deskmag.

[2] The research project was commissioned to the UdR TEMA of the Mantua Research Laboratory of the Politecnico di Milano—Mantova Campus by PromoImpresa Borsa-Merci—Mantova Chamber of Commerce.

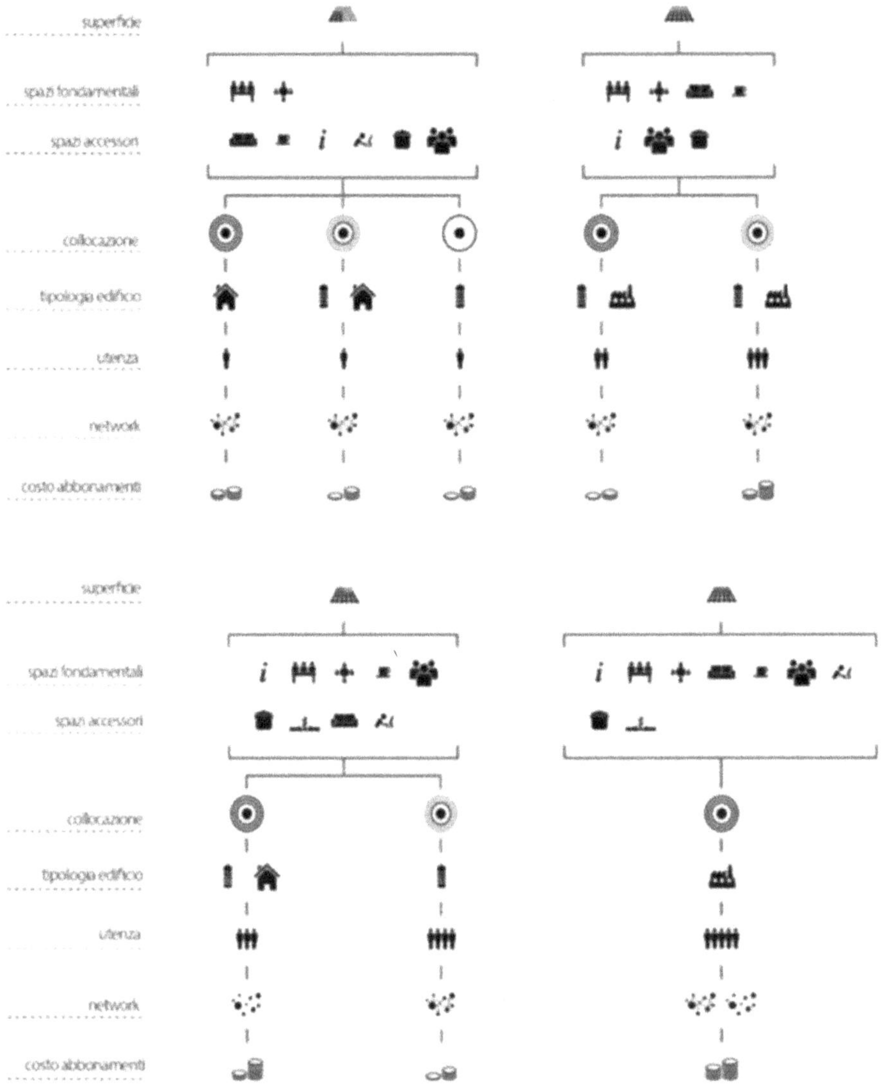

Fig. 1 Comparative matrix

the urban center (71%), followed by the peripheral areas (25%), while it is minimal in isolated contexts (4%). As for buildings, the tendency to recover buildings (90%) was recorded rather than the construction of new buildings; this observation supports the principle of sustainability at the core of the collaborative economy, which sees the redevelopment of what already exists as an opportunity to make these spaces active once more and reduce land consumption. As the coworking spaces are generally located in existing recovered structures, it was also interesting to note that around four-fifths of them refer to residential and commercial buildings with a slight prevalence of residential buildings, while only a small part is located inside industrial buildings.

The analysis showed that 72% of the containers have an area of less than 250 m^2, particularly between 50 and 100 m^2. Given the small surfaces, most of them can accommodate a small number of people (from 1 to 10); this size, while not contributing on the one hand to generating significant economies of scale, on the other hand, it does favor the creation of communities.

The essential functional spaces within the various containers surveyed have been traced back to four major categories: work spaces (meeting room, open space offices, study room, conference room), service spaces (reception entrance, kitchen), spaces for additional services (library, laboratory), and recreational spaces (refreshment area, relaxation area, outdoor space). Starting from the analysis of the existing realities, a hierarchy of these functions has been articulated based on their diffusion, which has allowed us to determine as open spaces of a coworking environment open space offices (easily adaptable and flexible spaces) that allow the users to work inside a large environment that stimulates collaboration, as opposed to a traditional office, and meeting rooms (necessary to hold meetings without disturbing other coworkers). Given the prevailing informal nature of these platforms, the relaxation areas and the refreshment areas (spaces equipped to encourage dialog between coworkers) are fundamental for the creation of an environment that favors socialization and sharing. Complementary to these spaces are the study rooms and private offices, or spaces intended exclusively for certain users, and the congress rooms structured to host presentations and events. In a smaller number of cases, the presence of a room equipped as a kitchen and spaces for library and laboratories was detected; in this case, it is a hybrid coworking platform, with features more common to the Fab labs.

With respect to the theme of space management, it was found that the manner is exclusively private, more than a quarter of the platforms analyzed adhere to a network and in only 10% of the cases analyzed, in order to make use of the spaces, a membership is required. Particularly, joining a network allows for the community of a coworking environment to increase exponentially by creating an ecosystem of relationships in which proposals are activated and contaminations develop in the entrepreneurial and professional sphere, particularly at the level of freelancers and small work teams. The advantages of belonging to a network are generally the use of a brand, having basic advice available for management and presence on the media and on social media, increasing the visibility and knowledge of the structure toward possible coworkers present in the territory.

The subscription costs that a user incurs per year to use the spaces are on average between €1000 and 3000; the peaks noted refer to platforms that do not adhere to the network, since adherence to networks generally leads to price control.

To obtain a cross section of the analyzed realities and to provide a methodological direction for the design of coworking spaces, a comparative matrix has been elaborated which has systemized the information concerning the functions with the surfaces, the location, the types of buildings hosting these activities, the number of users that can be hosted, network membership, and, finally, the annual cost of subscriptions. The reading of the matrix, consisting of four sections defined according to the extension of the surfaces of the collaborative platforms and their geographical location, has revealed that the spaces with reduced dimensions (0–250 m^2) find a preferential position in central areas, peripheral areas, and in isolated contexts, within residential and commercial building types. Since the platforms are small, they consequently have a reduced capacity and rely on existing networks to develop their business. The subscription cost is lower for spaces located in the suburbs or isolated areas. The spaces with medium-small surfaces (250–500 m^2) find a counterpart only in the center and on the outskirts where they are located within commercial and industrial buildings. Also in this case, joining a network is a characterizing element. Access to spaces has a higher cost in peripheral structures than in central ones. The realities that have medium-large surfaces (500–1000 m^2) are located in central and peripheral contexts, mainly occupying buildings for commercial and residential use and increasing the number of users that can be hosted. In this category, joining networks is not widespread. There is a noticeable difference in the cost of subscription between central and peripheral facilities. Platforms with large surfaces (more than 1000 m^2) are generally located in central areas within disused industrial buildings and provide a high number of workstations. The cost of subscriptions is medium-high and, as in the previous class, network membership is not a characterizing element. Finally, reading the information in a transversal manner, a number of elements characterizing the entire system emerge, such as the direct relationship between the increase in number of functions and the increase in surface area and between users and surface area, the preferential location in urban centers, the commercial building as prevalent building typology, the frequency of adhesion to a network, the proportion between the cost of the subscriptions proposed to the coworkers and the dimensions of the surfaces, and therefore of the functions offered, and the greater cost for access to platforms located in historical centers.

3 Proposal for the Definition of a Project-Management Concept

The analysis of the spaces present in the analyzed collaborative platforms made it possible to define the reciprocal relationships between the functions present in a coworking environment. The study of the relationships between the spaces has allowed us to conduct a synoptic reading of the different elements that structure the containers for a collaborative economy, and to define a concept of articulation of spaces, paths, and use of services over time (temporary, Fig. 2, medium, Fig. 3, and long, Fig. 4, term).

The spaces destined to be used by users on a temporary basis (e.g., daily use) are located near the entrance and are inserted along a path that allows users to reach only certain functions within the coworking system (open space office, refreshment area, services, conference room, and meeting room). Users who use spaces in a more structured way, but that are limited in time (e.g., weekly–monthly use), can benefit from additional services according to a growing level of accessibility to spaces (flexible open-space work area, kitchen, relaxation area), to the external space, to the library, and to the laboratory. Finally, users who use the space with greater

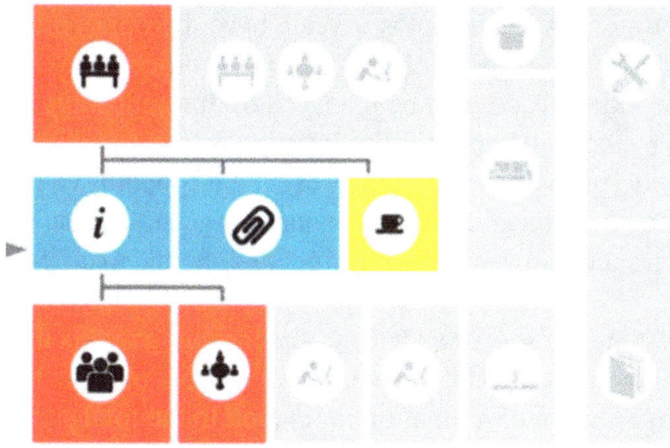

Fig. 2 Route and function diagram—temporary use

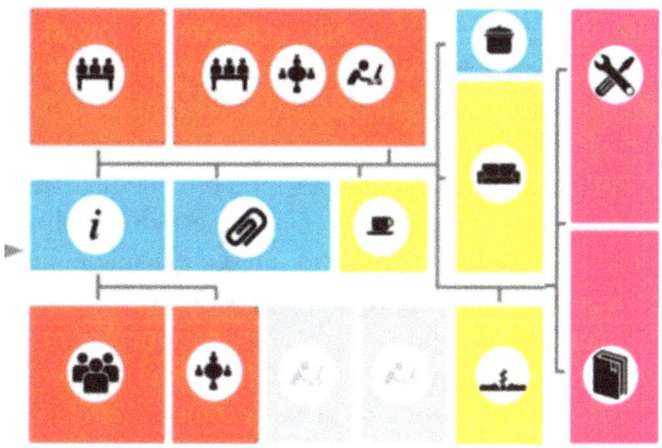

Fig. 3 Route and function diagram—use in the medium term

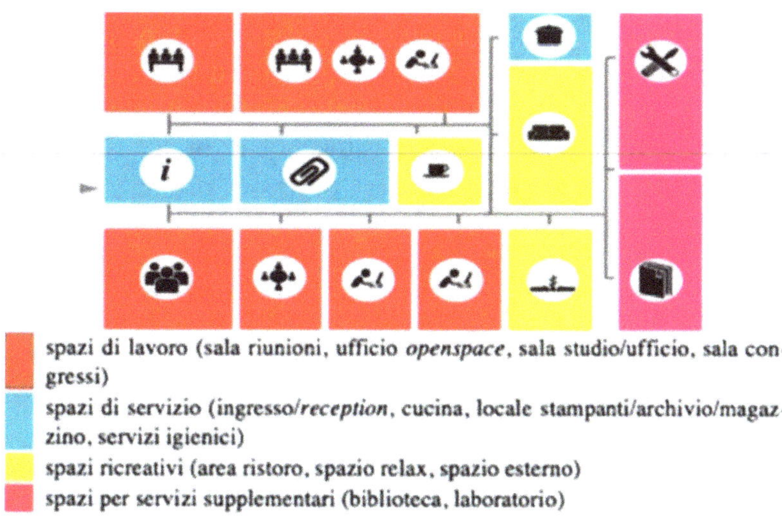

Fig. 4 Route and function diagram—long-term use

continuity over time (e.g., six months a year) have the opportunity to occupy the premises characterized by a greater level of privacy (offices).

The 24-h coworking spaces can be managed in different ways depending on the services offered by the platform. A basic operation is foreseen with daytime opening times from 7 am to 8 pm with the possibility of evening openings on certain occasions (exhibitions, events, meetings, etc.). A second management mode allows for the use of the spaces 24 h a day to allow access to workstations and to different services even at night.

The study saw the predisposition of a pre-dimensioning matrix that linked both the minimum reference surfaces with the maximum number of users that can be hosted and the percentage weight of a function in relation to the total surface. The reading of the matrix has revealed a number of observations regarding the surfaces: the extension of the work environments has a constant percentage weight in the different spatial solutions, while the surface of the service spaces decreases in proportion to the increase in the offer of activities. As the extension of coworking increases, the percentage of area used for recreational areas remains constant. Finally, the surfaces dedicated to paths are contained given the prevalent open-space aspect and the need to share the structure's spaces.

As described in the introductory passages, the refunctionalization interventions can constitute an effective response to the many questions of change expressed by the community, and although they are yet to represent a single narrative capable of communicating adequately with administrators, they prove to be a privileged field for the experimentation of models of public–private management of real estate assets and integration between economic activities and cultural and socioeconomic functions (Bacchella et al. 2015). The question of reuse becomes an architectural issue since the identification of the new functions cannot be separated from an evaluation of the architectural, typological, and technological characteristics of the building and the peculiarities that characterize the territorial area of reference. The presence of these endogenous and exogenous factors triggers specific problems: for buildings characterized by cultural values, a conflict is generated between the instances of conservation and transformation due to the inclusion of new activities. At the same time, new settled activities can produce positive effects on the surrounding area if they are able to trigger widespread recovery processes of underused areas or can have negative effects if not effectively managed (De Medici and Pinto 2012).

References

Bacchella, U., Bollo, A., & Milella, F. (2015). Riuso e trasformazioni degli spazi a vocazione culturale e creativa: un driver per lo sviluppo, ma a quali condizioni? In Giornale delle Fondazioni, Allemandi.

Baiani, S., & Cangelli, E. (2012). Valorizzazione e sviluppo sostenibile dei sistemi locali. In Technè n. 03/2012, Valorizzare il patrimonio edilizio pubblico.

Bolici, R., Leali, G., & Mirandola, S. (2015). Valorizzazione del patrimonio immobiliare dismesso o sottoutilizzato. Progettare per il coworking, report ricerca. http://www.polo-mantova.polimi.it/uploads/media/4_02.pdf.

De Medici, S., Pinto, M. R. (2012). Valorizzazione dei beni culturali pubblici e strategie di riuso. In Technè n. 03/2012, Valorizzare il patrimonio edilizio pubblico.

Maineri, M. (2013). Marta Mainieri: Ho inventato (e scritto) Collaboriamo!, per riunire tutti i servizi collaborativi italiani. In Che Futuro!, 28 marzo 2013,

Manzo, R. (2007). Il processo di rivitalizzazione del patrimonio pubblico. In R. Manzo & G. Tamburini (a cura di), *Il patrimonio immobiliare pubblico*. Nuovi orizzonti. Il ruolo dell'Agenzia del Demanio, Il Sole24Ore, Milano.

Ottone, F., Calvelli, S., Cocci Grifoni, R., Losco, G., Perriccioli, M., Rossi, M., et al. (2012). Rigenerare le città attraverso la valorizzazione del patrimonio pubblico: tecnologie ambientali e creatività. In Technè n. 03/2012, Valorizzare il patrimonio edilizio pubblico.

Ufficio Internazionale del Lavoro. (2012). "La crisi dell'occupazione giovanile: è il momento di agire. Risoluzione e conclusioni della 101a sessione", in Atti Conferenza Internazionale del Lavoro, Ginevra.

Public Health Aspects' Assessment Tool for Urban Projects, According to the Urban Health Approach

Stefano Capolongo, Maddalena Buffoli, Erica Isa Mosca, Daniela Galeone, Roberto D'Elia and Andrea Rebecchi

Abstract As part of the CCM2017 project titled "Urban Health," this paper describes the experience of developing and testing a multi-criteria, quali-quantitative assessment framework for Public Health aspects. The tool aims to evaluate urban transformation and regeneration actions, according to Urban Health strategies.

Keywords Urban health · Public health · Healthy urban planning and design strategies · Evaluation tool · Multi-criteria analysis

1 Introduction

Planning and management actions in urban contexts provide several opportunities for the protection and promotion of Public Health. Indeed, health conditions depend especially on environmental, economic and social factors (Fehr and Capolongo 2016), which are influenced by a correct design and management of the living environment. The concept of *Urban Health* has been introduced since the beginning of 2000, based on the definition of *Healthy City* which refers to the "*urban contexts able to support and improve constantly the physical environment and the social context, encouraging the development of economic and social resources, allowing people to mutually support each other in the development of daily life activities.*" (WHO 2016). From this concept derives the *Urban Health* strategy, which refers to the relationship between health promotion, disease prevention and the different interrelations with urban factors (Talukder et al. 2015). Indeed, *Urban Health* represents a complex issue as the actions aimed at improving the living conditions

S. Capolongo (✉) · M. Buffoli · E. I. Mosca · A. Rebecchi
Architecture, Built Environment and Construction Engineering—ABC Department, Politecnico di Milano, Milan, Italy
e-mail: stefano.capolongo@polimi.it

D. Galeone · R. D'Elia
Direzione Generale della Prevenzione Sanitaria, Ministero della Salute, Rome, Italy

S. Della Torre et al. (eds.), *Regeneration of the Built Environment from a Circular Economy Perspective*, Research for Development,
https://doi.org/10.1007/978-3-030-33256-3_30

of cities depend not only on the health sector, but also on urban planning decisions, as well on social, welfare, and education programs (Galea and Vlahov 2005).

In this regard, the *Erice 50 Charter* entitled *"Strategies for Disease Prevention and Health Promotion in Urban Areas"* by D'Alessandro et al. (2017b) defines ten goals useful to designers and policy makers, aimed to support the design of *Healthy Cities.* One of the most important goals for local government is the promotion of urban planning interventions that address citizens' healthy behavior and lifestyles (Capolongo et al. 2011; World Health Organization 2017).

Furthermore, the emerging environmental, social, and economic criticisms of the last years have given rise to a need for more specific objectives aimed at achieving *Salutogenic Cities* (Capolongo et al. 2018). In particular, the new objectives for healthy design and urban planning strategies have been defined, such as environmental and social sustainability of urban areas; adaptation to climatic changes and cities' urban resilience (Hickman and Banister 2014); new responses to the population's needs (Croucher et al. 2012; Active Living Research 2015).

In this regard, the support of urban planning becomes an important task to promote and protect different aspects as the health, wellbeing, and social inclusion of individuals who are directly influenced by their relationship with the built environment. Processes of validation, monitoring, assessment and formulation of strategic decision-making processes, through the application of mathematical tools and systems, are the basis of city regeneration actions as well as urbanized territory governance and *Public Health* promotion (Capolongo et al. 2016). Multi-criteria evaluation tools, updated with innovative strategies to reach *Urban Health* purposes are, therefore, needed in order to support planners and designers to achieve a healthier scenario. However, tools which evaluate how the design of cities can have an impact on people's health are still difficult to compare and apply, and they are primarily focused on quality and urban sustainability, neglecting the direct and indirect *Public Health* implications.

For this reason, the research starts from the current need to investigate the most recent and common urban quality evaluation tools, in order to understand which of them adopt performance criteria with direct or indirect relationships with *Urban Health.*

Within this context, the paper describes the advancements in the development of a multi-criteria evaluation tool based on a set of performance criteria (Capolongo et al. 2015). The tool was developed by an interdisciplinary working group which includes researchers from the DABC and DAStU Departments of the Politecnico di Milano and technicians from the Health Prevention Department of the Local Health Authorities (LHA) of Milan (Capolongo et al. 2013). The evaluation tool was developed with the main purpose of providing support to guide urban transformation and fostering the elaboration of strategic decisions on new planning interventions (Coppola et al. 2016). In addition, it is also aimed at monitoring advancements by evaluating changes over time. However, after the application of the tool, the need of extending its scale of intervention, from a local to a national level, defines the basis on which to review and improve the assessment tool, which is carried on by the DABC of the Politecnico di Milano and by the LHA of Bergamo, thanks to the funds of the National Center for Disease Prevention and Control CCM2017 regarding the project titled "*Urban Health: good practices for health impact assessment of urban and environmental redevelopment and regeneration interventions*." (CUP: C42F17000330001).

2 Methodology

Urban Health is characterized by a plurality of social and qualitative aspects derived by the relation between the built environment and its influence on *Public Health* and wellbeing. For this reason, *multi-criteria analysis* (Roy 2013) is adopted by the current research to systematically and scientifically develop the tool. This approach allows for both the analysis of the full range of aspects relating to a project and the simultaneous comparison of heterogeneous measures for evaluating a complex situation (Department for Communities and Local Government DCLG 2009). Furthermore, a *performance-based approach* characterizes the assessment method, aimed to overcome the traditional prescriptive regulations by means of the achievement of objectives based on urban quality. Finally, the direct contribution of experts in analyzing and evaluating projects was an essential component to guarantee new evidence-based knowledge. For this reason, LHA technicians were involved in both the tool development and the updating by means of brainstorming, aimed at discussing the most important criticisms emerging from the hygienic–sanitary evaluation of urban plans and projects (Capasso et al. 2018; Gola et al. 2017).

The research is developed through different phases, shown in the diagram (Fig. 1); after defining the main objectives to consider, a collection of best practices was supported by a literature review aimed to investigate the current and existing studies on urban quality evaluation methods and tools. A set of criteria was selected among the analyzed studies, fixing the basis for the development of the tool's framework and the evaluation method (Capolongo et al. 2016). The multi-criteria evaluation tool was applied and tested to have feedback on its effectiveness in two cities of the Lombardy region: in Milan since 2011 and for one year in Lecco. The reliability of the instrument was confirmed, while the applicability of certain evaluation criteria was considered critical. For these reasons, the tool is currently under review for an update and improvement of its criteria and performance scales, thanks to the funds provided by the CCM2017 project.

The on-going review will foster the possibility to apply the tool from local to national level and to increase public awareness regarding the relationship between *Public Health* and urban quality according to the *Urban Health* strategy (Rebecchi et al. 2016).

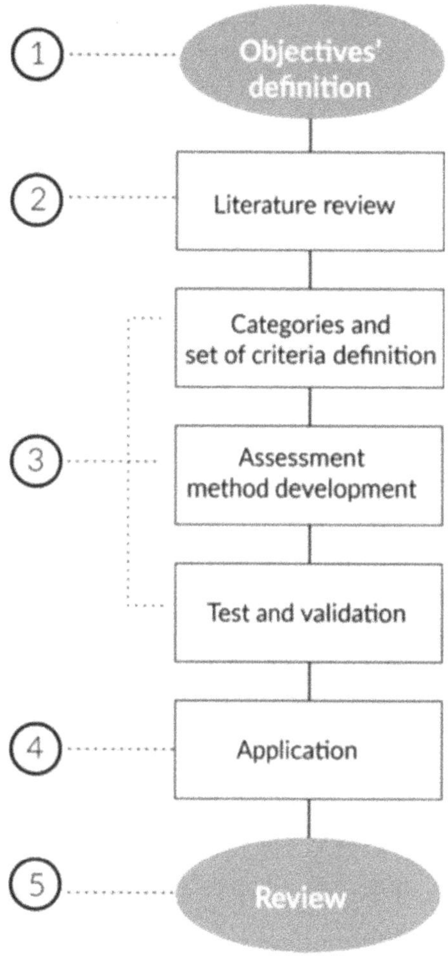

Fig. 1 Methodology flow chart (authors' elaboration)

3 Results

A significant number of European initiatives, aimed at measuring the level of sustainability and urban quality using different sets of criteria, based on a variety of factors such as environmental, social, and economic issues were found. For this reason, the literature review was useful to collect data for the categories and criteria for the tool's development.

Articles were selected from online databases by using specific keywords. The studies, selected and compared by means of eligibility criteria, have been used to include or exclude articles from the analysis.

Specifically, the literature review considered the following projects and tools:

- Indicatori Comuni Europei. Verso un profilo di sostenibilità locale. Ambiente Italia.
- Progetto Città Sane. Comune di Milano.
- A healthy city is an active city: a physical activity planning guide, Who Europe.
- Healthy City Project Technical Working Group on City Health Profiles, City Health Profiles.

- The Urban Audit. Toward the Benchmarking of Quality of Life in 58 European Cities. European Commission.
- Audit Commission Local Quality of Life Indicators supporting local communities to become sustainable. A guide to local monitoring to complement the indicators in the UK Government Sustainable Development Strategy, Office of the Deputy Prime Minister.
- Ecosistema Metropolitano, Ambiente Italia, Provincia di Milano.
- Green Building Tool—GBTool.
- Protocollo Itaca per la valutazione della qualità energetica ed ambientale di un edificio, Istituto ITACA.
- Progetto S.I.S.Te.R.

Furthermore, the most recent available neighborhood-level certification protocols were also included in the review. Starting from 46 selected studies, the eligibility criteria allowed researchers to reduce the analysis down to the following seven protocols: for America,

- LEED-ND. For Europe, the English protocol
- BREEAM for Communities, the French protocol
- HQE UPD, and the German protocol
- DGNB. For Asia, the Japanese protocol
- CASBEE UD and the protocol of members of the Persian Gulf
- GSAS. Finally, for Oceania, the Australian protocol
- GREEN STAR COMMUNITIES. All these tools were analyzed and compared in order to collect criteria that will form the evaluation framework of the instrument.

The multi-criteria evaluation tool, based on a set of performance criteria and aimed to promote *Public Health* purposes from the quality of the built environment, was developed in this way.

3.1 The Multi-criteria Evaluation System

The literature review, together with various brainstorming activities and focus groups with the technicians of the LHA of Milan, has allowed us to identify the 206 most frequently used criteria using the tools found in the literature, and to support the development of a new evaluation system.

The final assessment framework (Fig. 2) is formed of six thematic issues (environmental quality and wellbeing; waste; energy and renewable resources; mobility and accessibility; land use and functional mix; quality of urban landscape) and a set of 23 criteria, as Fig. 2 synthetizes.

Each criterion was developed in a specific evaluation data-record that includes the expected output to achieve, its impact on health (Oppio et al. 2016), a performance evaluation on both neighborhood and urban scale, a selection of best practices supported by pictures, notes and references.

Thematic issues	*Criteria*
1 Environmental quality and wellbeing	1 Air 2 Noise 3 Water 4 Ionizing radiations
2 Waste	5 Solid waste management 6 Liquid waste management
3 Energy and renewable resources	7 Energy consumption and monitoring 8 Passive technical systems for sustainability 9 Active technical systems for sustainability
4 Mobility and accessibility	10 Distances to parks and local services 11 Public transport system 12 Availability of pedestrian and bicycle paths 13 Links between existent mobility system and new settlements
5 Land use and functional mix	14 Functional and social mix 15 Urban density 16 Filtering areas 17 Protection of sensitive users 18 Hazardous and nuisance activities
6 Quality of urban landscape	19 Quality of outdoors areas 20 Urban equipment 21 Visual comfort 22 System of urban green areas 23 Parkings for inhabitants

Fig. 2 Assessment framework (elaboration by the authors)

In order to measure the achievement's level of the qualitative criteria, constructed attributes (Bouyssou et al. 2000) were used. The performance values are expressed with a qualitative score rating from 0 (inadequate performance) to 3 (good practice).

The current performance evaluation scale represents the basis of the evaluation report, as well as a guidelines manual for designers and urban planners with regards to Public Health (Table 1). Each score, defined by teams of experts, is explained through a reference judgment that points out the requirements that are mandatory for reaching the highest score. Since the score achieved by each thematic issue is given by the average of the scores gained in each criterion, the performance values of plans/projects are defined according to one of the following ranges:

- negative ($0 \leq$ performance value ≤ 1.5);
- critical ($1.5 <$ performance value ≤ 2.25);
- good ($2.25 <$ performance value ≤ 3).

The results of the tool are provided by different graphic means (Fig. 3) that underline strengths and weaknesses of the urban development proposals under evaluation. In particular, a spider diagram shows the score achieved by each thematic issue, while three histograms show: the overall score of the urban plan/project; the scores of the thematic issues and the score achieved by each criterion (Capolongo et al. 2015, 2016).

Table 1 Performance judgments for environmental quality and wellbeing on a neighborhood-level for a healthy urban planning tool (elaboration by the authors)

Issues	Criteria	Performance values
Air	Presence of pollution sources, coexistence of the following strategies – Location of sensitive users in protected areas and far from the pollution sources – Strategies for limiting emissions at source and/or reducing the diffusion of pullutants	Good
	Presence of only one of the strategies listed above Absence of the strategies listed above	Critical not sufficient
Noise	Presence of noise sources, introduction of the following strategies – Location of sensitive users in protected areas and far from the noise sources – Strategies for limiting noise at source and/or reducing the noise transmission from fixed or mobile sources	Good
	Presence of only one of the strategies listed above Absence of the strategies listed above	Critical not sufficient
Water	Coexistence of the following strategies – Efficient water supply system – Reducing waste and saving drinking water	Good
	Presence of an efficient water supply system Absence of the strategies listed above	Not sufficient critical
Ionizing radiations/non ionizing radiations	Presence and/or absence of possible sources of ionizing/not ionizing radiations, coexistence of the following strategies – Location of sensitive users and users with residence time higher than 4 h away from ionizing/non ionizing radiations; absence of sensitive users close to power lines – Strategies aimed to remove or to mitigate ionizing/not ionizing radiations	Good
	Presence of only one of the strategies listed above Absence of the strategies listed above	Critical not sufficient

3.2 Validation and Development

The evaluation tool was applied in the Lombardy region by the LHA of Bergamo, Milan, and Lecco with the aim of evaluating the procedure to be able to extend its use in other contexts. In particular, the application took place in Milan since 2011 and it is still in use, and for one year the tool was tested in Lecco. From these analyses, although the reliability of the instrument was confirmed, the applicability of a number of evaluation criteria was considered critical or limited by a lack of information.

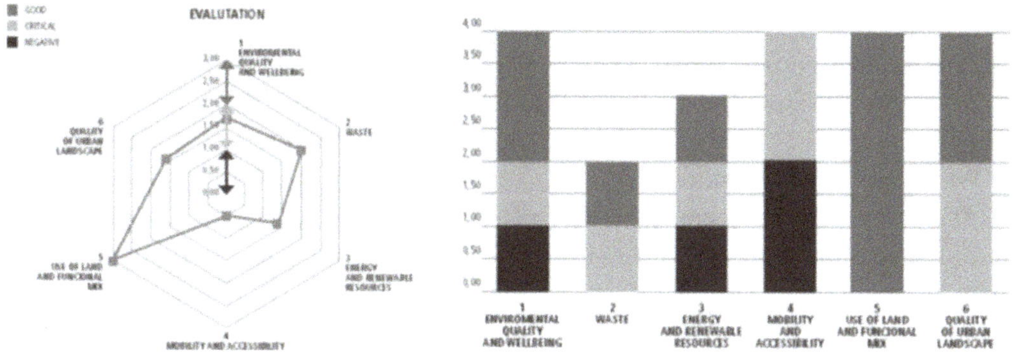

Fig. 3 Output of the evaluation through the different graphic means of the assessment tool (elaboration by the authors)

These results highlight the need to update certain criteria according to the new requirements of the *Urban Health* strategy (D'Alessandro et al. 2017a), and to introduce new ones, for instance regeneration of the abandoned areas and the contaminated site (ground and underground); geological, hydrogeological, and seismic risk prevention; social equity; universal design and design for all (European Institute for Design and Disability—EIDD 2004).

In particular, the last criteria refer to social wellbeing, since healthy cities are considered inclusive places, where planning and policy-making incorporate the views, voices, and needs of all communities (WHO 2016). This concept is assumed by the design for all strategy defined in 2004 by the European Institute for Design and Disability (EIDD), aimed to achieve cities where people diversity, social inclusion and equality represent the main drivers for Urban Health promotion (Mosca et al. 2019). Design for all's purpose is to develop functional and comfortable environments that can be used independently by the greatest number of users as possible, overcoming the concept of architectural barriers. The purpose is to provide the same experience of the space, even with various solutions, to different people, regardless of their abilities, disabilities, age, sex, and culture. The application of design for all concerns the involvement of a plurality of stakeholders (both experts and final users) from the beginning of the design process. This strategy is fundamental in order to understand and satisfy the physical, sensorial, and cognitive needs of the individuals by means of a prescriptive approach (Mosca et al. 2019).

Considering these new criteria, concerning the relationship between people's wellbeing and the quality of built environments, a review of the tool to make it more flexible and efficient in practice is required. After the update of the criteria, the following step will be to modify the performance scales and benchmarks of some criteria according to different territorial features. Furthermore, the outcomes of the survey suggest assigning different weights to the criteria in relation to their potential effects on *Urban Health*.

For these reasons, the tool is currently under review in order to update and improve its criteria and the performance scales by means of a project of two years (2018–2020) entitled "*Urban Health: good practices for health impact assessment of urban and environmental redevelopment and regeneration interventions.*" funded by the CCM, as previously mentioned.

The research team is coordinated by the Lombardy region (national proponent) and involves four Italian regions: Lombardy (LHA of Bergamo and ABC Department of the Politecnico di Milano); Piedmont (LHA3 of Turin and SCaDU, the regional epidemiology unit); Tuscany (LHA of Tuscany Nord Ovest); Apulia (LHA of Taranto).

The current review will foster the possibility of applying the tool from a local to a national level, and to increase public awareness regarding the connection between *Public Health* and urban quality according to the *Urban Health* strategy.

4 Conclusions

The review process both highlights the responsiveness of the evaluation tool to the current *Urban Health* issues and strengthens the effectiveness of the assessment process. Thus, in light of the most recent goals and requirements (D'Alessandro et al. 2015, 2016) the criteria review will provide several possibilities to expand the influence of the urban quality assessment tool from the local to national scale.

Furthermore, the overall contribution of the instrument includes, as one of its main objectives, increasing public awareness about the link between urban quality and *Public Health*, fostering the opportunities for a more effective relationship and training among designers (urban planners and architects) and *Public Health* professionals. Indeed, the instrument aims to be adopted both for supporting the assessment task of technicians of the LHA and as a guide for designers and planners in the design of interventions concerning social and healthy environments. The project funded by CCM2017, therefore, could be the opportunity to demonstrate new insights from the current review of the tool.

References

Active Living Research. (2015). Promoting activity-friendly communities. Active living research (pp. 3–7). San Diego, CA, USA.

Bouyssou, D., Marchant, T., Pirlot, M., Perny, P., Tsoukias, A., & Vincke, P. (2000). *Evaluation and decision models: A critical perspective* (Vol. 32). Springer Science & Business Media.

Capasso, L., Faggioli, A., Rebecchi, A., Capolongo, S., Gaeta, M., Appolloni, L., et al. (2018). Hygienic and sanitary aspects in urban planning: Contradiction in national and local urban legislation regarding public health. *Epidemiologia e Prevenzione, 42*(1), 60–64. https://doi.org/10.19191/EP18.1.P060.016.

Capolongo, S., Battistella, A., Buffoli, M., & Oppio, A. (2011). Healthy design for sustainable communities. *Annali di Igiene, 23*(1), 43–53.

Capolongo, S., Buffoli, M., & Oppio, A. (2015). How to assess the effects of urban plans on environment and health. *Territorio, 73,* 145–151.

Capolongo, S., Buffoli, M., Oppio, A., & Rizzitiello, S. (2013). Measuring hygiene and health performance of buildings: a multidimensional approach. *Annali di Igiene, 25*(2), 151–157. https://doi.org/10.7416/ai.2013.1917.

Capolongo, S., Lemaire, N., Oppio, A., Buffoli, M., & Roue Le Gall, A. (2016). Action planning for healthy cities: The role of multi-criteria analysis, developed in Italy and France, for assessing health performances in land-use plans and urban development projects. *Epidemiologia e Prevenzione, 40*(3–4), 257–264. https://doi.org/10.19191/EP16.3-4.P257.093.

Capolongo, S., Rebecchi, A., Dettori, M., Appolloni, L., Azara, A., Buffoli, M., et al. (2018). Healthy design and urban planning strategies, actions, and policy to achieve Salutogenic Cities. *International Journal of Environmental Research and Public Health, 15*(12), 2698. https://doi.org/10.3390/ijerph15122698.

Coppola, L., Ripamonti, E., Cereda, D., Gelmi, G., Pirrone, L., & Rebecchi, A. (2016). 2015–2018 Regional Prevention Plan of Lombardy (Northern Italy) and sedentary prevention: A cross-sectional strategy to develop evidence-based programmes. *Epidemiologia e Prevenzione, 40*(3–4), 243–248. https://doi.org/10.19191/EP16.3-4.P243.091.

Croucher, K., Wallace, A., & Duffy, S. (2012). *The influence of land use mix, density and urban design on health: A critical literature review* (pp. 3–25). York, UK: The University of York.

D'Alessandro, D., Appolloni, L., & Capasso, L. (2016). How wakable is the city? Application of the walking suitability index of the territory (T-WSI) to the city of Rieti (Lazio Region, Central Italy). *Epidemiologia e Prevenzione, 40,* 237–242.

D'Alessandro, D., Appolloni, L., & Capasso, L. (2017a). Public Health and urban planning: A powerful alliance to be enhanced in Italy. *Annali di Igiene, 29,* 452–463.

D'Alessandro, D., Arletti, S., Azara, A., Buffoli, M., Capasso, L., Cappuccitti, A., et al. (2017b). Strategies for disease prevention and health promotion in urban areas: The Erice 50 Charter. *Annali di Igiene, 29*(6), 481–493. https://doi.org/10.7416/ai.2017.2179.

D'Alessandro, D., Buffoli, M., Capasso, L., Fara, G. M., Rebecchi, A., & Capolongo, S. (2015). Green areas and public health: Improving wellbeing and physical activity in the urban context. *Epidemiologia e Prevenzione, 39,* 8–13.

Department for Communities and Local Government (DCLG). (2009). Multicriteria analysis: A manual London. http://eprints.lse.ac.uk/12761/1/Multi-criteria_Analysis.pdf.

European Institute for Design and Disability—EIDD. (2004). Stockholm Declaration. http://dfaeurope.eu/what-is-dfa/dfa-documents/the-eidd-stockholm-declaration-2004/.

Fehr, R., & Capolongo, S. (2016). Healing environment and urban health. *Epidemiologia e Prevenzione, 40*(3–4), 151–152. https://doi.org/10.19191/EP16.3-4.P151.080.

Galea, S., & Vlahov, D. (2005). Urban health: Evidence, challenges, and directions. *Annual Review of Public Health, 26*(1), 341–365.

Gola, M., Capolongo, S., Signorelli, C., Buffoli, M., & Rebecchi, A. (2017). Local health rules and building regulations: a survey on local hygiene and building regulations in Italian municipalities. *Annali Istituto superiore di sanità, 53*(3), 223–230. https://doi.org/10.4415/ANN_17_03_08.

Hickman, R., & Banister, D. (2014). *Transport, climate change and the city*. London, UK: Routledge.

Talukder, S. Capon, A., Nath, D., Kolb, A., Jahan, S., & Boufford, J. (2015). Urban health in the post-2015 agenda. Lancet, 385, 769.

Mosca, E. I., Herssens, J., Rebecchi, A., Froyen, H., & Capolongo, S. (2019). "Design for All" manual: From users' needs to inclusive design strategies. *Advances in Intelligent Systems and Computing, 824,* 1724–1734.

Oppio, A., Bottero, M., Giordano, G., & Arcidiacono, A. (2016). A multi-methodological evaluation approach for assessing the impact of neighbourhood quality on public health. *Epidemiologia e Prevenzione, 40,* 249–256.

Rebecchi, A., Boati, L., Oppio, A., Buffoli, M., & Capolongo, S. (2016). Measuring the expected increase in cycling in the city of Milan and evaluating the positive effects on the population's health status: A community-based urban planning experience. *Annali di Igiene, 28*(6), 381–391. https://doi.org/10.7416/ai.2016.2120.

Roy, B. (2013). *Multicriteria methodology for decision aiding* (Vol. 12). Springer Science & Business Media.

World Health Organization. (2016). Health as the Pulse of the New Urban Agenda. United Nations Conference on Housing and Sustainable Urban Development. Quito, October 2016. Available online: http://apps.who.int/iris/bitstream/handle/10665/250367/9789241511445-eng.pdf;jsessionid=07F882D99F1E1AF399B57D5546EEB2BB?sequence=1.

World Health Organization. (2017). *Towards more physical activity in cities transforming public spaces to promote physical activity—A key contributor to achieving the sustainable development goals in Europe*. Copenhagen, Denmark: BMC Public Health.

A Development and Management Model for "Smart" Temporary Residences

Liala Baiardi, Andrea Ciaramella and Stefano Bellintani

Abstract The text describes the features of the project for developing and managing smart temporary residences in a circular economy vision, Eco System, Temporary House—ESTH, winner of the Smart Living Tender in the Lombardy region. The research project aims to create a development and management model for "smart" temporary residences by applying a circular economy vision to the construction, furnishing and services industry. The development involves the application to an existing building subject to functional, construction and energy redevelopment through innovative construction and digital technologies. The property's redevelopment is based on a centralised management model for building (property and facility management) and users, thanks to use of the IoT (Internet of things).

Keywords Building management · IoT · Process model · Valorisation · Smart living

1 Introduction

The ability to organise programmed strategies for the redevelopment of building systems plays a fundamental role within the strategy of enhancing the real estate assets and the urban fabric.

L. Baiardi (✉) · A. Ciaramella · S. Bellintani
Architecture, Built Environment and Construction Engineering—ABC Department, Politecnico di Milano, Milan, Italy
e-mail: liala.baiardi@polimi.it

S. Della Torre et al. (eds.), *Regeneration of the Built Environment from a Circular Economy Perspective*, Research for Development,
https://doi.org/10.1007/978-3-030-33256-3_31

40% of residential buildings in European Union countries were built before 1960, and almost 84% are at least 20 years old. For this reason, a large majority of buildings are in a poor state of conservation and unable to meet the basic requirements dictated by user needs and the current legislative framework (European Union—EU 2010).

The need for redevelopment is also strongly motivated by the fact that residential buildings are responsible for a third of the world's final energy consumption (International Energy Agency 2013). It is, thus, essential to rethink energy adjustment to take a major step towards the achievement of environmental objectives in the medium and long term, and therefore create sustainable urban renovations. This requires vigorous policies, as well as effective and conscious actions to reduce the costs associated with the construction industry, in terms of operational and incorporated energy use and related emissions. The International Energy Agency (IEA) aims to achieve an 80% reduction in global emissions by 2050, which thing led European countries to focus their efforts on the optimisation of energy performance (Passer et al. 2016).

In this respect, the European Commission (EC) has identified the life-cycle assessment (LCA) as the most suitable methodology that is currently available to evaluate the potential environmental impacts and the performance of construction products and buildings (Kylili and Fokaides 2017).

The products have a life cycle that can be defined according to two different approaches: technical and economic. Generally, products with low-quality and economic value are scrapped at the end of their life cycle. For those defined as durable, the possibility is envisaged of carrying out repairs (which do not exceed the value of the product) before finally terminating the life cycle. Finally, for high-value and technically complex products (which make reproduction difficult), maintenance and functional adjustment activities can be initiated that are such as to restart a new life cycle.

The latter is the typical case of real estate products that, generally with a high economic value and low reproducibility, become the object of redevelopment or enhancement. This process consists in the intervention on the building that has become obsolete in order to restart a new technological and economic life cycle for it.

The requirement for a design praxis enhances the significance to the governance of both creative and constructive process, placing the question of method in a multidisciplinary and multi-objective dimension aimed at responding to the rapid change in the quality demand underlying the project itself.

It outlines a file rouge within the cultural debate of the area, making the topic of "method" a key issue of the disciplinary approach.

Indeed, it explains the systemic and complex vision of the design thinking; the procedural nature of operations; the hierarchical structure of the information/decision ratio in project organisation; the capacity of mediating constraints deriving by both the built environment; the biological cycles and the will of responding to the most advanced aspirations of society (Lucarelli and Rigillo 2018).

The activities of buildings valorisation, compared to traditional restructuring activities, represent an innovative approach with particular attention to processing potential of the property well and putting it in relation to the urban context and the target market needs.

Its fundamental goal is to increase in profitability through the design and construction of a "new and precise identity" of the property.

Starting from the analysis of the characteristics and transformative potential of the building (both from the urbanistic, architectural, layout, plant engineering point of view), we must define the potential need to change the destination in order to obtain the maximum efficiency of performance and profitability.

In particular, the organisation of a process of property enhancement aims to successfully identify and subsequently determine the proportion of unexpressed real estate value, i.e. what can be identified only by fully grasping the characteristics and the potential of the specific asset in relation to market demand in that particular context (Manfredi and Tronconi 2012).

Through a well-structured analysis and design activity it is, thus, possible to identify the opportunity that can best satisfy the cost/performance ratio with respect to the entire life cycle of the building.

Based on this, the text explains the underlying principles of the Eco System Temporary House (ESTH) Works Experimentation and Innovation project funded by the Lombardy region within its Smart Living program. Starting from the desire to enhance an existing building, the project aims to create a management development model for real estate assets.

This approach refers to the actual debate on the relevance of the building balance to the global sustainability, as described by environmental, social, economic and political aspects, that is linked to the restoration of existing buildings.

2 The Eco System Temporary House (ESTH) Project

Eco System Temporary House (ESTH) represents an innovative company for the development and management of smart temporary residences through the functional, constructive, energy and seismic redevelopment of existing buildings with innovative construction and digital technologies as well as recycled and recyclable materials in a circular economy vision.

Reconnecting to the principles of resilience management (Walker et al. 2006), the project implements design practices aimed at developing innovation of both product and process, according to the new "eco" paradigm coming from scientific debate (also including those of the ecological engineering and eco-technologies).

The renovation project involves structural consolidation by means of the technique of static strengthening and also the improvement of energy performance.[1]

Simultaneously are taken into consideration issues such as reducing carbon dioxide emissions, water conservation, rainwater and wastewater management and reuse.

Important aspects for the owner and the handler, not only for the environmental benefits and comfort that follow each other but also for the reduction of energy consumption and cost savings it brings.

The project includes the elaboration of a centralised management model for building (property and facility management) and users (services to the person) thanks to use of the IoT (Internet of things).

The IoT has the potential to allow communication between real and virtual devices in daily life using the Internet. It also focuses on providing information on changes to the state of things in real time. It can be compared to the nervous system in terms of the exchange of information, because the connection between the sensors and actuators that communicate networking suggests the development of intelligent environments (Isikdag 2015).

The IoT, together with detector devices, allows us to extract the "big data" (data and information) directly from the user-building system and reuse it for "continuously improving" the building-eco-system and the performance of services (monitoring the service-level agreement—SLA).

The residences will be allocated to particular categories of users who need to rent a house for a short to medium period, such as workers ("visiting professors" and researchers, entrepreneurs and corporate reality managers), people who need to stay for medical treatment or to care for sick relatives and tourists.

On the basis of a research carried out by Mckinsey on temporary residences, there is a growth in demand for spaces with smart features on the part of freelancers but also companies, small entrepreneurs or innovative start-ups (McKinsey Global Institute 2011).

Places, which have characteristics sometimes halfway between a home and an office, with work spaces and gathering spaces in which you can access, thanks to flexible subscriptions that allow you to occupy single locations, but also offices with

[1]The structural redevelopment requires seismic screening solutions by:

- seismic investigation,
- seismic redevelopment intervention aimed at the seismic certification according to the DDL 2017 budget law (in accordance with the "Guidelines for the classification of seismic construction risk"),
- structural and vibrational monitoring for the assessment of safety conditions in the course of the executive and post-intervention phases.

Environmental redevelopment requires energy screening such as:

- thermal investigation of shell dispersions and thermal bridges,
- adaptation of the Nzeb Nearly Zero energy building with integrated intervention at building level, plant engineering and low power consumption choice in respect of Leadership in Energy and Environmental Design (LEED) and Lombardy region directives (DGRX 3868).

multiple desks, meeting rooms and conference rooms for the time you need: a day, a month or more.

This temporary form of use began in America at the beginning of the century and then spread to the major cities of the world.

An example is the American case of WeLive, a widening product of the We Work philosophy based on community and flexibility where the users of the residences have access to the leisure and co-working areas and a wide range of additional services.

In Italy today, the answer to such residential needs in the free market offer shows some weaknesses of both a regulatory and contractual nature and a building nature, i.e. with types unsuited to the housing needs of the reference target.

In line and by way of implementation of the provisions in the PON GOVERNANCE and PON SMART CITY European Directives, Regional Law No. 31 of 28/11/2014, which predict a 25–30% reduction in land use by 2020, the project is designed to recover existing buildings with zero land consumption.

The concept is based on Corporate social responsibility that is guided towards a circular economy model of the construction and services sector, involving the PEOPLE-PLANET-PROFIT and ECONOMICS OF HAPPINESS sustainable principles through the humanisation of the elements of technological innovation.

3 The Operational Model

Planning E.S.T.H. ITALY intends to meet the needs of the hospitality market for serviced apartments as an alternative to traditional hotel rooms.

These kinds of accommodation generally consist in small furnished apartments available for short- or long-term-stays that provide, in addition to cleaning, a range of services for guests and include the price of taxes and utilities.

The "serviced" apartments offer services very similar to those of a traditional hotel, but with more space, comfort and privacy by replicating a more homely environment.

They have a private kitchenette, larger living/sleeping areas than most standard rooms, and often have access to gyms, restaurants, meeting rooms and other services depending on the "residence" target.

For the preparation and experimentation of the model, an abandoned property was chosen in the municipality of Milan whose redevelopment and enhancement are envisaged without demolishing the main structure and with the use of materials and components that can be easily removed, disassembled and reused.

The model contemplates a protocol that has the following as strategic and consequential points:

- the technical–economic due diligence for functional building repurposing;
- the development of the project with BIM aid, the recovery of the building with the functional adaptation of the internal layout to the new housing needs;
- centralised and advanced management with the introduction of value-added services for users.

The approach is systemic and sees all the envisaged elements as necessarily and systematically interdependent.

The technical–administrative due diligence (planning and construction) includes the investigation of structural and energy diagnostics, thermal bridges and 3D BIM output modelling.

In order to reconfigure and make real estate products on the market attractive, it is necessary to develop the project to match the expectations of potential demand as much as possible.

For this reason, it is necessary to carry out a suitable analysis of the competitive supply and demand in the reference sector.

A functional benchmarking analysis was thus conducted in support of the identification of best business practices applicable to the Eco system Temporary House model.

The underlying philosophy of the Benchmarking process consists of four elements/work phases:

- Knowing one's activities;
- Knowing the business leaders or competitors;
- Incorporating the best;
- Achieving excellence in managing one's activities (Ciaramella and Bellintani 2008).

The identification of the objectives/performance principles the building must attain provides important information for the definition of the project, and as a result, for the building-installation sub systems to be intervened on.

The building is designed as a highly technological eco-system designed in an integrated manner in its architectural, structural and installation parts, thanks to the use of Building Information Modelling software (BIM).

A BIM model not only represents the geometry of the project, but it contains within it all the technical, scientific, commercial and economic information that allows us to have a complete virtual representation of the work planned as the final result, with all the benefits arising from it.

The use of BIM also contributes to the creation of a database capable of containing technical and economic information.

This form of archiving makes it possible to correlate the considerable amount of information necessary in order to maintain an active management of the real estate assets. This information can provide further support in forecasting and monitoring of maintenance activities.

Building information management is the basis of the standards and requirements applied to the data aimed at the use of BIM. The continuity of data allows an effective exchange of information in a context in which sender and receiver understand the information (Va BIM Guide 2010).

The mitigation of the impact on the territory in terms of lower emissions is pursued by applying a "circular" system to the building sector system translated into energy and structural redevelopment interventions, choice of materials and products designed to be circular.

In this phase, the choices regarding the use of new materials and new construction technologies (e.g. carbon fibres and graphene) are made to facilitate the implementation of "light" structural interventions such as making the structure earthquake-proof and energy efficient.

As implementation of the BIM proceeds in the various phases of the project's life cycle, even the connected models evolve, with a constant enrichment of information. This progressive set of models is sometimes defined using different naming conventions. A common convention in the sector ranks the models as follows:

- the concept stage model (also called the mass model);
- the design stage model (also called the design model—in the case of a construction project we can also talk about an architectural model, a structural model, a MEP model, etc.);
- the construction stage model (also defined as the construction model);
- the operation and maintenance stage model (also defined as the final model).

The application of a centralised management model for building (property and facility management) and users (personal services) is implemented via the use of the IoT (Internet of things).

The IoT, together with detector devices, allows us to extract the "big data" (data and information) directly from the user-building system and reuse it for "continuously improving" the building-eco-system and the performance of services (monitoring the service-level agreement).

Use of the IoT combined with building automation technologies, attention to customer experience (through the use of a dedicated app for iOS and Android smart phones) enable us to meet consumer needs more effectively and manage the environments more efficiently.

The management model involves configuring a property management system (PMS) and the control room.

Property management system is a software programme used to manage room planning, check-in and check-out activities, accounts, and invoicing by accommodation facilities.

The control room represents a "reference model" that can also be used from remote, able to communicate with the BIM and conduct a census (in an interactive and structured manner) on technical/energy, building registry, accounting and tax data, as well as data on maintenance works and guarantees, with the ability to monitor on a remote basis (for example, by means of sensors and Webcams) and return information about individual devices at different levels of detail.

Through the application of the property management system and the interaction with the control room in the building, it is possible to plan and control the location of the units, handle the volumes of incoming and outgoing data, create links to internal and external systems such as hall and utilities systems, and generate reports capable of providing support to the operational and revenue management choices.

4 Innovative Aspects and Possible Developments

Innovation, which starts from the management model for the property (property and facility) and the services to the person, obliges us to rethink the entire construction process from design to implementation and monitoring: the approach of the initiative is systemic and sees all the envisaged elements as necessarily and systematically interdependent.

Thanks to a centralised governance of the data (platform—software—app) and an intelligent management of information, it is possible to extract the big data from both processes, through the use of sensors and control units that represent cognitive systems properly so-called (internal acoustic control, use of home automation and building automation systems), and users, translating them into a holistic view, achieving a continuous improvement of operational processes (service-level agreement—SLA), improving performance and thus ensuring user satisfaction, in addition to ensuring continuity of the 24 h service.

5 Conclusions

The project, in its final phase, leads constructing and testing a model that can be reproduced to meet the demands of a growing market, thereby contributing to the socio-economic development of the community.

The combined use of BIM and IoT technologies plays an important role for increasing the efficiency in customer services and facility management. For this reason, our future efforts will continue in this direction and will focus on investigating the feasibility of this integration with different approaches in building management.

In this research, real-time data from the sensors can be provided and tracked from the web browser. Analysis and visualization of the data from the sensors will be important for manage the building, particularly in view of comfort analysis.

Based on the research work and on the case study illustrated, we can conclude that applying an opportune centralised management model, real estate strategy must prove able to support the building reuse and relocation.

The choice of a correct and adequate definition of spaces and the provision of services to the enterprise and to the organisation is true strategic decisions that can influence the success of a project.

The case study highlights the tight relationship among the, real estate needs, and the material contribution given by the right strategy implemented by the FM or the Real Estate Management departments.

Managers have the responsibility to govern the whole process through its individual stages, involving the participating subjects and allocating the necessary resources. Facility managers are asked to monitor the correct development of the process and, if necessary, to intervene promptly.

The main indicator of their efficiency is the successful achievement of the set targets within the set deadlines and costs.

Acknowledgements The Eco System Temporary House (ESTH) is funded by the Lombardy region within the context of support to the integrated high-tech building supply chain: manufacturing, services and technology "Lombardy 5.0: policies for the consolidation and enhancement of lombardy's excellent supply chains" known as smart living.
PG Seven S.R.L., Guffanti Group & partners S.R.L., Universal Selecta S.p.A are partners in the project.
Members of the working group from the Politecnico di Milano: Andrea Ciaramella, Liala Baiardi, Stefano Bellintani, Marzia Morena, Angela Pavesi and Valentina Puglisi.

References

Ciaramella, A., & Bellintani, S. (2008). "L'audit immobiliare", Ed Il sole 24 Ore, Milan 2008.

European Union. (2010). European Union (UE) Directive 2010/31/EU of the European Parliament and of the Council of 19 May 2010 on the energy performance of buildings (recast). *Official Journal of the European Union*, 13–35. https://doi.org/10.3000/17252555.L_2010.153.eng.

International Energy Agency. (2013). World energy Outlook, OECD/IEA, Paris. Retrieved from https://www.iea.org/publications/freepublications/publication/WEO2013.pdf.

Isikdag, U. (2015). BIM and IoT: A synopsis from GIS perspective. In *Joint International Geoinformation Conference, 10* (pp. 33–38). Kuala Lumpur: International Archives of the Photogrammetry.

Kylili, A., & Fokaides, P. A. (2017). Policy trends for the sustainability assessment of construction materials: A review. *Sustainable Cities and Society, 35*, 280–288. Retrieved from https://www.sciencedirect.com/science/article/pii/S2210670717303773?via%3Dihub.

Lucarelli, M. T., & Rigillo, M. (2018). Resilience and technological culture of design: The centrality of method. *Techne, Journal of Technology for Architecture and Environment, 15/2018. Italy, 60/64.*

Manfredi, L., & Tronconi, O. (2012). La valorizzazione immobiliare, Maggioli editore, Sant'Arcangelo di Romagna.

McKinsey Global Institute. (2011). Urban world: Mapping the economic power of cities. Retrieved from https://www.mckinsey.com/featuredinsights/urbanization/urban-world-mapping-the-economic-power-of-cities.

Passer, A., Ouellet-Plamondon, C., Kenneally, P., John, V., & Habert, G. (2016). The impact of future scenarios on building refurbishment strategies towards plus energy buildings. *Energy and Building, 124*, 153–163. Retrieved from https://www.sciencedirect.com/science/article/pii/S0378778816302432?via%3Dihub.

Regional Law dated 28th November 2011, no. 31, provisions for reducing the use of space and for rehabilitating degraded land, (BURL n. 49, suppl. del 01 Dicembre 2014). Retrieved from http://normelombardia.consiglio.regione.lombardia.it/NormeLombardia/Accessibile/main.aspx?iddoc=lr002014112800031&view=showdoc.

US Department of Veteran Affairs. (2010). The VA BIM guide, US Department of Veteran Affairs, Washington DC. Retrieved from www.cfm.va.gov/til/bim/BIMGuide/terms.htm.

Walker, B., Gunderson, L., Kinzig, A., Folke, C., Carpenter, S., & Schultz, L. (2006). A handful of heuristics and some propositions for understanding resilience in social-ecological systems. *Ecology and Society, 11*(13).

Extra-Ordinary Solutions for Useful Smart Living

Elisabetta Ginelli, Claudio Chesi, Gianluca Pozzi, Giuditta Lazzati, Davide Pirillo and Giulia Vignati

Abstract The project 'cHOMgenius. PrototipeSystem and SharedProject. Soluzioni straordinarie per l'abitare intelligente' studies a modular constructional system and experiments with design solutions, examining constructive, structural and plant engineering techniques for OFF-GRID dwellings featuring home automation control and managed by digital tools with relevant verification and monitoring instruments, in a logic of complete disassembly, reuse and recycling according to the most recent European directive. This project, which includes as partners two Lombard companies together with the Politecnico di Milano, is supported by 20 national and international companies and by the UNI 'Ente Italiano di Normazione'. The OFF-GRID prototype consists of entirely 'clamping' technical-constructive solutions, digital management/energetic solutions, innovative maintainability solutions for seismic safety and economic sustainability, in relation to the high-energetic performance offered and the technical solutions adopted. cHOMgenius is a shipping container building totally placing itself within the circular economy, through the reuse of HC 20′ and 40′ containers made of corten steel as supporting structure of the dwelling. The approach to the theme of circular economy pursued is intrinsically linked to the 3Rs concept, understood as: (i) reduction of material in terms of quantity, embodied energy and time, resulting in a better use of products and giving them a multi-functionality character; (ii) recycling of products and materials through the use of dry technologies, offering the option to use decoupling materials in order to avoid not only dismantling costs, often uneconomical, but also to avoid polluting industrial cycles due to recycling; (iii) reuse/reapplication, seen as the most evident plus of the circular chain as it is considered synonymous with the increase of products' life.

Keywords Accomplished project · Industrialization · Useful life cycle costs · Experimentation sharing · Evolutionary process · Recombining innovation · Prediction

E. Ginelli (✉) · C. Chesi · G. Pozzi · G. Lazzati · D. Pirillo · G. Vignati
Architecture, Built Environment and Construction Engineering—ABC Department, Politecnico di Milano, Milan, Italy
e-mail: elisabetta.ginelli@polimi.it

S. Della Torre et al. (eds.), *Regeneration of the Built Environment from a Circular Economy Perspective*, Research for Development,
https://doi.org/10.1007/978-3-030-33256-3_32

1 Introduction

This paper shows a project funded by the 'Smart Living' call promoted by Regione Lombardia, which supports development and innovation projects carried out by partnerships in the construction, wood home furniture, appliance and high-tech sectors in collaboration with the universities, implementing the Regional Law 26/2015 'Manifattura diffusa, creativa e tecnologia 4.0' ('Creative and common manufacture and Technology 4.0') and developing the "LOMBARDIA 5.0" strategy. The aim is to address the evolutionary dynamics of productive sectors and especially to favour the qualification of the economic system through the stabilization and enhancement of 'excellent supply chains' as development drivers.

Timeline:

- February 2017 open call
- June 2018 starting date of the project—design phase
- July 2019 realization of the mock-up
- September 2019 monitoring phase
- December 2019 end of project.

2 Cultural Framework

On an institutional level, the construction sector and that of production, in general, have to act within a scenario marked by environmental issues, which must sensitize the designing and fulfilment actions of building interventions.

The proposal here illustrated is placed in such context and is representative of a design process, chiefly aiming at enhancing the energy used throughout the life cycle (Adalberth 1997) of a single-family residential building with a permanent residential function.

The project is based on the research and development of an industrial modular building system model (Kotnik 2008; Kramer 2015) offering high-energy performances (OFF-GRID) but also entailing current market costs. It proposes the construction of a residential prototype, based on industrialization, recycling and the eco-efficiency of natural, productive and professional resources criteria.

It focuses on the principles of hybridization and contamination between different productive sectors which, upon reaching shared objectives and results, translate into fruitful carriers of renewal and economic potentiality, for the purpose of contributing to a revival of the construction sector according to a proactive interpretation of the sustainability rules (environmental, social, economic and institutional).

The reference scenario related to sustainability is defined by the UNI 11277 standard and by the UNI PdR13[1] and its integration with CAM,[2] the relationship between energy saving and comfort, and the awareness in the use of resources provided by the principle of the 3Rs (reduction, reuse, recycling) (Huanga et al. 2018; Islam et al. 2016).

In a nutshell, the guideline of the study is based on the desire to innovate residential production by harnessing 'transfer' products as well as multifunctional solutions and products (i.e. products with multiple functions), combining the existing production know-how with advanced technologies to provide a 'system/product' in use with no CO_2 production.

3 Tools and Methods

The aforementioned programmatic scenario influences the method and choice of the tools applied in this study, within the cultural sphere of technological and environmental architecture design.

The approach we intend to pursue is meta-planning and is meant to provide guidelines. The immaterial invariants of the project determine the established performance for the resulting design and can be summarized as follows: time variable management: quick building times, rapid response times to external system stimuli, rapid dismantling and reuse or swift recycling times; transferability: the solutions (techno-typological, morphological, structural, plant-related) must be transferable in other geographical and demanding contexts; design and production innovation: transfer and/or adaptation from sectors dealing with the current manufacture of products, techniques and knowledge, building practice and other fields; qualitative multifunctionality of the architectural system, understood as the possibility to use in multifunctional terms both the whole system and the individual components, where the latter establish multifunctional relations for maximizing the use of the system potentiality; constructive reactive system: from a structural point of view (active anti-earthquake systems), from an energy point of view (integrated building/plant management) and from a technical point of view, in relation to the entire life cycle of the building and its components.

The invariants, in turn, have been translated into technological and functional resource requirements and objects, due to their strong circularity in the use and reuse of the involved resources and because they give substance to the concept of 'active resilience' of the project, read as the regeneration capacity of its intrinsic value

[1] UNI/PdR 13.1:2015 Sostenibilità ambientale nelle costruzioni—Strumenti operativi per la valutazione della sostenibilità (Environmental sustainability in buildings—Operative tools for sustainability assessment).

[2] DECRETO 11 ottobre 2017. Criteri ambientali minimi per l'affidamento di servizi di progettazione e lavori per la nuova costruzione, ristrutturazione e manutenzione di edifici pubblici (Minimum environment criteria for the allocation of design services and works related to the new construction, restructuring and maintainance of public buildings).

Table 1 Main resilience requirements for the project, as keywords

Resilience requirements for the project	
Technological-functional requirements	Examples of object requirements
Flexibility (Ginelli 2010)	Convertibility (Bologna 2002)
Predictive and adaptive project	Smart object
Reactive project	Durability (Jourda 2010), re-functionalization
Redundancy of systems	Multi-functionality reliability fault-tolerant design
Replicability	Industrialization and prefabrication (Ginelli and Pozzi 2017)
Sharing	Communication guarantee
Technological flexibility	Accessibility, maintainability, substitutability and transformability

(Ginelli and Pozzi 2017). The greater the intrinsic capacity of a building to accept changes and modifications to achieve a new given performance picture, the lower the cost of this upgrading and thus the greater its active resilience.

The same applies to embodied energy: the project has the intrinsic capacity to make energy available for time $t(0 + x)$—a time in future—whose conditions are still unknown, but which mandatorily require the right strategy (active resilience) to afford changes.

This active resilience generates invariants and requirements for the project. Such requirements are a priori strategies valid for each project and can be used so that the building, regardless of individual materials and specific products, can be resilient and thus actively respond to physiological changes or unforeseen events.

These requirements are attributed to the project in its general aspects, constitute the cultural approach that is essential to the project and originate techno-functional conditions. Each of them has been associated with prerequisites that objects must have, thus, giving rise to object requirements which are consequently related to the building material components and play a specific role in the logic of an active resilience project (Table 1).

Another important concept the project has been pursuing is 'recombining innovation'. It is defined as the capacity to create value by connecting products and know-how in a smart way, since this project could create the right conditions for companies and designers to produce 'better' ideas and outputs thanks to the network they establish with others (Fig. 1).

4 Results: The Project

Before proceeding with the specific description of the system, we wish to highlight some tenets regarding the design of the dwelling, divided into the different phases of the construction's life cycle:

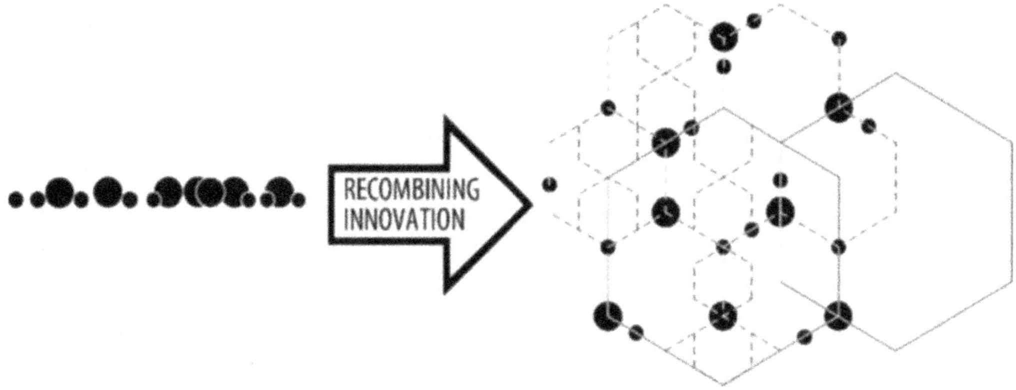

Fig. 1 Added value that recombining innovation can give to products, creating positive networks

1. Construction of the building and its components: dry technology with 'tightening' techniques (Giordano 2010); use of shipping containers as a structural system of the building organism and casing structure; use of a screw foundation system that guarantees the reversibility of the ground condition by dismantling; use of elements already pre-assembled in workshop, including counter frames, window frames, systems, fixed equipment, etc., use of prefabricated elements, such as prefab bathroom, staircase; minimum work on-site: assembly of coatings, some 'fragile' components, connections, etc., reuse of part of the container's removed metal sheet to be reinserted in the building for other purposes;
2. Management of the building and its components: independence from electric and gas networks (OFF-GRID); minimization of thermal losses; simplified system management: simplified interface for end users; self-learning of electromechanical equipment (from climate management to small household appliances); system performance and technological adaptability: system tested for different climatic area, from the Mediterranean to the continental one; substitutability of structural joints: in the event of an earthquake the only possible deformations are concentrated in the joints between the containers, which are monitored by specific sensors; therefore, it is possible to highlight the damaged joints and easily replace them;
3. 'End of life' of the main function, which stands for the convertibility of the system: reuse of the container module: the basic structure can be reused without heavy interventions; component multi-functionality: the structure of the container performs both structural and closing functions, while providing a considerable mass for thermal inertia; expandability: the structural module does not correspond to the living cell, meaning that it can be used for infinite compositions; possible new reconfiguration of the system: the easy disassembly and reassembly of the joints ensures an easy and quick reconfiguration of the structural modules; module transformability: the structural module can be used in different configurations, some of which require minimal interventions; module durability: the structural module is in corten steel, which is guaranteed to resist extreme conditions, including saltiness; energy recovered at the end of the function: all the

employed corten steel, which has high levels of embodied energy, can be used without additional energy for other functions (the structural module can become something else without other processes);

4. End of building life (Faludi et al. 2012): reversibility of the foundation system: once unscrewed the screw foundations, the ground returns to its original state without any damage; disassembly of the components: all connections are made with clamping and thus easily separable systems; reuse of the container: the basic structure can be reused without heavy interventions; reuse of the casing components: both the finishes and the thermal insulation are mechanically fixed, so that they can be easily dismantled and reused; recycling of container components: as a last opportunity, the container is made of corten steel which can be used as a second raw material;
5. 'End of life' of the main function. Transformation of its component parts: disassembly of the components; reuse of the envelope components; reuse of parts of the container's metal sheet.

The project uses the container as a structural resource. The employed module ensures high-structural performances, without introducing additional elements for the system stability (Bernardo et al. 2013).

We have studied operations to make this structure habitable. First, living space has been well conformed through the right aggregation of basic modules. Subsequently, the right functions have been included into the structure and the essential spatial characteristics have been applied. We followed the basic principle of maintaining a high degree of techno-typological and spatial flexibility for each space, while also guaranteeing the possibility of future extensions or changes in use.

4.1 The Mock-Up

The mock-up we are assembling is a 2-storey building. It consists of 4 HC 40′, linked by an 'other space' made of a steel autonomous structure (Kotnik 2008; Kramer 2015). It will simulate different technical solutions and real-use conditions. It will be placed in eastern Milan suburbs (Fig. 2).

From a *structural* point of view, the main purpose is containing goods. Containers (Giriunas et al. 2012) have to provide a suitable resisting structure as well, so that no meaningful change in shape can occur under the effects of both weight and the different actions which may take place during the various phases of transportation and movement. Looking at the terminology, indeed, the term 'box' applies to the main function as well as the structural scheme. The main goal of the project is to limit additions to frames around the cuts and to avoid braces: for this reason, we have obtained the maximum hole the metal sheets are able to bear in normal and earthquake conditions in relation to buildings.

The *foundation* system is based on totally reversible screw poles, without concrete or other non-easily dismountable solutions. With respect to seismic protection, we

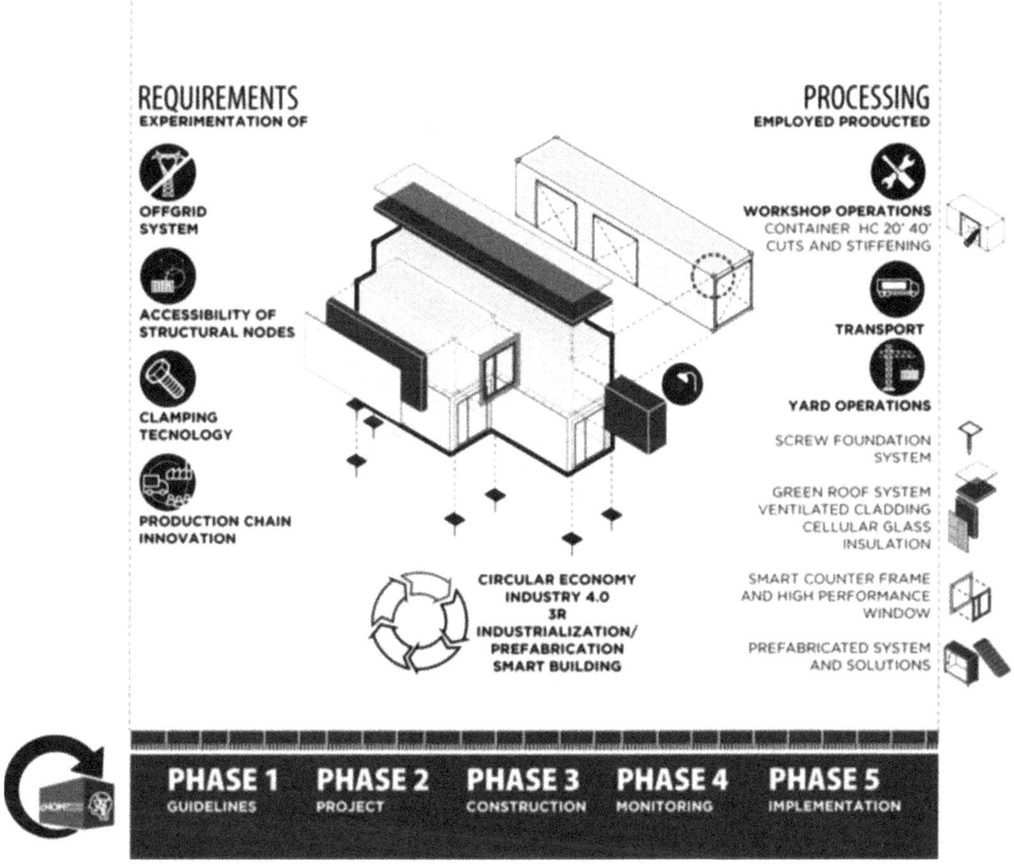

Fig. 2 Constructive scheme of the cHOMgenius mock-up

are developing a patentable device in which active sensors monitor the effects of horizontal forces and highlight possible damages; in addition, the seismic isolator is completely replaceable without uplifting the building.

Regarding the *aggregation* of modules, the boxes are jointed only at the corners and structural reinforcements are inserted only if an entire vertical sheet is cut away.

From the point of view of *energy systems*, the building is completely OFF-GRID thanks to a high-performance shell and 24 V electric plants that do not need converters. It is based on a bio-fuel cogenerator, linked with a 24 V heat pump, photovoltaic cells and a battery as storage (Fig. 3).

As regards the *envelope*, the containers are generally supplied without thermal insulation, and thus are not able to meet the energy performance requirements according to the legislation for NZEB buildings. The absence of a massive envelope also implies that buildings simply made up of containers have a low-thermal capacity. A change in the external temperature quickly leads to excessive cooling or overheating of the internal temperature with an extremely reduced delay time. Therefore, containers used for residential purposes require an insulation layer which must be placed outside the container, to avoid loss of internal surface and thermal bridges. For these reasons, we have considered cellular glass as the best material for such application: it is waterproof, able to stop the passage of steam, incombustible, resistant to harmful

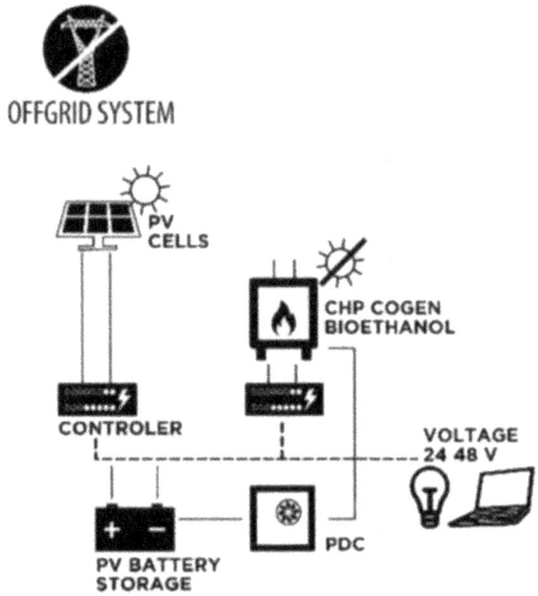

Fig. 3 Scheme of cHOMgenius energy plants

agents, acids and compression, non-deformable and easy to process. It is clamped to the sheet and sealed by removable adhesive.

5 Conclusion: Potential and Future Developments

Certainly, the proposal presents some weaknesses, but we have put forward possible solutions.

Firstly, the current normative apparatus based on traditional construction techniques is quite strict and not keen to recognize innovations. The difficulty to introduce the container system into the world of structural construction legislation could be solved through a structural safety assessment tool to validate the system in compliance with current legislation, as well as a tool for monitoring and reporting possible difficulties during use.

Another critical aspect is the need for an ad hoc design via technical, plant and structural solutions which are not available in current production. We have solved this problem by presenting innovative proposals to upgrade existing and consolidated products, according to the attainment of high performances combined with management and monitoring aspects, especially concerning anti-seismic and energetic/plant solutions.

The proposal may also present threats that could spoil the result. Among them, for example, a generalized vision linked to a negative perception of 'living in a container' with possible problems of acceptability. Such obstacle is easily overcome as the container is used as a structural system and, as far as permanent housing solutions are concerned, with guaranteed performances. Moreover, it is not visible unless the user chooses otherwise.

One potentiality of this solution is the availability of containers as a second resource, offering facilitated handling, high availability and durability. In addition, the design strategies for the replicability of work in the workshop and on-site are the project's other advantages. The proposal could trigger the following opportunities: (a) the evolution of the construction sector in terms of energy, new trends related to performance requirements, forms of living space use, costs, turnover, technologies and construction techniques, products, components and systems, at national and international scale (by type and materials used); (b) the current period characterized by new cultural and operational environmental challenges, requiring a healthy competitive ability to meet differentiated needs with adequate, appropriate and timely responses; (c) the transition to Industry 4.0; (d) the need to reduce waste and the obligation to use resources consciously; (e) the growth of real-estate market for unconventional building solutions and the resilience of the certified high-performance housing market; (f) the possible regulatory evolution in terms of performance for buildings with incremental performances, advanced technical and innovative structural solutions and energy/environmental, functional, usability and maintainability levels; (g) the harnessing of tax incentives in the field of energy self-consumption.

The sustainability of this system certainly depends on the environmental benefit of used materials, products and methods. However, it depends mostly on the ability to bind information through a multi-criteria structure, in order to produce benefits not individually, but rather as a system, from the perspective of an accomplished project.

References

Adalberth, K. (1997). Energy use during the life cycle of single-unit dwellings: Examples. *Building and Environment, 32*(4), 321–329.

Bernardo, L. F. A., Oliveira, L. A. P., Nepomuceno, M. C. S., & Andrade, J. M. A. (2013). Use of refurbished shipping container for the construction of housing buildings: Details for the structural project. *Journal of Civil Engineering and Management*, 1–9.

Bologna, R. (a cura). (2002). *La reversibilità del costruire*. Rimini: Maggioli Editore.

Faludi, J., Lepech, M. D., & Loisos, G. (2012). Using life cycle assessment methods to guide architectural decision-making for sustainable prefabricated modular buildings. *Journal of Green Building, 7*(3), 151–170.

Ginelli, E. (2010). La flessibilità tecno-tipologica nelle soluzioni progettuali e costruttive. In E. Bosio & W. Sirtori (Eds.), *Abitare. Il progetto della residenza sociale fra innovazione e tradizione*. Santarcangelo di Romagna: Maggioli Editore.

Ginelli, E., & Pozzi, G. (2017). Safety and energy controlled prefab building system. In *Conference and proceedings of SGEM VIENNA GREEN 2017* (Vol. 17, Issue 63, pp. 503–510). ISBN 978-619-7408-29-4/ISSN 1314-2704, 27–29 November 2017. https://doi.org/10.5593/sgem2017h/63/s26.064.

Giordano, R. (2010). I prodotti per l'edilizia sostenibile. La compatibilità ambientale dei materiali nel processo edilizio. Napoli: Esselibri S.p.A.: 243.

Giriunas, K., Sezen, H., & Dupaix, R. B. (2012). Evaluation, modeling, and analysis of shipping container-building structures. *Engineering Structures, 43,* 48–57.

Huanga, B., et al. (2018). Construction and demolition waste management in China through the 3R principle. *Resources, Conservation and Recycling, 129,* 36–44.
Islam, H., et al. (2016). Life cycle assessment of shipping container home: A sustainable construction. *Energy and Buildings, 128,* 673–685.
Jourda, F. H. (2010). *Petit manuel de la conception durable.* Paris: Archibooks + Sautereau.
Kotnik, J. (2008). *Container architecture.* Barcellona: Links.
Kramer, S. (2015). *The box, architectural solution with container.* Salenstein: Braun Editore.

Rethinking the Building Envelope as an Intelligent Community Hub for Renewable Energy Sharing

Andrea G. Mainini, Alberto Speroni, Matteo Fiori, Tiziana Poli, Juan Diego Blanco Cadena, Rita Pizzi and Enrico De Angelis

Abstract The widespread use of electric vehicles is hampered by the lack of an adequate charging points network. Likewise, and depending on the use, there could be a lack of correspondence between energy use and production in buildings equipped with renewable energy production systems. For these reasons, a modular device, which could be fully integrated into the building envelope, has been developed. The aim of the project was both to regenerate the existing building envelope and to enhance the newest one, adding new functions. The main goal will be the support of the growth of an electric power-sharing attitude capable of promoting the widespread use of electric vehicles of electric vehicle (EV), supporting strategic actions to retrofit/convert a private building in shared spaces for EV mobility, ensuring enough coverage for charging devices and reducing costs for public administration.

Keywords Building envelope · EV · Sharing BiPV · Ventilated façade · Electric mobility

1 Introduction

The building sector, currently recovering from a recession that has affected it in recent years, is in the need to enter overwhelmingly into the circular and digital transformation. The development of interconnected buildings and micro-grid neighborhood, in terms of management and service provision, will soon take place for the benefits of all building users, vehicle users and pedestrians (related to what today has been identified as the great transition to the Internet of things (IoT) and smart city). This driving force is generating product innovation, contextualized within the sharing

---

A. G. Mainini (✉) · A. Speroni · M. Fiori · T. Poli · J. D. Blanco Cadena · E. De Angelis
Architecture, Built Environment and Construction Engineering—ABC Department, Politecnico di Milano, Milan, Italy
e-mail: andreagiovanni.mainini@polimi.it

R. Pizzi
Dipartimento di Informatica Giovanni degli Antoni, Università degli studi di Milano, Milan, Italy

S. Della Torre et al. (eds.), *Regeneration of the Built Environment from a Circular Economy Perspective*, Research for Development,
https://doi.org/10.1007/978-3-030-33256-3_33

economy scheme, that is, the decision to share spaces in exchange for additional services that can be integrated and shared within locals and/or condominiums. This new paradigm is in fact, possible thanks to the introduction of newly available, scalable and modular technologies that meet the user demands (safety, security, monitoring and management).

The research project INCASe, funded by Regione Lombardia, makes part of this reference scenario. Its primary objective is to integrate modular shared charging points for light electric vehicles and within façades and/or enclosure systems in order to blend these systems into the urban fabric (see Fig. 1 for the set-up installation process and Fig. 2 for the device completeness detailing). The generated impact is the diffuse development of the neighborhood electrical vehicle (NEV) in urban areas and the creation of an interface to a scalable micro-smart grid by providing condominium recharging system. The project delivers, in addition to the development and integration of a charging device implemented within a building envelope system, the creation and application of a platform for managing and accounting the charging use by private individuals, through the use of a mobile app.

Fig. 1 Installation of the prototype module as a stand-alone device within the campus of Università degli studi di Milano

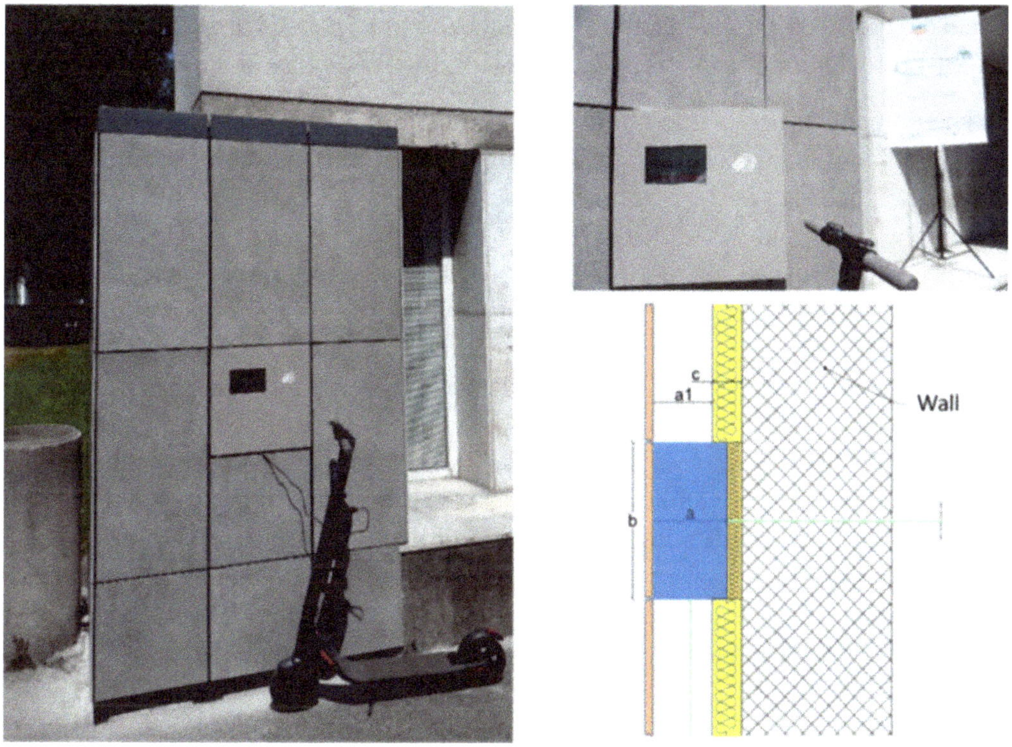

Fig. 2 Device completeness perspective, in situ demonstrator view (left and top right) and cross section (bottom right) where **a** and **b** are the dimension of the charging box, **a1** is the air gap dimension, **c** the insulation thickness

2 INCASe, Significance, Effect and Obtained Results

With the project INCASe (Integrated shared ChArge points for Smart buildings), software and hardware IoT have been developed, tested and perfectly immersed within a modular building element. This will enable the building to interface and communicate with the electrical grid, behaving then as a hub of the micro-grid acting as a shared sharing point for electrical vehicles. A scalable building component/device system prototype for electric mobility has been developed The proposed solution is the predisposed for intelligent electricity use and for the exploitation and enhancement of renewable resources used in the building aiming to reduce the need of use of the electricity grid for EV charging. Within the context of nearly zero energy buildings (NZEB), the device is able to:

Connect to both the electricity grid and to the private renewable energy sources produced in the building;

Recharge and manage electrical vehicles such as bicycles, scooters and mobility equipment for the disabled. The number of vehicles charged contemporarily will depend on the network availability; however, it will be optimized by power-sharing technologies;

Connect via open-communication protocols (i.e., Open Charge Point Protocol (OCPP) for additional app-based services).

The component is intended to be adaptable either to new buildings construction or to renovation interventions on existing buildings. In addition, it is suitable to be installed outdoors in parking areas, aside cycle paths, public access areas or can be installed as a stand-alone device. In this last solution, the system will be constructed using certified recycled material to maximize the reduction of ecological footprint. In Fig. 1, a series of photographs show the process of construction and integration of a portion of the new building envelope equipped with the INCASe module.

The system makes available and easily usable, by every individual user, fundamental information for the monitoring, optimization and enhancement of the electricity produced. Additional services that improve the building operation performance will be foreseen. Within these additional services, the following can be included: security control of the area, remote authorization for building access and the storage of orders placed with the courier. Likewise, the municipality would be able to have available shared charging spaces for the electrical mobility, guaranteeing the sufficient territory cover and reducing costs of implementation and management. In this way, the system is an alternative to the road infrastructure conversion and allows the efficient management of municipal spaces for free or paid parking otherwise necessary for recharging. The activities of sharing electrical vehicles or electricity provision will directly benefit the citizens by enhancing the use of these spaces, also due to the reduced costs of construction and maintenance.

3 Conclusions

The project is immersed within the context of the development of advanced sensor implementation for IoT devices, with the capabilities to be integrated for building automation at building scale through the installation of elements into a modular façade component enabling innovative interventions primarily on existing buildings.

The system will allow the acquisition of granular data coming either from the condominium's interior or from external affiliations of electrical vehicles that will be accessible for monitoring via the app-based environment and the cross-communication link with the device. Different techniques applied, would allow the real-time adaptation of the implemented functionalities for off-line analysis and profiling aimed at improving the service provided. Accordingly, it will be possible to allow the interaction of the device both with the electric vehicles plugged or with those registered for connection and with smart elements for building automation present in the condominium, primarily energy storage technologies (i.e., aside photovoltaics systems) and personal devices.

Acknowledgements The project, funded by Regione Lombardia for the call of proposals SMART LIVING—"Manifattura diffusa, creativa e tecnologica 4.0," was developed thanks to the participation of a large number of partners: Route220 srl—Evway (project leader); S&H Software & Hardware srl; Department of Informatics—Università degli Studi di Milano; Department of Architecture, Built Environment and Construction Engineering—SEEDLAB.ABC—Politecnico di Milano. All partners wish to thank AdermaLocatelli Group for the contribution and support given for the realization of the first prototype and sample exhibited at the Festival of Sustainable Development 2019.

Bibliography

Buonomano, A., Calise, F., Cappiello, F. L., Palombo, A., & Vicidomini, M. (2019). Dynamic analysis of the integration of electric vehicles in efficient buildings fed by renewables. *Applied Energy, 245,* 31–50.

Camarinha-Matos, L. M. (2016). Collaborative smart grids—A survey on trends. *Renewable and Sustainable Energy Reviews, 65,* 283–294.

Geelen, D., Reinders, A., & Keyson, D. (2013). Empowering the end-user in smart grids: Recommendations for the design of products and services. *Energy Policy, 61,* 151–161.

Kahrobaeian, A., & Mohamed, Y. A. R. I. (2012). Interactive distributed generation interface for flexible micro-grid operation in smart distribution systems. *IEEE Transactions on Sustainable Energy, 3*(2), 295–305.

Kılkış, Ş., & Kılkış, B. (2019). An urbanization algorithm for districts with minimized emissions based on urban planning and embodied energy towards net-zero exergy targets. *Energy, 179,* 392–406.

Pelletier, S., Jabali, O., & Laporte, G. (2019). The electric vehicle routing problem with energy consumption uncertainty. *Transportation Research Part B: Methodological, 126,* 225–255.

Salpakari, J., Rasku, T., Lindgren, J., & Lund, P. D. (2017). Flexibility of electric vehicles and space heating in net zero energy houses: An optimal control model with thermal dynamics and battery degradation. *Applied Energy, 190,* 800–812.

Wang, Y., Nazaripouya, H., Chu, C. C., Gadh, R., & Pota, H. R. (2014). Vehicle-to-grid automatic load sharing with driver preference in micro-grids. In *IEEE PES Innovative Smart Grid Technologies, Europe* (pp. 1–6). IEEE.

Wei, J., & Yu, Z. (2011). Load sharing techniques in hybrid power systems for DC micro-grids. In *2011 Asia-Pacific power and energy engineering conference* (pp. 1–4). IEEE.

Adaptive Exoskeleton Systems: *Remodelage* for Social Housing on Piazzale Visconti (BG)

Oscar E. Bellini

Abstract To promote the renewal and sustainable requalification of social housing in Lombardy means to carry out research in order to identify solutions as efficient and effective as possible, which do not involve the demolition of the building but promote its enhancement. Today it is possible to intervene on existing buildings with new strategies which give all-round and multipurpose solutions to the general issues, using techniques that go beyond punctual interventions and extend the useful life cycle of the built environment. The seismic upgrade must be at the basis of every project within construction. Thanks to an adaptive exoskeleton system it is possible to innovate the architectural image, to support an equitable and sustainable development based on the prevention and risk management connected to unexpected seismic events and to guarantee aspects of structural safety and physical integrity of the users, to improve the morphological, spatial and typological organization of buildings. By using an exoskeleton system, it is possible to innovate the architectural make-up, to support an equitable and sustainable development based on the prevention and the risk management connected to unexpected seismic events. A way to take into due consideration the now unavoidable aspects of structural safety and physical integrity of the users. This paper, part of a Departmental Study, presents the first guidelines to the renewal of social housing buildings owned by Aler Bergamo, Lecco, Sondrio on Piazzale Visconti in Bergamo.

Keywords Social housing · Exoskeleton · Built environment · Integrated design · Resilience

O. E. Bellini (✉)
Architecture, Built Environment and Construction Engineering—ABC Department, Politecnico di Milano, Milan, Italy
e-mail: oscar.bellini@polimi.it

S. Della Torre et al. (eds.), *Regeneration of the Built Environment from a Circular Economy Perspective*, Research for Development,
https://doi.org/10.1007/978-3-030-33256-3_34

1 A New Strategy to Build In and On the Built

> We are an extraordinary and beautiful country but at the same time very fragile. [The landscape is fragile and Cities are fragile, especially suburbs where no one has spent time and money to maintain them. But it is precisely the suburbs that are the city of the future, [...] one that we will bequeath to our children. We need to carry out a monumental project of "mending" and we need ideas. (Piano 2014)

This important statement by the Italian architect Renzo Piano underlines the strategic importance of intervening in the obsolete construction of our suburbs and introduces the imperative and need to put forward new ideas to pursue the objective now recognized on the political, economic and disciplinary level to intervene in the built environment[1] (Murie et al. 2003).

Few are the designers who have the skills and professionalism to know what to do about the enormous, at least in terms of size, built heritage present in these realities starting from the great real estate assets, such as public housing. This enormous building heredity, which dates back to the second post-war period, now constitutes a significant part of our suburbs in terms of quantity, and it must be "adjusted", in line with a much needed responsible initiative.[2] This paper describes a pragmatic proposal for the redesign of post-Second World War buildings based on the most recent international experiences and provides an operational instrument for the "integrated" and "adaptive" redevelopment of built environments: on a structural, technological, typological, morphological, functional, performance, economic and social level of social housing real estate.[3]

2 Integrated Design in Social Housing: Looking for a New Balance

According to scientific literature, there are different ways of intervening on built environments without resorting to demolition. These methods can be traced back to key attitudes, which must absolutely be integrated with one another, so that the

[1] In 2017, the European Union Prize for Contemporary Architecture—Mies Van der Rohe Award was awarded to a Dutch project for the renovation and rental of a social housing building. The award was given to NL Architects, XVW Architecture kleinburg DeFlat, Amsterdam, 2013–2016. Although in Italy social housing is less developed than in other European countries, it still represents a far from negligible asset with performance deficits that are largely the same as those of private assets. This means the study field should extend to include the entire housing sector.

[2] Building rehabilitation projects are interventions to create new dwelling habits, new uses, new functions and new aesthetic and architecture solutions.

[3] The European Committee for the Promotion of Housing Rights considers social housing as services provision for those without access to the housing market in order to reinforce their position within the community. It is possible to associate the term "social housing" with the public housing sector.

project intervention can have value (Zambelli 2004; Grecchi 2008; Malinghetti 2011; Ascione 2012; Perriccioli 2015; Paris and Bianchi 2018).

The priority intervention concerns the structural system of the building. In a country with a high seismic risk like Italy, it is essential to approach constructions by facing this criticality, in which many situations present itself as a priority that could undo all the other retrofit actions of the building, starting from economic ones. An adaptive exoskeleton can be used to improve this aspect, promoting these actions and improving the situation. It is a device inspired by the external structure of certain invertebrates, similar to medical prosthetic support, which intervenes in the deteriorated parts, restoring and implementing its characteristics and performance.

Applied to buildings, it defines an independent volumetric expansion, thanks a structure of autonomous foundations, to be juxtaposed to the façades, where it creates new spaces and volume. It can act as a support to a new rooftop architecture, additional shaped boxes or new floor surfaces to rethink dwellings.

The adaptive exoskeleton can help interventions on a variety of levels: structural, as a system for static and seismic strengthening; energetic, as a device used to reduce consumption and the environmental impact and to increase living comfort; typological, in terms of an opportunity to reorganize and redesign dwelling-sizes; functional, as an opportunity for the inclusion of new horizontal and vertical connections and architectural, for the technological rethinking of the interface between the inside and outside of the building.[4]

In order to use the exoskeleton system, we must carry out an accurate analysis with regards to feasibility analysis and convenience of the intervention, not only for economic reasons but also for an ecological opportunity, in order to take into account, the environmental "costs" resulting from any demolition or reconstruction (Boeri and Longo 2012). In terms of energy eco-efficiency, adaptive exoskeletons are to be preferred to a "radical construction solution"—which demolishes in order to reconstruct—since they minimize, from the initial stages of the design, the use of raw materials and reduce yard waste debris.

Today, the main techniques for seismic reinforcement are referable within a local approach, which consists in the consolidation of the structure with a punctual strengthening of the frame nodes, beams and pillars and in the global approach, in which the building is retrofitted using the addition of earthquake-resistant elements.

While punctual reinforcement interventions are very expensive, invasive and destructive, the adaptive exoskeleton is applied from the outside of the building and can be economically more convenient if integrated with other retrofitting interventions. The exoskeleton structure can be added to buildings working from the outside in the form of a double skin. This can be designed in two alternative ways: (a) integrating additional bracing walls within the exoskeleton (walls solution); (b) designing the exoskeleton itself as an earthquake-resistant box-shaped system (shell

[4]This constructive solution is very similar to the design research and the works of the French architects Lacaton and Vassal.

solution). The choice of the structural solution depends on the initial stiffness of the building and may be conceived as over-resistant or dissipative. The box-shaped solution allows for the reduction of the stresses in the elements, by reducing the thickness of the additional skin and the adoption of specific elements with the double objective of improving energy efficiency along with the safety of the building. The wall solutions include, among others, the use of braces or walls with rigid or dissipative connections, walls hinged at the base, rocking walls, adaptive seismic walls and dissipative braces. The shell solution involves the creation of a new skin, a diaphragm in which the entire façade structure becomes an earthquake-resistant element (e.g. upgrade of grid shell and curtain wall or coating with resistant panels) (Marini et al. 2016; Passoni 2016; Scuderi 2016).

These techniques, integrating and overlapping on a holistic basis, can produce a lot of effects and benefits at different levels. They (a) allow for the upcycling of the building structure, improve seismic resistance and resilience; (b) reduce the environmental impact associated with seismic risk; (c) increase real estate value; (d) protect the long-term economic investment, which could be compromised by the damage caused by earthquakes; (e) reduce the cost of restructuring due to increased resilience; ensure the coexistence in a single construction site of the architectural, structural and energy renovation; (f) cancel out costs for the relocation of residents during the work by intervening on the outside; (g) allow for the addition or expansion of housing (rooftop, addition, etc.), thanks to new indoor and outdoor surfaces, the sale of which can partially compensate the renovation costs; (h) promote urban densification policies, through volumetric expansions, by reducing the consumption of land; allow for the morpho-techno-typological redefinition of the building, that can be redesigned in its vertical and horizontal connecting elements; (i) promote urban regeneration; create more pleasant, sustainable and resilient environments (Bellini et al. 2018). To increase the environmental value of the renovation, it is fundamental to reconsider the operational approaches within the life cycle thinking, aiming at maximizing performance and minimizing the impacts and environmental costs of the building life cycle (Antonini et al. 2011; Bellomo and Pone 2011; Paris and Bianchi 2018).

In addition to protecting the static aspects and monitoring the borderline states of the system (performance-based design), the structural design refers to the choice of materials—eco-efficient and recyclable—and technologies—prefabricated, dry, reparable and adaptable—according to principles of minimization of the environmental and economic impacts (life cycle assessment and life cycle costs), implementing the concepts of system sustainability and resilience (Bellini et al. 2018).

3 Objectives and Aims of the Research and Sourcing Process

The Departmental Study, financed by Aler[5] Bergamo, Lecco, Sondrio and entitled "Preliminary guidelines for seismic resilience and urban regeneration, through an adaptive exoskeleton, of the settlement of public social housing on Piazzale Ermes Visconti", aims to explore the possible technical solutions to improve the housing, quality and technological performance of the buildings in Bergamo, without resorting to total demolition and subsequent reconstruction from scratch.[6]

The Aler's need is above all to identify constructive guidelines to be used on buildings without having to relocate the tenants residing in their own homes.

In this context, after a series of studies and analyses of the buildings, a multifaceted approach was proposed to Aler. The aim of the work is to investigate the solutions and systems to rehabilitate Aler real estate and to verify how it could be implemented by adopting an innovative strategy: a sort of prosthesis, an *adaptive exoskeleton* to be applied to the social housing buildings.

Aler wanted to use a paradigmatic solution that was adaptable to its decaying buildings. A solution that can easily be modified over time to integrate new social, economic and urban conditions. An open system that helps buildings respond to environmental, economic, functional and social challenges. Not a solution that crystallizes the building's image and prepares it for its future obsolescence but a "radical solution". A design process and method that increases the settlement density of the urban block, without consuming new ground. The guidelines proposed to use an adaptive exoskeleton: an independent but collaborative anti-seismic structure.[7]

The first step is to improve the quality of the buildings and to facilitate the new functional and typological layouts required over time by the local users. This system is designed to extend the building's life cycle through a gradual adaptation that reduces the effects of environmental stress on the building and spreads it out over a longer time span. This system is a structure of metal scaffolding that can be applied and connected to the buildings that require rehabilitation. It is important to emphasize how this technology relies on "dry assembly" and reversible technological solutions that allow for cost reduction and recycling of building materials and provide a viable alternative to the building replacement and its high environmental impact.

---

[5]ALER (Agenzia Lombarda Edilizia Residenziale) is an Agency that promote and manage social housing in the Lombardy Region.

[6]The urban block covers an area of about 5,500 m^2 and occupies a strategic position at "Villaggio degli Sposi". It has a regular shape and a good supply of vegetation. The urban block is entirely occupied by social housing which are not well maintained nor well preserved. The buildings are arranged in an L shape and are composed of 24 (16 + 8) houses with stairs and no elevators. The buildings were built with a masonry structure made of blocks of load-bearing bricks in the early '50s and they are critical from an energetic, structural and technologic point of view.

[7]Norme tecniche per le costruzioni, NTC, 2008. D.M. January 14, 2008.

The exoskeleton may perform both a two-dimensional action through the definition of façade refurbishment (recladding, refitting and overcladding) and a three-dimensional action defined by volume additions (individual boxes, bioclimatic greenhouses towers and continuous or overall additions) (Guidolin 2016).

The guidelines proposed by Visconti aim to be a pursuit of cross-disciplinary design instruments for the achievement of "holistic and integrated regeneration" for public social housing. They want to be an articulated map of mediations and insights about strategies to build in and on the built environment, based on two fundamental aspects: the first is supported by sociological positions according to which a refined and careful designed environment produces a sense of place implicitly as its own, it follows that the rehabilitation action assumes a value of raising the social position even before the economic value of the area or of the building. The second—the maximization of resources—is part of the broader theme of respecting the environment which is supported by actions such as attention to land use and the definition of technical/technological solutions aimed at active and passive energy saving.

The rehabilitation project has shown that the interpretation of emotional and physical roots of the inhabitants in relation to their everyday life becomes a plus towards both the housing and the urban landscape transformation if in addition to these results there are clear and well-defined strategies in terms of execution, reliability, management and funding. This study's primary aim is to show the feasibility of the building rehabilitation approach not only in energetic terms but primarily in relation to the quality increase of structural safety and housing services.

The definition of the metadesign intervention for the "Remodelage"[8] of the Aler lodgings on Piazzale Visconti was based on the following aspects: (a) general aspects: the process of building rehabilitation can be an interesting topic from several points of view because it is closely related to other issues such as economic recovery and employment, urban regeneration, cohesion and social participation. The recovery of social unease in the social housing of Piazzale Visconti must be tackled minimally with the simple building recovery of dwellings bordering on the urban decay. The provision of outdoor collective spaces in agreement with the dignity of the person and designed for "public social housing" can lead, as well as to social assistance programs, to an improvement of their condition. (b) Technical aspects: the energy aspect is only one important variable in the process as it has many funding opportunities, but at times, it can seem to limit.[9] Thus, the first action that has been proposed to Aler concerned the structural system of the buildings on Piazzale Visconti (Figs. 1 and 2).

[8]The team was created by Roland Castro for the regeneration of the Grands Ensembles in the French banlieues. Castro and Denissof (2005), [Re]modeler, Métamorphoser, Le Moniteur, Paris.

[9]Instead the systemic approach is most evident in this project: the REHA-PUCA French program which aims at identifying innovative solutions suitable for building rehabilitation of sample buildings through a competition open to groups made up of designers and contractors. Three guidelines are identified: diversification, management and densification, interpreting the economy of territorial space in order to avoid further land use.

Fig. 1 Urban block of Piazzale Visconti with five buildings dedicated to public social housing. The three identical buildings are owned by the Municipality of Bergamo; the others belong to Aler

Fig. 2 Topographic survey of the Piazzale Visconti block and quantification of the new building volume. The entire block is intended for public housing

This leads to preventive practices that reduce structural vulnerability to seismic actions, planning methodologies that promote a rational use of resources, an enhancement of the built environment and the preservation of human life (Marotta and Zirilli 2015). Interventions that provide an alternative to the traditional "scrapping/demolition" and transcend the practice of "abandoning what does not work". It is possible to exceed the ideological dilemma between demolition/conservation and inaugurate a "third way". A design method which today is prefigured in Parasite, Rooftop and Hybrid architecture (Boeri and Longo 2012; Angi et al. 2012; Angi 2016a, b; Montuori 2016).

The project contents go beyond the conventional methods that define sustainability as related just to an energy upgrade, by introducing solutions on the structural safety and stability aspects relating to the increasingly frequent seismic phenomena as well (Marini et al. 2016). The sustainability of an intervention is also related to the impacts of damage and collapse due to possible earthquakes during the life cycle of the retrofitted building (Murie et al. 2003; Feroldi 2014; Belleri and Marini 2016).

In the disciplinary debate, ranging from "scrapping" to "mending", it appears reasonable to use the potential of the adaptive exoskeleton system (Marini et al. 2017). In this way, it is possible to integrate a design approach that allows to implement the resilience of buildings. This device improves the performance, through an external supporting and cooperating prosthesis, which is not simply earthquake resistant, but also technological, considering that it facilitates the realization of "double integrated skin solutions" with which to obtain a new frontier between exterior and interior, in order to improve energy efficiency and promote the architectural restyling of the building (Guidolin 2016). The use of the exoskeleton facilitates the morpho-techno-typological rethinking of the existing structure and allows for the activation of urban densification policies (Boeri and Longo 2012) and for the urban regeneration of the social and functional substrate (Di Giulio 2013).

4 Conclusions

The research on social housing buildings on Piazzale Visconti aims to demonstrate the potential to use innovative technical strategies for the rational maintenance of real estate directed at the architectural recovery and reconfiguring of social housing stock, improving the performance and quality of the environment built.

Today, it is possible to apply retrofitting processes in opposition with demolitions and reconstructions, above all in terms of social and environmental costs.

We have articulated social, economic and technological critical situations, in which it is possible to adopt external structures to help the integrated refurbishment. This device is the exoskeleton system.

It allows for construction from outside the building minimizing inside work within the housing unit. It is an "innovative device" to connect technological and social issues in the organization of a particular building site management process. It allows for the regular execution of building functions, thus containing the costs of the building site.

The exoskeleton systems can have different configurations. It allows users to achieve sufficient settlement density, creating the possibility of carrying out new housing. It is an external structural grid that gives the designer and user a certain level of customization freedom, above all in terms of the morphological and functional configuration of the façade, which can be read as an interface system between private interior space and public space.

The adaptive exoskeleton systems are able to create balconies, greenhouses, etc.; technological elements for shading control can be added; the architectural morphology and typology can be reconfigured and some customized functions can be considered. It is possible to get a new building: a new architecture (Fig. 3).

The integrated rehabilitation actively involves users and designers, through a device that connects technological innovation and social need for involvement, in order to assign an active role to the user in a process through which they are strictly interested in providing a new aesthetic identity to buildings. A design process that requires significant disciplinary skills: skills that today Department of Architecture, Built environment and Construction engineering of the Politecnico di Milano can provide.

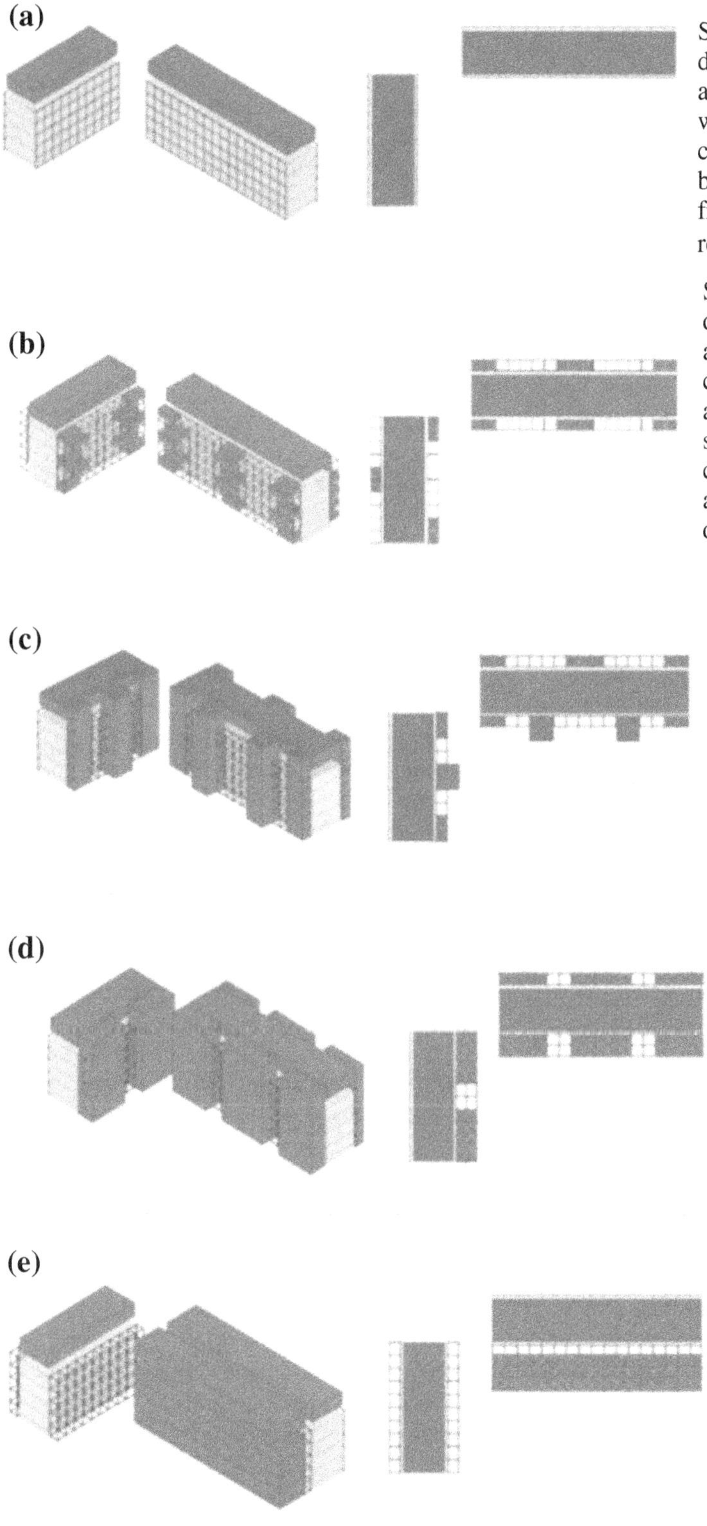

(a) Solution for two-dimensional exoskeleton application solution, in which to apply rooftop architecture, façade refurbishment, recladding, refitting, overcladding for retrofit.

(b) Solution for three-dimensional exoskeleton application, where the concept is to build rooftop architecture, punctual box-shaped (box, loggias, balconies, greenhouses etc.) and to redesign indoor dwellings.

(c) Solution for three-dimensional exoskeleton application, where the concept is to build rooftop architecture, new boxes, loggias, balconies, greenhouses etc., to redesign indoor dwellings and staircases, lifts etc.

(d) Solution with a three-dimensional exoskeleton application, where the concept is to build rooftop architecture, to double up floor levels creatinine a new gallery,

(e) Solution with a three-dimensional exoskeleton application, where the concept is to build rooftop architecture, doubling floor levels with a central corridor building type and new dwellings increasing urban density and residents

Fig. 3 Five morpho-techno-typological solutions obtainable by adaptive exoskeleton system

References

Angi, B. (2016a). *Amnistia per l'esistente. Strategie architettoniche adattive per la riqualificazione dell'ambiente costruito*. Siracusa: LetteraVentidue Editore.

Angi, B. (Ed.). (2016b). *Eutopia urbana/Eutopia Urbanscape*. Siracusa: LetteraVentidue.

Angi, B., Botti, M., & Montuori, M. (2012). "Eutopia urbana. La manutenzione ragionata dell'edilizia sociale" Abitare il nuovo/Abitare di nuovo ai tempi della crisi, Clean Edizioni. In *Abitare il nuovo/Abitare di nuovo ai tempi della crisi*, 12–13 dicembre 2012 (pp. 1771–1785). Università degli Studi di Napoli Federico II—Dipartimento di Progettazione Urbana e Urbanistica.

Antonini, E., Gaspari, J., & Olivieri, G. (2011). "Densifying to upgrading: Strategies for improving the social housing built stock in Italy". *Techne*, *4*, 306–314.

Ascione, P. (2012). Cognitive study and upgrading of the 20th century architectonic heritage: Experiences and methodologies. *Techne, 3,* 250–261.

Belleri, A., & Marini, A. (2016). Does seismic risk affect the environmental impact of existing buildings? *Energy and Buildings, 110*(1), 149–158.

Bellini, O. E., Marini, A., & Passoni, C. (2018). Adaptive exoskeleton systems for the resilience of the built environment. *Techne, 15,* 71–80.

Bellomo, M., & Pone, S. (2011). Technological retrofit of existing buildings: Dwelling quality, environmental sustainability, economic rising. *Techne, 1,* 82–87.

Boeri, A., & Longo, D. (2012). From the redevelopment of high-density suburban areas to sustainable cities. *Architectoni.ca, 2,* 118–130.

Castro, R., & Denissof, S. (2005). *[Re]Modeler, Métamorphoser*. Paris: Le Moniteur.

Di Giulio, R. (2013). *Paesaggi periferici. Strategie di rigenerazione urbana*. Macerata: Quodlibet Studio, Città e Paesaggio.

Feroldi, F. (2014). *Sustainable renewal of the post WWII building stock through engineered double skin, allowing for structural retrofit, energy efficiency upgrade, architectural restyling and urban regeneration* (Ph.D. thesis). University of Brescia.

Grecchi, M. (2008). *Il recupero delle periferie urbane. Da emergenza a risorsa strategica per la rivitalizzazione delle metropoli*. Rimini: Maggioli.

Guidolin, F. (2016). Taxonomy of the redevelopment methods for non-listed architecture: From façade refurbishment to the exoskeleton system. In A. Caverzan, T. M. Lamperti, & P. Negro (Eds.), *A roadmap for the improvement of earthquake resistance and eco-efficiency of existing buildings and cities, Proceedings of Safesust Joint Research Centre* (pp. 97–102). Ispra.

Malinghetti, L. E. (2011). Recupero edilizio. Strategie per il riuso e tecnologie costruttive, Il Sole 24 Ore, Milano.

Marini, A., Passoni, C., Belleri, A. Feroldi, F., Preti, M., Metelli, G., et al. (2017). Combining seismic retrofit with energy refurbishment for the sustainable renovation of RC buildings: A proof of concept. *European Journal of Environmental and Civil Engineering*, 1–20.

Marini, A., Passoni, C., Belleri, A., Feroldi, F., Preti, M., Riva, P., et al. (2016). Need for coupling energy refurbishment with structural strengthening interventions. In B. Angi (Ed.), *Eutopia urbanscape. The combined redevelopment of social housing* (pp. 83–115).

Marotta, N., & Zirilli, O. (2015). Disastri e Catastrofi. Rischio, esposizione, vulnerabilità e resilienza. Milano: FrancoAngeli.

Montuori, M. (2016). E pluribus unum, in Angi B. (a cura di/edited by). Eutopia Urbana/Eutopia Urbanscape. Siracusa: Lettera Ventidue, pp. 11–43.

Montuori, M., Angi, B., Botti, M., & Longo, O. (2012). "The rational maintenance of social housing (with a warlike modesty)". In *Cities in transformation. Research & stamp; design, Housing and the shape of the city* (65–68), Politecnico di Milano, 7–10 giugno 2012, Milano.

Murie, A., Knorr-Siedow, T., & Van Kempen, R. (2003). *Large housing estates in Europe: General developments and theoretical backgrounds*. RESTATE report. Urban and Regional Research Centre, Utrecht University.

Paris, S., & Bianchi, R. (2018). *Ri-abitare il moderno. Il progetto per il rinnovo dell'housing*. Macerata: Quodlibet.
Passoni, C. (2016). *Holistic renovation of existing RC buildings: A framework for possible integrated structural interventions* (Ph.D. thesis). University of Brescia.
Perriccioli, M. (2015). *Re-cycling social housing, Ricerche per la rigenerazione sostenibile dell'edilizia residenziale sociale*. Napoli: Clean.
Piano, R. (2014). Il rammendo delle periferie. IlSole24 Ore, domenica, 26 gennaio.
Scuderi, G. (2016). Adaptive building exoskeletons. A biomimetic model for the rehabilitation of social housing. *International Journal of Architectural Research, 9*(1), 134–143.
Zambelli, E. (2004). Ristrutturazione e trasformazione del costruito, Il Sole 24 Ore, Milano.

Assessing Water Demand of Green Roofs Under Variants of Climate Change Scenarios

Matteo Fiori, Tiziana Poli, Andrea G. Mainini, Juan Diego Blanco Cadena, Alberto Speroni and Daniele Bocchiola

Abstract Green roofs are a resource for the city: they mitigate pollution, decrease the urban heat island effect (UHI), and regulate storm runoff. Within a climate change scenario, green roofs might instead become an issue, and in particular, in mitigating UHI at mesoscale level. The aim of the contribution is to define the water balance and thus the water consumption of a typical green roof, considering its variation when immersed into different climate scenarios that took place in the past five years (Linked with the following research projects: (1) *Research title*: 2016, *Fondazione Minoprio/Politecnico di Milano, Dipartimento ABC (ongoing)*, *Research type*: Convention, *Responsible*: Matteo Fiori. (2) *Research title*: 2018, Harpo Contract (ongoing), *Research type*: Funded by third parties, *Responsible*: Matteo Fiori. (3) *Research title*: 2018, Soprema Contract (ongoing), *Research type*: Funded by third parties, *Responsible*: Matteo Fiori. (4) *Research title*: 2018, ASSIMP T-dry Contract (ongoing), *Research type*: Funded by third parties, *Responsible*: Matteo Fiori).

Keywords Climate change · Green roof · Sustainable water management

1 Green Roof Water Demand and Climate Change

The content of water in green roofs affects the thermal performance of the roof surface layer, given the modified conductivity of the ground layer and the evaporative effect generated by the water state change. Green roofs have proven to be a good strategy for reducing the urban heat island effect, the storm water runoff in low water permeability surfaces areas, air pollutant concentrations, plus the reduction of solar gains from the roof exposure (Demuzere et al. 2014).

M. Fiori · T. Poli (✉) · A. G. Mainini · J. D. Blanco Cadena · A. Speroni
Architecture, Built Environment and Construction Engineering—ABC Department, Politecnico di Milano, Milan, Italy

D. Bocchiola
Department of Civil and Environmental Engineering—DICA, Politecnico di Milano, Milan, Italy

S. Della Torre et al. (eds.), *Regeneration of the Built Environment from a Circular Economy Perspective*, Research for Development,
https://doi.org/10.1007/978-3-030-33256-3_35

Nevertheless, climate change is threatening the efficiency of these alternatives, given the strong heat stress, the large amplitude of the temperature variation to which the vegetation is exposed, and/or the increase of water vapor and decrease of liquid water in warm seasons (i.e., higher air's water vapor carrying capacity) (Wong et al. 2012). In consequence, some vegetation might not withstand the climate variations undergone at their location, modifying the thermal properties of the green roof (Paolini 2015). Fiori et al. (2013) and Simmons et al. (2008) have studied green roof performance for different green roof types, obtaining significant variance according to the combinations of soil, vegetation, and irrigation. Simmons et al. (2008) explored the variance of green roof maximum runoff retention and thermal properties at different water contents, for different green roofs' layer composition. Farrell et al. (2012) studied the survival of green roofs' vegetation when subjected to drought, testing their tolerance to limited irrigation, highlighting the importance of proper selection of the type of vegetation according to the climate.

Environmental alterations have been witnessed during the last five years (Wong et al. 2012); thus the way the green roof would respond for delivering the desired heat rejection. The research intends to show how the green roof has adapted to the variations in the temperature changes along the past decade and how these variances could be aided by the control of water content delivered to their vegetation and stored within the soil.

The following study has been presented and developed by SEEDLab.ABC, ABC Department, and Politecnico di Milano. All data has been surveyed thanks to the sensor installation done by METEOLab.ABC, and the data monitoring is carried out by SEEDLab.ABC. From the stored data, outdoor temperature, relative humidity (RH), total solar radiation, surface temperatures, and water content have been inspected for a green roof of a two-story office building in Milan, Italy (45° 28′ 47″N; 9° 13′ 47″E). The green roof is divided into eight parcels with different vegetation, plus a gravel-filled reference parcel, representing the original finishing of the roof. Each layer temperature has been surveyed to establish the heat transfer through them. A plan view of the green roof is shown in Fig. 1. The sensor distribution is described in the roof slab cross section as shown in Fig. 2. The data collected has been confronted to see how the local climate variances have affected the heat transfer.

2 Weather and Green Roof Condition Variance

All the data gathered has been condensed into three typical days for summer, mid-season, and winter. From the average value encountered for the 24 h of June, March, and December, this was done for green roof parcels 5 (i.e., vegetation layer as sedum on moss) and 6 (i.e., vegetation layer as sedum on lapillus), during 2012, 2017, and 2018. Air temperature, relative humidity, and total solar radiation data, gathered from an on-site weather station, have been screened, together with the surface temperatures. Figure 3a shows how the fluctuation on solar radiation is high for March (i.e., ~1.5 times higher in 2012 than in 2018), but the air temperatures are approximately

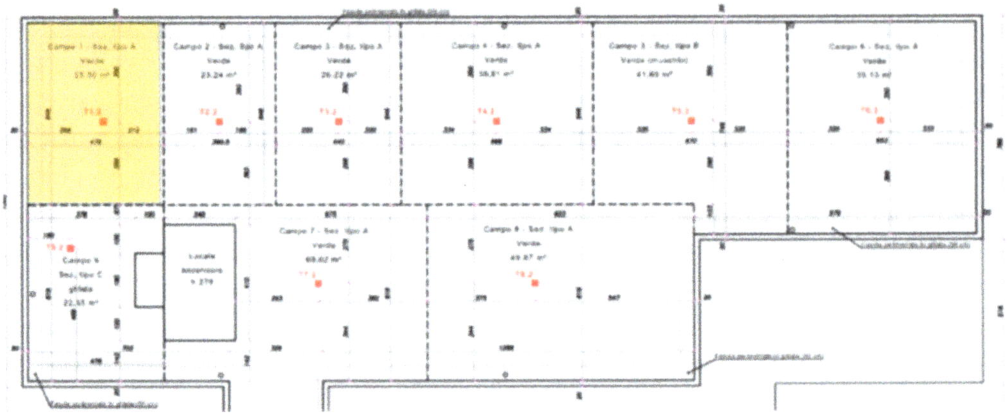

Fig. 1 Green roof plan view specifying sensor location. This work has concentrated on roof 5 and 6 (i.e., sedum on moss and sedum on lapillus). All dimensions are presented in cm by © SEEDLab.ABC, ABC Department, and Politecnico di Milano. Vegetation type is then described beside Fig. 2

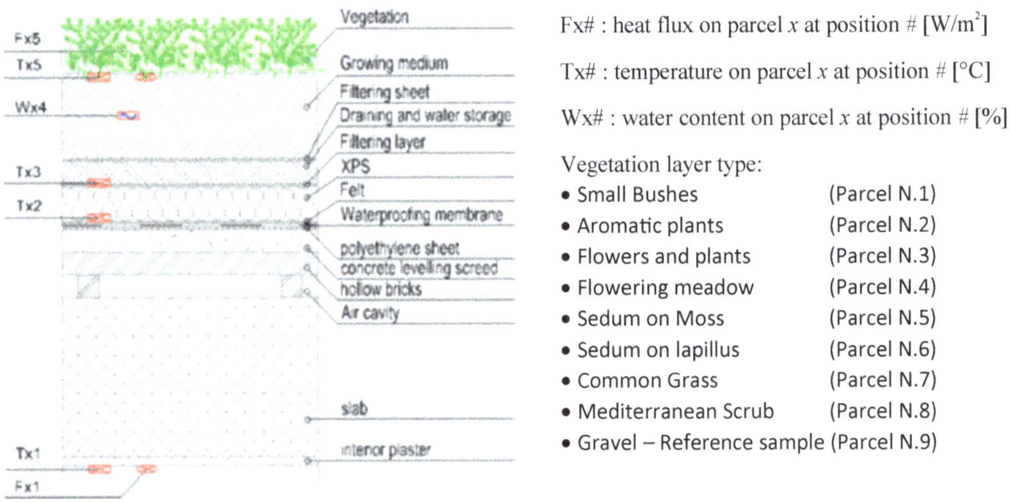

Fig. 2 Roof construction layer configuration, sensor location, and labeling. On the right, the description of the vegetation layer type for every parcel

similar for all three years (i.e., 2012, 2017, and 2018). Meanwhile, for air temperature during December, a difference of ~2° and ~3° was found from 2012 to 2017 and 2018, respectively (Fig. 3c), for a rather similar solar radiation exposure. The most significant behavior fluctuations can be seen for March and June (see Fig. 3a, b) for the heat flux F65, installed at greenery level on the exterior surface, monitored from 2012 to 2017 and the surface temperature T55 surveyed from 2012 to 2017 or 2018. Even at rather similar air temperatures and solar radiation average values, not only the amplitude of the hourly average during a day is significant (especially for the former) but also there is a notorious different trend (in particular, from T55-2012 to T55-2017 or 2018). This could be explained given the notorious difference on water

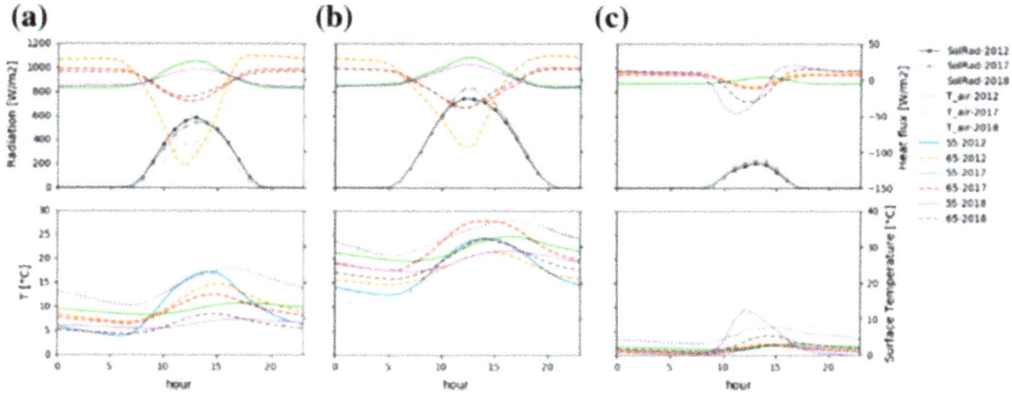

Fig. 3 Air and surface temperature, solar radiation, and heat transfer behavior ([+] toward environment, [−] toward room) for a typical day in **a** March (mid-season); **b** June (summer); **c** December (winter)

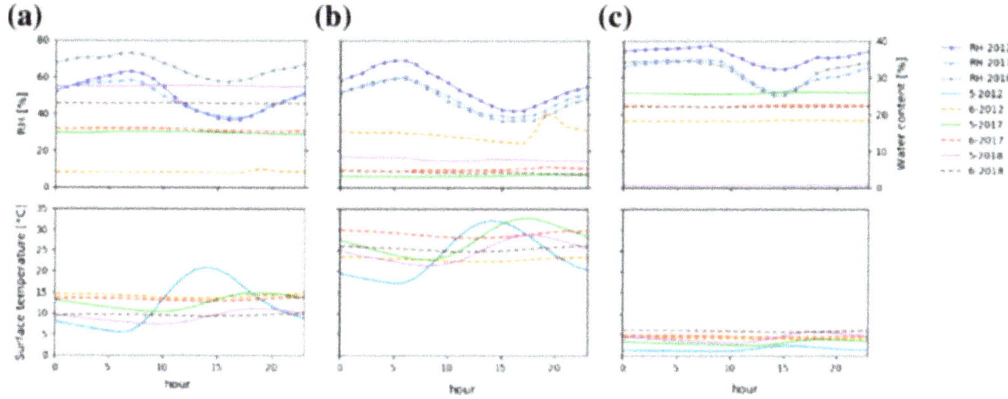

Fig. 4 Soil water content and external side of the insulation layer temperature behavior on a typical day for **a** March (mid-season); **b** June (summer); **c** December (winter)

content of the soil from 2012 to 2017, that is from ~4 to ~15% probably supplied throughout irrigation (hence, the similar values of RH; see Fig. 4a).

From Fig. 4, it can be concluded that most of the soil's water content was given by the water input transported through irrigation, as there can be seen almost no influence of the air's RH.

3 Heat Influx Behavior Change

As internal air temperatures are designed to fluctuate within a range, it is normal to find a moderately constant behavior of ceiling surface temperature as shown in Fig. 5. Only the visible oscillations go along the trend of the external air temperature.

On the other hand, the heat flux read by the sensor at the interior surface has a very particular behavior for March and December (see Fig. 5a, c), with a peak on

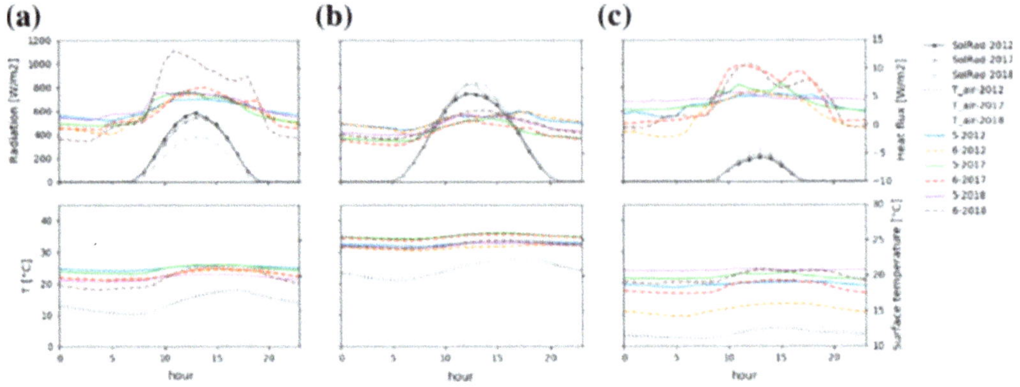

Fig. 5 Internal surface temperature and heat transfer behavior variance for a typical day in **a** March (mid-season); **b** June (summer); **c** December (winter)

the early occupancy hours and by the end of occupancy hours that correspond to the presence of internal heat gains combined with the most direct beam solar radiation entering the room beneath the roof surface. In 2018 and 2017, with a higher water content on the soil, it is noted that the heat flux from the interior to the exterior is larger; meanwhile, the heat coming from the exterior is lower.

It shall be noted as well how the two different types of vegetation (greenery and moss) on the green roofs behave in terms of inward heat flux, especially for March and June (see Fig. 3a, b). The green roof type 5 seems to have a greater water content retention (presents higher water content), thus, a lower peak amplitude, and it turns positive around midday. In contrast, green roof type 6 presents a much higher amplitude, in particular for March and June of 2012 (>−90 W/m^2) given its vegetation's high evaporative properties, and it is always on the opposite flux trajectory.

4 Conclusions

Green roofs are key passive strategies that bring great benefit in terms of sustainability to the urban scale and of energy savings to the local building scale. It must be noted that it is not a strategy that behaves equally throughout the year; it varies in accordance with the soil water content and the vegetation cover.

The significant variance of the green roof behavior at different water contents has been presented, and how climate fluctuations alter the green roof's thermal performance, requiring higher water input that determines different thermal conductivity values of the soil.

Further studies are foreseen to evaluate the water input required per each roof, maintaining a constant water content and how the roof's thermal performance varies throughout the year; measure roofs' vegetation proliferation and compare the thermal performance at normalized vegetation density conditions; and compare the aging effect on the roof's performance for green and cool roofs exposed to the same weathering conditions. Moreover, additional work is expected when more data is collected, that is after ten years of exposure and data collection, evaluating the presumed climate change effect on sustainable building passive strategies.

References

Demuzere, M., Orru, K., Heidrich, O., Olazabal, E., Geneletti, D., Orru, H., et al. (2014). Mitigating and adapting to climate change: Multi-functional and multi-scale assessment of green urban infrastructure. *Journal of Environmental Management, 146,* 107–115.

Farrell, C., Mitchell, R. E., Szota, C., Rayner, J. P., & Williams, N. S. G. (2012). Green roofs for hot and dry climates: Interacting effects of plant water use, succulence and substrate. *Ecological Engineering, 49,* 270–276.

Fiori, M., Paolini, R., & Poli, T. (2013). Monitoring of eight green roofs in Milano. Hygrothermal performance and microclimate mitigation potential. In *39th World Congress on Housing Science Changing Needs, Adaptive Buildings, Smart Cities* (pp. 1365–1372). Milan, Italy: PoliScript, Milano.

Paolini, R. (2015). An overview on the performance over time of cool and green roofs as countermeasures to urban heat islands. *Tema: Tempo, Materia, Architettura, 1*(1), 9–14.

Simmons, M. T., Gardiner, B., Windhager, S., & Tinsley, J. (2008). Green roofs are not created equal: The hydrologic and thermal performance of six different extensive green roofs and reflective and non-reflective roofs in a sub-tropical climate. *Urban Ecosystems, 11*(4), 339–348.

Wong, S. L., Wan, K. K. W., Yang, L., & Lam, J. C. (2012). Changes in bioclimates in different climates around the world and implications for the built environment. *Building and Environment, 57,* 214–222.

Comparison of Comfort Performance Criteria and Sensing Approach in Office Space: Analysis of the Impact on Shading Devices' Efficiency

Marco Imperadori, Tiziana Poli, Juan Diego Blanco Cadena, Federica Brunone and Andrea G. Mainini

Abstract Indoor occupant comfort has been related to total building energy consumption, and some of its components (lighting, heating, and cooling mainly), together with carbon production, also with occupants' productivity, learnability, and health. However, few works relate comfort to the circular economy and are barely related to the circularity of the selected building materials or systems. This work is intended to evaluate how the dynamism of a building envelope (triggered by different comfort preferences) disturbs the efficiency of the building and maintenance activities (Linked with the following correlated research projects: (1) *Research title*: Imaging processing on determining eye strain (ongoing), *Participant research groups*: VELUXlab & SEEDLab.ABC).

Keywords Interactive buildings · Visual comfort · User-centered approach · Building operation maintenance

1 Occupants' Comfort and Energy

A significant share of the energy consumed by buildings is intended for delivering proper indoor conditions for most of its occupants. These proper indoor conditions are generally referred as comfort conditions, which have been defined by ASHRAE 55 as "*…condition of mind which expresses satisfaction with the environment….*" Therefore, it encompasses different components, namely thermal, visual, acoustic, air quality, layout distribution, and others.

The indoor environment depends on the combination of various physical parameters, and hence, multiple plant systems are needed for managing all of them in parallel. Most of the plant systems have a dynamic operation, with the intention of properly handle the physical parameter variations, generated by mutable weather

M. Imperadori · T. Poli (✉) · J. D. Blanco Cadena · F. Brunone · A. G. Mainini
Architecture, Built Environment and Construction Engineering—ABC Department, Politecnico di Milano, Milan, Italy
e-mail: tiziana.poli@polimi.it

S. Della Torre et al. (eds.), *Regeneration of the Built Environment from a Circular Economy Perspective*, Research for Development,
https://doi.org/10.1007/978-3-030-33256-3_36

conditions during the building lifetime. To do so, there must be a performance criterium, or criteria, to rate the efficiency of the processes carried out by the system and to trigger an intervention when the goals set are not met.

As the closest element to the exterior, the building envelope is the most influential building system for providing well-being indoors, and in particular the transparent portion (defined as the quickest path for heat, light, sound, and pollution transfer). Additional shading devices have been employed to increase the dynamism and performance of the envelope, boosting the façade composition. The adequacy of the design, functional model, and control logic would depend on the type of activity held indoors, but most importantly the type of occupants hosted.

Not all occupants perceived similarly and prefer, require, or demand the same indoor environmental conditions. Thus, depending on what the designers' choice is:

- The building could perform badly if a manual control has been envisaged without any correction or adaption (Masoso and Grobler 2010).
- An autonomous building could not provide enough satisfaction, if the performance criteria are not adjusted to the occupants' requirements, and they would feel underrated if no sense of control is given (Belafi et al. 2017; Langevin et al. 2015).
- An adaptive building could operate decently in a mixed-mode, allowing occupants' interaction and overriding the initially set activation thresholds (Gunay et al. 2014).

The type of operation affects the energy consumption of the building (i.e., environmental gains) and the frequency of activation, hence the fatigue on the materials, and the maintenance activities. Further replacement, or maintenance, interventions would enlarge the embodied energy of the system threatening its circular economy.

2 Shading Requirement

Taking into consideration only the lighting requirement for reading and writing activities, sufficient illuminance shall be provided under daylighting (when available) and artificial lighting. Starting from the minimum threshold established of 300 lx and a maximum of 1000 lx (following sDA and ASE lower and upper limits established by LEED v4 (2014)) to avoid the risk of glare and modifying it according to the needs of the occupant (i.e., aged eye, protected eye, and younger eye); see Table 1.

Shading requirement has been set as the need for a lower/higher glass transmittance of the transparent portion of the building façade to regulate the daylight influx, and this would only be used when the values obtained indoors do not comply with the settings set. However, these settings were diversified to encompass a more realistic preference of different building users, and also to cover what the design regulations do not clarify: maximum illuminance values (i.e., there are only lower thresholds).

An office space (2.95 × 5.10 × 3.17 m) in Milan, Italy (45° 28′ 47″N; 9° 13′ 47″E), with 30% window-to-wall ratio (WWR) oriented toward South, was used as a case study, in which the illuminance was computed at an analysis grid at 0.8 m from the

Table 1 Frequency hours of shading and lighting activation according to the lower and upper illuminance thresholds

Condition	E_{min} (lx)	E_{max} (lx)	Artificial lighting (%)	Shading (%)	Total no. activation hours (%)
Normal	300	1000	22.86	49.94	27.20
Younger occupants[a]	400	650	27.92	61.54	10.54
Older occupants[b]	354	1180	25.70	46.08	28.22
Glasses worn occupants[a]	265	600	21.42	63.36	15.22

[a]Average value for a neutral condition obtained from a qualitative survey performed at Politecnico di Milano (18–22-year-old students)

[b]Assumed value, considering the ~18% decay of stimulus at the 550 nm wavelength of light (see Turner and Mainster 2008)

floor. The optical properties of the materials were the following: glass $\tau_{vis} = 0.65$; ceiling $\rho_{vis} = 0.8$; internal walls $\rho_{vis} = 0.5$; and floor $\rho_{vis} = 0.4$.

The obtained values for different criteria were confronted against the traditional E_h evaluation; that is, what was found from analyzing preferences of a qualitative survey applied to bachelor students and what has been suggested by Turner and Mainster (2008) due to the eyesight decay. The frequency of activation and the variances obtained due to these values have been collected and presented in Table 1, additionally in Figs. 1a and 2 annual heat maps have been included to see the behavior of illuminance and required activation during the year.

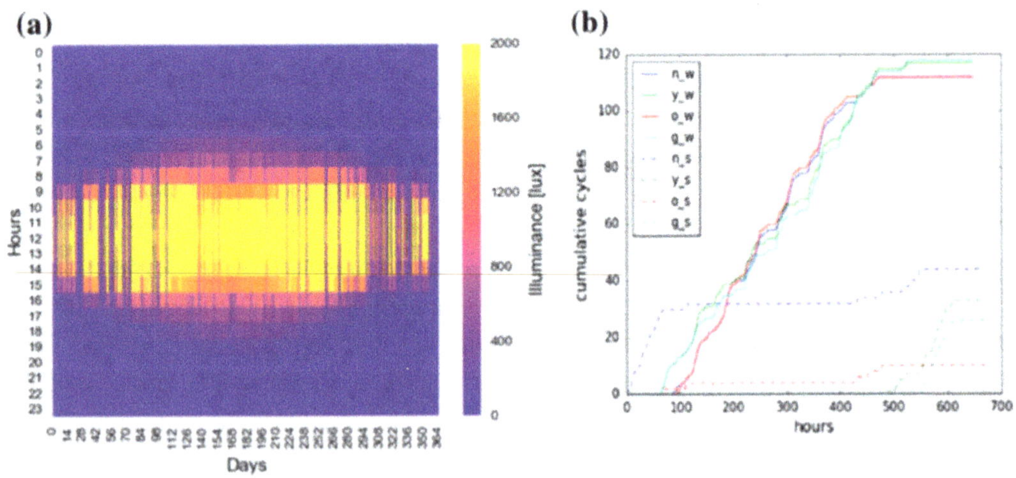

Fig. 1 Average room surface illuminance value along the year (**a**) and shading cycle occurrence cumulative sum throughout 3 months (i.e., summer June–Aug (s) and winter Jan–Mar (w)) for normal considerations (n), young (y), older (o), and glasses worn occupants (**b**)

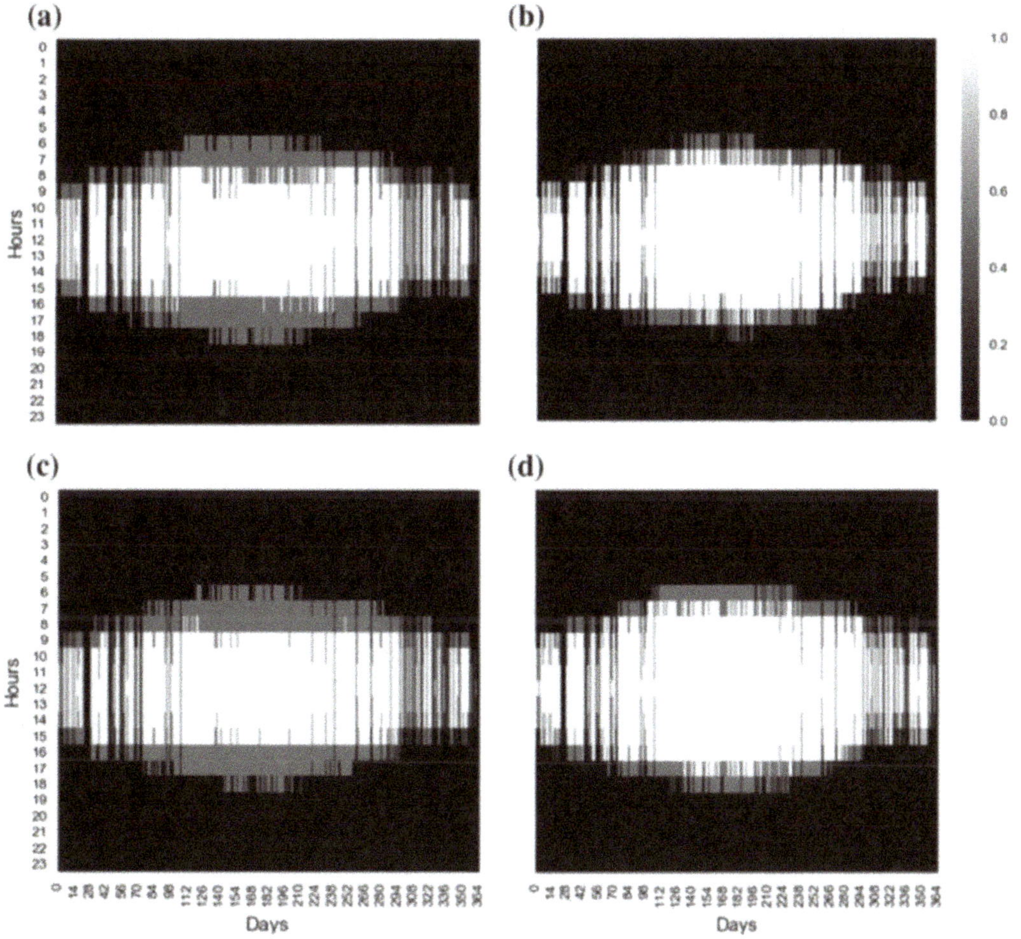

Fig. 2 Activation controls for artificial lighting (value 0), for shading (value 1) and no activation required (value 0.5). For **a** normal consideration, **b** younger occupants, **c** older occupants, and **d** glass worn occupants

2.1 Frequency of Use

The frequency of use of both shading and lighting appliances has been estimated from an annual simulation using the validated ray-tracing software radiance presented by Ward and Shakespeare (1998). It has been assumed that the values reported in Table 1 are a hypothetical ideal case in which the shadings are correctly operated by the building, and in which they have been adapted to a more realistic hosted occupancy type.

3 Conclusions

The need for clarifying the type of occupancy indoors is clear, as the variance of the activation hours of the electrical appliances and/or shading can reach a difference of ~13% generating a much larger quantity of cycles that could reduce the life expectancy of the building systems. Moreover, the hours of comfort have a well significant difference when considering one range or the other, for instance, for occupants wearing glasses the number of hours in which no intervention was required was ~15%; meanwhile for the established benchmark (i.e., between 300 and 1000 lx), it was ~27%. In terms of cycles, it is clear how the number of activations varies from one occupancy type to the other, given what is shown in Fig. 1b. For summer, the amount of cycles is reduced as they are mainly ON; meanwhile for the winter, a higher variance is noted due to lower daylighting availability and the perpendicularity of the light influx.

Further studies are foreseen to establish a more reliable visual comfort range for the horizontal illuminance that would allow to improve the building design. Additional surveys on diverse occupant samples are expected to assess different influential physical features.

Standards and Laws

American Society of Heating, R. and A. C. E. (ASHRAE). (2013). ASHRAE Standard 55-2013 Thermal Environmental Conditions for Human Occupancy. Ashrae, 2004.

Council, US Green Building. LEED v4 for building design and construction. USGBC Inc. (2014).

References

Belafi, Z., Hong, T., & Reith, A. (2017). Smart building management versus intuitive human control—Lessons learnt from an office building in Hungary. *Building Simulation, 10*(6), 811–828.

Gunay, H. B., O'Brien, W., Beausoleil-Morrison, I., & Huchuk, B. (2014). On adaptive occupant-learning window blind and lighting controls. *Building Research and Information, 42*(6), 739–756.

Langevin, J., Gurian, P. L., & Wen, J. (2015). Tracking the human-building interaction: A longitudinal field study of occupant behavior in air-conditioned offices. *Journal of Environmental Psychology, 42*, 94–115.

Masoso, O. T., & Grobler, L. J. (2010). The dark side of occupants' behaviour on building energy use. *Energy and Buildings, 42*(2), 173–177.

Turner, P. L., & Mainster, M. A. (2008). Circadian photoreception: Ageing and the eye's important role in systemic health. *British Journal of Ophthalmology, 92*(11), 1439–1444.

Ward, G., & Shakespeare, R. (1998). *Rendering with radiance: The art and science of lighting visualization.* Morgan Kaufman.

www.ingramcontent.com/pod-product-compliance
Lightning Source LLC
LaVergne TN
LVHW080016210926
848481LV00011B/3042